D0918816

Religion in the Southern States

A HISTORICAL STUDY

Religion in
the Southern States

A Historical Study

edited with an introduction by
Samuel S. Hill

Mercer University
Press
Macon, Ga. 31207

BR
535
.R44
1983

ISBN 0-86654-045-4

All books published by Mercer University Press are produced
on acid-free paper which exceeds the minimum standards set by the
National Historical Publications and Records Commission

Library of Congress Cataloging in Publication Data

Religion in the southern states.

Bibliography
1. Southern States—Church history—Addresses,
essays, lectures. 2. Christian sects—Southern States—
Addresses, essays, lectures. 3. Southern States—
Religion—Addresses, essays, lectures. I. Hill,
Samuel S.

BR535.R44   1983   277.5   82-23979
ISBN 0-86654-045-4

Table of Contents

Dedication

In honor of
Walter Brownlow Posey
Pioneer in the study
of specialized areas
within the religious South

Preface

While preparing the *Encyclopedia of Religion in the South,* I came to the realization that one set of its ingredients made up a book in its own right. The 16 state histories constitute a significant and quite distinctive approach to the study of Southern religious history. They add up to a unique story very much worth telling.

Thus, in anticipation of the *Encyclopedia's* publication, we are issuing this fascicle. Thanks are due to each author for cooperating in the decision to give dual exposure to the fruits of his labor. Each seems to have shared the editor's notion that this collection could quite beneficially have a life of its own.

Which states to regard as Southern states proved to be a question that touched on several issues. One criterion seemed finally the most compelling: the prevalence of the dominant pattern of Southern religious geography. That means a Baptist-Methodist-Presbyterian primary strength. This left the status of a few states to be determined, namely Louisiana, Florida, Maryland, Missouri, and West Virginia, perhaps also Oklahoma. But each was finally assessed as qualifying since each resembled more than it diverged from regional patterns.

No common plan of organization was assigned to the authors. Accordingly every one is different, in line with each historian's tastes and chosen procedure—in addition to the unique contours of each state's history. The historical survey essay that concludes this volume also relects no other schema than the one its author imposed upon the data.

Samuel S. Hill
Gainesville, Florida
12 November 1982

INTRODUCTION

The study of American history by regions is a highly interpretive and rather controversial enterprise. A number of topics of course can be addressed quite profitably in this way; for example, the effect of immigration on the New England states, economic developments in the Great Plains states, or agriculture in the Pacific Northwest. But the collections of states referred to in those cases are rather artificially created; they represent a certain coherence, yet they are closer to being geographical conventions than identifiable cultural or social units. In doing regional studies, the trouble arises when it is supposed that a region is a cultural unit.

The South may be the only solid exception, but that does not lessen the controversial and troublesome nature of the undertaking. The South is an identifiable cultural and social unity—well, mostly, in certain ways, some parts of it. What occasions and justifies treatment of it as such is its peculiar history, centered about the sectional clash over slavery, an agricultural economy, and states'-rights politics. The existence of the Confederate States of America, although short-lived, symbolizes and confirms the reality of the South as a cultural unity. For a half-century before its formation and more than a century since, a human complex called Southern society has had a recognizable life of its own. Its people have known that to be a fact as they traveled elsewhere and engaged in comparisons of customs, values, and cultural features. Outsiders have been aware of it too. Few better confirmations may be found than the similarity of reactions felt by a great variety of "Northerners" to the experience of the South and its people. As different as Iowans are from Vermonters, they have known how much more different South, Southern, and Southerner are from "Northern culture"—whatever that is in its great diversity—than those two states are from each other.

This collection of articles on the history of religion in each of the sixteen Southern states is predicated on the claim that the region does have distinctive cultural identity—even though that is a "limited distinctiveness." Also a significant degree of cultural cohesion has prevailed. Notwithstanding that reasoning, this is a rather bold claim. What does Maryland have in common with Oklahoma? Louisiana with West Virginia? Missouri with South Carolina? And even, most surprisingly, Alabama with Georgia? (Never mind comparisons of Florida with anything!) Geographers and students of regional cultures in America do finally depict this sprawl of states and communities as some kind of region, with reference to religion as much as to any single factor. Succinctly stated, an Anglo-Saxon Protestant hegemony prevails in numbers and in influence. The Baptists, the Methodists, and the Presbyterians, usually in that order, are the dominant religious bodies. Any area where that pattern is disrupted is referred to as an exception; as, for example, Roman Catholic strength in Louisiana and Texas; German Protestant visibility in parts of Texas, Virginia, and the Carolinas; or sectarian profusion in the Appalachian highlands. The point is underscored by Campbellite formidability in certain places. Whether the Disciples of Christ in Kentucky or the Churches of Christ in Middle Tennessee is the group in question, the strength of the Campbellite movement is not thought of by the populace or by scholars as particularly strange. These after all are people of Anglo-Saxon stock and their religion recognizably left-wing Protestant and cozily American. Moreover, all of these generalizations apply to the region's significant black population and culture as well as to the white, even if black cultural variation is somewhat curtailed on the side of traditional Christianity and expanded on the side of innovation.

Very likely, this study of religion in the Southern states, state by state for sixteen is the first effort of its kind. (This book's editor does not have any difficulty figuring out why this task has not been conceived before.) Paradoxically, the juxtaposition of these unit histories both confirms and disputes the fruitfulness of the undertaking. Doing so shows how extensive Southern culture is and at the same time how discrete its parts are, both large parts like whole states and small parts like areas within states.

But in addition to highlighting one question, Is there a Southern religious region?, this collection tackles another, Is there much to be gained from studying a state's religious history? In what sense does any *state* have a religious history? That task too has rarely been approached. Denominational histories for states abound. We have histories of religion for the entire country. There are even studies of religion within regions in certain frames of time. But few if any state histories of religion—that is, of all communities of faith—have been attempted.

This, then, is something of a pioneering effort, and in two respects. It canvasses an entire region's religious history. In addition, it uses discrete state units as the primary means for doing so. One long essay by the editor at the end seeks to provide a panorama of the entire scene. It aims to comprehend major religious developments from Maryland to Texas and Missouri to Florida from 1565 and 1607 until the 1980s. That venture too is a pioneering one; it is hardly free from peril. Nevertheless both approaches have merit and—it is hoped—the two together inform and illuminate.

Since these state religious histories were assigned originally as contributions to the *Encyclopedia of Religion in the South*, their composition reflects the independence and tastes of each author. An encyclopedia, most notably one on the subject of religion, is not the same as a dictionary, after all. No format was prescribed; each historian has constructed his own design. Accordingly sixteen unique ways of tackling the job are to be found. Yet a number of concerns, topics, and issues show up across the sweep of this material. And all follow a basically chronological approach. But the parts of the story highlighted by each author differ from state to state as befits the singularity of each state's history.

Of course, any scholar analyzes the subject at hand in line with his or her own training, interests, and judgments. This series of essays reflects that predictability like a textbook case. Where it is demonstrated most directly is in the penchant for concentrating on earlier periods of historical development. For one thing recent history is difficult to assess and chronicle. More pertinent in the Southern instance, however, is the standard preoccupation with the nineteenth century, especially the Old South, the antebellum decades. The Civil War, Reconstruction, and New South era ranks second for importance. But the colonial period claims much attention in studies of the seaboard states from South Carolina northward. A disproportional share of the narrative, then, will be associated with certain periods, and these will vary somewhat from one set of states to another. But it will be observed by most readers, and should be emphasized in any case, that rhythms differ. What was early for Arkansas is "late" for Virginia. Anglo-American history had hardly got going in the southwestern states before the Civil War.

It is very suggestive to note concurrency—and its absence—as well. Perhaps the principal lesson to be learned from doing regional history this way is how greatly rhythms differ. One is instructed—and his imagination enlivened—by asking what was happening during a given period to the general basic culture, the South as a whole, within which states A, B, and C were in quite different phases.

It can be argued that state boundaries are artificial as far as culture is concerned. To be sure, the people in adjoining counties of northwest Alabama, northeast Mississippi, and west south central Tennessee are apt to prepare the same foods, speak with the same accent, and be affiliated with the same denominations. Just the same, the political organization of those culture-kin, even blood-kin, people into three separate states makes for concrete differences in the ways their lives are ordered. State borders are somewhat more than political constructions. This may even be true in religious patterns, especially when an area was settled after state lines were drawn and the denomination within a state planted mission work inside its boundaries. Also, the plain truth of the matter is that the career of religion has been different in every state—less specifically so than political history perhaps, yet discernibly different. The point at which boundaries come closest to being artificial is where they cut through culturally homogeneous zones, as for example in mountain areas, the District of Columbia suburbs, or the "black belt" territory of southern Mississippi and Alabama.

It is suggested to readers that they examine two or more chapters of this book at the same sitting. One learns more than twice as much by pondering the history of religion in North Carolina and in Louisiana during a single afternoon. The benefits are truly enhanced if you read about quite different parts of the South in that same sitting. The comparative study of the history of a single culture is uncommonly productive.

As for the final chapter which aims at a synthesis, a historical overview, that should probably be considered last. But whether then or earlier, its material should be seen in dialectical relation to the discrete units. And one will soon detect the biases of that survey chapter. They are slanted toward the older Southern states and toward the period from the settlement at Jamestown to the 1920s. In the last analysis it may be that this particular book's most telling lesson is that most of us who deal with the South have given little attention to its western reaches. It may also follow that the freshest contribution of this work is an introduction to the religious life of the people of Texas, Oklahoma, and Arkansas in particular.

Alabama

J. Wayne Flynt
Auburn University

The itinerant preacher arrived about 1817 in St. Stephens to proclaim the gospel. The population of Alabama's territorial capital on the banks of the Tombigbee River was quite satisfied with conditions as they were and did not desire religious provocation. When the zealous minister persisted, ignoring the town's ban against such preaching, the people of St. Stephens set him adrift on the river. As he floated downstream, he turned back toward the town and shouted: "St. Stephens be damned. I came unto you and you received me not. I now confine this den of iniquity to the snakes, bats and owls." Within months of this curse, Cahaba was made the new capital, and St. Stephens began a decline which left no remains except tangled garden figs and crepe myrtles intertwined beneath oaks that once lined city streets.

Although St. Stephens is the only recorded incident of an Alabama town consigned to perdition for rejecting repentance, it could have been a frequent occurrence on Alabama's nineteenth century frontier. Between 1800 and 1820, pioneers poured into the newly opened cotton lands of the Tennessee and Tombigbee valleys. Life was primitive, conditions squalid, the intrepid settlers often uneducated and profane. Although Alabama would later pride itself as the heart of Dixie's Bible Belt, descriptions left by the first generation of preachers were not flattering. An early Methodist leader depicted Washington County settlers as "grossly worldly and extremely wicked," who "could no more be impressed with the obligations and benefits of the Christian religion than could the beasts of the forests in which they lived." A Presbyterian report from the Tennessee

Valley in the 1820s concluded that "no part of our country is more destitute of spiritual instruction, nor perhaps does any part open a wider door of usefulness."

Even nominally religious people were condemned for backsliding and moral depredations. A pioneer Presbyterian missionary believed that although there were many professing Christians (principally Methodists and Baptists, he added smugly), most had lost their first love. Their "sinful propensities" led them into fashionable amusements. Such Christians damaged the gospel even more than avowed infidels. Nor were Presbyterians immune to such temptations. The North Alabama Presbytery answered with stern advice a query concerning ministers and laymen who sent their children to dancing school: "Dancing as ordinarily practiced in society is almost invariably connected with scenes, company and indulgencies of a character decidedly gay, worldly and adapted to lead to many and serious evils." The Presbytery appended to its diatribe against dancing further admonitions against theatres, circuses, jugglers' performances and similar carnal exhibitions.

Perhaps the most enthralling entertainment that remained on that harsh and lonely frontier was religion. Although Jesuits undoubtedly had accompanied transient Spanish expeditions and had settled in the French outpost of Mobile, the Rev. Lorenzo Dow is the earliest recorded Protestant to penetrate the dangerous and sparsely populated plains of the Tombigbee. Braving Indians, weather, and godless whites, Dow began preaching in the Tensaw settlements in 1803. Although he was not ordained and the Methodist Church rejected his requests for support, he was doctrinally a disciple of Wesley and considered himself a Methodist notwithstanding. An enthusiastic preacher who parted his hair in the middle and let it hang to his shoulders, Dow soon was known throughout the territory as "Crazy Dow." Driven by a fanatical zeal to spread the word of universal atonement and free salvation, he took his message to Canada, Ireland, and England, as well as to the remote wilderness of the Tombigbee. Between 1803 and 1812, Dow crisscrossed Washington County ten times preaching salvation or damnation, depending upon mood and congregation.

Because churches were scattered and poorly organized, ministers relied upon the camp meeting as an effective device for evangelizing the godless. Methodists and Baptists in particular, and Presbyterians to a lesser extent, imported the strategy of the great Cane Ridge, Kentucky, camp meeting of 1801. Their task was to save sinners, and neither doctrinal creeds, formal education, nor denominational differences must interfere. Disagreements over methods of baptism or predestination were contained by generally good-humored toleration. One Baptist layman claimed that his Methodist wife believed in falling from grace but never fell, whereas he believed there was no fall, but fell daily.

Canaan Baptist Church in Jefferson County conducted a camp meeting in October 1831. The "tents" which communicants inhabited surrounded a brush arbor where the meetings were held. One witness described the proceedings:

> It is not unusual to have a large portion of the congregation prostrated upon the ground; and, in some instances, they appear to have lost the use of their limbs. No distinct articulation could be heard; screams, cries, groans, shouts, notes of joy, all heard at the same time, made much confusion—a sort of indescribable concert.

Whatever the physical manifestations, the meeting began a revival which resulted in three churches baptizing 500 people within 12 months' time.

Two Methodist sponsored camp meetings in the Tennessee Valley resulted in more than 400 conversions during a six-month period of 1828. Decatur, Courtland, Tuscumbia, and Florence were "all in a flame." James W. Faris, Methodist pastor in the Franklin Circuit of the Tennessee Valley, electrified the congregations with his preaching. Oftentimes called "Faris, the eccentric," what he lacked in education he made up for in ardor. One contemporary acknowledged that Faris had no education but added that "as an orator he swept all the chords of the human soul. He touched the emotions and swayed the vast throngs of a camp meeting as absolutely as the storm sways the trees of the forest." Similarly successful Methodist camp meetings were established at Oakbowery (1837), Fredonia (1838), Bethlehem (1843), and Hillabee (1847).

Despite their predestinarian theology, Presbyterians were also active on the camp meeting circuit. Their most famous facility was at Hatchet Creek in east-central Alabama. The mountainous terrain of that area was settled by hardy Scotch-Irish Presbyterians following Indian removal in the 1820s and 1830s. Presbyterian farmers built a fence to enclose the horses, mules, and oxen which hauled inquirers to the meetings. On hills behind the church, they constructed 25 cottages, each with four rooms and a hall. As interest grew and crowds increased, they built a large pine arbor abutting the small Presbyterian church. Years passed and the soul-

its size. Congregations such as that of St. John's Church in Montgomery often furnished the state's governors and senators, and enrolled its wealthiest planters and merchants. Nonetheless, the church developed a distinctly low church orientation that allowed it to blend easily into the religious mainstream.

Other denominations were limited by geographical or ethnic factors. The Cumberland Presbyterians and Disciples of Christ established congregations mainly in the mountainous northern counties. Catholics were generally confined to the extreme south, where families of French and Spanish extraction held defiantly to the old faith. Mobile was the Catholic capital of Alabama, and Protestant work advanced slowly in that port city. Presbyterianism flourished only among Scotch-Irish in the foothills of the lower Appalachians and later among Scottish coal miners in the Birmingham district. Despite its early successes in rural camp meetings, the Presbyterian movement was quickly confined to larger towns and cities, leaving the countryside to the more democratic Methodists and Baptists.

The primary barrier inhibiting Presbyterians was a centralized church structure which maintained strict standards for licensing and ordination. For instance, the North Alabama Presbytery found unacceptable a sermon by John K. Wallace in the 1820s. Although the sermon demonstrated "considerable labour," the Presbytery did not think that there was "sufficient closeness of attention." Members also pronounced it "faulty in precision and perspicuity, and that there are too many redundant words." The South Alabama Presbytery spent two entire days examining another candidate for the ministry.

Once licensed, the Synod selected the theological seminary which the aspiring minister would attend and often paid his expenses. Upon requesting ordination, the Presbytery administered grueling examinations. During the 1850s one Alabama presbytery warned applicant R. W. Shive to be prepared to discuss the Greek New Testament, Virgil's *Aeneid* (all six volumes), the Odes of Horace, Alexander's *Evidences of Christianity*, Mosheim's church history, Kurtz's treatise on church government, and Picket's theology. After recounting such arduous standards, a pioneer Alabama Presbyterian historian concluded: "No wonder the Baptist farmers who ploughed until Saturday, mounted their horses, then rode across the woods to their Sabbath appointments . . . found entering the ministry a simple event by comparison with a Presbyterian youth."

High intellectual standards were a premeditated policy aimed at a more cultured audience. The chairman of home missions for the Presbyterian denomination in the state commented on the changing conditions within the state in his 1859 report:

> There are numerous communities of the wealthy and intelligent throughout our bounds. The whole country is indeed highly prosperous. Learning is rapidly advancing, seminaries springing up at every step . . . .
>
> The religious teachers of the people have hitherto been, generally, uneducated men, following the common avocation of life, while to the best of their ability they preached the gospel. But the recent rapid developments of the human mind are beginning to throw light upon the darkest and most remote corners of all this land. It is reported to us from every quarter that there is a general longing after a different order of things.

Perhaps he overestimated the religious sophistication of Alabama's masses.

Although such accounts demonstrate that the religion of the head was by no means unknown to the Alabama frontier, they also explain the relative lack of success of the Presbyterian Church. Throughout the nineteenth century, Presbyterians found it impossible to staff their churches adequately. The Talladega Presbytery died for lack of ministers. In 1872 the Tuscaloosa Presbytery numbered 25 churches, 13 of them without a pastor. In 1829 only 30 Presbyterian ministers shepherded 1,713 members. In 1880 the church actually had fewer members than in 1860. After more than a half-century of activity, only 5,800 Presbyterians worshipped in 117 churches. There were numerous counties without a single Presbyterian church in 1860.

Although Alabama's Protestant churches defined their mutual tasks in similar ways, they all experienced internal factionalism and schism. The chief sources of division were familiar: race and theology.

Methodists and Baptists had been especially successful at enrolling slaves in their churches. Although white ministers usually tended these biracial blocks, black ministers were ordained and sometimes even gained renown and freedom. The Rev. Caesar Blackwell, a black minister living near Montgomery, was sought by both white and black congregations for revivals. So popular did he become that the Alabama Baptist Association

(Montgomery County) purchased his freedom and provided for his old age.

As slavery became a heated issue, denominations widely stereotyped as apolitical assumed surprisingly active public roles. The Alabama Baptist Convention first defended slavery at its 1835 convention. Thomas Griffin, a prominent Methodist leader, told the 1826 Methodist General Conference that he was displeased by the opposition of some Northern Methodists to slavery: "It appears to me that some of our Northern brethren are willing to see us damned, rammed, crammed, and jammed into a 46 pounder, and touched off into eternity."

By 1844 tempers had risen to such a point that the Methodist Quarterly Conference, meeting in Tuscaloosa, passed a resolution which argued that "peaceable secession is greatly to be preferred to ceaseless denunciation, distrust, and strife." The male members of the Uniontown Methodist Church resolved in July 1844, that "a division of the M. E. Church is indispensably necessary and that under existing circumstances we cannot be satisfied without it . . . " The decision of Southern Methodists to form a regional church in 1844 and the Baptist decision to do likewise a year later met with overwhelming approval in Alabama. The Christian Church divided in 1854 and the Presbyterians in 1861. By 1861 church leaders were involved deeply in rationalizing the South's racial, political, and economic systems. In fact, they could hardly have been more deeply involved in secular politics. In January 1861, three prominent Methodist ministers addressed a Montgomery political rally and called for Alabama's immediate secession. Dr. Basil Manly, a Baptist pastor and former president of the University of Alabama, assured the 1861 Alabama Baptist Convention that Baptists were ready to defend the state's sovereignty and independence. Throughout the Civil War, ministers served not only as chaplains and soldiers but as Dixie's apologists, bolstering morale and imploring God's blessings on the Confederacy's righteous cause.

Theological conflicts as well as political ones troubled Protestant groups. New School and Old School factions of Presbyterians waged internecine war in the Tennessee Valley. But the most divisive internal dispute occurred between missionary and anti-missionary Baptists.

Many predestinarian Baptist congregations in Alabama opposed missionary, educational, benevolent, and temperance activities. Strongly anti-institutional, they even opposed the state convention and Sunday Schools. Although centered in the hill counties of northern and eastern

Alabama, they had some strength throughout the state. By the 1830s disagreements within churches and associations became so intense that many split. The oldest Baptist fellowship, the Flint River Association, contained a majority of anti-missionary churches. In such cases, the mission advocates usually withdrew, forming new congregations and associations. More than 100 Baptist churches in the 1960s carried names such as "Liberty," "Friendship," "Fellowship," "Harmony," "Freedom," or "Union," and most dated from this divisive era.

So strong were the Primitive Baptists (as the anti-mission churches came to be known), that they threatened the life of the newly formed state convention. The 1837 meeting received a report that 12 of Alabama's 21 Baptist associations were divided over the missions issue, four associations had fallen to the anti-missionists, and only three were clearly mission-minded.

The rapid spread of Alexander Campbell's movement into north Alabama in the 1830s also sapped Baptist energies. The Disciples of Christ established strongholds in the same general areas as the Primitive Baptists.

By the 1850s the anti-mission dispute subsided, to be replaced by the Landmark controversy. Containing some elements of the earlier conflict, Landmarkism was an attempt to assert traditional authority (hence the term "landmarks"), which supposedly had once characterized the church, but was now being lost. Led by J. R. Graves of Tennessee and James M. Pendleton of Kentucky, this faction opposed denominational boards and agencies, "alien baptism," open communion, or any non-Baptist minister preaching in a Baptist church. Arguing the primacy of the local congregation, they traced Baptist traditions back to the time of Christ and contended that it was the only true church. Although Southern Baptists withstood this assault also, it left deep doctrinal scars. The remaining Landmark churches finally separated from the Southern Baptist Convention (SBC) in 1905, but many Southern Baptist churches retained anti-institutional and ideological positions, refusing to contribute to denominational agencies or causes, rejecting "alien baptism" or ecumenical cooperation.

Theology constituted only one element of this struggle which also involved class structures and geography. North and east Alabama, where both Primitive and Landmark Baptists were strongest, was a land of remote hollows and mountains. Outside the fertile Tennessee Valley, there were few plantations or slaves. The counties were inhabited mainly by yeomen and poor whites who eked out a subsistence existence on small farms. They resented the political dominance of the wealthy central Alabama counties. Education was not greatly valued and was difficult to provide the scattered mountain people. Hence, they resented educated people who were sometimes haughty and arrogant.

Further to the South, Baptists and Methodists enjoyed unprecedented prosperity in the 1840s and 1850s. As the frontier receded, they began to build schools and colleges for their young. Baptist academies were established in Moulton, Greensboro, Cusseta, Six Mile, Tuskegee, Evergreen, Tucsaloosa, LaFayette, and Ruhama. They founded Judson College for women in 1839 and Howard College for men in 1842, both located in the Black Belt town of Marion. Methodists were even more active, establishing "female colleges" in Huntsville, Tuscaloosa, Tuskegee, Auburn and Athens, and Southern University at Greensboro, Wesleyan University at Florence, and the East Alabama Male College at Auburn. Because the state provided little public education, Methodists also established many academies. Such institutions produced well educated leaders who quickly upgraded Baptist and Methodist intellectual life, and provided Alabama many of its most talented teachers, lawyers, politicians, and women.

The Civil War interrupted the prosperity and success of Alabama's churches. Theologically, it forced white Protestants to wonder why God had visited his wrath upon a cause which they considered righteous. Typical of the dilemma was an 1862 resolution proposed by a committee of the East Liberty Baptist Association: "The present civil war which has been inaugurated by our enemies must be regarded as a providential visitation upon us on account of our sins." Following heated debate, the resolution was modified by insertion of the phrase: "Though entirely just on our part."

Reconstruction provided little time for pondering the theological implications of such weighty matters. The status of the freedmen was as vexatious an ecclesiastical problem as a political one. White Protestants were by no means of one mind regarding their black brethren. Some were delighted to see them withdraw, but others tried to preserve a biracial church dominated by whites. The 1865 Alabama Baptist Convention contended that the altered civil status of blacks did not necessitate any ecclesiastical change: "While we recognize their right to withdraw from our churches and form organizations of their own, we nevertheless believe that their highest good will be subserved by their retaining their present relation to those who know them, who love them, and who will labor for the promotion of their welfare."

One Baptist association offered to provide for the religious and educational welfare of blacks, who would be allowed to select their own pastors and teachers "from among the whites." Black Christians ignored such paternalism.

Instead, blacks organized their own schools, churches, and colleges. Some 600 blacks, who constituted two-thirds of Montgomery's First Baptist Church, withdrew under the leadership of the Rev. Nathan Ashby. In December 1868, Ashby became president of the newly organized Colored Baptist State Convention. Twelve years later, in 1880, delegates from across America met in Montgomery to organize the National Baptist Convention, which soon enrolled the majority of black Christians in the United States.

Methodists experienced similar withdrawals. The Florence District of the Methodist Church had 829 black members in 1860, but only 309 by 1865.

Despite the efforts of missionaries representing northern white churches—Congregational, Presbyterian, Roman Catholic, Methodist, and Baptist—more than 90 percent of Alabama's black Christians enrolled in their own Methodist and Baptist churches. Outside groups made a greater contribution to the educational opportunities of blacks by sponsoring numerous colleges. From black churches and denominational schools came a generation of political, religious, educational, and business leaders.

Methodists experienced more internal divisions during Reconstruction than any religious group. Many living in north Alabama had opposed secession. In 1867 some of them organized the Alabama Conference of the Methodist Episcopal Church. The Methodist Episcopal Church, South, viewed this new group not with fraternal brotherhood, but as a meddling interloper and pawn of "Radical Reconstruction." The new church experienced trouble, especially in the Black Belt and east Alabama. The presiding elder of the Demopolis District wrote of "persecutions, sore and constant ostracism, and threats of violence . . . " The head of the East Alabama District reported that "one of my preachers . . . was assassinated by a band of ruffians and his son seriously wounded . . . " Another pastor approaching his church found a skull and crossbones posted on the door and a threatening mob outside.

In such tumultuous times, church growth slowed. After an initial increase owing to returning soldiers who had been converted in the revivals which swept the Confederate armies in 1863-1864, some denominations actually lost members because of withdrawal by blacks.

Economic change was as traumatic as racial upheaval. The "New South" crusade transformed north Alabama into one of the major industrial regions of the South. The Birmingham district attracted not only rural dwellers to industrial jobs, but also many foreign immigrants. By 1889, 18.7 percent of the state's coal miners were foreign born, mostly from England, Ireland, and Scotland. In the years from 1890 to 1910, more immigrants came from southern and eastern Europe.

Presbyterians organized a church among Scottish miners at Pratt Mines village in 1883 and immediately encountered the problems wrought by a new industrial order; no funds could be raised because the miners were on strike. The influx of Scottish miners helped explain the rapid increase in the Presbyterian Church, from 5,800 members in 1880 to 12,000 by 1897.

The infusion of eastern and southern Europeans also brought growth to less traditional Alabama religious groups. The Catholic population of Birmingham climbed with the arrival of more than 5,000 Italian steel workers. Greek and Russian Orthodox congregations were organized in Jefferson County, formed primarily by Slavic coal miners. Jewish communities grew rapidly, especially in Birmingham and Montgomery, where peddlers established mercantile houses. Although such groups never represented more than a small fraction of Alabama's religious population, they did create a more variegated religious landscape and triggered increasing nativism and anti-Catholicism.

More immediately troubling was the decline of the rural church as whites moved to the city. Ministers tended to follow them, assigning high esteem to urban pastorates and seizing the first opportunity to relocate in town. During the last 12 years of the century every name except 10 on the roster of the Presbyterian Synod changed, and one denominational historian chided the tendency of ministers "to leave a country field so soon as a city pastorate beckoned."

In the mid-1880s rural Baptist churches began criticizing the state mission board for directing too much money and attention to urban churches. They finally forced the resignation of the secretary of the mission board over this issue in 1885. Most rural Baptist churches could not afford a resident, full-time pastor and met only once a month. They had no Sunday School or educational program, or if they had one, it met only a few months a year. As late as 1898 only 744 white Baptist churches conducted a Sunday School, while 995 had none.

The Baptist dispute over mission board policy was symptomatic of a more profound division within Protestant denominations. Each of them combined several dissimilar groups. Growth occurred among more prosperous, better educated residents of bustling towns and cities. But in the country, times were hard and getting worse. As crop prices plummeted, railroad freight rates and bank interest went up, and children left the land for more promising opportunities, farmers became frustrated and angry. Denominational leaders identified more closely with the new urban business and industrial leaders. But many rural, bi-vocational pastors and laymen drifted into agrarian protest movements.

The Rev. Samuel M. Adams, a Baptist pastor in Bibb County, served as president of the Farmers' Alliance, as head of the Populist Party, and as a state legislator. One conservative journalist heard him speak and declared that "he is so full of politics that it was a hard matter for him to keep in the road." The editor of *The Alabama Baptist*, noting divided congregations and declining contributions, warned in 1892 that Baptist pastors had "gone wild over politics."

Presbyterians attributed their financial problems in the early 1890s to the divisive gubernatorial campaign between Populist Reuben F. Kolb and Democrat Thomas G. Jones. The Church had been forced to curtail its work because of the "prevalence of great political excitement," the "heated political campaign," the "depression of the times and the political differences of our people." Despite class and theological conflicts, the nineteenth century was an era of spectacular growth.

Numerically, Baptists and Methodists dominated the state at the end of the century. Alabama was 97 percent Protestant: Baptists and Methodists stood at almost equal strength, 46.2 percent to 43.4 (counting whites only, the Southern Baptists numbered 17.5 percent of the total church population, the Methodist Episcopal Church, South, 15.7 percent); Presbyterians enrolled 3.8 percent of the total church population; Roman Catholics 2.4; the Disciples, 1.6; and Episcopalians 1.1. Fifteen years later, Baptists had made rapid gains to 54.9 percent, Methodists had declined sharply to 30.9, Presbyterians and Episcopalians had remained at almost exactly the same percentage of the total church population, and immigration had increased Roman Catholic membership to 5.1 percent. Although often ignored in statistical surveys, Negro Baptists outnumbered all religious groups in the 1916 census, with 30.8 percent of the total church population compared to Southern Baptists, who held second place with 20.6 percent.

The urban growth pattern was even more remarkable. In Birmingham, the state's largest city, the most numerous religious group in 1906 was Roman Catholic, which counted 28.9 percent of total church membership, followed by National Baptists (14.6 percent), and the Methodist Episcopal Church, South (14.2 percent). Southern Baptists were a distant fifth (7.5 percent).

Chaotic urban and industrial activity left in its wake grievous social and economic problems. As churches tried to cope with urban problems, they became increasingly engaged in social ministries. Alabama's Protestant churches had never been as apolitical as their critics have sometimes charged. No element of southern life had tried harder to rationalize slavery and secession.

Temperance had required an even longer involvement in politics. The Alabama State Temperance Society had been organized in 1834 by Methodists, Presbyterians, and Baptists. Toward the end of the century, the denominations combined in a major campaign against "demon rum." The 1881 Alabama Baptist Convention announced that it was "in profound sympathy with all movements which look to the suppression of the sale and drinking of intoxicating liquors." The 1882 conference of the M. E. Church, South, adopted a report of its Committee on Temperance declaring that a "very large proportion of human misery, including poverty, disease, and crime, is induced by the use of alcohol . . ." As associations and individual churches mobilized, Protestants gained increasing skill as effective political lobbyists. Conservative Democrats resisted as best they could, but the political clout of organized Evangelicals finally swept away all opposition and instituted prohibition at both county and state levels.

Prohibition was a broadly conceived social movement designed to deal with poverty, crime, and disease. Having entered politics on behalf of that cause, Protestants remained to champion other reforms consistent with the Progressive impulses of the times. Most notable was their vigorous crusade against child labor. The Rev. Edgar Gardner Murphy, an Episcopal priest ministering to textile workers in Montgomery, actively publicized the exploitation of children. The North Alabama Conference of the M. E. Church, South, adopted a resolution in 1901 calling for a ban on all labor of children under the age of 12. Frank W. Barnett, editor of *The Alabama Baptist*, condemned child labor as nothing less than murder, demanded that pulpits ring with denunciations, and vowed to defeat any state legislator who voted against reform. The shaken Alabama legislature passed landmark child labor legislation in 1907.

That same year the M. E. Church, South, appointed a Commission of Social Service Movements which subsequently addressed a wide range of controversial issues. Its 1910 report denied that "social salvation" could replace individual regeneration but endorsed the social gospel as an invaluable tool against "syndicated sin." The 1911 report argued that the church should modify the entire social fabric so as to "make a kingdom of God among men . . . "

Mrs. J. B. Cumming, a leader of the Baptist Woman's Missionary Society, made her agency an instrument for reform. She believed that the root of human suffering could be found in the social and industrial order: exploitation of children for profit, poor housing for workers, excessive hours of labor, inadequate pay, and unsanitary factories and shops.

Editor Barnett of *The Alabama Baptist* chided churches that "frequently shut their eyes to the struggles of labor to get a minimum living wage; and have not heard the cry of the children who were being sacrificed in our mills; or cared when a fight was being made for shorter hours and better working conditions." The chief foe of reform was "industry and property," which sought "to rob the workmen and the tenant of life and health because it happens to be more profitable at the time."

Energized by such social visions, urban churches undertook extensive social ministries. Methodists established several settlement houses in industrial sections of Birmingham and Mobile. These provided free kindergartens, adult literacy classes, home economics classes, and free medical care. Some Baptist congregations established "institutional churches" with extensive social ministries. Presbyterians began a settlement house among Birmingham steel workers, and the city's Independent Presbyterian Church provided a "Fresh Air Farm" for poor, inner city white children, a public health nurse, and an employment service.

White Baptists, Methodists, and Presbyterians also appointed special committees to examine relations with their black brethren. The 1912 conference of the North Alabama Methodists asked for creation of a Commission on the Social Condition of the Negro to improve black housing, education, social and religious life. That same year the Woman's Auxiliary of the Presbyterian Synod of Alabama held a conference for Negro Women at Stillman College, which began a long educational ministry to that black institution. By the early 1920s, they had expanded their program to provide biracial women's Bible study.

Even attitudes toward women began to change. The small, largely rural Methodist Protestant Church led the way in its 1887 state conference voting 23 to 7 that, since "in Christ there is neither male or female," "all members, whether male or female, above the age of 21 and of good standing, are alike entitled to vote in all church elections." A similar measure introduced at the 1913 North Alabama Methodist Conference was tabled. Five years later in 1918, the Alabama Conference adopted such a resolution by a vote of 136 to 20. The Alabama Baptist State Convention allowed women delegates to vote at its 1913 meetings.

Although the Social Gospel made significant inroads among Alabama Protestants, another of the current religious trends, liberal theology, had little influence. An occasional minister such as Dr. Alfred J. Dickinson of Birmingham's First Baptist Church, L. L. Gwaltney, editor of *The Alabama Baptist*, or Dr. Henry M. Edmonds of the city's Independent Presbyterian Church might be tainted with "higher criticism" at a northern college or theological seminary. But the result was usually ostracism or worse (Edmonds was fired for heresy by South Highlands Presbyterian Church before forming his new congregation).

Denominational moderates tended to dominate annual meetings and maintained a shaky truce during the Woodrow, Toy, and Whitsitt controversies in the late nineteenth century. But the Fundamentalist conflict forced divisions. Only shrewd maneuvering by Baptist leaders prevented biblical tests for teachers at the denomination's Howard College. The 1914 conference of the M. E. Church, South, attacked its book concern for publishing "mere novels and unreligious literature," and expressed alarm "at the silence of our church press in the face of this relentless propaganda of higher criticism in print and in school." So outraged were delegates by 1918 that they concluded, "Let us have a book burning." The 1923 North Alabama Conference condemned "modernism," and the 1929 meeting adopted a memorial which would "prevent any man or woman from preaching or teaching in our institutions of learning, churches, training schools, or Sunday Schools, or from editing any of our connectional literature, or from holding any other place or position in our church, who does not believe in the inspiration of the Scriptures, the Virgin Birth, the death and resurrection of Jesus Christ, according to the Bible statements."

By the 1920s, theological controversies, anti-Catholicism, and excessive focus on the single issue of prohibition narrowed the range of Protestant activities. Baptists continued to grow more rapidly than other denominations, perhaps because they were less affected by theological controversy, and they remained more conservative and rural. Their bi-vocational ministers gave them strong identification with the common folk moving into urban areas, especially coal camps and mill towns. Between 1916 and 1926 the number of churches in Alabama increased by only 5.3 percent. Yet in only half that time, 1918-1924, Southern Baptists established 81 new churches, and increased membership by 22 percent. The Southern Baptist Convention's 75 million campaign, begun in 1919, raised 2.5 million dollars over five years for Alabama Baptist mission and benevolence causes, compared to only 825,000 dollars contributed over the previous five years. State Baptists, in fact, overexpanded and went heavily into debt, a situation not corrected until the mid-1940s.

Both Baptists and Methodists launched major drives to construct hospitals in urban areas during the 1920s, though Methodists were somewhat hampered by lagging finances. As one Methodist official put it in 1924: the problem was the "gratification of bad and useless habits at the expense of the church treasury with the result that a few hundred dollars are collected for benevolent purposes, while thousands are spent for chewing gum, dope, tobacco, movies, joyriding, and the high cost of swimming."

The 1930s were years when survival not growth was uppermost. Enrollments generally remained stable, while finances collapsed. In 1934 baptisms reached the lowest point in Baptist churches since 1918. Ministers accepted substantial salary cuts and were thankful to have jobs at all. The last denominational academies and high schools were closed, replaced by the expanding public school movement. The Alabama Temperance Alliance, a coalition mainly of Methodists and Baptists, succeeded in containing the legalization of alcohol to 24 counties, while keeping 43 dry.

The religious legacy of the Second World War was mixed. Even during the war there had been racial strife in Alabama's war industries. The return of thousands of black veterans intent on a better life posed new challenges for the church.

Consistent with its antebellum heritage, white Protestant churches rationalized segregation and provided considerable assistance to politicians who vowed to resist racial desegregation. Although the state's

Southern Baptists belatedly established a Department of Work with Negro Baptists in 1951 and contributed financially to several black Baptist schools, they bitterly attacked the 1954 Brown decision and resisted integrating their churches. Leon Macon, editor of *The Alabama Baptist*, wrote that the desegregation decision had "jarred to the foundation a Southern institution." John H. Buchanan, pastor of the influential Southside Baptist Church in Birmingham, concluded that the Supreme Court "from its cloistered chambers has overlooked the reality of the situation" and complicated and damaged race relations. The 1954 North Alabama conference of the M. E. Church, South, resolved that "it is our honest conviction that it is for the good of whites and Negroes that separate schools be maintained."

Black Christians saw the issue quite differently. Although black churches across Alabama finally became involved in the Civil Rights Movement, congregations in Montgomery pioneered many of the strategies later adopted nationwide. In December 1955 Montgomery black leaders met at the Holt Street Baptist Church and formed the Montgomery Improvement Association. The Rev. Martin Luther King, Jr., who had become pastor of Dexter Avenue Baptist Church in September 1954, was elected president.

King's major assets were an excellent education (Morehouse College, Crozer Seminary, Boston University), unusual oratorical skills, and kinship networks to Atlanta's influential religious community. After arriving at Dexter Avenue, King created a Social and Political Action Committee because "the gospel of Jesus is a social gospel . . . seeking to save the whole man . . . " Together with black labor leader E. D. Nixon and fellow Baptist pastor Ralph D. Abernathy, they organized the Montgomery Bus Boycott. Despite provocative violence directed at them by some whites and more widespread economic intimidation, King and his associates maintained a remarkable degree of unity and non-violence. Drawing upon the religious metaphor of the suffering Savior, King articulated the most powerful idiom of the American Civil Rights Movement in his sermon to that first meeting at Holt Street Baptist Church just before Christmas, 1955:

> If you will protest courageously and yet with dignity and Christian love, when the history books are written in future generations, the historians will have to pause and say, "There lived a great people—a black people—who injected new

meaning and dignity into the veins of civilization." This is our challenge and our overwhelming responsibility.

This animus led King to crusades in Birmingham and Selma which altered American society in fundamental ways. Although King soon became a national figure, he waged his first campaign from the black churches of Montgomery.

Racial change was not the only evidence of a new world aborning. The location of war industries and training facilities in the South between 1940 and 1945 transformed Dixie into a relatively prosperous region, at least for most whites. Congregations of the M. E. Church, South, and the Southern Baptists became steadily more "mainstream," especially in the cities. Their ministers were more likely to have formal education and less likely to elicit emotional responses from their congregations.

Southern Baptists proved best able to maintain traditional evangelical zeal while assimilating middle class values. The Department of Evangelism and Enlistment, recreated in 1950, devised ingenious programs to enlist and retain members. Beginning in 1948 a state evangelistic conference was held annually. A simultaneous revival conducted by all Southern Baptist Convention churches in 1955 resulted in a record of nearly 29,000 baptisms in Alabama. In 1946 the state convention launched a city missions program under the direction of a superintendent of missions for each city. Between 1950 and 1963, 125 new SBC churches were begun in Alabama's six largest cities. The increase in Baptist membership was spectacular: Huntsville, 117 percent; Mobile, 99 percent; the Tri-Cities (Tuscumbia, Sheffield, Florence), 72 percent; Birmingham, 54 percent; Montgomery, 53 percent; Gadsden, 51 percent. Financial contributions increased a staggering 185 percent between 1944 and 1951.

The Alabama Baptist was an effective tool for promoting such causes. By 1961 its circulation was the second largest of any state journal in the Southern Baptist Convention, reaching 115,000 homes. Its readership throughout the state was second only to the secular *Birmingham News* in Alabama. Some 1,900 churches included subscriptions for all church members in their budgets.

Baptists also tackled the problem of enlisting rural whites who were moving to towns. In 1954 the state convention sponsored a "Transfer of Church Membership Week" to persuade new arrivals in industrial cities to move their church membership along with their furniture. Yet the denomination retained 1,600 churches in Alabama's open country in 1945, thus maintaining its traditional rural base.

To train the ministers necessary for its numerous congregations was a demanding task. In 1947 Howard College (now Samford University) began its Extension Division of Christian Training to take religious education to the people. A pioneer venture in adult education, it operated through church centers. Most of the teachers were local pastors or college graduates who received only actual expenses. Classes met one evening a week. Between 1947 and 1957 more than 10,000 different people enrolled in the courses, including hundreds of bi-vocational ministers for whom it was the sole opportunity for formal theological training. As late as 1980 Alabama had more bi-vocational Southern Baptist pastors than any state (1,211, or 40.3 percent of the state's total). In 1956 the extension program operated out of more than 50 centers with 2,000 students, 500 of them pastors with little education. Academic standards were never high, and the program declined rapidly after 1958 when a college accrediting agency refused to allow the college to offer academic credit for its extension courses. Nonetheless, the extension concept provided better trained leaders during a critical period of Baptist growth, and modified versions of the Howard Extension were adopted by Baptist colleges in several other states.

By the mid 1960s Southern Baptist growth finally subsided. The 30,476 baptisms reported in 1959 was a new record, but the statistically conscious denomination had little to brag about for the next few years. Baptisms declined to 25,000 in 1965, the smallest number since 1952. Sunday School enrollments also declined.

By the 1970s, the SBC was the superpower of Alabama religion. Its sophisticated medical centers in Birmingham were among the best in the state, its computer operations modern, and its three colleges thriving. Nearly one of every three residents of Alabama was a Southern Baptist in 1971 (30.6 percent). Members of SBC churches constituted more than half the white church membership in all but six of Alabama's 67 counties. Only in Macon County did any white denomination outnumber them.

Other denominations had pockets of strength corresponding to historic patterns. Catholics numbered more than eight percent of the total church membership in six mainly urban or extreme south Alabama counties. But black and white Methodists and Baptists were the only groups with strong support statewide.

Although confined mainly to the hill counties, the most rapid postwar growth occurred among the Church of God, Cleveland, Tennessee.

This mainly white, rural Pentecostal denomination was the third largest church in 17 of Alabama's 67 counties by 1971. In many areas it was rapidly replacing Southern Baptists as the church of the plain white people.

The cycle of nearly two centuries entered a new phase. White Baptists had joined Methodists in middle class respectability but at the price of evangelical fervor. Black Baptists and Methodists often felt more in common with Pentecostal white churches than with their more sedate brethren. But the long-standing Baptist hegemony seemed as pervasive as ever, supported since 1945 by people who wielded increasing political and economic power.

Bibliography

Alabama News of the Church of God and Alabama Kingdom Builders News.

Bureau of the Census, *Religious Bodies, 1906, 1916, 1926, 1936.*

Daniel L. Cloyd. "Prelude to Reform: Political, Economic, and Social Thought of Alabama Baptists, 1877-1890," *The Alabama Review* 31 (January 1978): 48-64.

Aleathea T. Cobbs. *Presbyterian Women of the Synod of Alabama.*

Mark H. Elovitz. *A Century of Jewish Life in Dixie: The Birmingham Experience.*

Zelia S. Evans and J. T. Alexander, editors. *Dexter Avenue Baptist Church, 1877-1977.*

Walter L. Fleming. "The Churches of Alabama During the Civil War and Reconstruction," reprinted from *The Gulf States Historical Magazine,* by W. M. Rogers and Co., Montgomery, Alabama, 1902.

Wayne Flynt. "Organized Labor, Reform, and Alabama Politics, 1920," *The Alabama Review* 23 (July 1970): 163-80.

_____ . "Dissent in Zion: Alabama Baptists and Social Issues, 1900-1914," *The Journal of Southern History* 35 (November 1969): 523-42.

_____ . "Religion in the Urban South: The Divided Religious Mind of Birmingham, 1900-1930," *The Alabama Review* 30 (April 1977): 108-34.

_____ "Alabama White Protestantism and Labor, 1900-1914," *The Alabama Review* 25 (July 1972): 192-217.

Douglas W. Johnson, et al., *Churches and Church Membership in the United States: An Enumeration by Region, State and County.*

Michael Kenny. *Catholic Culture in Alabama: Centenary Story of Spring Hill College, 1830-1930.*

Marion E. Lazenby. *History of Methodism in Alabama and West Florida.*

James W. Marshall. *The Presbyterian Church in Alabama,* Robert Strong, editor.

Thomas M. Owen, compiler. *The Methodist Churches of Montgomery.*

B. F. Riley. *A Memorial History of the Baptists of Alabama.*
A. Hamilton Reid. *Baptists in Alabama: Their Organization and Witness.*
George H. Watson. *History of the Christian Churches in the Alabama Area.*
Anson West. *A History of Methodism in Alabama.*

ARKANSAS

ORVILLE W. TAYLOR
GEORGIA COLLEGE

The first Christian religious service in Arkansas was conducted in 1541 near present-day Helena by Catholic priests accompanying Hernando de Soto on his journey of exploration across the South. No priest appeared again until 1673, when the French Jesuit explorer Father Marquette visited an Indian village a few miles above the mouth of the Arkansas River. In 1682 Father Membre, a Franciscan accompanying the explorer La Salle, also conducted services there.

A base for more permanent Catholic work was established when the French seigneur Henri de Tonti founded Arkansas Post, the first European settlement in the lower Mississippi Valley, in 1686 near the site of the earlier visits. De Tonti gave land to the Jesuits, and up to the end of the French period various priests held services for the few French traders, hunters, and farmers in Arkansas and did mission work among the Indians.

Few records of Catholic activity in Arkansas during the Spanish period after 1762 have survived. It is known, though, that the church at Arkansas Post was named St. Esteban's, and that priests there performed marriages and baptisms and carried out other priestly functions.

After Arkansas became part of the United States in the Louisiana Purchase of 1803, Catholic work was placed under control of Archbishop Carroll of Baltimore, who appointed Father William Dubourg administrator. Dubourg became Bishop of Louisiana and the Floridas in 1815 and entrusted Catholic work in Arkansas to the Lazarists, who remained until the arrival in 1844 of Andrew Byrne, bishop of the new Diocese of Little Rock.

In 1833 secular priests also began to work in what since 1819 had been Arkansas Territory. They founded St. Mary's Church, oldest permanent Catholic church in Arkansas, at the thriving French settlement of the same name five miles below Pine Bluff on the Arkansas River. At least 50 Catholic families lived there, with others scattered along the valley at Little Rock, Pine Bluff, New Gascony, French Town, Plum Bayou, Arkansas Post, and Napoleon. Prominent priests included Father Dupuy, Father Richard Bale, and Father P. K. Donnelley. Sisters of Loretto led by Mother Agnes Hart established a school at St. Mary's in 1838.

When he arrived in Little Rock in 1844 Bishop Byrne found only 700 Catholics in the diocese, most still in the lower valley, but a few in every county. The state (admitted in 1836) had a population of only 100,000, and Little Rock, the capital, was a small frontier village. Setting out to strengthen Catholicism in the state, Bishop Byrne solicited funds from foreign and American organizations, built the first St. Andrew's Cathedral, recruited priests from the East and abroad, and led in the founding of churches in Fort Smith, Fayetteville, Rocky Comfort, and other towns, and schools in Little Rock, Fort Smith, and Helena. Byrne attempted to arrest the relative decline of Catholicism in the state in the face of the flood of predominantly Protestant immigrants by attracting European Catholic settlers. His only success, however, was in recruiting 300 Irish Catholics to settle on 640 acres he purchased at Fort Smith. Some died of "shipboard fever" and others settled in Little Rock and St. Louis, but most went to Fort Smith to become the nucleus of the Catholic community there. Contributing to the general failure of Bishop Byrne's project was the anti-foreign, anti-Catholic Know Nothing movement. During its height the Catholic church at Helena was burned in 1854 and an unsuccessful effort was made to invalidate purchase of the Fort Smith property.

Thus Catholicism in Arkansas was still far from thriving, with only nine priests, a few nuns, and 1,000 parishioners, when Bishop Byrne died in 1862. Rejuvenation would have to await the coming of more-welcome Catholic immigrants after the Civil War.

Protestants rapidly overtook Catholics in number in Arkansas after 1803. Particularly prominent were Methodists and Baptists, with smaller numbers of Presbyterians and Episcopalians and a few members of other denominations.

The Methodist Church was the largest denomination in the state before the Civil War. Its simplicity of doctrine and worship appealed to the frontier population, and its centralized organization made it possible to send ministers into new areas. The Methodist pioneer in Arkansas was William Stevenson of Belleview, Missouri, who preached in 1813 in the northeast and between 1814 and 1816 along the Ouachita, Caddo, and Red Rivers in the southwest. In 1816 he organized Spring River Circuit, the first in Arkansas, centered in Lawrence County in the northeast. The next year he led a colony of Methodists from Missouri to Mound Prarie in the southwest, which became an early center of Arkansas Methodism. Stevenson became presiding elder of all Methodist work in Arkansas, but moved about 1825 to Louisiana.

From its beginnings along the northeast-southwest highland line, Methodism expanded into the eastern lowlands and the western hills and mountains. The 92 members of 1815 increased to 1,634 in 1831, 5,034 in 1840, and 24,164 in 1861. By 1861 there were about 500 churches, those in important towns such as Little Rock, Camden, Fort Smith, El Dorado, and Bateville served by full-time pastors and the remainder organized into circuits.

The structure of the Methodist Church in Arkansas became more complex as membership increased. The single district within the Missouri Conference was divided in 1832 into Arkansas District in the north and Little Rock District in the south. Arkansas Conference was created in 1836, and Ouachita (now Little Rock) Conference, covering southern Arkansas, in 1854. Overall control was in the hands of the national General Conference, which assigned bishops to Arkansas. The first was Thomas A. Morris; among others before the Civil War, all non-resident, was James O. Andrew, whose ownership of a slave precipitated the split in the Methodist Church in 1844. There would be no resident bishop until the election of H. A. Boaz in 1926.

Even before 1844 the Methodist Protestant Church had separated from the Methodist Church (1830) in protest against the power of bishops. The first church in Arkansas of this new denomination was formed at Cane Hill in the northwest, and an Arkansas Conference was organized in 1837. By 1860 there were only about 2,000 Methodist Protestants, mostly in the northwest.

Baptists began work in Arkansas only slightly later than Methodists and also in northeastern Arkansas. Although by the twentieth century they would become the largest denomination in the state, they grew more slowly than Methodists in the early period. Contributing factors were the lack until 1848 of a centralized organization and disruption of some early churches by anti-mission, anti-organization forces, including the Camp-bellites, later known as the Disciples of Christ. On the positive side, Baptist churches could be formed without outside authorization or officially-recognized ministers, and also had simple doctrines and forms of worship.

Salem Baptist Church, the first in Arkansas, was organized in 1818 on Fourche-a-Thomas River in present-day Randolph County by James P. Edwards, a missionary from Bethel Association in Missouri, and Benjamin Clark and Jesse James. Bethel Association helped organize several other churches in the area in the next few years. Baptist work expanded southward in 1819 with the foundation by local residents of Pecannerie Church on the Arkansas River.

The most vigorous founder of early Baptist churches was David Orr, a missionary of the American Baptist Home Mission Society. He founded at least ten churches, including Rehobeth and Little Fork in Lawrence County and Rocky Bayou in White County, and organized Spring River Association in 1829. The first Baptist church in Little Rock was organized by Silas Toncray, a minister-jeweler, in 1824. The same year Toncray formed Little Rock Association, first in the state. After Toncray moved to Memphis in 1829 the church was taken over by Campbellites, and Baptist work would not resume in Little Rock until the present First Baptist Church was organized in 1858.

Stimulated by increased immigration after 1836, a wave of revivalism, and the organization of the Arkansas Baptist State Convention in 1848, Baptist membership grew to 372 in 1839, 2,989 in 1848, and 11,341 in 1860. The 321 churches of 1860 were mostly rural but some existed in the major towns.

Although autonomous, Baptist churches voluntarily formed associations for mutual support and concerted evangelistic effort. By 1860 there were 16 associations; they met after crops were gathered for reports of committees, worship services, and socializing among the delegates from the often-isolated churches. The need for a more comprehensive organization was filled by the Arkansas Baptist State Convention, organized in 1848 at Tulip in south-central Arkansas. Composed of delegates from churches and associations, the convention had no official ecclesiastical jurisdiction, but devoted itself primarily to promotion of missions and ministerial education. It soon affiliated with the Southern Baptist Convention, formed in 1845. Despite some tension between the state convention and churches over the question of ultimate authority, the convention operated successfully until it became inactive during the Civil War. Two other conventions arose in the 1850s, White River State Convention in northern Arkansas and the General Association of Eastern Arkansas. Neither was revived after the Civil War.

Presbyterians were the third largest denomination in pre-Civil War Arkansas. Cumberland Presbyterians, who had split from the national Presbyterian Church in 1810, began work at Cane Hill in northwestern Arkansas in 1825 under the leadership of John P. Carnahan, and a church of the major Presbyterian group was organized in Little Rock in 1828 by James W. Moore, a missionary from Pennsylvania. Gradually Presbyterians came from the older states, some clustering in colonies around Jacksonport and Batesville on the White River and Scotland and Mt. Holly in Union County. By 1860 there were about 60 churches with about 2,500 members, plus a smaller number of Cumberland Presbyterians. Primarily rural at this time, Presbyterians later became increasingly urban.

Arkansas Presbytery, organized in 1835, and Ouachita Presbytery, formed in 1849 and covering the southern half of the state, comprised the Synod of Arkansas, constituted in 1852 with W. K. Marshall as first moderator. Previously Presbyterian work in Arkansas had been under control of the Synod of Memphis. Primary concerns of the synod were evangelism, establishment of a college, support of the work of the Presbyterian Church, especially foreign missions, and the state of religion in the churches.

Organized activities of the Episcopal Church in Arkansas began in 1838 with the election of Leonidas Polk, later famous as a Confederate general, as Missionary Bishop of the Southwest. The few Episcopalians in Arkansas previously were so scattered that no parishes had been formed. The number would remain small since most Episcopalians were members of the very small upper economic and social class.

Before becoming Bishop of Louisiana in 1841, Polk made two arduous missionary journeys through Arkansas and aided in organizing Christ Church, Little Rock, and St. Paul's Church, Fayetteville. Slow growth continued under the succeeding missionary bishops, James H. Otey, George W. Freeman, and Henry C. Lay, and by 1860 the 12 organized parishes had about 400 members. Most of the congregations were very small and without their own buildings and rectors.

The few Christian churches in the state not related to major denominations were mostly in the hills and mountains of the northwest. Total membership probably did not exceed a thousand.

Early religious life in Arkansas was influenced by the frontier conditions which continued until well after the Civil War. The population was small, scattered, and mostly rural, the few roads were little more than cleared tracks, and few bridges spanned the numerous streams. The state had less than 100 miles of railroad in 1860. Most houses and other buildings were built of logs or rough planks, even in the towns, the largest of which, Little Rock, had only 3,727 people in 1860.

Many churches originally held services in homes or open shelters, then typically built one-room log buildings and later frame churches. There were few brick or stone churches until much later.

Most churches had services only once or twice a month, although the two and three hour sermons compensated for the infrequency. Salaries of pastors were very low; in 1833 Methodist ministers received $34 per year if single and $68 if married. Consequently many preachers were also farmers or primarily made their living in other ways. The general level of ministerial education was very low, especially among Baptists and Methodists, who valued a divine "call" above education. Many early preachers suffered real personal hardship, often riding horseback hundreds of miles a year through swamps and forests to reach their remote, scattered churches.

Camp meetings were a common feature of frontier religious life. Held in the summer after the crops were "laid by," they lasted from a week to a month and often were conducted jointly by the Protestant churches of the area, with their preachers rotating in delivering the four or five sermons a day under brush arbors or tabernacles. People came from miles around to hear the preaching and to sing, pray, testify, shout—and perhaps be converted. The accompanying social life was an almost equally important part of the camp meeting. Facilities at camp meetings usually were crude and temporary, but semi-permanent buildings were erected at some camp grounds. Some still function, and present-day assemblies such as Arkansas Baptist Assembly at Siloam Springs, Western Methodist Assembly at Fayetteville, and the Assemblies of God Ozark-Lithia Camp Ground at Hot Springs are simply more elaborate versions of the frontier camp ground.

Most of the denominations carried on mission work among the Indians who lived in sizable numbers in Arkansas until the 1830s. The best-known mission was Dwight Mission, founded in 1820 on Illinois Bayou in western Arkansas by Cephas Washburn and other Congregational missionaries but abandoned in 1829 after most Arkansas Indians were removed to Indian Territory. During the 1830s the churches often ministered to the thousands of Indians passing through on the several branches of the "Trail of Tears" leading to Indian Territory.

Jewish people began to enter Arkansas in the 1830s, but not yet in numbers large enough to organize congregations. The first were Jacob Hyman and Levy Mitchell, who came to Little Rock from Crakow, Poland, in 1838. Edward Czarnikow arrived in Fort Smith from Posen, Poland, in 1842, and was soon followed by others from that city. The first Jew in Pine Bluff was a man named Wolf (1850) and the first in Hot Springs was Jacob Kempner (1856). Living exclusively in the towns, almost all Jews were merchants. Those in Fort Smith traded extensively with the Indians. Descendants of some of the earliest Jewish families are still prominent in Arkansas.

All of the Christian denominations in Arkansas worked among the slaves, who by 1860 comprised a quarter of the population of 435,450. Three-quarters of the slaves lived on the cotton lands of the southeastern half of the state. The motives were both spiritual and pragmatic; it was believed that white Christians were obligated to share the gospel with slaves, but also that religious slaves were more likely to remain in peaceful subjection.

Slave church members sometimes attended services with white members and sometimes separately. There were no separate official slave churches, although occasionally slave members had separate meeting places and slave preachers. Wesley Chapel was built in 1854 in Little Rock for slave members of the First Methodist Church, with the slave preacher William Wallace Andrews in charge.

Along with encouraging slaves to become members of the regular churches, all denominations also carried on mission work among them, especially in rural areas with many slaves. Methodists had at least 10 missions at various times, including one on the Red River where absentee ownership was prevalent. Baptist mission work was also extensive, if less well-organized until formation of the state convention. In its first year the convention appointed a missionary to slaves on the Red River. Associations also did mission work; Red River had as many as four at a time. Presbyterians and Episcopalians also did mission work among slaves on a smaller scale, and in small numbers slaves continued to be baptized into the Catholic church.

Despite such efforts, no more than seven percent of Arkansas slaves in 1860 were formally affiliated with the churches. But slaves also frequently held secret services unrelated to organized churches, although all secret meetings were illegal. The rapid emergence of separate black churches after emancipation demonstrated that "underground" churches were stronger and more widespread than had been popularly believed.

Only about 18 percent of the white people of Arkansas were members of slaveowning families, but many others had strong ties to slavery. By the Civil War pro-slavery sentiment was dominant, although a strong minority opinion existed in the north and west. Most of the churches and ministers reflected the general approval. Sermons often cited biblical justification and asserted that Christian whites had been given control of slaves for the purpose of converting them.

Ministers frequently were slave owners themselves. Baptist farmer-preachers owning a few slaves were not uncommon, and at the upper end of the scale Bishop Leonidas Polk owned 400 slaves, although not in Arkansas. In 1850 a tenth of the Methodist ministers who were members of the Arkansas Conference held slaves, including the presiding elder of the Washington District with 15. More than a fourth of the local preachers owned slaves.

A few ministers and church members spoke out against slavery, especially before the Abolitionist movement crystallized pro-slavery sentiment. The Methodist Jesse Haile, who became presiding elder of Arkansas District in 1825, spoke so militantly against slavery that a number of Methodists joined other denominations. As a result Haile was transferred in 1830 to Illinois.

Sentiments such as Haile's had little influence upon most Arkansas churches, which readily endorsed the divisions in their denominations over slavery. In 1845 Arkansas Methodists declared allegiance to the new Methodist Episcopal Church, South, and soon after it was organized the Arkansas Baptist State Convention affiliated with the Southern Baptist Convention. Southern Presbyterians and Episcopalians split from the national churches at the beginning of the Civil War (the latter reunited in 1865). Since there was no separate American Catholic Church, Catholics did not officially divide along sectional lines.

Division of the denominations would have profound effect upon religion in Arkansas. It would help bring on the Civil War, which in turn would lead to serious weakening of the churches for a time, emergence of separate black denominations, and, for Methodists, Baptists, and Presbyterians, continued alienation from similar denominations outside the South for decades to come.

The Civil War severely disrupted life in Arkansas. Only three states had more battles and engagements, and at least 75,000 men, including most of the white males of military age, served in the Confederate and Union armies and state troops. About a fifth were in the Union army. Others served as irregular troops as the tides of war surged across the state. Among those who served were most of the male members of the churches, and thus, in that male-dominated day, most of the leaders, lay and clerical. Women often carried on as best they could, but the churches shared in the general disruption.

Numerous ministers became chaplains, and others ministered to troops as campaigns passed their way. Among well-known chaplains were Horace Jewell, later author of a history of Arkansas Methodists, and Ebenezer Lee Compere, who left the First Baptist Church of Fort Smith to become chaplain to General Stand Watie's Confederate Indians. Some ministers also became ordinary soldiers.

The war took its toll of church buildings, often expropriated by the armies, then damaged or destroyed. Particularly offensive to Southern Methodists was seizure of some of their churches under the Stanton-Ames joint policy of the Union army and the Northern Methodist Church. The policy provided that as an area was occupied Southern Methodist churches would be turned over to Northern bishops. In Arkansas Bishop Ames took over churches in Little Rock, Pine Bluff, Fort Smith, Fayetteville, Helena, and elsewhere and organized an Arkansas District of the Methodist Episcopal Church. But Union generals did not always cooperate or chose to use the buildings themselves, Southern Methodists in the loyal border states protested strongly, and soon after the war President Johnson returned most of the buildings to the Southern owners.

The Civil War also damaged the human spirit, leaving a legacy of bitterness, hatred, and divisiveness which would persist for a very long time.

At the end of the Civil War the first task facing the churches was reestablishment of organized religion at all levels. Along with recovery and subsequent growth, the chief developments in religion in Arkansas during the remainder of the century were the choices by the churches of continued separation or reunion with the Northern branches, the emergence and growth of separate black churches, the strengthening of the Catholic and Lutheran Churches by the coming of ethnic immigrants, the founding of schools and colleges, and the "Landmark" controversy leading to a major split within Arkansas Baptist life in 1901.

Methodists revived their conferences, appointed pastors, and sent delegates to the General Conference of the Methodist Episcopal Church, South, at New Orleans in 1866. The conference moved toward democracy by authorizing lay representation, which became policy despite adverse votes by the Arkansas conferences. Laymen steadily assumed leadership; George Thornburgh, for example, was secretary of White River Conference, formed in 1870 and dissolved in 1914, business manager of the *Arkansas Methodist*, and superintendent of the Arkansas Methodist Orphanage in Little Rock. Women would not gain full laity rights until 1918. Ladies Aid and women's missionary societies and increased emphasis upon Sunday Schools also date from this period. Such innovations enabled Methodists to resume their growth.

Many Baptist churches were revived and new ones were organized, but others would never recover. Associations, which had declined from 16 in 1860 to only six, were quickly reestablished, and by 1868 there were 23. The Arkansas Baptist State Convention was revived in 1867 by a handful of delegates in Little Rock, and despite limited funds, continuing criticism from anti-mission elements, and the perennial Baptist struggle between centralization and decentralization, slowly regained the strength which would insure its position as the focus of Baptist work. Among those responsible for the revival and growth of the convention were W. M. Lea, pre-war president reelected in 1867, J. B. Searcy, General Missionary Agent and convention secretary for many years, and James P. Eagle, Confederate soldier and officer, minister, governor of Arkansas 1888-1893, president of the convention 21 times, and president of the Southern Baptist Convention three times.

The Presbyterian Synod of Arkansas resumed meeting in 1866, but there were other interruptions during Reconstruction, and at one time a proposal was made to abolish it. But it survived and by 1877 the 60 churches of 1860 had increased to 83.

Bishop Lay provided some continuity for Episcopal work since he had been elected in 1859 and remained 10 years. During the war he had visited the small, scattered congregations when possible, but at war's end most had to be revived.

Coordinated Catholic activity, which had almost ceased with the death of Bishop Byrne, resumed in 1867 upon arrival in Little Rock of Bishop Edward Fitzgerald, at 33 the youngest Catholic bishop in the nation. At that time there were only four functioning parishes, five priests, and schools at Little Rock and Fort Smith operated by the Sisters of Mercy. As Bishop Byrne had done, Bishop Fitzgerald encouraged Catholic immigration to Arkansas. He would eventually be highly successful, but only after the worst of the political turbulence and economic depression of Reconstruction. One of the chief monuments to Bishop Fitzgerald is the impressive present St. Andrew's Cathedral, dedicated in 1882. Very independent-minded, he cast one of only two votes against adoption of the doctrine of papal infallibility at the Vatican Council in 1870.

Additional Jews came to Little Rock during and after the war, and organized Jewish religious life began in 1866, when Congregation B'nai Israel was organized with Morris Navra as president. After meeting for several years in a single room, in 1872 the congregation built a brick temple and elected its first rabbi, Jacob Bloch. In 1873 Rabbi Bloch represented the congregation in the Cincinnati convention when it became one of the 32 charter members of the Union of Hebrew Congregations, parent organization of Reform Judaism. Meanwhile Jews moving into other towns and cities were also forming congregations.

Of the five denominations in Arkansas which had split, officially or unofficially, from their northern brethren by the beginning of the Civil War, two reunited quickly and three remained separate. Catholics simply resumed participation in the councils of the church, and Episcopalians sent delegates to a single General Conference, where reunification was achieved easily. Neither church insisted that its southern dioceses treat blacks as equals.

Early efforts to reunify Northern and Southern Baptists and Methodists were unsuccessful, for the animosity and suspicion most Northerners and Southerners had toward each other continued after the war. The Southern Baptist Convention resumed normal activities after the war, in 1868 officially stating that it was a permanent institution, and the Arkansas Baptist State Convention reestablished the pre-war relationship.

The eventually successful effort of the Methodist Episcopal Church, South, to remain separate was accompanied by rancor and bitterness on both sides, to a great extent because of the attempts of the Northern church to "recolonize" the Southern church through the Stanton-Ames policy. Even though the policy was revoked, Southern Methodists were indignant and resentful.

Even earlier, incensed at what they considered the high-handed tactics of Northern Methodists, the Southern bishops declared in August, 1865, that the Methodist Episcopal Church, South, would not succumb to absorption. Delegates to the 1866 General Conference, including those from Arkansas, voted overwhelmingly to continue, and the Southern Methodist Church proceeded to carry on its affairs as before the war.

Any hopes of speedy reunification of Presbyterians were dashed when the Northern church announced in 1865 that the price of reunion was recantation of their errors by Southern Presbyterians, now named the Presbyterian Church in the U. S. (PCUS). Reunion became even less likely when in 1870 the PCUS charged that the Northern church, renamed that year the Presbyterian Church in the U.S.A. (PCUSA) was doctrinally unorthodox. Eventually harsh attitudes were modified somewhat, and official fraternal relations were established in 1883. But, despite such efforts as the request in 1887 by three Southern synods, including the Synod of Arkansas, that closer relationships be sought, reunification would never come.

As Arkansas came under the control of the Union army and the slaves were freed, separate black churches began to emerge. A few people hoped that racially-integrated churches could continue, but the desire of the newly-freed slaves to manage their own affairs and the continuing antipathy and condescension of most Arkansas whites toward blacks determined that most blacks would soon be worshipping in black churches.

Most black Methodists found their way into one of four groups. The first was the Methodist Episcopal Church (northern). This church had several advantages in seeking black adherents—its history of opposition to slavery, support of the Republican Reconstruction government, and a vigorous educational program through its Freedmen's Aid Society, which founded numerous schools in Arkansas. Nevertheless, the church failed to attract many blacks.

The largest black Methodist group was the African Methodist Episcopal Church, founded in Philadelphia in 1787, which began to attract or organize congregations in Arkansas at the end of the war. In 1868 it organized an Arkansas conference with Bethel Church, founded in 1865 by the well-known free black Nathan Warren, as the nucleus.

The second-largest black Methodist group was a direct offshoot of the Methodist Episcopal Church, South. Soon after the war its black congregations were authorized to form quarterly conferences, and in 1870 by mutual agreement black churches in Arkansas and other states withdrew and formed the Colored Methodist Episcopal Church at Jackson, Tennessee. Blacks were given the buildings they were using, and white churches sometimes assisted them. Colored (now Christian) Methodist Episcopal members often were held in contempt by other black Methodists because of their fraternal relationship with their former masters. For many years the church operated Haygood Institute and Seminary in Arkansas.

Smallest of the black Methodist groups was the African Methodist Episcopal Zion Church, founded in New York in 1796.

Black Baptists were less fragmented, partially because northern white Baptists, who had no true convention organization until 1907, did not attempt to organize or attract black Baptist churches. One of the first organized was the First Baptist Church of Little Rock, which traces its origin to a slave congregation in 1845. The new churches soon formed associations, the first the First Missionary Baptist Association in 1867. By the 1880s there were nine and a state convention. An Arkansas minister, E. C. Morris, was the first president of the national convention to which most black Baptist churches in Arkansas still belong, the National Baptist Convention, U.S.A., Inc., formed in 1895. Although black and white state conventions maintained fraternal relationships, prospects for organic union became increasingly dim.

A technically separate black Southern Presbyterian Church eventually was formed, but records show no Arkansas churches affiliated with it. The number of black Presbyterians in the state has always been small. No separate black Catholic and Episcopal denominations were formed, although increasingly there were separate congregations for black members.

The disruption of the Civil War followed by the instability of Reconstruction slowed immigration into Arkansas to a trickle. The state's population, which had more than doubled in the pre-war decade, increased by only 11 percent to 484,000 in 1870. But after the end of Reconstruction in 1874 immigrants attracted by cheap land being opened up by new railroads again poured into the state to increase the population to 806,000 in 1880, 1,128,211 in 1890, and 1,311,564 in 1900. This near-tripling of population in 30 years profoundly affected religion in Arkansas, accounting for great growth among well-established churches, rejuvenation of the Catholic Church, and growing prominence of other denominations. By the end of the century Arkansas had dozens of denominations in addition to the half-dozen present there prior to the war.

Most of the immigrants were Anglo-Saxon Protestants from the older South, but substantial numbers were of European Catholic and Lutheran background. The only pre-Civil War Lutheran church in the state, organized at Long Prairie south of Fort Smith in 1852 by Germans from Saxony, was inactive during the war but was revived in 1868 as the First Lutheran Church of Fort Smith. The same year the First Lutheran Church of Little Rock was organized by predominantly German people with such well-known Little Rock names as Kramer, Geyer, and Riegler. Between 1876 and 1900 churches still existing were founded, mostly by German farmers from Germany, Russia, and the American Midwest and Northeast, in widely-distributed towns, some with the appropriate names of Ulm, Waldenburg, Stuttgart, and Augsburg.

Catholics established new churches at Pocahontas and Lake Village in the immediate post-war period while reviving the inactive churches, then founded no fewer than 33, most still existing, from 1875 until 1899. They generally fall into three categories. Some were founded in such non-ethnic towns as Brinkley, Forrest City, Little Rock, and Paragould, although sometimes for immigrants, a few were established for German railroad workers.

Five churches were formed by ethnic groups other than German. Immaculate Heart of Mary Church at Marche north of North Little Rock was organized in 1878 by Poles. The community continued to thrive until World War II, when the federal government bought much of the farm-land for expansion of nearby Camp Robinson. But the thriving church atop Jasna Gora (Blue Hill) is a familiar sight in northern Pulaski County. Bohemians founded a church near Dardanelle in 1895, but after a few years it dwindled for lack of clerical leadership. In 1898 Slovacs organized Sts. Cyril and Methodius Church at Slovac in eastern Arkansas. Two churches were formed by Italians, the first in 1895 at Sunnyside near Lake Village by immigrants brought to farm the fertile cotton lands. Malaria soon killed many of the colony of 250 families, and most of the survivors drifted away, especially to Tontitown in more climatically favorable northwestern Arkansas where under the leadership of their priest, Father Bandini, they founded a second colony and church which still thrive. The Sunnyside community and church succumbed to the boll weevil in 1912.

Almost half of the new Catholic churches were organized among German immigrant farmers, all but two, at Stuttgart in eastern Arkansas and Engelberg near Pocahontas, in the upper Arkansas River Valley. The chief motivating forces behind this movement, which greatly changed the religious composition of that section, were the Little Rock and Fort Smith (now Missouri Pacific) Railroad and Bishop Fitzgerald. The railroad widely advertised the large grants of land it had received to finance construction, and attracted thousands of mostly Catholic Germans to the largely undeveloped region. The railroad company and Bishop Fitzgerald, realizing that German-speaking priests and nuns would attract German settlers, cooperated in inviting several orders, especially the Benedictine Fathers and the Benedictine Sisters, to establish work in the valley. Benedictine Fathers from Indiana founded St. Benedict's Priory in 1878 on a square mile of land in Logan County given by the railroad. The Benedictines soon organized churches and schools in the German communities, some on land also given by the railroad. Despite early poverty and hardship, the priory prospered, serving as the nucleus of Catholic work in the valley, especially by training pastors for the churches. In 1891 it became an independent abbey named New Subiaco with Swiss-born Father Ignatius Conrad as abbot. The abbey outgrew its rambling frame quarters and in 1902 moved into the massive five-story hollow-square stone structure it still occupies.

Also in 1878 German Benedictine Sisters founded St. Scholastica's Convent and School at Shoal Creek (New Blaine) on land given by the railroad twelve miles east of the abbey. Convent Maria Stein was founded at Pocahontas in 1888, but was moved to Jonesboro in 1898 and renamed Holy Angels Convent.

The ethnic communities have dissipated somewhat, especially since World War II, but as late as 1935 German-language services were still being held in some of the churches. The churches have remained strong, and have provided a greater variety in religious life than had been known previously in Arkansas.

A need for denominational schools and colleges became increasingly apparent as life in Arkansas became more settled and sophisticated in the last third of the nineteenth century. Public schools were inadequate, and colleges were needed for ministers and other leaders. There were not even state-operated institutions of higher education prior to the opening of the University of Arkansas at Fayetteville in 1871.

Schools of various denominations had existed before the war, but most were weak and short-lived. The closest approximation to a true college was Cane Hill College, established in 1834 by Cumberland Presbyterians. After a long lapse following the war, it was revived at Clarksville in 1891 as Arkansas Cumberland College, and later became the present College of the Ozarks, now controlled by the PCUSA. Presbyterians also operated schools before the war at Spring Hill, Mt. Holly, Lonoke, and Batesville.

Baptists sponsored schools at Mine Creek (Nashville), Arkadelphia, and Camden, while Methodist schools existed at Fayetteville, Pine Bluff, Batesville, Washington, Tulip, Arkadelphia, Centre Point, and Van Buren. Wallace Institute at Van Buren, founded in 1854 and endowed with $10,000 from the estate of Mr. and Mrs. Alfred Wallace, succumbed to the war as the other schools did. But its endowment somehow survived, and in the 1930s, grown to $25,000, went to Hendrix College.

After the war the denominations resumed their efforts to found colleges. Again the Presbyterians took the lead. In 1872 Dr. Isaac C. Long founded Arkansas College in Batesville, still operated by the Synod of Arkansas of the PCUS.

Baptist associations opened schools, some aspiring to the status of state Baptist college, in the 1870s. Best known were Judson University at Judsonia, Shiloh Institute at Springdale, Red River Academy and Arkadelphia High School at Arkadelphia, and Buckner College at Witcherville near Fort Smith. Meanwhile the state convention had resumed its strong pre-war interest in ministerial education and the establishment of a college. In 1870 it authorized payment of annual subsidies of $150 to young ministers and designated Mississippi College, Clinton, as the official Arkansas Baptist college; subsequently a number of Arkansas ministers studied there and elsewhere.

But this was only an interim measure, and in 1886, after delay because of economic depression and lack of enthusiasm by many of the generally poorly-educated Arkansas Baptists, the convention opened Ouachita Baptist College in Arkadelphia. By then all of the other Baptist schools had expired except Buckner College, which came under Episcopal control from 1887 until 1890 and was transferred in 1904 to the General (Landmark) Baptist Association. Ouachita College prospered under its first president, J. W. Conger, enrolling 476 students by the end of his administration in 1907. The strong beginning helped it to weather later economic problems and competition from other Baptist colleges to become the Ouachita Baptist University of today. Ouachita was coeducational from the first, but pressure from the women's movement of the period influenced the convention to found Central Female College at Conway in 1892.

The next year White River Association opened Mountain Home College in the town of that name.

Arkansas Methodists also opened numerous short-lived schools after the Civil War, including Camden Male College, Arkansas Female College in Little Rock, and twenty district high schools thoughout the state between 1871 and the 1890s. All of the latter were replaced by public high schools. But Quitman College in north-central Arkansas gave creditable college work, enrolling 3,000 students, including 30 who became Methodist ministers, from 1871 until it fell victim in 1899 to its location away from a railroad.

In 1888 an educational commission proposed that Arkansas Methodists operate only two colleges, the male Central Collegiate Institute at Altus (renamed Hendrix College in 1889), founded in 1876, and a new female college to be built at Searcy. Despite the recommendations, within two years there were four Methodist colleges. Galloway Woman's College opened at Searcy in 1889, and coeducational Arkadelphia Methodist College in 1890. The same year Hendrix was moved to Conway, where under the presidency of Dr. A. C. Millar it began to develop into one of the best small liberal arts colleges in the South.

Thus by the end of the century white Presbyterians, Baptists, and Methodists were attempting to operate many more colleges than they could support.

Three black denominational colleges still in existence were founded in Little Rock during this period. Philander Smith College was opened in 1877 by the Methodist Episcopal Church (Northern) as Walden Seminary. Arkansas Baptist College began in 1884 as a ministerial institute related to the new black Baptist state convention. Shorter College, opened in 1886 as Bethel Institute by Bethel African Methodist Episcopal Church, later moved to Arkadelphia and then to North Little Rock.

From the beginning many Arkansas Baptists opposed centralized efforts in missions and other activities, emphasizing instead the primacy of churches and associations. In the 1850s this faction became associated with the Southern Baptist "Landmark" movement led by James R. Graves, editor of the *Tennessee Baptist*. Graves was very popular in Arkansas, and for a time his paper was designated as the official Arkansas Baptist paper. Landmark adherents also believed that Baptist churches were the only true churches, descended in an unbroken line from those of the New Testament. Thus they practiced closed communion and rejected alien immersion. They were predominantly rural and generally suspicious of an educated clergy.

As activities of the Arkansas Baptist State Convention grew after the Civil War, Landmark leaders became increasingly vocal. At the 1888 convention meeting they insisted that boards and conventions were heretical and opposed appointment of a paid corresponding secretary. The controversy came to a head at the 1901 convention meeting in Paragould over renewal of the appointment of A. J. Barton as missionary secretary. Barton was reelected, but with great difficulty. Landmark reaction to this defeat led to the organization in 1902 of the General Association of Arkansas Baptists, dominated by the Rev. Ben M. Bogard for fifty years. Although churches and associations began immediately to declare allegiance to association or convention, many vacillated, and not until the 1920s was the schism complete. Separate statistics were not published until 1921, but in the early years the convention probably lost 60 percent of its churches, mostly small and rural, and a third of its members. By 1921, however, as a result of vigorous efforts by convention churches and of concessions to Landmark sympathizers, only 30 percent of the churches and 25 percent of the members were affiliated with the association.

In 1905 the Arkansas association joined with similar groups to form the American Baptist Association. A schism in 1950 resulted in organization of a second Landmark group, the Baptist Missionary Association. Although both are now national in scope, the core of Landmark strength is in Arkansas. In 1971 a dozen counties, more than in any other state, had more Landmark than Southern Baptist Convention members. Landmark Baptists have acquired many of the organizational characteristics against which they rebelled in 1901-1902, while many convention ministers and churches cling to elements of Landmark belief.

A general census of religious bodies in the United States in 1906 reveals the great growth of church members and denominations in Arkansas after the Civil War. Baptists had overtaken Methodists as the largest denomination, reporting 193,244 members. The 94,204 black Baptists, including 840 Primitive Baptists, outnumbered convention Baptists (about 61,000) and Landmark Baptists (about 30,000) combined. Small groups such as General, Freewill, Primitive, Seventh-Day, and Two-Seed-in-the-Spirit Baptists comprised the remaining 8,000.

Of the 142,569 Methodists, 81,699 were in the Methodist Episcopal Church, South, the largest single group in the state. There were 40,873 members of the separate black Methodist groups (AME 26,903; CME

11,506; AME Zion 2,404), 12,569 members (including some blacks) of the Methodist Episcopal Church, 6,658 Methodist Protestants, and 830 Congregational and Free Methodists.

With 32,307 members, Catholics had replaced Presbyterians as the third largest denomination. The 21,156 Presbyterians were divided as follows: Cumberland Presbyterians, soon to diminish sharply in a partial merger with the PCUSA, 11,990; PCUS, 7,357; Associate Reformed Presbyterians, 854; PCUSA, 809; and United Presbyterians, 1, 461.

The Churches of Christ, first recognized in the 1906 census as a separate denomination, had 11,006 members, followed by the Christian Church (Disciples), from which they had split, with 10,269. The Churches of Christ had been the conservative wing of the Christian Church, and since the mid-nineteenth century had been moving toward separation based on objection to creation of missionary societies, introduction of musical instruments in services, and growth of liberal biblical scholarship. Episcopalians numbered 4,315, Lutherans 2,080, and Jews 673.

Among the remainder of the 53 individual denominations, all with small numbers, were the Seventh Day Adventists, the Church of Christ, Scientist, the Church of the Brethren, the Amish, the Salvation Army, the Unitarian-Universalists, the Latter Day Saints, and three still-existing denominations founded in Arkansas. The Church of the Living God was organized in 1889 at Wrightsville near Little Rock by the appropriately named ex-slave William Christian, who taught that "Freemason religion" was the only true religion. The Church of God in Christ, which now has almost a half-million members, was founded in 1895 by two Baptist ministers who believed that holiness is necessary for salvation. The Free Christian Zion Church of Christ, whose headquarters is in Nashville, Arkansas, was organized in 1905 at the equally appropriately-named town of Redemption by dissident black Methodist and Baptist ministers. There were also a few independent churches.

The 425,000 church members of 1906 comprised about 30 percent of the total population of about 1,400,000, more than twice the percentage of 1861. Almost 80 percent were Baptist or Methodist.

In the period before World War I Arkansas was still one of the most rural states in the nation. Only 12.9 percent of the 1910 population of 1,574,449 was urban, living in towns of 2,500 or more. Little Rock, by far the largest city, had a population of only 45,941, although it was an important regional center. Population growth had tapered off and would be only moderate up to 1940, when a period of decline would begin. The black population had increased from the 25.6 percent of 1860 to 28.1 percent, but thereafter would steadily decline. There was a good railroad network except in the mountains, but most roads were still unpaved. Agriculture, especially cotton growing, and lumbering dominated the economy, with manufacturing and processing increasingly important.

The churches were correspondingly rural, with at least 90 percent in the open country or small towns. Rural churches averaged little more than 50 members and town and city churches less than 200. Most rural and some town and city churches were still served by half-time or quarter-time pastors.

In this predominantly rural setting, which continued until 1970, the denominations would grow at varying rates. Of the older denominations, Baptists and Methodists would grow substantially, while Catholics, Presbyterians, Episcopalians, and Disciples would level off. Other groups showing growth were the Churches of Christ and the various Pentecostal-Holiness churches, white and black. Growing denominations tended to be more evangelistic and emotional in appeal and forms of worship.

Just before World War II a major new denomination was organized in Arkansas. In April, 1914, 300 delegates from Pentecostal churches which had sprung up across the United States in the previous 20 years met in Hot Springs and formed the Assemblies of God. Despite insistence that it was not a new church, the group soon emerged as a distinct denomination with paid officials and a headquarters in nearby Springfield, Missouri. It has become the largest Pentecostal body, with Arkansas one of its strongest states.

Another development of the time resulted in further fragmentation, rather than consolidation, of churches. In 1915 a dissident faction broke away from the black National Baptist Convention, U.S.A., Inc. to form the National Baptist Convention of America. A second schism in the original group in 1961 resulted in formation of the Progressive Baptist Convention, Inc. Thus Arkansas now has three black Baptist conventions, the Consolidated Missionary Baptist Convention, the Regular Baptist Convention, and the Progressive Baptist Convention. The first, affiliated with the original national convention, is by far the largest.

Ministers and members of Arkansas churches almost universally supported World War I. A later study of attitudes of ministers in non-German, non-pacifist churches found none in Arkansas who opposed the war. But while supporting that particular war, religious organizations such as the Arkansas Baptist State Convention sometimes deplored war in general and expressed concern for the spiritual welfare of the enemy.

Support was demonstrated in various ways. Church members and ministers served as soldiers, officers, and chaplains. Civilian ministers preached, taught Bible classes, distributed tracts and Bibles, and visited the sick on military installations, especially Camp Pike near Little Rock. As the war went on, however, the War Department restricted the activities of civilian ministers on the posts, prompting the Baptist State Convention to oppose appointment of military chaplains as a violation of the principle of separation of church and state.

In the churches, though, there was little separation. Pastors preached in support of the war, sometimes using government-supplied propaganda, and promoted Liberty Loan drives, Victory gardens, and even enlistment. Members responded with equal patriotism. After the war the churches were the focal point of fund-raising drives for relief of victims of the war in Europe.

Arkansas enjoyed a measure of prosperity in the 1920s, although less than in most of the nation and fading more quickly. Least affected were farm workers, more than two-thirds of whom were tenants or share-croppers often living little above the subsistence level. The per capita income of rural Arkansas in 1922 was only $210.

Nevertheless the churches prospered moderately, especially in the towns and cities, where some new buildings were constructed. Most rural churches still had small, one-room buildings without electricity. Financial support of churches increased; members of Baptist State Convention churches, for example, gave $468,000 in 1919, but $1,300,000 in 1924.

But the short-lived prosperity was not an unmixed blessing. Some churches had difficulty paying for new buildings, and denominations overextended themselves in building, expanding, and operating schools, colleges, hospitals, and orphans' homes. The Baptist State Convention founded an ambitious but ill-timed system of six mountain academies, closing several within a few years and the remainder during the Depression. Presbyterians had a more modest system of two mountain schools; one was closed in 1931 and the other continued to operate on a limited scale.

The full-scale arrival of the automobile age in Arkansas in the 1920s had distinct influence upon religious life. More affluent rural people could now attend church more conveniently, while urban people could more easily ignore church activities to participate in the growing variety of secular pleasures. Part-time pastors found it easier to get to their scattered churches. But the state would not have a good rural road system until after World War II.

The Great Depression of the 1930s affected everyone in Arkansas, but especially the 80 percent who were rural. The churches felt the full effect, as shown by gifts to Baptist State Convention churches. After the peak of $1,300,000 in 1924 they remained almost level until 1930, then dropped by nearly half to $685,000 in 1933. As a result of such declines salaries of some pastors of all denominations were reduced or not paid at all, denominational employees were terminated and programs curtailed, and church buildings and other facilities were not maintained properly.

Particularly hard hit were denominational institutions, especially colleges. In 1930 the Catholics closed Little Rock College, founded in 1908 by Bishop John B. Morris, successor in 1906 to Bishop Fitzgerald. Methodists transferred Henderson-Brown (formerly Arkadelphia Methodist) College to the state in 1929, then closed Galloway College in 1933. Officially, at least, the two were merged with Hendrix College. In 1934 Harding College, founded at Morilton in 1919 by the Churches of Christ, occupied the Galloway property at Searcy.

Baptists closed Mountain Home College in 1933 and Jonesboro Baptist College, founded in 1903, in 1935. Ouachita College survived under the leadership of Dr. J. R. Grant, but only by such drastic measures as cutting faculty salaries and paying debts from endowment. Central College also weathered the Depression, but not the effects of World War II, and after shifting to North Little Rock for two years was closed in 1950. In 1948, however, the state convention had assumed control of Southern Baptist College at Walnut Ridge, which had been founded at Pocahontas in 1941. The Landmark Association of Missionary Baptists opened a Central College on the Conway campus in 1952.

Both Presbyterian colleges survived, but remained small and financially hard-pressed. An attempt in 1951 to merge the PCUSA College of the Ozarks and the PCUS Arkansas College failed because of denominational differences and local possessiveness. The state's black denominational colleges had even greater difficulty in surviving the Depression.

In the long run religious higher education in Arkansas benefitted from the closing or divestiture of at least some small, impoverished colleges, making possible more effective use of always limited funds.

One of the most traumatic economic effects of the Depression was the near-bankruptcy of the Baptist State Convention. Its debts of the expansive 1920s grew by 1934 to the unmanageable total of $1,126,000, and when vigorous fund-raising campaigns, including collection of old gold and silver and a "God's Acre" plan, netted little, in 1936 the convention negotiated a settlement of 35 percent. By 1938 the convention was legally, at least, debt free. But it later demonstrated its moral integrity by paying the remainder of the debt between 1944 and 1952. The persistence of Dr. B. L. Bridges, executive secretary from 1931 until 1958, was largely responsible for this.

Along with hardships and setbacks there were two Depression successes, the renaissance of the Episcopal Diocese of Arkansas and the reunification of the Methodist Church. The Episcopal diocese, as a result of the Depression and years of ineffectual leadership by very elderly bishops, had become so weak and disorganized one writer described it as "the most tragic diocese in the American church." When Richard Bland Mitchell became bishop in 1938 there were only 36 parishes and missions—a third without clerical leadership, fifteen priests, and 4,592 members, few more than in 1906. Contributions were small, property had been sold for operating expenses, and worship services differed little from other Protestant churches. Bishop Mitchell revived and established churches, recruited clergy, reestablished Episcopal forms of worship, and promoted giving. When he retired in 1956 churches, clergy, and contributions had increased greatly, membership had doubled, and a new pride in the diocese had emerged which would enable it to more than double again by 1980.

Arkansas Methodists were on the cutting edge of the successful 1939 reunification movement. Sentiment was generally favorable, and over the years there had been some reunification without waiting for official action. For example, in 1913 Northern and Southern churches in Eureka Springs combined into a single Southern church, and in 1920 the Rev. Claude E. Holifield of the Methodist Protestant Church joined the North Arkansas Conference of the Southern church.

Although an earlier plan of union failed in 1925 for lack of a 75 percent majority in the Southern conferences, the Arkansas conferences approved it by a three-to-one margin. Only three of 445 delegates voted against the final plan. The immediate effects of reunion were small and felt mostly by the former Methodist Episcopal and Methodist Protestant Churches, each of which had Arkansas memberships of only about 5,000. A few church buildings were closed and a few irreconcilable members withdrew; the few blacks from the Methodist Episcopal Church were placed in a separate Southwest Conference, where they remained until it was merged with the white Arkansas conferences in 1973. The serious material effects of the Depression were accompanied by some worthwhile spiritual effects. Church membership grew as people sought solace from temporal woes. Church members helped each other, unfortunates in the community, and the many destitute transients. And, as one minister said later, the dire circumstances caused many people to be more conscious of God.

As another war loomed, some Arkansas churches expressed their opposition to militarism and its consequences. As early as 1928 the Arkansas Baptist State Convention condemned war, and in 1934 went on record against compulsory military training in denominational colleges, although Ouachita had required such training for many years. Shortly before Pearl Harbor a convention committee was expressing the hope that the world's problems could be solved without further resort to arms.

But when World War II came the churches supported it, just as they had World War I. Many more members went away to the bigger and longer war, including many ministers who served in the military chaplaincy. Since the war a number have continued to serve as career chaplains.

On the home front churches of all denominations, especially in cities located near army camps and air bases, welcomed and ministered to the many servicemen trained in the state. They also helped finance and operate social centers for the military. But the churches did not minister as enthusiastically to another large group in the state during the war—the 10,000 Japanese-Americans from the West Coast confined in War Relocation Centers at Rohwer and Jerome. Major denominations made pronouncements of welcome and concern and urged tolerance, but did little in an organized manner to minister to the spiritual and physical needs of the detainees.

The churches were affected not only by loss of members to the military, but also by sharp shifts in the population. The state's many armament plants and other defense industries at Little Rock, Pine Bluff, Bauxite, Camden, and elsewhere attracted large numbers of rural people, and from 1940 to 1950 the urban population grew by half to 33 percent of the total. During the same period, however, people left the state, especially for California and Northern industrial states, in such numbers that the total population dropped by two percent to 1,909,511. Blacks left at a much higher rate than whites, and by 1950 had declined to 22.4 percent, less than a hundred years earlier. As a consequence rural churches, especially black churches, declined and town and city churches grew. Despite the population loss, overall church membership increased.

War prosperity raised giving to the churches dramatically. Income of Arkansas Baptist State Convention churches, for example, rose 258 percent to $3,314,104 during the war years. Coupled with restrictions on building this would lead to a building boom after the war.

Demographic and social trends have continued to affect religion in Arkansas since World War II. The population in 1960 was 1,786,272, down 6.5 percent from 1950. But efforts to stem outward migration, attract new people, and eradicate the image of Arkansas as backward and racist began to bear fruit, and by 1970 population was up 7.7 percent—but still lower than in 1940. The state reaped the harvest of its efforts by 1980, when the population of 2,285,513 represented a 19 percent gain, one of the highest in the South. By 1970 Arkansas had as many urban residents as rural. The trend has continued, modified by growth of population in the Ozark and Ouachita Mountains, one of the four most rapidly growing non-metropolitan regions in the United States.

By 1980 blacks comprised 16.3 percent of the population, little more than half of the peak year of 1910. The percentage decline since 1970 was contrary to Southern and national trends, but the actual number increased by 20,000. The relative decline of blacks has not been uniform, and the percentage in the central portions of larger cities, especially Little Rock, has increased.

Demographically, Arkansas in 1980 was growing and increasingly white and urban, but with blacks in some of the larger cities increasing more rapidly than whites. Thus both the number and membership of the churches are increasingly urban. From 1951 to 1978 the number of rural Baptist State Convention churches remained stable and membership increased 74 percent, while urban churches increased 222 percent in number and 207 percent in membership. Although only 28 percent of the number, urban churches had 60 percent of the membership.

The larger cities have undergone "white flight" to the sprawling suburbs. Some of the many new suburban churches merely followed their membership, while others seek to fulfill new needs. Another religious response to demographic change has been the founding by various denominations of new churches in resort and retirement communities, including Cherokee Village, Bella Vista, Horseshoe Bend, Hot Springs Village, and Fairfield Glades.

Growing affluence also has had great effect upon the churches. Although Arkansas continues to rank near the bottom nationally in per capita income, contributions to churches have increased more than ten-fold since World War II. One of the first effects of the prosperity after the war was a building boom. Few churches have not constructed new buildings or additions or renovated older facilities. Even accounting for inflation, increase in value of church property has been spectacular. In 1944 the value of all white Methodist Church buildings and parsonages was $9,000,000, but by 1974 was $93,000,000. Arkansas Baptist State Convention churches increased in value from $25,000,000 in 1951 to $281,000,000 in 1979. This was not just an urban phenomenon; open country Baptist churches gained in value from $2,000,000 to $40,000,000 as wooden one-room buildings were replaced with modern brick and stone structures.

Many of the new churches were elaborate, containing carpeted sanctuaries, spacious educational facilities, social halls, wedding chapels, and parking lots for the almost totally-mobile generation. A few were truly grandiose, with facilities on large plots far beyond the older concept of a church—gymnasiums, jogging tracks, arts and crafts and game rooms, reducing salons, and snack bars. Much post-war church architecture is undistinguished, but a few notable buildings in traditional and modern styles have been constructed. Not all churches have shared in the general prosperity, though, and old and unkempt buildings may still be seen throughout the state.

Growth of physical facilities has been accompanied by growth in the number and variety of paid staff members. Associate pastors, ministers of education, ministers of music, and others are common in medium-sized and large churches. Similarly, programs of churches have expanded to include musical activities for all ages, activities for "senior citizens," radio and television ministries, and youth programs featuring social and recreational activities, drama, and musical productions sometimes using religious rock and folk music. The increasing attention to youth has meant that in most Protestant churches more people enter the church through Christian nurture than by the revivalistic "sawdust trail" of the past. In response to a great increase in working mothers many churches operate kindergartens and day-care centers.

The innovative church programs have to some extent counteracted a steady decline since the 1950s in participation in traditional activities such as Sunday School. Only 55 percent of the members of Baptist churches attend Sunday School now as compared to 75 percent in 1954.

The new affluence has also permitted state denominational organizations to renovate or build new facilities for their colleges, hospitals, children's homes, and assemblies, and to establish new activities such as retirement homes. A notable example is the Good Shepherd Retirement Home in Little Rock, opened in 1979 and operated by the Methodist, Episcopal, and Catholic Churches. Denominational programs have grown to include prison and industrial chaplaincies, work with Indochinese and Cuban refugees, migrant workers and Hispanics, and increased emphasis upon work with college and university students. Student organizations sponsored by Methodists, Catholics, Episcopalians, convention and association Baptists, Assemblies of God, and others are common at the state's colleges and universities. Many have their own facilities with full-time directors, while others are coordinated by local pastors.

By 1980, 60 percent of the people of Arkansas, double the percentage of 1906, were church members. Of the approximately 1,350,000 members about 750,000, or 55 percent, are Baptists, whose growth since World War II, largely due to continuing emphasis on evangelism, has been great. More than 400,000 are members of churches of the Baptist State Convention, by far the largest single group in the state, and about 150,000 of churches of the two Landmark groups, the American Baptist Association and the Baptist Missionary Association, whose growth has kept pace with that of convention Baptists.

The 150,000 black Baptists comprise only 20 percent of the total, as compared to 40 percent in 1940. Smaller groups such as Freewill, General, and Primitive Baptists account for the remainder.

Methodist growth has leveled off in recent years. All Methodists combined, including United Methodists with about 175,000 members, the three black groups, and small numbers of Free and Wesleyan Methodists, number about 230,000, or 18 percent of all church members.

The Churches of Christ, third largest denomination in Arkansas, have grown steadily since separation from the Christian Church (Disciples) to a membership of 85,000, eight times that of 1906. Churches of Christ are found in all counties, but are most numerous in the central and northern sections of the state. The largest concentrations are in Little Rock, Searcy, Paragould, Jonesboro, Fort Smith, and Nashville. Of the 700 churches 48, almost all urban, have predominantly black memberships. The Christian Church has increased only 27 percent since 1906 to 14,000.

Catholic membership, almost level from 1906 until World War II, has since doubled to 62,000. The Assemblies of God have about 45,000 members, as do the various branches of Presbyterianism combined. There are about 17,000 Episcopalians, 10,000 Nazarenes, 12,000 Lutherans, more than 5,000 Jews, and varying numbers of many other denominations, including the United Church of Christ, the Unification, Spiritualist, and Greek Orthodox Churches, and the Black Muslims. Jehovah's Witness, the various Churches of God and other Pentecostal-Holiness groups, and the Church of Christ of Latter Day Saints have all shown substantial growth in recent years. Northwestern Arkansas has long had some members of the Reorganized Church of Jesus Christ of Latter Day Saints, whose headquarters is in adjacent Missouri.

Ministers and members of most Arkansas churches have tended to be theologically conservative, although there has been a small liberal minority. This is illustrated by the controversy over teaching of the theory of evolution which has periodically appeared in the state since the 1920s.

In 1924 the Baptist State Convention passed a resolution requiring employees of the convention to sign a statement denying the theory of evolution and upholding the basic tenets of Christian fundamentalism—plenary verbal inspiration of the Bible, virgin birth, substitutionary atonement, bodily resurrection, and literal second coming. Most convention employees signed the statement unquestioningly, but the board of trustees of Ouachita College substituted a milder one it defended by saying that although teachers in Baptist schools should subscribe to basic Christian beliefs, "we do not sit in judgment upon the scientific views of teachers of science." But under the heat generated by the Scopes trial in Tennessee in 1925 the Ouachita board succumbed to conservative pressure and insisted that faculty members sign the convention statement. Later six refused, including the president, Dr. C. E. Dicken, who then resigned because he believed the convention had no right to require the faculty to sign when there was no evidence in the college of lack of belief in the Bible.

Meanwhile other denominations were enunciating somewhat milder positions on the issue at stake in the Scopes trial. The *Arkansas Methodist* believed that the Tennessee law forbidding the teaching of evolution would be upheld and that what is taught in the schools should be left to the state legislatures, but that Christians should not be concerned whatever the outcome, because the trial would not decide whether there is a God. The *Guardian*, the state Catholic paper, hoped that the Tennessee law would be declared unconstitutional, but as to the relationship of the Bible and science Catholics should not be disturbed since the meaning of the Bible is determined by the infallible voice of the church.

Fundamentalists in Arkansas, encouraged by the fact that although Scopes' conviction was reversed the constitutionality of the anti-evolution law was not ruled on, attempted to get a similar law passed. After one failed to pass in the state legislature in 1927, the Rev. Ben M. Bogard organized the American Anti-Evolution Association, which succeeded in submitting the law to a public referendum in 1928. Arkansas citizens approved it by a vote of 108,000 to 63,000.

A few religious leaders opposed the law, most notably Dr. Hay Watson Smith, pastor of the Second Presbyterian Church of Little Rock, who from 1924 until 1934 successfully resisted repeated efforts to convict him of heresy for pro-evolution statements.

The Arkansas anti-evolution law was not enforced, and little was heard of it until Susan Epperson, a high school biology teacher in Little Rock, challenged its constitutionality in 1966. In 1968 the case reached the U. S. Supreme Court, which ruled the law unconstitutional on grounds that it was contrary to both the First and Fourteenth Amendments.

The *Arkansas Gazette*, which had opposed the law from the beginning, optimistically said that the Supreme Court decision marked the end of the era of anti-evolution laws. But a more correctly prophetic note was sounded by the Rev. M. L. Moser, pastor of the independent Central Baptist Church of Little Rock, who said that teaching the biblical account of creation along with the theory of evolution should be permitted. In 1981, with fundamentalist support, the Arkansas legislature passed a new law requiring schools which teach the theory of evolution to give equal treatment to creation science. After the law was challenged in the courts Governor Frank White claimed that mail to his office was running five to one in favor of it.

Arkansas churches and their leaders also have tended to be conservative on social issues. Generally they have favored prohibition or restriction of the sale and use of alcoholic beverages and have opposed gambling, commercial activities on Sunday, liberal divorce laws, abortion, and the Equal Rights Amendment. Although women have long played active parts in church life, few have been given positions of genuine responsibility in either local churches or denominational organizations.

There are relatively few ordained women ministers in the state; most are in the various Pentecostal and Holiness churches.

Racial attitudes have moderated somewhat in recent years and blacks and whites maintain generally friendly relationships. But there has been little integration of local churches, black or white. Since the period of the controversy over integration of Little Rock Central High School in the late 1950s some churches have operated private schools which are mostly segregated in fact, if not legally. Private schools are not as common in Arkansas, though, as in the Southeastern states.

Bibliography

The Arkansas Baptist.

The Arkansas Gazette.

The Arkansas Methodist.

Kenneth K. Bailey. *Southern White Protestantism in the Twentieth Century.*

John L. Ferguson and J. H. Atkinson. *Historic Arkansas.*

Conrad N. Glover and Austin T. Powers. *The American Baptist Association, 1924-1974.*

The Guardian.

E. Glenn Hinson. *A History of Baptists in Arkansas.*

Historical Commission, Diocese of Little Rock, *A History of Catholicity in Arkansas.*

Histories of the Arkansas Churches of the Lutheran Church-Missouri Synod.

Woodie D. Lester. *The History of the Negro and Methodism in Arkansas and Oklahoma.*

Margaret S. McDonald. *A History of the Episcopal Diocese of Arkansas.*

Frank S. Mead. *Handbook of Denominations in the United States.*

New Catholic Encyclopedia.

H. L. Paisley (ed.). *Centennial History of Presbyterianism (U. S.) in Arkansas.*

Ira E. Sanders and Elijah E. Palnick. *The Centennial History of Congregation B'nai Israel.*

Orville W. Taylor. *Negro Slavery in Arkansas.*

Ernest T. Thompson. *Presbyterians in the South*, 3 vols.

Walter N. Vernon. *Methodism in Arkansas, 1816-1976.*

Albert W. Wardin. Jr., *Baptist Atlas.*

FLORIDA

SAMUEL S. HILL
UNIVERSITY OF FLORIDA

'Is Florida a Southern state?' is an abiding question and one that refers to religious as well as to other dimensions. A negative response to it has greater validity in the 1980s than at any time since La Florida belonged to Spain, but the question has been pertinent since the colonial period. The geographical location of the "Sunshine State," somewhat marginal to the region, puts large distances between its population centers and those of other states. Its tropical climate distinguishes it from every other state not only in the region but also from the entire nation as well. In some respects Florida belongs as much to a warmth-hungry Northeast and Midwest as to the South. Its diverse population, permanent and winter-temporary, reflects that fact.

Florida's history helps explain its uniqueness. And the history of religion is one of the better clues to its special development. The usefulness of religious patterns as a clue is suggested when Florida's social-political units are compared with those of the nation at large. But the uniqueness of its religious patterns are dramatically clear when they are set alongside historical developments in neighboring, and other Southern, states.

With a comparative approach in mind, the religious history of Florida can be divided into five chronological periods: (1) Old World Church-State Patterns, 1564-1821; (2) Diversity in Discrete Units, 1821-1879; (3) Southern Patterns Take Over, 1870-1921; (4) Phasing into Radical Pluralism, 1921-1945; (5) Radical Religious Pluralism Prevails, 1945-. The accelerating succession of periods, each shorter than the previous one especially over the past half-century, highlights the complexity of Florida culture in the 1980s.

Old World Church-State Patterns, 1564-1821

Florida did not become a legal part of the United States until 1821 when it was purchased from Spain as a Territory. Admitted to statehood in 1845, it was the last of the Southeastern states to enter the Union. From 1565 until 1763 and again between 1783 and 1821 it was La Florida, a colony of Spain. The British period provided a 20-year interlude. From its founding until the Revolutionary era it was on the "rim of Christendom," an isolated, sparsely populated area where cultural patterns remained European longer than in the other seaboard colonies.

Actually Spain had made six attempts to establish settlements for God and King before the first permanent settlement was successfully staked at San Agustín in 1565, five of them on the Gulf coast between Charlotte Harbor and Pensacola, the sixth in the Chesapeake Bay area far to the north of the Atlantic coast but still within Spain's presumed La Florida. The formation of permanent St. Augustine itself did not come easily. A year earlier Huguenots had landed at Fort Caroline on the south bank of the St. John's River near present-day Jacksonville to claim the area for France but a skirmish between the French and Spanish a few miles south of San Agustín the next year assured Spain's control of the area. Nombre de Dios was the name given to the site, later to the Mission on the site, by Pedro Menendez de Aviles, on 8 September 1565.

The ascription "Name of God" tells quite a lot. In that political-social climate what was done for country was *ipso facto* done for God. Also at this place Christendom was planted as an extension of Europe's long-held assumption that land, people, and customs all were inextricably bound up with the Church—religion incorporated them all. La Florida was an outpost of Spanish culture, not simply a possession of the Spanish government. From this planting a harvest was meant to be reaped, especially of the souls of the pagan Indians, the area's only inhabitants for many centuries. The Church's tilling of the soil was done rather impressively. The diocese first sponsored these missions to the Indians, then the Jesuits did so, later the Franciscans. And these successive agents went far to fulfill their commissions, all the way north to Virginia and west to Texas. Most importantly, the social policy of these Spanish Christian evangelizers was commendably humane; they sought to instruct and persuade response to Christianity rather than to coerce it. And they sought to leave Indian culture intact. Their policy of respecting indigenous cultures extended to instructing Indian Christians, rather gradually and with some depth, so that they would be in position to catechize other Indians. This was an organized and rather aggressive mission to the native peoples of central and northern La Florida, not the coercive Christianization of heathen people practiced by Catholics and Protestants alike in America and elsewhere.

Such an aggressive style of operation was indeed to occur; in fact, it brought the missionary enterprise largely to an end, but not until the passing of the "golden age of Florida missions," which covered most of the seventeenth century. From 1595 forward for a century, the Franciscans carried out a successful Christianizing effort with the result that by 1700 some 26,000 Indians had been taught the Christian religion. There was of course some hostility on the part of Indians toward the Christian newcomers and cultural intruders, with 17 priests and lay brothers having been martyred by 1600. However, the undertaking was constructive in both quantity and quality. It should be borne in mind too that the several hundred Spanish settlers, mostly in St. Augustine, made up part of the Catholic population who were served by diocesan priests. In due course the golden age gave way to a period of sharp decline.

After 1675 good times phased into bad times for the cause of the Christian religion. Paradoxically, this had to do with the encroachment of Christian civilization upon La Florida—a different kind than the Spanish Catholic civilization that had prevailed from the beginning of the European settlement among an uncivilized Indian population. It is likely that the positive state of religion and civilization would soon have eroded from the force of internal conditions anyway. But the rate of deterioration was accelerated by another form of European Christian civilization, the English, that both diverged from and was inimical to Spanish Catholicism. By 1675 English settlers were to be found as far south as Charleston in Carolina; only 25 years later an English hegemony held the territory all the way to the Georgia-La Florida border. This arrangement was soon to spell the beginning of the end of the 150-year Spanish culture in a remote part of the New World. The "rim of Christendom" fell into the field of an inexorably centripetal force. As the British culture permeated American life, there was less and less room for a European alternative.

La Florida's Indian population—a large one—continued to occupy a central role in the drama. These natives abandoned loyalty to the Church rather quickly, most going over to the English side by the time of the War of Spanish Succession (Queen Anne's War) in 1702. After the conflict, Governor James Moore of Carolina attacked St. Augustine and many other villages. A number of churches were destroyed in his raids of 1702-1704. The decline was rapid after that: by 1708 all missions had disappeared; more than 10,000 mission Indians were deported as slaves to Carolina; the number of priests in La Florida dropped to 25 in 1738 and to as few as 10 in 1759. At the time of Spain's cession of Florida to Britain in 1763, no more than eight Catholics, all lay, lived on the Peninsula, and not many more in the Panhandle. While Florida was not quite on the rim of Christendom any longer, it had moved only a little closer to the expanding civilization of Protestant America. Even though a British colony for 20 years, it shared few qualities with the society with which its future lay.

Although the English government pledged religious freedom to Catholics who remained, many from St. Augustine and Pensacola exiled themselves to Cuba and Mexico. The Church of England appeared, but its ministrations were limited to the few English settlements and garrisons. At one time or another, nine Anglican clergymen were licensed to work in Florida. An Anglican house of worship existed in St. Augustine but neither it nor the cadre of English churchmen lasted long after the Spanish retrocession in 1783. Roman Catholicism did take a new lease on life—small but permanent—with the arrival of a colony of Minorcans in 1768. After 10 years at New Smyrna, a company of some 600 moved up the coast to St. Augustine. Until the great migration from the north in the 1920s, no infusion of Catholics was to occur, with the exception of a Cuban settlement in Key West from 1868 and the Cuban, Spanish, and Italian immigrant settlement in the Tampa area in the late 1800s.

As if a sign of the religious situation to come, a few Protestant settlers straggled into northeast Florida before 1821. They tended to be referred to indiscriminately as Lutherans, but they were mostly Presbyterians, Quakers, and Baptists. The first Baptist church was founded in 1821 in Nassau County, making it the first denomination to form a permanent congregation. Presbyterians followed in 1824. Actually, a sizable proportion of Florida's 10,000 white residents in 1821 (3000 of them in St. Augustine) were of Protestant heritage. And they were accorded a measure of religious freedom, being required only to have their younger children baptized. In actual practice because of distance and the paucity of priests even this minimal regulation was enforced infrequently.

The closing of the period of "old world patterns" found the population small and the civilization only slightly advanced. But an era had come to an end and the future of Florida was to resemble the culture near it, no longer the Spanish one which had established and sustained it for two and a half centuries.

Diversity in Discrete Units, 1821-1870

When Florida became an American Territory in 1821 and a state in 1845, its incorporation into the United States both mirrored and enhanced its new social and cultural condition. Spain's domination had amounted to little since the beginning of the British period in 1763; indeed it was virtually insignificant throughout the eighteenth century. Despite its geographical isolation, Florida was certain to be an extension of the United States, politically, socially, and culturally. The last two dimensions included the religious factor. For more than a century it was to be homogeneously American, in fact regionally American. Until its own peculiar forms of population in-migration took place beginning in the 1920s—as late as that, it was quite similar to other Southern states.

But Florida's case is its own. Population was small and scattered. No towns of any size stood within its boundaries and none was approaching urban status. Furthermore little tradition had developed, meaning that no strong sense of identity and pride had appeared. What there was was a sprinkling of farms, villages, and small towns from Pensacola in the west and Tallahassee in middle Florida to St. Augustine on the east, with the peninsula almost totally uninhabited except for some Indians and a Cuban colony at Key West (the state's largest town in 1850). It was a classic frontier society.

The religious life of Florida is described as functioning in discrete units. What was happening in one area had relatively little bearing on what was happening in other places. Churches existed here, there, and at the next place but with a minimum of interaction. What was true of the church life of Florida was also true of citizen's relations to other dimensions of society. In a manner of speaking there was no Florida, that is, a state with a cohesive life of its own, or anything like a "state of mind" which elicited loyalty and provided identity. Yet this amorphous society had enough public shape to enter the nation as a state and, 16 years later, to secede. Nevertheless the ascription, "frontier society," is powerfully accurate.

But there were people all about and many of them were Christians. Any clustering of adherents to a particular persuasion seemed to organize fairly soon into a congregation. As the local units multiplied, denominational developments appeared: the first presbytery came into being in

Tallahassee in 1841; the Florida annual conference of Methodism dates from 1845 at a meeting in the same city; the first Baptist association near Lake City in 1835. But cooperative efforts of these kinds reflect a somewhat later and slightly more fully developed church life. What happened first was the founding of local churches.

The first Baptist church, as we have noted, dates from 1821 in northeast Florida. There had probably been Baptists in the area somewhat earlier, among them runaway slaves from neighboring states. Population growth was small in the counties where the earliest congregations formed. Accordingly Baptist membership was also small, but that planting was to grow to 4740 in 1870, 2.5 percent of the state's population of just under 200,000. These beginnings, small and simple, befitted a tradition that favored localism, placed low value on education, and attracted the common folk.

Presbyterian beginnings sound more impressive, though they hardly were, owing to the more literate and cultivated sensibilities of Presbyterian people. Scots filtered into the Panhandle from North Carolina after 1820. The first church was organized in 1824 in St. Augustine (a town with a white population of 300 in 1821, or ten percent of the Territory's). Having appeal to families steeped in the Calvinist heritage, few in numbers they remained but influential. In no Southern state east of the Mississippi River were there so few Presbyterians in the nineteenth century. In Florida, the least populous of the states at mid-century, 177 organized churches were to be found, only 16 being Presbyterian (compared to 87 Methodist and 56 Baptist churches). Among its public ventures were: a concern to catechize slaves; outspoken hostility to Roman Catholicism; and reasonably close cooperation with the northern Presbyterian Church.

Methodists, the largest Christian body, can trace their origins to classes and societies in northeast Florida from 1820 on. Expansion and movement were facilitated here as in other states by evangelical zeal and a ministerial system, referred to as circuit-riding, that promoted mobility, a system well suited to demographic conditions. At first attached to the Georgia Conference, Florida's Methodists constituted their own Conference in 1845. The following year when the national church split over slavery, they aligned with their Southern neighbors in the Methodist Episcopal Church, South. Membership totals were impressive, jumping from 6874 in that year to almost 14,000 in 1860. Also, in Florida as elsewhere, Methodists devoted much energy to the evangelization of the slaves. As the Civil War opened, 6649 Negro members were reported by the Florida Conference. Eleven years later, not a single Negro belonged; the exodus of black Christians into separate denominations, three of them Methodist incidentally, was rapid and complete. The African Methodist Episcopal Church and the A.M.E., Zion, Church came south and reaped a huge harvest. The Colored Methodist Church was of Southern origins.

The Protestant Episcopal Church made its appearance during the British period but the founding of the first parish church did not occur until 1825 in St. Augustine. Soon thereafter Pensacola and Tallahassee (1827), Key West (1832), and Jacksonville (1834) could point to an Episcopal presence. With roots going back to the first convention in 1838, the Diocese of Florida was formed in 1851 and a bishop was elected. Ten churches could be counted that year and the Episcopal Church was in Florida to stay; however, its effectiveness was largely confined to life-long Episcopalians, a small company. Alone among Florida's Protestant communions, the Episcopal Church never really divided into Northern and Southern branches, notwithstanding a brief formal affiliation with a symbolic Confederate Church (P.E.C., C.S.A.).

Jews, later to be so strong in numbers and influence, acquired a bit of visibility in this period of diversity in discrete units. Before Territorial status was achieved, a few Jews had arrived in Pensacola in 1764 and St. Augustine in 1783, plus a handful of others here and there. As late as 1881, only 722 Jews lived in the state, with a single organized congregation, Pensacola's, dating from 1874. Anti-Semitism, absent in the early decades, had appeared by the 1840s and is thought by some to have contributed to the adding of a last name, Yulee, to "David Levy," the Jew (later a convert to Christianity) who in 1845 became the first Jew to serve as a United States Senator.

Southern Patterns Take Over, 1870-1921

After the Civil War, though not directly because of it, an identifiable Florida society took form. Discrete units—in religious terms, Methodist and Baptist, and Presbyterian and Episcopal, with a sprinkling of Catholics and Jews—representing a mild diversity were about to yield to a new configuration. In the place of that simple complex, a recognizable Southern pattern appeared. Now Southern society straddled the boundary Florida shared with Georgia and Alabama. Apart from certain features of flora and fauna and a coastline, Florida differed only in minor ways from the neighboring states.

Not only did cultural cohesion make its first appearance, but the period of 1870 to 1921 marks the era of greatest cohesion ever in Florida's history. For those decades, it was unmistakably a Southern state, society, and culture. Dominant, even normative, patterns prevailed. Peoples and mores were evaluated by standards almost universally accepted inasmuch as they were taken for granted. The peculiar character of the culture of the American South is not to be blamed for this development, since cultural cohesion and dominance are a common human condition. The point is that in Florida this condition made its first appearance and its shape was that of the South.

We should therefore not be surprised that this was also the period of Florida's most hostile response to departures from social norms or challenges thereto. It is the nature of human culture in "sacred" societies that intrusions are resented; "purity" is prized. Impurity in this period of Florida's history was to come in the form of Roman Catholicism—not really from Roman Catholics of whom there were very few.

The traditional denominations remained the largest and most influential. It is not at all accidental that Florida's major Protestant communities were the South's: Methodist, Baptist, Presbyterian, and Episcopal. The state's population had migrated mostly from other Southern states where those were the prominent bodies. Also extension work or domestic missionary activity was carried on by those groups that had strength near by. The near-duplication of the Deep South's patterns by Florida developments is demonstrated by the overtaking of the hitherto largest body, the Methodist, by the Baptists, who surpassed them in size in 1906.

Of greatest importance for the churches in this period was the growth of population in the state. Few settlements of any size existed south of Gainesville and Ocala at the time of the Civil War. But increase and expansion showed signs of promise in the decade of the 1870s and became pronounced by the 1880s. The Methodist Episcopal Church, South, with its circuit-riders in the vanguard, pursued the expanding population as it moved southward. As the Tampa and central Florida areas expanded in the 1880s, soon to be followed by the formation of permanent towns down the state's spine, then along both coasts, before and after the turn of the century, Methodists were present to found churches. The largest numerical change took place between 1867 and 1885, there being 12,380 members (all white) in the latter year, up from 6266 (whites and blacks) in 1867. The membership figures from Reconstruction to 1900 highlight three major developments within Florida Methodism.

First, blacks withdrew or were withdrawn from a previously unified (if unequal) constituency. Always active in missions to the Negroes, the Methodist denomination lost those members to separate black denominations, with no reported Negro membership in the M.E. Church, South, by 1872. Second, growth was substantial before 1890, that is, as long as rural demography and culture patterns remained. Third, statistics leveled off in the 1890s and, in relative terms, decreased, as the "circuit-rider dismounted" and the denomination failed to adjust very sensitively to new conditions. Moreover in this period the Church was challenged by other denominations which had made a belated start in Florida. Even so there were nearly 20,000 members in the main body in 1900, as well as several thousand Negro brothers and sisters and a sprinkling of (sectarian) Methodist Protestants and northern co-religionists (the Methodist Episcopal Church).

Consolidation marks this period. The Conference was more maturely structured, districts were organized and developed, church agencies began emerging and taking firm shape. In 1902 in Lakeland, the denomination's educational institution was opened, being named Florida Southern College in 1906. A denomination that had sowed seeds early, broadcast widely, and reaped quite a harvest, was on the landscape as far as the eye could see. Henceforth its rhythms were to be those of stability and ubiquity, not rapid growth or exuberant vitality.

These same traits characterized the early second runners, the Baptists, who have been Florida's largest Protestant community throughout this century (although without the power they have attained in other Southern states). Lacking any kind of connectionalism, the Baptist churches suffered severely in the War's aftermath. The poverty of the Baptist people was reflected in the shortage of ministers and the incapacitation of churches to do anything on an organizational scale. Yet, in spite of severe curtailment of opportunity, churches grew. By using the advantages of the Baptists' associational system, they pooled resources and confronted concerns. It is admirable that so bereft a people could found a college, establish a state paper, and create missionary agencies.

Stetson University was founded at DeLand in 1888. Notwithstanding shortage of funds and depth of financial commitment, the state's Baptists had the vision to found and see to the continuation of a center for the training of the young, lay and clergy alike. The *Florida Baptist Witness* began in 1873 and has enjoyed unbroken service. Local congregations banded together to form area units called associations; in turn, these joined to become a state convention to carry out the will and vision of the smaller units. Of the greatest importance is the decision made in the 1880s to side with the Home Mission Board of the Southern Baptist Convention in preference to the American (Northern) Baptist Home Mission Society which had come on the scene through ministries it undertook on behalf of the recently freed Negroes. Henceforth Florida's Baptists were to be as solidly in league with the Southern Baptist organization and outlook as those of any other state.

A strong sense of denominational identity was emerging, obviously. These advances on the organizational front mirror that fact. Those in turn are tied to growth in Baptist size. Of the total state population of 520,000 in 1900, Baptist membership stood at 23,136. Twenty years later the figure had increased to 57,078 in a state population just under one million. In this period Baptist growth was greater than the state's growth.

These are Southern Baptist Convention churches' totals, it should be noted. Negro Baptist Churches had begun to dot the Florida landscape from 1880. The reports of 1883 reveal 16,857 members in Negro Baptist congregations—with virtually no racially mixed congregations. Between 1885 and 1920 most of these affiliated with one or another newly organized Negro Baptist denomination.

Presbyterian church life in this period was notably undistinguished. Reeling from the economic blows brought on by the War and its aftermath, Southern Presbyterians talked cooperation with their Northern brothers and sisters, but merger did not occur (nor had it by 1982). The more prosperous Northern body did aid the devastated Southern church financially on a number of occasions.

Florida Episcopalianism appears brighter in this era than Presbyterianism, because being sacramental it externalizes its life. Growth and development were hardly impressive, however. There was a fair amount of work done among the freedmen especially with a view to education and training. Bishop John Freeman Young's tenure (1867-1885) was notable for its efforts to build a strong sense of Churchmanship and mission. But the big news of the period is associated with 1893 when the new "missionary jurisdiction of Southern Florida" saw the light of day. Population was increasing on the southern three-fourths of the peninsula and new parishes and missions were being formed to serve Episcopalians moving there. A glance at the list of congregations existing in the state in the 1890s tells quite a story: (a) Most of them in the territory from Ocala south were to survive and even flourish. (b) In the north and northwest, most of the rural and small town parishes were to remain small or die out, while those in the larger towns were to become the strength of the Church's life in those parts of the state.

Other religious bodies took their place on the Florida scene during this period. A Shaker colony appeared in Osceola County in the 1890s. The Church of the Brethren was in evidence from the 1880s and acquired some strength on the lower half of the peninsula after 1910 as Pennsylvanians, Buckeyes, Hoosiers, and others migrated to the state. Similarly Lutherans and Congregationalists, the latter's presence made notable by its founding of Rollins College in Winter Park in 1885, the state's first institution of higher learning to have a continuing life.

Jews and Catholics continued to be a minority presence. The earliest Jewish congregations were formed in Pensacola (1874), Jacksonville (1882), and Tampa (1894). In 1881, only 772 Jews resided in Florida, of whom 130 were in Jacksonville. Jewish population expansion was to await the immigration, tourist, and economic boom of the 1920s. Roman Catholicism was better represented, there being 24,658 communicants in 1916, less than three percent of the state's population of 921,618. Its fame far outdistanced its size, however. (Notoriety is a more apt description.)

Nativism surfaced in the South much later than it had in the Northeast and Midwest. A function of high-level immigration totals, the nativism that took anti-Catholicism form in the North was vigorous for the 30 years preceding the Civil War. That virulent movement's day in the South occurred during the 1910s as resistance to all sorts of "isms," few making any real impact at all on Southern society. The percentage of Catholics living in Florida was as tiny as that prevailing in other Deep South states. But an ominous threat was seen on the horizon.

Anti-Catholicism in Florida was short-lived, bubbling up by 1913 and mostly out of sight by 1919. Its appearance came to focus in the election of Sidney J. Catts to the governorship in 1916. A Baptist preacher and lawyer recently moved from Alabama to the Panhandle, he ran on the Prohibition Party ticket and won in one of the state's most surprising elections ever. A few proposals passed the House but died in the Senate: e.g., a "garb" bill that would have prohibited priests and nuns from wearing religious clothing or insignia while teaching in public schools; and prohibition acts that would have deprived churches of the use of sacramental wine. Other bills passed were never actually enforced, for example, convent inspection legislation aimed at providing for checking out suspected wrongdoings as "closed" convents and parochial schools. A bill was enacted that prohibited white people from teaching Negroes in white schools (and vice versa); it was enforced once, with the arrest of three sisters teaching at the St. Joseph's school in St. Augustine. Far down state in 1915 popular animosity toward Roman Catholicism was strong enough in Fort Lauderdale to remove a teacher of that faith who had been appointed to a public school position (by a vote of 181 to 7).

Florida, thus, made it into the twentieth century a little late and rather gracelessly. Its culture was that of the Deep South, positively and negatively. The Florida that has come to people's minds since World War II is a product of events and developments no older than the years following World War I.

Phasing into Radical Pluralism (1921-1945)

Florida's history was typically Southern throughout the nineteenth century and for the first two decades of the twentieth. Since then it has reverted, in a manner of speaking, to the eccentric character its colonial career manifested. The angle of divergence is of course far smaller for the past half-century. But Florida was becoming a "rim" once again between 1921 and 1945—though perhaps "hub," of the tourist tastes of Eastern Americans—is a better image. Still more Southern than anything else or culturally amorphous, Florida was developing its own personality, a complex of people, economy, life-style, and religion, that turned it into a veritable region of its own.

One indicator of its divergence was the early appearance of economic disaster in the 1920s, an occurrence that was Florida's alone. The rest of the country moved ahead in times of relative security and prosperity until the last quarter of the decade's final year, but Florida had already "boomed" and "busted." Americans from the upper Midwest to New England, all the way south to the bordering states were discovering the "Sunshine State." Tourists were coming in ever greater numbers, their forays facilitated by railroads that crisscrossed the state and extended past Miami out to Key West (until a hurricane destroyed some key bridges in 1935). An even greater contributing factor was the construction of a statewide system of public roads. The growing popularity of the family automobile prompted short and long visits to the peninsula over roads that had not existed two or three years earlier.

Some of the tourists and numbers of prospective permanent residents took the bait being dangled by a small army of land developers. "Runaway inflation in land sales" accompanied the crescendo of the Florida fever.

But boom turned to bust in 1926. Three years later Florida staggered from the blow of the entire nation's financial calamity. As if those buffetings were not enough, lethal hurricanes struck the southern parts in 1926 and 1935. These major setbacks notwithstanding, Florida became a new society during the 1920s. Population totals rose from 968,470 in 1920 to 1,468,211 in 1930. The people who came, especially those who stayed, brought their culture with them, their religious affiliations and tastes included.

Radical diversity and radical pluralism happened to Florida almost simultaneously. That is to say, so many newcomers were appearing on the scene, representing such a variety of social and cultural backgrounds, that they swamped the existing complex, especially over the lower two-thirds of the peninsula. In religious terms, Roman Catholics, Jews, and Northern Protestants—Lutheran, Congregational, United Presbyterian, among them—now lived alongside the Southern denominations, diluting their impact and challenging their cultural hegemony. Subtly, Methodism—the closest thing to a "national church,"—was coming to reflect Northern as well as Southern traditions and styles. During one and the same era, Florida came to be a conglomerate of peoples and a diffused culture. Southern identity was beginning to give way quite decisively to "Florida culture," an unique, somewhat amorphous, yet locatable version of American life.

Southern culture had not yet been totally forsaken, however (nor has it in the 1980s in the northern tier of counties and the entire northwest). The influence of that way of life was prominent in the 1928 presidental election and campaign that pitted Democratic Governor Alfred E. Smith of New York against Herbert Hoover of the Republican Party. In the South, this amounted to a single issue election, over prohibition and religion, the two fusing into one. Methodist Bishop James Cannon itinerated from Washington throughout the South and beyond to promote the anti-liquor forces against Smith's election. Florida was not left bereft of his services; on 4 August 1928, he journeyed to Jacksonville and departed after organizing "dry Democrats." The Protestant churches gave much support to that cause. Doubtless the Baptist, Methodist, Presbyterian, and sect peoples made a major difference in Florida's popular vote. Feelings ran very high, there being many Hoover clubs and anti-Smith clubs. A prominent speaker to such groups and many public rallies was the Rev. John Roach Straton, fundamentalist pastor of Manhattan's Calvary Baptist Church, who had grown up in Alabama and Georgia and attended a Southern Baptist college and seminary.

Thus, the Hoover *versus* Smith campaign of 1928 reflected the lingering impact of Southern culture, its values and its religion, upon Florida. While it is excessive to speak of these events as the last gasp of regional influence, they do stand as a kind of watershed. The Republican presidential aspirant won in the state, but the rest of the ticket went to the Democrats. Nor did the two-party system return to Florida in that year. It was becoming a steadily less Southern state, but this era witnessed only a "phasing into radical pluralism," not an accomplished social transformation. Sheer population statistics reveal how clear its new course was coming to be, however. Between 1920 and 1930, the percentage of increase was 51.6; during the 1930s it dipped to 29.2. (Then with the Depression past and World War II in process and finished, the percentage of population increase soared to 46.1 in the 1940s.) Since most of these newcomers were from non-Southern states, regional strength was indeed diffused and the old cultural hegemony broken up.

Radical Pluralism Prevails (1945-)

The Florida that Americans think of as Florida did not exist before the 1920s and really not until after World War II. Once again the percentage of population increase is revealing. As if the 1940s figure of 46.1 percent were not enough, the 1950s record is overwhelming.

The number of residents in the state rose from 2,778,000 at the beginning of the decade to 4,952,000 in 1960, a growth rate of 78.7 percent. Now what had been incipient from 1920 forward was an accomplished fact. Florida had become unique. It was Southern and not Southern. It resembled other states attractive to retirees and tourists, California and Arizona, yet it was very different from them. It was an amorphous society and culture but it had a kind of shape, tradition, and dynamic of its own. There were at least two units, "the other Florida," from Gainesville north and west, and the mystique-laden peninsular Florida, yet a kind of identity bound all the state's citizens together.

A glance at the religious membership statistics of 1971 affords some clues. (This compilation includes only Christians and not all of that constituency since some black denominations and someother sects were not keeping or reporting detailed records.) In that year 41.2 percent of all Floridians owned some kind of Christian membership. Within that large company the size of three denominations reached double digits, the Roman Catholic Church with 32.8 percent of the total number of Christian adherents, the Southern Baptist Convention with 28.8 percent, and the United Methodist Church with 13.8 percent.

Why these? For one thing, all of them have massive national memberships. In fact, they rank first, second, and third among all American Christian bodies. Are we to infer from this that Florida is a microcosm of American religiosity? Probably not, but the correspondence is striking and suggestive. What it means has two aspects. First, it was predictable that a state that attracted hundreds of thousands of immigrants from the Northeast and Midwest where Catholic numbers are great would show a strong Catholic membership. But it must be remembered also that Florida experiences in-migration from the south as well. New residents especially Cuban, also other Latin citizens, have moved to Florida in large numbers—and these are "99 percent Catholic."

Second, Florida's religious patterns reflect its Southern heritage, with the result that the region's "big two" are prominent in their deepest southeastern penetration as elsewhere. After all, the Southern patterns that virtually constituted the state down to 1920 were not displaced or replaced, only supplemented. Moreover a healthy proportion of those who have moved into Florida over the past six decades have come from the contiguous region (as did most of the Anglo- and Afro-Americans who settled the area in the early nineteenth century). In the Methodist case, as mentioned earlier, that denomination's size and its general distribution throughout the Northern home territories of new Floridians assured that quite a company of Methodists would be joining their Southern religious cousins in the towns and cities of the Sunshine State. It is thus more intriguing and coincidental than factual that Florida's three largest denominations are also the nation's. Yet we learn quite a lot about both its distant past and its recent history by observing that phenomenon.

Pursuing that point a step further, we note that the nationwide Catholic tendency to be very strong where it is strong at all persists in Florida. Similarly the Southern Baptists. In 1971 four counties could claim a Catholic proportion above 50 percent of the total number of Christian adherents. All four—Dade at 62.1 percent, Broward at 58.7, Monroe at 57.7, and Palm Beach at 53.6—are concentrated at the southern tip of the peninsula, closest to Cuba and, in a manner of speaking, also to the Catholic strongholds of Northern areas. (In Florida you "go south to go north.") The obverse is true as well. Where Catholicism is weak, it is almost non-existent. Six Panhandle counties could count fewer than one percent of their residents as members of the Church, and rural Sumter County, some 50 miles north of Tampa, held none.

Southern Baptist Convention size, high and low, is inversely correlated with Catholicism's. All of the state's most Baptist counties are in "the other Florida," the Panhandle mostly. The percentages there are staggering, in the 80s for four, in the 60s and 70s for eight others. The least Southern Baptist counties are all down south in tourist and northern immigration centers, such as Miami, Key West, Sarasota, West Palm Beach, and St. Petersburg. These percentages range from 10.1 in Broward to 18.1 in Collier.

Methodism's place in Florida is almost routinely akin to its position all over the country: rarely dominant, almost never weak, typically of moderate strength. The greatest proportions (in the 20s) of Methodists appear in such rural counties as Flagler, Franklin, and Jefferson. But they stand between 10 and 20 in almost all the other 65 counties, south and north, urban and rural, coastal and inland. America's "national church" is also Florida's.

From these three to the other denominations the statistical gap is quite wide. The two major Presbyterian bodies account for 6.1 percent of the total number of Christian adherents. The Episcopal Church percentage stands at 5.4 and the three largest Lutheran groups total 4.1. Moreover in the cases of all three, no part of the state reflects a heavy concentration, although Lutherans are mostly found in centers for immigration from Lutheran strongholds.

The picture of Florida's religious culture and the religious dimension of its general culture are misrepresented, however, by exclusive reliance on the size of its largest Christian groups. For one thing, Jews are numerous and their place in the culture is substantial. The estimated Jewish population in the state in 1980 was 455,000 or 5.1 percent of all inhabitants. Only New York and California have a greater number of Jews; in percentage of total population, Florida is surpassed only by New York (12.1), the District of Columbia (6.1), and New Jersey (6.0).

A pronounced pattern of concentration is evident in the state. Miami and Miami Beach are home to 225,000 Jews. Along the rest of the southeast "Gold Coast" totals reach 180,000. Some 17,500 Jews reside in Tampa and St. Petersburg. Other centers are: Orlando with 12,000, Sarasota with 6200, and Jacksonville with 6000. Elsewhere no sum surpasses 1000 save Daytona Beach's 1200. Also, quite apart from quantity, the impact of Jewish life on the state may be seen in the extent of its philanthropy and in the increasing scope of its representation in the political life of the state—in the Legislature, a recent United States Senator, and a recent gubernatorial candidate, for example. Jewish presence and prominence have come a great distance since 1920.

Hardly less significant for the recent religious history of Florida is the rampant diversity that has developed there. One element in the larger picture is secularism; that major force that surely is America's most popular posture since World War II. When defined as the "practice of the absence of God," secularism is readily seen as related to religion, not its denial but rather its non-practice in the midst of some avowal. Secularism abounds in American society; it is scarcely any stranger to Florida. What is so telling about its strength there is its resemblance to Northern urban life. A curious mixture of Southern rurality and Northern urbanity, Florida is sometimes culturally indistinguishable from New York, Chicago, or Philadelphia. Whereas Southern secularists are often conversant with religious faith and apologetic for their indifference to it, the type associated with a less Evangelical and more urban manner of living has simply lost sight of religion, conceptually and experientially—though still without denying it. At bottom, any such view of religion cares too little about it to discredit it any more than to affirm it.

Major Protestant bodies, Roman Catholics, Jews, and secularists are prominent, then, in contemporary Florida society. But they are joined by myriad sects, cults, black denominations, and small religious bodies. A glance at the Saturday religion section of any urban newspaper reveals both a remarkable quantity of religious organizations and an incredible diversity. "You name it, Florida has it," might almost be the state's religious motto. All traditional denominations are present, also Judaism, every conceivable sect and independent congregation, and a plethora of religious science and divine wisdom bodies. It is doubtful that such an abundance in number and variety may be found anywhere else except for southern California. In Florida metropolitan areas, a fantastic confluence occurs: northeast, midwest, southern, and Caribbean; urban, rural, and small town; traditional, recent upstart, and as-new- (and perhaps as-ephemeral-) as-yesterday; ethnic patterns of all kinds; and so on. Many come to Florida searching; there is plenty to shop for in that remarkable culture, for old and young, for the ill and the adventurous, seemingly for everyone. And secularism is an ever-present force.

One of the surest ways to ascertain a religious body's strength in a locale is to note its commitment to educating its own in that locale. Church colleges were founded by the Congregationalists (Rollins at

Winter Park in 1885), the Southern Baptists (Stetson at DeLand three years later), and the Methodists (Florida Southern at Lakeland in 1902). In the 1930s Roman Catholics organized Barry and Biscayne in Miami, but St. Leo's College had been planted in Pasco County in 1889. Florida Presbyterian College (now Eckerd) dates from 1960. Black denominations contributed Edward Waters College in Jacksonville in 1891 (African Methodist Episcopal), Bethune-Cookman in Daytona Beach in 1923 (Methodist), and Florida Memorial College in Miami in 1879 (American Baptist), all springing from earlier foundations. Independent or loosely affiliated Bible colleges and schools dot the state, (noteworthily) at Dunedin, Zellwood, Boca Raton, Temple Terrace (Churches of Christ), and Graceville (Southern Baptist). The Church of God (Anderson, Indiana) has Warner Southern College in Lakeland. Independent Christian schools are to be found state-wide, with some offering post-high school course work. Clearwater is the home of the second largest center of the Church of Scientology for training its leaders and counseling its members. The Krishna and Unification Church movements have made the smallest inroads into Florida but their evangelists may be found in the state's largest airports. And much more.

The story of religion in Florida is fascinating. Never very "normal" by American standards except for its Southern period from 1821 until 1921, it is hardly "normal" now. Yet in certain ways it may be more predictive of things to come in America at large than might have been thought—or than many would like to believe. Florida has become the model of a pluralistic society. In religion, its centers of gravity are Southern traditions, conservative leanings, new movements, and special kinds of immigrants, from Northern states and Caribbean societies. Thus it has its own peculiar forms of pluralism, making for a unique blending. That is why "religion in Florida" as a subject for study demands more attention than it has received. It may be a laboratory for twenty-first century America. It certainly is a topic that Floridians need to be well informed about, since knowledge of religious history and patterns could facilitate better human understanding and even aid in the formation of public policy for all the citizens of the state.

Bibliography

William E. Brooks, ed. *From Saddlebags to Satellites: A History of Florida Methodism.*

Joseph D. Cushman, Jr. *A Goodly Heritage: The Episcopal Church in Florida 1821-1892.*

———*The Sound of Bells; The Episcopal Church in South Florida 1892-1969.*

Leonard Dinnerstein and Mary Dale Palsson, eds. *Jews in the South.*

Michael V. Gannon. *The Cross in the Sand: The Early Catholic Church in Florida 1513-1870.*

———*Rebel Bishop: The Life and Era of Augustin Verot.*

Douglas W. Johnson, Paul R. Picard, and Bernard Quinn. *Churches and Church Membership in the United States, 1971.*

Edward Earl Joiner. *A History of Florida Baptists.*

Cooper Clifford Kirk. "A History of the Southern Presbyterian Church in Florida, 1821-1891" (unpublished Ph.D. dissertation, Florida State University, 1966).

Charlton W. Tebeau. *A History of Florida.*

GEORGIA

WAYNE MIXON
MERCER UNIVERSITY

Among the first inhabitants of the land that was later known as
Georgia, everyone was his own priest. The unremitting struggle merely
to survive, by requiring all to devote their energies to finding food,
prohibited the rise of a priestly class; so, the aborigines, who arrived
around 8000 B.C., engaged in individual worship of nature spirits. Within
3000 years, as the food supply became more dependable, a few people
who were paid by others with food were designated as witch-doctors;
their function was to control the spirits. Some 5000 years later, an exalted
class emerged as the religious and secular leaders. By 1000 A.D., religious
ceremonialism was becoming more sophisticated as great temple mounds
were built in the theocratic city-states of Etowah, Ocmulgee, and Kolo-
moki. After 1300, these societies gave way to the Creek Confederacy, a
political rather than a religious unit. Nevertheless, religion remained
important among the various tribes comprising the Creek league, and the
high priest of each wielded much political power. Paying homage to
fire-and-water deities, these Indians celebrated each summer a festival of
first fruits during which they performed rites of sacrifice and purification.

Such was the form of worship the Jesuit missionaries of Catholic
Spain found when they arrived among the people of Guale, a region of the
Georgia coast, in the 1560s. Within six years, the Jesuit effort to make
Christians of the Gualeans had failed, the victim of native indifference
and Spanish parsimony. In 1573, one year after the last Jesuits had left
Guale, Franciscan friars arrived. After a shaky start, the zealous Francis-
cans, more strongly supported by civil authorities than the Jesuits had

been, firmly established their missions. By 1606, having weathered a major Indian revolt, the Franciscans claimed some 1500 converts. During the next fifty years, the Spanish missions along the coast grew without interruption, and new missions were established to the west in Apalache. With some success, the padres taught the natives European ways. By 1702, however, growing Franciscan complacency and attacks by hostile Indians, pirates, and English settlers in Carolina had caused the nine coastal missions to be abandoned. Twenty-six years later, the Apalache missions fell to Carolinian and Creek depredations.

The Englishmen who settled Georgia shortly after the Spaniards' expulsion were by and large less concerned with the souls of the Indians than with their wampum. Moreover, many of the colony's early clerics soon found that advancing the cause of religion among white Georgians was a hard enough task.

The weakness of the Church of England particularly vexed the colony's officials. Anglican clergymen were partly responsible for that situation. Ministers were few, and of those few many were profane, intemperate, and licentious. Moreover, those priests who were virtuous were often contentious, most notably John Wesley and his brother Charles, who served briefly in the 1730s. Rare was someone like Bartholomew Zouberbuhler, a man of exemplary character who served his Savannah parish effectively for 20 years.

The elitism of the Church of England also turned many Georgians against it. Preaching subordination within a hierarchical social order rather than equality in Christ, Anglican clerics sometimes exhibited contempt for poorer Georgians. The adversarial relationship that often resulted hampered Anglican growth.

The Church of England not only failed to profit from the Great Awakening that aroused many Georgians from spiritual lethargy early in the 1740s but in the long run suffered from that revival of religion. Some Anglican leaders opposed the work of the foremost awakener, George Whitefield, an Anglican priest in Savannah. Whitefield's Calvinistic theology, his animated style of preaching, and his willingness to associate with those who rejected the Church of England rendered him unacceptable to many of his fellow Anglicans.

Fifteen years after Georgia's settlement, there were only 63 Anglicans in Savannah. Ten years later, the establishment of the Anglican church as the official, tax-supported church failed appreciably to enhance its popularity. As revolutionary fervor intensified in the 1770s, the association of the Anglican church with British authority severely diminished its appeal. By 1775, there were no more than five Anglican churches in the colony.

For much of Georgia's colonial period, those Christians who dissented from the beliefs and practices of the Church of England outnumbered Anglicans. In 1748, there were probably six dissenters for every Anglican in Savannah. On the eve of the American Revolution, dissenters comprised a clear majority of the colony's churchgoers.

Several factors contributed to the growth of dissenting denominations. Although interested in the welfare of Anglicanism, many of the Trustees who supervised Georgia's settlement were just as concerned that their colony grow. Consequently, Georgia was designed to be a haven for persecuted European Protestants. Moreover, the colony's Anglican establishment, even if it had wanted to, was too weak to trouble dissenters, who were allowed to worship freely. Finally, some Georgians, indifferent to religion altogether, did not care what one's faith was. Tolerance was the rule in colonial Georgia.

Some of the European Protestants who came to Georgia stayed only a short time. The Moravians, who began to arrive in 1735, never numbered more than 50; they left in 1740 when civil authorities commanded them to fight the Spanish.

Other Protestants from Europe established themselves permanently. In 1734, Lutherans from Salzburg settled at Ebenezer where they thrived until their leader, the Rev. John Martin Bolzius, died in 1765; thereafter, the Salzburgers, numbering about 500, were rent by factionalism. Two years after the founding of Ebenezer, Presbyterians from Scotland established Darien.

Still other Presbyterians came, many from other colonies. In 1752, settlers from South Carolina founded Midway along the coast and built Midway Church which, if Congregational in name, was Presbyterian in fact. Three years later, in Savannah, a congregation independent of the Church of Scotland was formed; that church subsequently enjoyed considerable influence because its pastor, John J. Zubly, was the colony's foremost dissenting cleric. By 1770, Scots-Irish had begun to settle the backcountry around Augusta, but a scarcity of pastors and neglect by itinerant preachers retarded the growth of Presbyterian churches there. Five years later, there were some six Presbyterian congregations with 600 members throughout Georgia.

Shortly after Presbyterians came to the backcountry, Baptists arrived there, too. Twenty years earlier, a small group of Regular Baptists had worshipped in Savannah but had left no church. In 1773, a Regular Baptist minister, Edmund Botsford, established a church south of Augusta. A year older than Botsford Church and the first Baptist church in Georgia was Kiokee Church west of Augusta, which was organized by Separate Baptists under the Rev. Daniel Marshall.

The Separates, who came to Georgia from the Carolinas and Virginia, traced their origins to the Great Awakening in New England. Growing out of a revivalistic faction in the Congregational church, Separates restricted membership to those who had undergone the overpowering, specific experience of conversion and maintained that baptism, by mode immersion in water, should be received only by believers who had been born anew in Christ. Moderately Calvinistic, Separates believed that man was innately depraved and could be saved from eternal damnation only by divine grace. Unlike most Regular Baptists and Presbyterians, however, the Separates either denied or ignored the Calvinist doctrines of election and limited atonement. More aggressive and more emotional than the Regulars, the Separates won more converts. In the fluid, harsh society of the Georgia backcountry, the Separates offered settlers comfort and order through the church without condescension. Within three years of the founding of Kiokee Church, there were perhaps 750 Baptists throughout the colony. It was the Separates who "Baptistized" Georgia.

In addition to the Baptists and the Presbyterians along the frontier and the Anglican congregation in Augusta, there was, after 1768, a settlement of Quakers at Wrightsborough in the backcountry. Peopled largely by Friends from North Carolina, Wrightsborough grew into a thriving community of 600 by 1775.

Although many different Christian churches had adherents in colonial Georgia, Roman Catholics were conspicuously absent. Centuries of English hostility toward the Church of Rome coupled with Georgia's proximity to Catholic Florida prompted the Trustees to prohibit the entry of Catholics. In 1747, there were only four Catholics in Georgia, although a few years later the colony was temporarily home for 400 Acadians, who were allowed to worship privately.

Not only did the Trustees wish to keep Catholics out of Georgia, some wanted to ban Jews also. Yet, when 42 Jews arrived in Savannah in 1733, James Oglethorpe allowed them to stay. Sectarianism soon divided the group, and fear of Spanish invasion prompted mass emigration. That threat ended in 1742, many Jews returned, and Savannah's Jewish community endured, largely because of the leadership of Benjamin Sheftall.

Although no synagogue was built in the colonial period, Georgia's Jews worshipped freely in their homes.

If many early Georgians lacked religious commitment, by 1775 religion nevertheless exerted some influence in the life of the colony. Georgia's very settlement resulted in considerable measure from the opportunity most people had to worship freely. Moreover, after 1758, religion had a direct impact on government, for Anglican vestrymen were not only church officers but civil officials as well. Furthermore, the few schools that existed were run by clergymen, the most noteworthy being Whitefield's Bethesda Orphan House near Savannah. Finally, religion imparted to some Georgians a moral code to live by and made them better people.

The American Revolution stopped the progress of organized religion in Georgia. Politics divided denominations, particularly the Anglican, Lutheran, and Presbyterian, each of which contained a substantial minority loyal to the Crown. As fighting intensified in Georgia after 1778, ministers were compelled to flee, congregations were dispersed, and sanctuaries were destroyed. When the fighting ceased in 1782, churches throughout the young state were in disarray.

Nevertheless, developments that would encourage church growth had occurred. The relationship between church and state was fundamentally altered. In 1777, Georgia's first constitution enhanced religious liberty by disestablishing the Anglican church. Subsequent changes in the state's basic law made religious freedom complete. By the end of the century, all religious tests for holding public office had been abolished as had all restrictions on freedom to worship.

The history of religion in Georgia since the Revolution is largely the story of the growth of Evangelical Protestant denominations, especially the Baptist and the Methodist. The denominational diversity that existed in 1775 had been severely diminished by 1800. The Protestant Episcopal church, the American legatee of the Church of England, had only one active congregation. The Lutheran community at Ebenezer was greatly reduced as a result of wartime division and the subsequent defection of younger members to the Baptists and the Methodists. The Quaker settlement at Wrightsborough fell victim to the war and subsequent developments.

The hegemony of the Evangelicals in Georgia's religious life resulted from their theology, their social ideology, and their methods of spreading the gospel. By the end of the eighteenth century, theological similarities overshadowed differences among Baptists, Methodists, and Presbyterians. Each denomination—the Methodist with the greatest fidelity—embraced Arminianism, which meliorated the harsh doctrines of Calvinism by espousing the idea of unlimited atonement and by contending that the human will played an active part in the process of salvation.

Although Georgia's Evangelicals emphasized man's depravity, they also stressed the importance of the individual in the sight of God. Even if poor, female, or black, each person was a child of God and, however despised by man, was beloved of Him. The new birth in Jesus Christ made it possible for the reborn to reject social canons in favor of moral understanding founded on religious experience. Extending the kingdom of God on earth became more important than gaining acceptance in the eyes of the world. The Christian might improve the society he lived in by trying to diminish worldly corruption through pious example.

In all likelihood, Evangelical Protestantism attracted Georgians who were dissatisfied with society as they found it and who yearned for an alternative sphere in which to assert themselves. And yet, the primary reason for one's joining an evangelical denomination was not social but religious—to be saved from sin, to live the holy life, and to go to heaven. Fervently, evangelical preachers stressed the urgency of salvation and outlined its plan: conviction of sin, repentance of that sinfulness, and, through God's grace, conversion to a life in Christ. That message was spread in regular church services and, more dramatically, in periodic revivals.

More than anything else, the Second Great Awakening of the early nineteenth century advanced the cause of Evangelical Protestantism in the young state of Georgia. Begun in Kentucky in 1799, the Great Revival reached Georgia two years later. If Presbyterians pioneered the Kentucky awakening, Baptists and Methodists benefited most from the Great Revival in Georgia.

Back in 1786, John Major and Thomas Humphries, Methodist itinerants, had established their church's first congregations in Georgia. Fanning out over the settled portions of the state in the 1790s, Methodist circuit riders took the gospel to frontiersmen who seldom, if ever, had heard it before. These itinerants, who traveled great distances under difficult circumstances for paltry pay, soon seized upon an innovation of the Great Revival to advance Christianity. The camp meeting, though used effectively by Georgia's Baptists, was the stock-in-trade of the state's Methodists in the first half of the nineteenth century.

Made to order for a scattered population of plain folk, the camp-meeting provided an occasion for small farmers, who sometimes traveled fifty miles to reach the site, to come together and enjoy the society of one another. Important as the social aspects of the camp meeting were, its prime purpose was to aid in the conversion of sinners. Usually held when crops had been either laid by or harvested, the camp meeting in all its features was designed to keep pressure upon those wrestling with the Holy Spirit. The believers who preached, exhorted, sang, and prayed for the unrepentant with mounting intensity expected the convicted to give evidence of the Spirit's workings. And they usually did by whining, barking, jerking, dancing, and falling to the ground. Thousands of Georgians—men and women, white and black together—attended camp-meetings, from the first ones in 1802 until their decline in the 1840s.

The Great Revival swelled the ranks of the Methodists and the Baptists. By 1805, the Baptists, with some 9500 adherents, had nearly tripled their strength of 1790, and the Methodists, 5000 strong, had increased threefold their numbers as of 1800. Once the emotional intensity that helped effect these conversions had subsided, many of the newly saved fell away from the church. Nevertheless, the impact of this awakening upon Georgia was lasting, for it further democratized religious life, elevated individual morals, and diminished vices such as brutality, drunkenness, and fornication that were once rife in the backcountry.

With the camp-meeting institutionalized and with the number of circuit riders increasing, the Methodist church continued to grow, if occasionally fitfully, after the Great Revival. In 1830, when the Georgia and Florida Conference was formed, the state's Methodists numbered some 20,000. Fifteen years later, at the formation of the Georgia Conference, there were slightly more than 50,000 Methodists. The tenfold increase since 1805 resulted largely from the permanent itineracy used by the church, which was better organized and more effective than the *ad hoc* system employed by Baptists and Presbyterians. By mid-century, 140 Methodist circuit riders carried their message to all parts of the state.

Although the sevenfold increase among Georgia Baptists between 1805-50 failed to match the rate of Methodist growth, the Baptists achieved those results without the benefit of episcopal organization. Nevertheless, although each Baptist congregation prized its autonomy, statewide organization emerged in 1822 with the formation of the General Baptist Association, which five years later became the Georgia Baptist Convention. Charged with promoting missions and with coordinating Baptist work, the state convention was built upon voluntary organizations of regional churches, the first of which was the Georgia Association formed in 1784. Composed of two associations at its founding, by 1850 the convention consisted of more than 20 associations with more than 600 churches containing nearly 55,000 members. An additional 15,000 Baptists belonged to churches within associations independent of the state convention.

Georgia's other significant evangelical denomination, the Presbyterian, grew much more slowly than either the Baptist or the Methodist church largely because of Presbyterian insistence upon an educated clergy and reluctance to employ emotionalism. In 1796, when the first presbytery, which included the whole state, was organized, it contained only 14 small churches. The Great Revival, which rejuvenated the Baptists and Methodists, did little for the Presbyterians. In 1810, that church counted just slightly more than 200 communicants, fewer than in 1775. Over the next 20 years, however, vigor replaced dormancy—largely because of the work of a few zealous evangelists such as the Princetonian Remembrance Chamberlain—and by 1830 Presbyterians numbered nearly 3000. At mid-century, five years after the formation of the Synod of Georgia, the church claimed more than 5000 communicants.

The 105,000 white Georgians who belonged to the Baptist, Methodist, and Presbyterian churches made up 20 percent of the state's white population in 1850. Therefore, their views on social issues carried considerable weight. In the first half of the nineteenth century, evangelical leaders saw much in Georgia that needed improving. Although their belief in the separation of church and state caused them to shun direct political action and although they doubted the efficacy of broad social reform without individual regeneration, Georgia's Evangelicals did believe that the improvement of individuals might lead to the betterment of society.

Acting upon that belief, some evangelical ministers in the backcountry, as early as the 1790s, promoted education, notably the Methodist Hope Hull, the Baptist Silas Mercer, and the Presbyterian Moses Waddel. Although none of the schools that those men conducted lasted, their very founding showed the intentions of some clerics. As the new century began, church-sponsored schools continued to open and then to close, the most ambitious being the Rev. Henry Holcombe's Baptist academy. Nevertheless, 30 years later, education under Evangelicals achieved permanence in the form of colleges. At the urging of such ministers as Jesse

Mercer, Silas's son, and Adiel Sherwood, the Georgia Baptist Convention established Mercer University in 1833. Three years later, Methodists chartered Emory College, and in 1839, assumed control of Wesleyan Female College. A year earlier, Presbyterians, who had dominated the staff of the state university in its early years, opened their own college, Oglethorpe University.

Often, the work at these institutions was hardly of collegiate quality. Yet their faculties included such able people as Augustus Baldwin Long- street of Emory, a man of many accomplishments; James Woodrow of Oglethorpe, a Harvard-and Heidelberg-trained scientist; and John Lead- ley Dagg of Mercer, an eminent theologian. If the men who established Mercer, Oglethorpe, and Emory did so in part to train ministers, they also hoped to effect the general education of their people and to fashion a social order controlled by Christian leaders.

From the 1820s on through the 1850s, the scope of evangelical benevolence broadened. Churchmen formed anti-dueling societies, sup- ported Sabbatarianism, advocated better treatment of the handicapped, and ministered to the poor. Among the most popular of benevolent enterprises was temperance. Believing intemperance to be a social evil, not just an individual's sin, many Evangelicals worked hard to diminish or to eliminate the use of intoxicating liquors. Baptists in Eatonton led the way in this reform in 1827 by organizing the state's first temperance society. By 1830, Methodists and Presbyterians had begun to join the movement, and more than 40 local societies had been formed. Most Evangelicals refused to mix temperance with politics, however, because to do so would infringe upon the prerogative of the state. As a result, when a Methodist lay preacher ran for governor as the candidate of the Temperance Party in 1855, he received only five percent of the vote.

Antebellum Georgia Evangelicals attempted to extend Christ's king- dom and bring about moral improvement not only through the spoken but also through the printed word. Efforts to establish a permanent religious journal that theretofore had failed succeeded in 1833, when Jesse Mercer began publishing the Baptist Christian Index, a weekly paper that was among the more significant religious periodicals in the South. Four- teen years later, Georgia's Presbyterians played a major role in establish- ing the *Southern Presbyterian*, the journal of Southeastern synods, which was usually published in Milledgeville until 1853, when its offices were moved to Charleston. These journals, together with the Methodist paper published out of state, reported denominational activities, appealed for higher pay for ministers, adjured Christians to influence others by living righteously, encouraged benevolence, and promoted missions.

Many Georgia Evangelicals supported organizations to foster missions both in foreign countries and within the state among whites, Indians, and blacks. In the 1830s, Evangelicals began a systematic effort to spread the gospel among Georgia's slaves. Attempts by individuals to evangelize the slaves had long been made. In royal Georgia, the Anglican Zouberbuhler worked zealously in that cause. After the Revolution, Abraham Marshall, Daniel's son, helped organize, with the slave Andrew Bryan, the country's first independent Negro Baptist church among Savannah's slaves.

By 1830, nine percent of Georgia's blacks were either Baptists or Methodists. Evangelical Protestantism appealed to black Georgians for many reasons: it contained practices that paralleled African religion; it promised eternal reward or punishment without regard to one's color; it offered blacks one of their few opportunities to associate with whites on a level approaching equality; it imparted hope to a people who had much cause to despair.

After 1830, the mission to slaves received broader support largely because of the efforts of articulate, influential spokesmen. Particularly active in the movement were the Methodist minister James O. Andrew, elected bishop in 1832, and the Presbyterian divine, Charles Colcock Jones, the movement's chief theorist. Georgians who supported plantation missions hoped to encourage docility among the slaves, to advance religion among their white masters, to promote better treatment of the slaves, and, what was most important to the mission's leaders, to furnish the slaves the means of salvation. Although race prejudice minimized the success of the mission, it nevertheless contributed to the advance of Christianity among Georgia's blacks. By 1860, roughly 12 percent of the state's Negro population were church members, the great majority being Baptists and Methodists.

Although Jones and Andrew outspokenly advocated worship by whites and blacks together and mixed congregations were common, some Evangelicals of each race favored separate churches in the interests, they said, of space, propriety, and self-determination. Black Baptists had some 25 churches by 1860, the largest of which, Augusta's Springfield African, had 1600 members. Close behind was the oldest black congregation, Savannah's First African Baptist, whose pastor of 40 years, Andrew Marshall, was the preeminent black clergyman of the antebellum South.

Because relations between white and black Christians were usually amicable, the state's white Evangelicals were dismayed and angered by the rise of antislavery sentiment among Northern Baptists and Methodists. When Northern Baptists in 1844 refused to appoint a Georgia slaveholder as a denominational missionary, the state's Baptists helped form the Southern Baptist Convention in Augusta the next year. When Northern Methodists, also in 1844, voted to relieve Georgia's James Andrew of his duties as bishop for as long as he owned slaves, Georgian A. B. Longstreet, speaking for Southern Methodists, declared that the vote mandated separation. Not surprisingly, the following year Georgians helped organize the Methodist Episcopal Church, South.

If the mission to slaves, so prized by some Georgia Evangelicals, failed to allay antislavery sentiment in the North and to stay denominational division along sectional lines, the mere issue of missions sparked schism inside the state itself within the largest denomination. As early as the 1820s, some Baptists opposed missions that were supervised not by local churches but by central agencies. Such organization, those Baptists said, was unscriptural and unnecessary. So, too, they believed, was theological education, which would diminish humility and piety among ministers. By the mid-thirties, these conservatives had broken away from the Georgia Baptist Convention to preserve what they believed was pure, primitive Christianity. Within 15 years, anti-mission associations included almost 400 churches with nearly 12,000 members. Throughout the 1850s, Georgia's Primitive Baptists published the semimonthly *Southern Baptist Messenger*, the most influential Primitive journal in the Deep South.

The mistrust of ecclesiastical authority that provoked division among Baptists, and to a lesser degree among Methodists, also contributed to the appeal of the Campbellite movement, which was even so weaker in Georgia than in states to the north. By 1830, the followers of Alexander Campbell, the Disciples of Christ, numbered nearly 600 in Georgia. Thirty years later, after union with the Christian church, occasional visits by Campbell, and publication at Augusta of the short-lived *Christian Union*, the Disciples numbered 1100.

In addition to opposing centralized organization and authority, dissident Evangelicals criticized the increasing affluence and refinement of those Georgians within the parent denominations. Between 1830 and 1860, the Baptist, Methodist, and Presbyterian churches changed significantly. Although revivalism remained strong, the camp meeting gave way to the protracted meeting, an event held indoors with less emotionalism. Support of missions and education increased. Solicitude for the welfare of urban churches was more evident among churchmen who theretofore had directed their efforts largely at villagers and country folk.

The urban ministry of the Evangelicals enjoyed much more success than the rural ministry of the leading non-evangelical denomination, the Protestant Episcopal. Despite efforts by a few Episcopalians to broaden the scope of their church's ministry, that church remained confined largely to cities and grew but slowly between 1790 and 1840. In that year, the Diocese of Georgia, organized back in 1823, elected its first bishop, Stephen Elliott, Jr., who breathed new life into the church. With only six churches and 300 members in 1840, the denomination included almost 30 churches with 2000 members 20 years later. Even so, Elliott's advice to Episcopal clergy to employ more fervor and less erudition in order to enhance the church's appeal among rural Georgians met with little support.

Rejected by Georgians at large was the rationalistic message of Unitarianism and Universalism. By 1860, three attempts by Universalists to publish journals had failed, and Georgia's two Unitarian societies were dead.

Greater success greeted the efforts of Roman Catholics, although it can hardly be termed large. After the American Revolution, the Church of Rome benefitted from Georgia's new constitutional guarantees of religious liberty. In 1793, settlers from Maryland established Georgia's first Catholic church at Locust Grove in the backcountry. Seven years later, Catholics in Savannah built a church. In 1850, the Catholic church established the Diocese of Savannah under Bishop Francis X. Gartland to serve the state's eight congregations, virtually all of which were urban.

Georgia's Jews also benefitted from the increased religious liberty after the Revolution. Yet if the Jewish community grew, it was still confined largely to Savannah, which from 1786 to the middle of the next century had the state's only synagogue. Over the following 120 years Georgia's Jewish population would grow to roughly 25,000 and would remain concentrated in the cities, with Atlanta emerging as the chief locus.

As the 1850s advanced, Georgia's churchmen were increasingly caught up in the sectional conflict, despite the efforts of many to avoid involvement in the political disputes between North and South. Nevertheless, because most ministers believed that Scripture sanctioned slavery, they came to view the political conflict in religious terms. Yet, as late as 1861, many clergy, most notably Methodist Bishop George Foster Pierce, hoped that Georgia could remain in the Union. Six of the 10 ministers who sat in the secession convention opposed leaving the Union, but when the convention voted to take Georgia out, a majority of clerical delegates endorsed the decision. So it was in the state at large. Once the issue was decided, most clergy supported Georgia's stand.

After the Civil War began, Georgia's churches worked strenuously for the Confederacy. Congregations collected supplies and distributed them to soldiers. The major denominations jointly published religious literature for the army. Ministers frequently preached bellicose sermons that sometimes characterized the Confederate effort as a holy crusade against the Yankee infidel. Hundreds of clergymen served in the army, and others worked among the soldiers as missionaries or evangelists. Revivals were numerous, fervent, and often lengthy among Confederates fighting in Georgia. Until 1864, the churches enjoyed spiritual growth. Special services occurred frequently, and work among the blacks continued. In the wake of Sherman's march, however, came disruption as some churches were destroyed and others were confiscated for military purposes. The collapse of the Confederacy inflicted hardships upon the churches and the institutions they supported. Ultimately, Oglethorpe University failed to recover and closed in 1872.

Still, the churches endured, and after the war the religious establishment expanded. In 1870, there were 500 more churches than in 1860, and the value of church property had increased by $1,000,000. The pattern of church membership remained unchanged. Baptist and Methodist congregations comprised 70 percent of Georgia's churches in both years.

After the war, the state's religious leaders devoted a good deal of energy to defending their antebellum justification of slavery and to reproving northern churchmen for being religious carpetbaggers. Ill will was particularly evident within Methodism. Georgia's Methodists of the southern church accused missionaries of the northern church of trying to appropriate the pulpits of that state's southern churches and of sowing discord among Methodist freedmen.

For their part, the freedmen needed little prodding from northern missionaries to establish black organizations. The unwillingness of white Christians to associate with free blacks under conditions approaching equality together with the desire of black people to exercise leadership in God's house prompted an exodus of Negroes from churches controlled by whites. Within Methodism some blacks affiliated with the northern church, but many more joined black organizations. The African Methodist Episcopal church, which organized its first Southern congregation in Savannah in 1865 and formed a state conference two years later, was especially popular. A smaller number joined with the African Methodist Episcopal, Zion, church, which established a state conference in 1867, or with the Colored Methodist Episcopal church, the protégé of the Methodist Episcopal Church, South, which formed a Georgia Conference in 1870. Black Baptists, while adhering to congregational autonomy like their white counterparts, also left white churches en masse. Black Presbyterians, although many fewer in number than Baptists or Methodists, formed the first black presbytery in the United States in 1867. Those blacks, like most other Negro Presbyterians in Georgia, affiliated with the northern church, from which white southerners had separated six years before in Augusta.

The evangelical churches provided the principal training ground for black leaders, many of whom served as administrators and faculty of the denominational colleges that were being established in Georgia with the help of northern churchmen and philanthropists. By 1890, Atlanta, the major center of higher education for blacks in the entire country, housed the following institutions: Atlanta University (founded in 1869, sponsored by the Congregational Church); Clark University (1869, Northern Methodist); Atlanta Baptist College (1867, later Morehouse College); Atlanta Baptist Female Seminary (1881, later Spelman College); Gammon Theological Seminary (1883, northern Methodist); and Morris Brown College (1885, A.M.E.). In Augusta, Paine College (C.M.E.) offered higher education to blacks after 1882.

Although many black religious leaders in the state worked for the improvement of their race, their ideas of how best to achieve advancement varied widely. J. W. E. Bowen of Gammon Seminary advocated accommodation with white leaders; John Hope, president of Atlanta Baptist College, preferred protest to accommodation; Henry M. Turner, A. M. E. bishop, endorsed emigration as the only way for blacks to escape oppression.

For thousands of black Georgians, the church provided sustenance during the trying times after emancipation. Church membership, particularly among Baptists and Methodists, increased markedly. By 1890 black Baptists numbered 200,000; black Methodists, 125,000. Adherents of those denominations comprised almost 40 percent of the state's black population.

After the bitterness of Reconstruction had subsided, some white churchmen worked to strengthen the black church. Education, those whites believed, would serve that goal. Acting upon that belief, the Georgia Baptist Convention operated institutes between 1878 and 1895 to train black preachers and deacons. Among Southern Baptists, Georgians, along with Texans, enjoyed the greatest success in that work. In that same period, Georgia Methodism provided the greatest white advocate of black education in the South, the Rev. Atticus G. Haygood, who was successively editor of the *Wesleyan Christian Advocate*, president of Emory College, agent of the John F. Slater Fund, and bishop in the southern Methodist church.

Nevertheless, white evangelical leaders believed that Georgia's blacks should remain subservient. The *Christian Index* defended segregation, denounced social equality between the races, and, alone among Southern Baptist weeklies at the end of the century, justified lynching under certain conditions. By 1900, professors at Mercer University had characterized black suffrage as a blunder, black education as productive of evil, and the color line as an act of God. As Jim Crow tightened its hold, even Bishop Haygood retreated from his earlier position on the race issue, and Emory College, in 1902, eagerly accepted the resignation of a professor who had written that blacks had rights that whites should be made to respect.

After the Civil War, changes other than black separation from white churches occurred in Georgia religion. Among white Evangelicals, there was a diminution of the discipline that churches meted out to members and an increasing willingness to call upon the state to enact legislation that regulated behavior. By the end of the century, the two largest evangelical denominations were advocating the passage of laws to restrict athletic competition, gambling, worldliness on the Sabbath, and the grounds upon which divorce could be obtained. The greatest evangelical crusade for moral reform was the movement to prohibit the manufacture and sale of alcoholic beverages. That movement received great impetus in Georgia and elsewhere in the South from the persuasive Methodist revivalist, Samuel Porter "Sam" Jones of Cartersville, who believed that Prohibition would cure all of society's ills. Although some evangelical leaders condemned the growing tendency to mix religion with politics and contended that Prohibition was unscriptural, partly because of evangelical pressure, Georgia enacted local-option in 1883 and statewide Prohibition in 1907.

Efforts to persuade the state to sanction evangelical moral precepts by law reflected in some measure the unease that churchmen felt over changes occurring late in the nineteenth century. Georgia traditionalists feared the effect that the higher criticism, the Darwinian theory of evolution, and the rising industrial ethic might have on religion as they knew it, even though, paradoxically, evangelical leaders sometimes promoted industrialization.

Of those developments, only industrialization had any discernible impact on Georgia, and it did not prove inimical to organized religion. In fact, church membership increased by nearly 30 percent in the latter half of the nineteenth century. By 1906, 43 percent of all Georgians professed to be church members. Of that number, 92 percent were Baptists and Methodists.

With a view to ministering to the increasing number of members more effectively and to encouraging even further growth, Evangelicals developed more extensive organization. Between 1865 and 1900, the Georgia Baptist Convention, which represented the great majority of white Baptists, created the office of Superintendent of Sunday Schools, established the Board of Missions, organized the Women's Missionary Union and the Baptist Young People's Union, and opened an orphanage. During that same period, similar developments, particularly as regards Sunday School and women's work, occurred within the Southern Methodist church in the state. Moreover, after 1866, two conferences, the North Georgia and the South Georgia, carried out the duties that the Georgia Conference alone had performed since 1830.

Although Baptists and Methodists set the tone of Georgia's religious life at the beginning of the twentieth century as they had done through the previous century, other denominations grew significantly between 1850 and 1900. While Georgia's population more than doubled during those years, the growth rate of certain denominations was considerably greater. Membership in the Roman Catholic church increased at least fourfold; in the Presbyterian church, almost fivefold; in the Protestant Episcopal church, ninefold; and in the Christian (Disciples) church, thirteenfold. Denominational strength in 1906 was as follows:

Baptist	596,319
Methodist	349,079
Presbyterian	24,040
Roman Catholic	19,273
Christian (Disciples)	13,749

Protestant Episcopal	9,790
All Others	16,787
Total	1,029,037

Not only did the established denominations grow, there were at the end of the century short-lived colonies of Shakers in southeastern Georgia and Christian socialists near Columbus. Moreover, the seeds had been planted that would yield new sects early in the twentieth century.

After the Civil War, division afflicted Georgia's Disciples of Christ. Those poorer Disciples who believed that the denomination was capitulating to fashion, wealth, and unscriptural innovations such as instrumental music and missionary societies broke away and formed the Churches of Christ, which, by 1906, contained more than 1000 members.

During that same period, largely within Methodism, the Holiness movement gained many followers, making Georgia the banner holiness state in the South. Endorsed in varying degrees by such prominent Methodists as the aged Lovick Pierce, the bishop's father, and the young Warren A. Candler, holiness doctrine embraced the Wesleyan idea of Christian perfection that was attained through the post-conversion second blessing of sanctification. Advocates of Holiness formed a state association, published a journal, and established a camp meeting site.

Yet if many Methodist ministers countenanced Holiness, the movement incurred the opposition of Bishop Haygood who, in 1894, prompted the general conference of the southern church to denounce the Holiness faction. Despite that denunciation, some of Georgia's holiness Methodists remained within the church. Others, joined by the disaffected in other denominations, sought new organizational affiliations, and as a result holiness sects emerged. Prominent among the dissidents was Joseph H. King, erstwhile Methodist minister who became a leader in the Pentecostal Holiness church, which established headquarters at Franklin Springs, began publishing the *Pentecostal Holiness Advocate* in 1917, and two years later founded Emmanuel College. Some years before, in 1907, several Holiness congregations in north Georgia had affiliated with the Church of God based in Tennessee and embraced Pentecostalism. In addition to accepting the doctrine of baptism by the Holy Spirit, a third experience beyond conversion and sanctification, Georgia's Pentecostals believed that evidence of that experience could be shown in the gift of speaking in tongues that were normally unknown to the believer. It seems that the appeal of Pentecostalism was rather like the appeal of

Evangelicalism a century earlier. By and large, Georgians who were poor, lonely, anxious, disillusioned with the world around them, and dissatisfied with the religious establishment found the friendship and security offered by pentecostal fellowship particularly attractive. Pentecostalism would gain many adherents in the course of the twentieth century.

The many changes—industrialization, urbanization, a rising tide of foreign immigration, new intellectual currents—that weakened traditional religion in much of the country early in the twentieth century had less impact in Georgia and the rest of the South. The state's religious establishment remained firmly entrenched. Yet, partly out of fear of the forces of modernity, Georgia, as of the early 1920s, was one of only six states in the nation to require that the Bible be read daily in public schools.

If many of Georgia's Christians welcomed the Bible in the schools, they would bar the spirit of Charles Darwin. In all likelihood, a majority of Protestant clergy and church members opposed the teaching of the theory of evolution, especially in church-sponsored institutions. A Methodist petition of 1922 charged the dean of the Candler School of Theology with tolerating unchristian instruction. Two years later, Mercer University dismissed an instructor of biology whose stand on evolution was suspect. Nevertheless, no major denomination formally endorsed the proposals of militant Fundamentalists to prohibit the teaching of evolution by law. In fact, prominent clerics such as Methodist Bishop Warren A. Candler—whose stout orthodoxy caused him to oppose union with the northern church because he believed it to be permeated with modernism—and Baptist ministers M. Ashby Jones of Atlanta and John E. White of Savannah denounced attempts to use the church to dictate to the classroom. Partly because of the stand taken by such men, the Georgia legislature by 1925 had twice rejected anti-evolution bills.

Some Georgians who found aggressive Fundamentalism attractive also endorsed the Ku Klux Klan, although there was no organic connection between the two. Revived and housed in Atlanta after 1915, the Klan succeeded in clothing itself in the mantle of Evangelical Protestantism partly because some churchmen encouraged it to do so in the belief that the Klan's attacks upon foreigners, Roman Catholics, Jews, Negroes, and others who were considered morally deficient would purify America. The incident that adumbrated the revival of the Klan, the lynching of Leo Frank, an Atlanta Jew, had been obliquely condoned by the Baptist *Christian Index*. In the Klan's imperial city, prominent Baptist ministers and laymen were especially active in the hooded organization, serving as recruiters, national officers, and faculty of short-lived Lanier University, an "All-Southern" institution closely associated with the Invisible Order. Even so, numerous clergymen in Atlanta and elsewhere in the state opposed the Klan, notably Episcopalians C. B. Wilmer and Henry J. Mikell, Methodist Plato Durham, and Baptists M. Ashby Jones and Louie D. Newton, whose subsequent service to his denomination would earn him the title "Mr. Baptist."

By the late twenties, internal dissension had sapped much of the Klan's strength in Georgia, but the organization remained strong enough to campaign aggressively against Alfred E. Smith, Democratic presidential candidate in 1928. Many Evangelicals outside the Klan also opposed the candidacy of a man who criticized Prohibition and who belonged to the Roman Catholic church. Nevertheless, other Evangelicals, most notably Bishop Candler, condemned the involvement of their brethren in party politics. Unlike many other Southern states, Georgia remained in the Democratic camp and would likewise do so when another Catholic Democrat ran for president thirty-two years later.

If some churchmen feared their fellowman, others tried to help him. As the twentieth century advanced, many Georgians continued to suffer from poverty and the illness it bred, from ignorance, and from injustice. To fight those evils and to propagate the faith, the churches expanded their benevolent enterprises. Hospitals, orphanages, and homes for the aged were built or enlarged. From the Roman Catholic to the Pentecostal, churches operated schools at varying levels. In higher education, the more notable additions included Bessie Tift College and Shorter College, the former controlled by the Georgia Baptist Convention after 1898, the latter after 1902; Emory University with its Candler School of Theology, which was established in 1914 by a gift from Bishop Candler's brother, Asa, the Coca-Cola magnate; and Agnes Scott College, supported by the Presbyterian Synod of Georgia after 1922, and the Presbyterian Columbia Seminary, which after its move from South Carolina, opened in Decatur in 1927.

Care of the disabled and education of the young received wide support among Georgia's Christians. Less popular was the social gospel, a movement to use the church to change society. Many Christians, particularly Evangelicals, believed that the proper business of the church was to win souls to the Lord and then to encourage pious and moral living in preparation for the hereafter, and not to promote social reform.

Nevertheless, there was an articulate element within Georgia Protestantism that embraced social Christianity. Among Baptists, the Rev. John E. White served as vice-president of the Southern Sociological Congress, an agency organized in 1912 to call special attention to the evils of convict leasing, inadequate education, and racial injustice. The Rev. M. Ashby Jones, the foremost advocate of improved race relations in the Southern Baptist Convention, helped establish the Commission on Interracial Cooperation (CIC) in Atlanta in 1919. The Rev. Edwin C. Dargan served as first chairman of the state convention's Social Service Commission, which was created in 1911 to study, among other things, labor conditions and race relations. That commission became ever more aware of social ills under the chairmanship in the 1930s of W. W. Gaines, an Atlanta layman. Baptist women, who were assuming positions of responsibility within the denomination, were also concerned with social problems. Foremost among those women was Isa-Beall Neel, who had long been active in her denomination's benevolent causes and who, when elected in 1931, became the first woman to serve as vice-president of the Southern Baptist Convention. In the thirties, Mrs. Neel also served as state chairman of the Association of Southern Women for the Prevention of Lynching (ASWPL), a Southwide organization based in Atlanta that was composed largely of churchwomen.

Methodists were equally active in spreading the social gospel. In 1911, Mary De Bardeleben, the first Southern white woman to engage in such work, established a settlement house for Augusta's blacks. A few years later, the Rev. Will W. Alexander, having left the pastorate, helped found the CIC and served as its director throughout its 25-year existence. In the thirties, Dorothy R. Tilly of Atlanta worked diligently in behalf of the ASWPL. Subsequently, she served on the Southern Regional Council, the successor of the CIC, and organized the Fellowship of the Concerned to monitor the treatment accorded to blacks in the South.

There were also advocates of social Christianity among Presbyterians and Episcopalians. Early in the twentieth century, Atlanta Presbyterians began a spiritual and social ministry among blacks in the city's ghetto. Later, the Synod of Georgia established a special committee on moral and social welfare. For a short time in the second decade of the century, Episcopalians operated the La Grange Social Settlement to minister to textile workers. From 1918 to 1940, that denomination supported an industrial school for blacks in Fort Valley.

These attempts to proclaim the social gospel often suffered from popular indifference and inadequate funding. Nevertheless, the very presence of such efforts reflected an increasing willingness on the part of some church members to use religion to advance the cause of social justice.

Social Christianity received its greatest test after the Second World War. Theretofore, Georgia churchmen attempting to improve both the condition of blacks and relations between the races had refused to challenge the system of racial segregation, in part because they believed that such a radical position would hinder the attainment of their other goals. After 1945, the federal government and civil rights activists increasingly prodded white Georgians to decide whether they would accord the black man his rights under the law or continue to deny him those rights. Many Georgia Christians, victims of their history, opposed the civil rights movement.

The advice of some of the state's religious leaders to comply, in the spirit of Christian love, with the laws of the land sometimes went unheeded. In 1956, a grand jury in Sumter County censured the local ministerial association after the clergymen had condemned the use of violence against members of an integrated commune. Three years later, a Presbyterian pastor in Columbus was dismissed for his liberal stand on the race issue. In the early sixties, Baptist churches in Atlanta, Macon, and Albany turned away blacks seeking to worship, and townspeople rebuked faculty of denominational colleges that gave succor to civil rights workers. At the end of that decade, the editor of the Atlanta *Presbyterian Survey* was forced to leave his post because he supported the civil rights movement. And so it went.

All the while, however, many religious leaders continued to counsel moderation. When Atlanta was ordered to integrate its public schools in the late fifties, more than 300 of the city's ministers appealed for obedience and good will. During the same period, the *Christian Index*, seldom before an advocate of the social gospel, denounced violence against the black man, urged respect for his rights, and condemned politicians who sought to close the state's public schools rather than let them be integrated. In the early sixties, the Georgia Baptist Convention and the North Georgia Conference of the United Methodist Church likewise opposed closing the public schools. Although public schools remained open, a number of churches, angered further by federal prohibition of worship in those schools, abandoned them to establish private institutions where religious instruction was offered to white children only. If the moderation of church leaders was partly responsible for persuading Georgia's white Christians to acquiesce, albeit reluctantly, in the desegregation of secular society, by and large the churches remained segregated.

And they grew. In 1936, roughly 42 percent of the state's population were church members, a figure virtually unchanged since 1906. By 1971, however, at least 60 percent of the population professed allegiance to some Christian church. Denominational membership was as follows:

Baptist	1,792,256
Methodist	501,664
Roman Catholic	103,609
Presbyterian	102,169
Holiness and Pentecostal	78,960
Episcopal	39,780
Others	127,187
Total	2,745,625

Perhaps the major reason for the great increase in church membership since the Second World War is active evangelization on the part of certain denominations, particularly the Baptist. In 1936, Georgia churches within the Southern Baptist Convention had 265,630 members. Thirty-five years later, that number was 1,276,081. In 1971, Baptist dominance pervaded the state; in all but 10 of Georgia's 159 counties, Baptists accounted for a majority of church members.

As church membership increased significantly within the state after 1945, three notable Georgians—one Catholic and two Baptists—demonstrated to the rest of the world what being Christian and southern might mean. The great Catholic writer, Flannery O'Connor, showed that both she and the Protestant rustics of whom she wrote were haunted by God. The Rev. Dr. Martin Luther King, Jr., in the matchless oratory of the black evangelical tradition, stirred millions of people with his dream of social justice. The integrity and compassion of President Jimmy Carter, who like thousands of his fellow Georgians had been "born again" in Christ, caused millions elsewhere to ponder the meaning of the Christian rebirth that was central to Evangelicalism.

It is that belief in the possibility of Christian rebirth that is the great constant in the history of Georgia religion over the past 200 years. Many changes have occurred during that time: the education of ministers has improved; church buildings have gotten bigger and are more richly appointed; congregations have grown in size and in wealth; worship in the major denominations has become more sedate; groups with little connection to the dominant Protestantism, such as the Mormons and the Jehovah's Witnesses, have appeared; electronic media have carried wor ship in sermon and song to thousands of homes; some churches have adopted commercial methods to sell themselves; a charismatic move- ment, akin to Pentecostalism, has emerged; and secular diversions have multiplied.

Through all those changes, some things have stayed the same: revi- valism remains vital in many evangelical churches; the ministry of music continues to be an integral part of worship—even Sacred Harp, or shape-note, singing, introduced 140 years ago by B. F. White, can yet be heard, particularly in rural churches in south Georgia; the tradition of enthusiastic worship still lives, especially in the Holiness and in the black churches. What is most important, virtually all Georgia Christians, whether farmer or corporation executive, continue, as their forebears did, to believe in an omnipotent and personal God, who through His Son Jesus Christ can save man from sin and give him a heavenly reward.

Georgia's Christians, at their worst, can behave in unchristian fashion. They can be intolerant of differences, complacent amid wrongs, and smug in their sense of superiority. Yet, at their best, they have fostered learning, benevolence, and good will among men; they have taken seriously the charge to be their brothers' keepers; and in times of distress, of sickness and bereavement, they are a present help indeed. All in all, Georgia is a better place for their presence in it.

Bibliography

Kenneth K. Bailey. "Protestantism and Afro-Americans in the Old South: Another Look," *Journal of Southern History* 41 (November 1975): 451-72.

_____. *Southern White Protestantism in the Twentieth Century.*

T. Conn Bryan. "The Churches During the War," *Confederate Georgia.*

Emory Stevens Bucke, ed. *The History of American Methodism,* 3 vols.

Harold E. Davis. "Religion," *The Fledgling Province: Social and Cultural Life in Colonial Georgia, 1733-1776.*

John Lee Eighmy. *Churches in Cultural Captivity: A History of the Social Attitudes of Southern Baptists.*

Hunter Dickinson Farish. *The Circuit Rider Dismounts: A Social History of Southern Methodism 1865-1900.*

Douglas W. Johnson. *et. al. Churches and Church Membership in the United States: 1971.*

John Tate Lanning. *The Spanish Missions of Georgia.*

James Adams Lester. *A History of the Georgia Baptist Convention, 1822-1972.*

Ronald Wilson Long. "Religious Revivalism in the Carolinas and Georgia, 1740-1805," Ph.D. dissertation, University of Georgia, 1968.

Anne C. Loveland. *Southern Evangelicals and the Social Order, 1800-1860.*

Donald G. Mathews. *Religion in the Old South.*

William H. Sears. "The Pre-History of Georgia," *Georgia Review,* 6 (Winter 1952): 397-408.

George G. Smith, Jr. *The History of Methodism in Georgia and Florida, from 1785 to 1865.*

Rufus B. Spain. *At Ease in Zion: A Social History of Southern Baptists, 1865-1900.*

Henry Smith Stroupe. *The Religious Press in the South Atlantic States, 1802-1865.*

Vinson Synan. *The Holiness-Pentecostal Movement in the United States.*

Ernest Trice Thompson. *Presbyterians in the South,* 3 vols.

U. S. Department of Commerce, Bureau of the Census, *Religious Bodies: 1906-1936.*

KENTUCKY

FRED J. HOOD
GEORGETOWN COLLEGE

It is altogether possible that Kentucky has both the most denominationally diverse and the most religiously homogeneous population of all the Southern states. As is true of the South generally, the Baptist churches have the largest membership in Kentucky. Uncharacteristically southern, however, is the fact that Kentucky's second largest religious population is Catholic. Surprisingly, much of that is rural Anglo-Saxon; the remainder is centered in the urban areas of Covington and Louisville and made up of the descendants of the German and Irish who migrated to Kentucky before the Civil War. These people blend into the Kentucky cultural landscape with scarcely a discernible difference except for their Catholicism.

By contrast, Baptists and Baptist churches vary greatly with location, region, and social class. Methodists, the various branches of the Christian churches (Campbellite) and Presbyterians show a similar diversity. In fact, individual churches of these denominations may collect congregations as different in style as an Episcopal parish and a Pentecostal sect. While denominational loyalties may be strong, a mountain Baptist and Pentecostal church may be marked more by the common culture of the Applachians, or rural Baptists and Catholics in Washington and Nelson Counties more easily detected by the peculiar characteristics of the "Knob" culture. This cultural homogeneity and religious diversity should not be construed as merely secularism. It reflects more than anything a history that has been more dynamic religiously than culturally or at least in which religion has been formative.

The early settlement of Kentucky was notable for its religious dimension. Unlike colonial settlement patterns in the backwoods areas or the later migration patterns across New York and into the Midwest, many of the earliest Kentuckians arrived in already formed communities and brought their institutions of religion with them. The Baptists, suffering from restrictions under Virginia's establishment, migrated in large numbers in the 1780s. The largest group, known as the "Traveling Church," left Spottsylvania County, Virginia, under the leadership of the Rev. Lewis Craig. The more than 500 persons in this group formed the basis for a large number of Baptist communities in the Bluegrass region of central Kentucky. Maryland Catholics also came to the state in well organized communities of approximately twenty-five families. Most of these settled in and around Bardstown in what is now Nelson County. One such group stopped in the Bluegrass and survives to the present as a small but vigorous Catholic minority in Scott County. Presbyterians coming to Kentucky in the earliest period, although not as often in such large groups, tended also to settle contiguous areas. Bourbon County, on the eastern edge of the Baptist settlements in the Bluegrass, was populated almost entirely by Presbyterians. A second area of Presbyterian dominance emerged in the early 1790s with the settlement of Logan County in western Kentucky. On the western fringe of the Bluegrass region along the Salt River, a community of Dutch Reformed settled in the 1780s—a move that represented the second community relocation for these people. Thus the earliest religious landscape of Kentucky featured a significant denominational diversity, but with each denomination living in religiously homogeneous quasi-ethnic, communities.

The termination of the War for Independence from England and military victories over the Indian tribes to the north opened the way for a massive migration to Kentucky that was to disrupt this initial, and, from the point of view of the early settlers, desirable pattern. Virginia rewarded its soldiers of the revolution with warrants for lands in Kentucky. These warrants circulated as currency and produced an interesting pattern of land ownership in Kentucky which influenced both cultural and religious developments in the Commonwealth. Eastern speculators, including a number of Virginia aristocrats, bought these warrants and secured massive tracts of Kentucky land. In addition, the wealthiest of the immigrants who located before 1784, often acting as agents for speculators and absentee owners, were also able to build considerable estates. Among this new aristocracy were many of the earliest religious leaders.

The mass of the new immigrants to Kentucky were therefore not of the solid middle-class landowners, but of those less fortunate who were primarily attracted by a common five year free rent plan for clearing the land and building cabins on the claims of both resident and absentee owners. This pattern of land ownership produced a society with two distinct elites, often with conflicting values, a relatively small independent middle class, and a large number of the dependent classes, both slaves and white tenants. The elites may be called the Presbyterian-Nationalist and the Baptist-Localist.

Religiously and culturally the two Kentucky elitist sectors were quite dissimilar. The elite group created from the earliest settlers was primarily rural, poorly educated and otherwise deficient in "higher culture." Most of them migrated from the backwoods areas of the eastern states. Politically their concerns rarely extended beyond their own and neighboring communities, for which they believed that religion should be the primary instrument of social intercourse and order. The largest number of these leaders were Baptists, but the few Methodists in the state and some Presbyterians shared their essential values. The other elite group came more from the coastal plains and represented more old wealth and cultural sophistication. While land served as a basis of their wealth and they often lived on their estates, this elite was accompanied by a number of urban (town) enterprises, especially commerce and law. Their political interests were national in scope and they looked more to various agencies of government than to the churches as the proper means of social order. Most in this group were Presbyterian, Episcopalian, or Associate Reformed Presbyterian, with by far the largest number being Presbyterian.

During the 1790s the population of Kentucky tripled. Although a number of these new migrants represented the new commercial, manufacturing, artisan, and professional classes that populated the emerging towns, the greatest number were of the rural dependent classes. Most of these were religiously quite indifferent and their presence soon disrupted the religious orderliness which characterized the original settlements. Drunkenness, petty theft, and other activities branded as vices, such as gambling, horse racing, dancing, and "frolicking," rapidly increased. These forms of social disruption were perceived by the religious elites, especially of the Baptist-Localist variety, as a religious problem which could only be solved by an increased attention to religion.

From this set of circumstances came the "Great Revival." It began in Logan County in western Kentucky in 1799. The problem of maintaining order in this area was so severe in the 1790s that it was called "Rogues Harbor." The "first citizens" of the region, who were primarily Presbyterian but who reflected values similar to those of the central Kentucky Baptists, began praying for a revival in 1797. James McGready was a leading figure in this revival. Two of his three Presbyterian congregations, Red River and Gasper River, experienced mild revivals in 1799. The following summer all these congregations met at Red River in June to observe a communion service. Before the four day affair ended, Logan County experienced a rare religious phenomenon. On the final day, under the preaching of the Methodist William McGee, many people fell semiconscious to the floor under deep religious conviction.

The news of such extraordinary events spread with great rapidity, and elaborate plans were made for a similar meeting the following month at Gasper River. While one of Logan County's wealthiest citizens rode on horseback spreading the news of the forthcoming meeting to adjacent communities, other leading citizens bestirred themselves to Gasper River to prepare the campgrounds for the large crowds which were expected. This was the first great "camp meeting" in the United States. The greatest meeting of the Kentucky revival came the following year at Cane Ridge, in Bourbon County just a few miles east of Paris. Barton W. Stone, the Presbyterian minister, went to Logan County early in the summer of 1801 to investigate and planned a similar event at his church. Eye witnesses estimated the size of the crowd at Cane Ridge at between 12,000 and 25,000—or from five to ten percent of the entire population of Kentucky. At this meeting, preaching ran into the night, people collapsed as if in a coma, others were seized with what was described as the "jerks," while still others barked like dogs. Hundreds pointed to this meeting as the place of their conversion.

The revival produced lasting effects on religion and society in Kentucky, but it also accentuated the denominational diversity and religious homogeneity already observable from the earliest period. The Baptist churches were the largest gainers in the revival, tripling their membership to over 15,000. The Baptist experience illuminates the general tendencies inherent in the revival. The new converts represented an almost perfect cross section of the state's population in 1800. The largest number of converts came therefore from the poor white class and from black slaves. The revival thus integrated this population into the community structure and brought them under the oversight of the Baptist religious, social, and economic elite which continued to dominate the leadership roles in the churches. These leaders concentrated their energies on securing social order through the agency of church discipline. The rate of exclusions as the result of church trials quadrupled in the period after the revival and most of those excluded were among the poor whites and the blacks.

The Methodists, the second largest gainers among the established denominations, reflected the Baptist pattern in a rather curious way. Although the Methodist polity was centralized and hierarchical, early developments in Kentucky allowed local congregations to function very much like those of the Baptists. While the itinerant ministers provided certain ministerial services to these congregations, the real leaders of the churches were resident laymen who served as class leaders and patrons. These leaders occupied an economic and social status equivalent to the Baptist pastors and deacons. In his two extended tours through Kentucky, Bishop Francis Asbury usually lodged with these leaders, a benefit which gave them additional status as overseers of the social order of their communities.

The Presbyterians, on the other hand, were devastated by the revival, losing at least a third of their 2,700 members by 1810. This also meant a corresponding decline in the power and influence of the social, political, and cultural values of the Presbyterian-Nationalist elite in Kentucky. The Presbyterian clergy, represented by such men as David Rice and John Lyle, were generally highly educated, specialized and professionalized in their ministerial calling, more sensitive to national political and denominational concerns than to those of a particular local community, and suspicious of the genuineness and orthodoxy of the revival. Ultimately they concentrated their attention on attempting to eliminate suspected doctrinal and educational deviation among Presbyterian revivalists. The result was the formation of two new denominations in Kentucky, each reflecting more the concerns of the Baptist elite than those of the Presbyterian elite.

The first new religious group to emerge on Kentucky soil was the Christian churches under the leadership of Barton W. Stone. Stone and several other revivalistic Presbyterian ministers came under the suspicions of the Synod of Kentucky in 1803. They were accused of various excesses, Arminian heresies, and the lowering of educational standards for the ministry. When Richard M'Nemar was tried for heresy, he, Stone, Robert Marshall, John Dunlavy, and John Thompson withdrew to form the Springfield Presbytery which was soon dissolved. Many Presbyterian churches in central Kentucky split between loyal Presbyterians and the followers of Stone, who referred to themselves by the generic term "Christian." In the rural areas the newly formed Christian churches reflected rather precisely the Baptist pattern, even adopting adult immersion. They so strongly insisted upon the autonomy of the local congregation that the first twenty years of their history remains clouded, revealed only in the separate histories of each community. As among the Baptists, however, these churches represented the total spectrum of classes in Kentucky society, with the political and economic leadership of the community clearly reflected in the leadership of the churches. Most of the remaining struggling Presbyterian congregations, however, were made up primarily of representatives of Kentucky's small middle class.

The second new denomination in Kentucky was the Cumberland Presbyterian Church, formed in 1810 after a lengthy ecclesiastical battle between the Presbyterian revivalists of western Kentucky and the Synod of Kentucky. The revival created an increased demand for preaching and the pro-revival Presbytery of Cumberland responded to this demand by appointing "exhorters" and later by licensing and ordaining ministers not having the education demanded by traditional Presbyterian standards. This group, like the revivalists of central Kentucky, represented the interests of the economic and political elites of the local communities. Finis Ewing, the major figure in the movement, was the eighth and final child of western Kentucky's most prominent family. His older brothers were many times sheriffs, judges, and legislators who were credited bringing law and order to the entire region. McGready, who ultimately rejoined with the older Presbyterian body, was also a man of property whose lay associates were made up of the region's elite. While the Cumberland Presbyterians did not reflect the ecclesiastical pattern of the Baptist model as clearly as the Christians, the pattern of control by the local elite was pronounced. A loose presbyterial polity featuring circuit riders gave considerable autonomy to the local congregation.

That the Great Revival was primarily a movement of which the major tendency was to promote community order is perhaps most vividly portrayed in the emergence of Shakerism in Kentucky. After 1805 when three Shaker missionaries visited Kentucky, two communities were formed. Those people who became Shakers had earlier been participants in and supporters of the revival. In central Kentucky, three of the most prominent ministers in the Stone movement ultimately led most of their congregations into the Shaker commune at Pleasant Hill. The other major community in this village came from the peripatetic Dutch settlement of Mercer County. In western Kentucky, John Rankin, pastor of one of the earliest Presbyterian churches affected by the revival, led his people to form the nucleus of the Shaker commune at South Union. The Shakers pushed community order to its greatest extreme, devising rules and regulations concerning every aspect of life. Although a controversial and often maligned religious group in Kentucky for a century, the Shakers reflected in microcosm the major tendencies in Kentucky society in the early nineteenth century.

The only major group among the earliest settlers not affected by the Great Revival were the Catholics. Nelson County and the surrounding areas were largely spared the disorder of the 1790s, and the Protestant settlers tended to avoid the area. Catholicism thus prospered. From 1793 to 1797 the 300 Catholic families were served by a single priest, Stephen T. Badin. In 1810 Benedict Flaget was consecrated as the first bishop of the Diocese of Bardstown—which covered an area from Canada to southern Tennessee and from the Alleghenies to the Mississippi River. Under Flaget numerous new churches were built and the state was more adequately supplied with priests. He established St. Thomas Seminary in 1811 and in 1812 the Sisters of Loretto and the Sisters of Charity of Nazareth were founded, thus supplying teachers for the Catholic schools. The consecration of St. Joseph's Cathedral in Bardstown in 1819 symbolized the strength of Catholicism in Kentucky.

Although the revival essentially strengthened the existing power structures in Kentucky, it contained some countervailing tendencies regarding the state's slave population. First, it created a mild anti-slavery movement. Barton Stone himself became convinced of the evils of slavery and emancipated his few slaves. William Hickman, pioneer Baptist pastor of the Forks of Elkhorn church, also began preaching emancipation, for which he was dismissed. A small number of Baptist ministers and churches formed the Anti-Slavery Friends of Humanity Association. This movement was never very large and the majority of Kentucky's white religious population defended the institution of slavery. In fact, while religious Kentuckians later supported colonization and African missions, laws passed in the state legislature in 1801 during the height of the revival tightened controls on the state's slave population. Thomas

Campbell moved from Boone County in 1820 when he learned, through violations, that Kentucky law prevented the instruction of slaves.

More significantly, the revival stimulated Negro spirituality and increased the desires of blacks to have their own services of worship. These were generally perceived by the whites as potentially subversive, and frequently blacks caught preaching were disciplined by the white congregations, in which the blacks had no voice. Black preachers and hearers were so persistent, however, that many of the churches were forced to change tactics and allowed separate, albeit supervised, black services. The first independent black church, also a product of the revival, was established in Lexington. The minister, Peter Duerett, organized the church in 1801 from fifty of his recent converts. The white Baptists refused to ordain him or to recognize the baptism of his converts. He persisted, however, and after his death in 1823, the congregation was admitted into the Elkhorn Association as the First Baptist Church, Lexington, Colored, in 1824. Under the leadership of Elder London Ferrill and Elder Frederick Braxton the congregation grew to over 2,000 by the time of the Civil War. By then there were seventeen independent black Baptist churches in the state, most of which, however, were formed in the 1850s.

To some extent the emergence of independent black churches presaged the forces in Kentucky society which were soon to produce not only further denominational diversity but also a social, economic, political and religious diversity within denominations. The result was that by the time of the Civil War there was often a great deal of diversity within a single denomination but a remarkable similarity of groupings across denominational lines. During the 1820s and 1830s many of the earliest and most fully populated areas of the state developed into mature and relatively stable communities while outlying areas, forced to absorb the bulk of continued population growth, experienced continued disorder. The result was a growing regionalism within the state and a reordering of values and practices of the elites, especially in the more mature communities.

Denominationally this transition was most notable among the Baptists, who in 1820 continued to be the largest group. With over 30,000 members they outnumbered the Methodists two to one. Many second and third generation Baptists raised in affluence and positions of leadership began looking beyond the narrow community concerns of their fathers and expressed an interest in state and national affairs. In so doing they adopted a system of values which made them much more compatible with the earlier Presbyterian-National elite. Baptists now became governors, judges, and in 1828 Robert Johnson, son of the Scott County Baptist patriarch, became Vice President of the United States. At the same time, the vast number of Baptists remained rural and community oriented

The tensions inherent in this growing diversity among Baptists expressed themselves most forcefully in the long lasting controversy over missions. When Luther Rice, schooled in the tradition of the New England establishment but becoming Baptist along with Adoniram Judson, visited Kentucky in 1815 to raise funds for the General Convention of the Baptist Denomination in the United States for Foreign Missions, the lines were already clearly formed. The more affluent and better established Baptists immediately sensed the value of associated activity to foster their recently acquired ambitions while the majority resisted such activity as threatening their limited power in their communities.

The issues became considerably more complex and less focused until Alexander Campbell's influence began spreading through Kentucky after 1822. Campbell, a Presbyterian become Baptist and starting in 1823 editor of the *Christian Baptist*, initially came to Kentucky to debate baptism with a Presbyterian. His influence among Kentucky Baptists grew to prominence and within a few years became divisive. Campbell advocated the Bible as the only rule of faith and practice, baptism for the remission of sin, weekly communion, the right of any Christian to preach and administer the ordinances, and the supremacy of the local church over associated activities. While Campbell's teachings attracted persons from almost the entire sociological spectrum of Baptists, excluding only the entrenched leadership, they appealed particularly to those of moderate anti-mission sentiment. Aspiring leaders suspicious of the Baptist drift toward associated activity found a constituency prepared to receive Campbell's ideas. Although General and Regular Baptists had united in 1801 on the basis of the Bible as the only creed, a number of the more powerful churches continued to use the Philadelphia Confession. The general turning away from Calvinism also aided the "reformers," who, significantly, met for the first time the day before the session of the Baptist Missionary Association of Kentucky in 1824.

Before 1830 Baptists were divided into three discernible if overlapping groups—mission, anti-mission, and followers of Campbell. Beginning in 1828 churches and associations began to divide over the issues raised by Campbell. The anti-mission Baptists, especially in the outlying areas of eastern Kentucky, the Knobs, and sections of western Kentucky consolidated their positions in those associations, leading the way for a further fragmentation after 1830. Ultimately this strengthened the hands of the mission Baptists in the more established communities of the state because the associations gained greater authority and potential opposition was eliminated.

Alexander Campbell and his followers soon merged with the older Christian churches associated with Barton W. Stone to form yet another distinct denomination, which also incorporated a wide spectrum of religious belief and the sociological diversity becoming characteristic of denominations in Kentucky. Recognizing their commonalities, the Christians (Stone) and Disciples (Campbell) of Scott and Fayette counties discussed merger in 1831 and 1832. Both groups claimed the Bible as the sole rule of faith and practice, which was now becoming a topic of agreement among most Kentucky Protestants, and desired to restore the churches to the practice of primitive Christianity. Although each group was quite persistent in advocating its own "generic" title and the Disciples opposed "hired" preachers while the Christians continued to insist that only ministers could administer the ordinances, merger was gradually achieved through a process of agreement to tolerate differences.

The statistics for enrollment in the various denominations are approximate at best, but illustrate something of the distribution in the state. In 1832 there were 37,520 Baptists of all varieties with 25 associations, 442 churches and 289 ministers. The Methodists, prospering without as many internal disputes as the Baptists, had 77 preachers and a membership of 23,935. Combined, the Disciples and Christians in various stages of merger probably had 16,000 members. The Cumberland Presbyterians, now spread throughout the midwest, were the fourth largest denomination in Kentucky with about 10,000 members. The Presbyterians had 103 churches, 61 ministers and 7,832 members. The Catholics, having recently added German immigrants of Louisville and Cincinnati to their older population, had 30 priests. In the Episcopal vineyard five priests were laboring.

The 1830s and early 1840s represented a period of denominational consolidation and expansion. While no new bodies appeared, the evolution of the "popular" denominations left many of their natural constituents uncomfortable and ready to follow one of the many evangelical—more precisely, pentecostal-holiness—sects that emerged after the Civil War. Activities centered on various associated missionary and educational ventures. The earliest church-related higher education in Kentucky was sponsored by the Presbyterians, who founded Transylvania University in Lexington in 1797. Initially an institution of some quality, its early history was marked by extensive battles between the Presbyterians and proponents of "liberal religion" for control of the school. Liberalism never secured a firm rooting in Kentucky, however, and in the 1820s Transylvania returned to more conservative though not exclusively Presbyterian control. The Presbyterians chartered Centre College in Danville in 1825. The missionary (elite) Baptists by now felt they needed a professional and educated ministerial leadership and founded Georgetown College in 1829. The politically and socially aspiring Baptist trustees attempted to secure the aid of educators of national renown to teach at the new college. Appearing at the height of the conflict with the emerging Christian churches, the college became an area of contention until the Disciples formed Bacon College in 1836. Initially located in Georgetown, Bacon College moved to Harrodsburg in 1839 and was merged with Transylvania in 1865, with its control passing to the Disciples.

The second phase of denominational consolidation for Kentucky's largest groups witnessed the formation of several associations for missionary and other purposes. The Presbyterians, Cumberland Presbyterians, and Methodists of the state already had their machinery by virtue of their ecclesiastical organization. This was not the case with the Baptists and Disciples. The Kentucky Baptist Convention was formed in 1832. Although ultimately to become the most powerful religious organization in the state, from the outset the convention was controlled by a very small number of ministers. Most of the members of the 608 churches in the state were suspicious of such organizations and refused to support it through contributions or attendance. In an attempt to secure further support the name was changed in 1837 to the General Association of Baptists in Kentucky. The association supported Georgetown College and employed agents to preach across the state and raise funds. This change in title had little basic effect and it was not until the twentieth century that the General Association consolidated its control of the majority of Baptists in the state.

Christians, even more than Baptists, resisted organizations beyond the level of the local church. Yet certain leaders of this denomination, like their Baptist counterparts, felt that organization was essential to expansion. In 1849 the national American Christian Missionary Society was established and the following year the Kentucky Annual State Meeting was established, with representatives of only 62 of the 400 churches present. In the Christian churches, controversy over such organizations grew and occupied the attention of the denomination after the Civil War.

Consolidation and expansion were followed rapidly by further fragmentation which resulted in even greater denominational diversity. The issues leading to the Civl War and the war itself were more disruptive in Kentucky than in any other state. Although inhabitants of a border state, the vast majority of Kentuckians were proslavery and antiabolitionist in sentiment. In all the denominational schisms previous to the war, most Kentucky churchmen sided with their brethren to the south. Kentucky Presbyterians had historically nurtured a vocal antislavery minority, stemming from David Rice's arguments for a gradual emancipation clause in the Kentucky Constitution of 1792. The Synod of Kentucky in 1834 went so far as to approve, by a vote of 56 to 8, a resolution calling for gradual emancipation. This action was in advance of Kentucky public opinion, however, and the following year some members of the Synod were leaders in the movement to drive the abolitionist James G. Birney, a Presbyterian layman, out of the state. The division of Presbyterianism in 1837 into Old Side and New Side assemblies was more complex than the later divisions among Methodists and Baptists, but antiabolitionism was at least a significant factor. In the schisms, the Synod of Kentucky joined the South in supporting the Old Side. The Presbyterian antislavery minority continued to be vocal. Their forces were augmented in 1847 when Robert Jefferson Breckinridge returned to his native state. A vigorous Old Sider, he gave energy to the small antislavery group and in 1849 he and several other Presbyterians once again tried to have gradual emancipation placed in the Kentucky Constitution. Even the New Side Presbyterians, who at their peak could boast no more than 14 ministers, 22 churches and 1,000 members, resisted the antislavery tendencies of the national General Assembly. The Kentucky delegates to the assembly walked out in 1857 and formed an independent Synod of Kentucky, but within a year most returned to the Old Side.

The Methodist Episcopal Church, South, and the Southern Baptist Convention were both organized in 1845. The primary issue in each case was the debate over the proper role of the church on the issues of slavery and abolitionism. In each case the Kentucky churches stood overwhelmingly with the South. The state's delegates to the national Methodist General Conference in 1844 unanimously supported the South, even though Kentucky Methodist opinion, especially along the state's northern border, was somewhat divided. The South attempted to exert its influence in this region by holding its organizational meeting the following year in Louisville. When the Kentucky Conference of the Methodist Episcopal Church, North, was constituted in 1852, it claimed only 2,183 of Kentucky's approximately 50,000 Methodists. The transition to the Southern Baptist Convention was more easily accomplished among Kentucky Baptists because they had a looser organization and a weaker antislavery heritage. While Kentucky was not represented at the organizational meeting in Augusta, Georgia, in 1845, the General Association of Baptists in Kentucky, meeting later that year at Georgetown, agreed to dissolve its connection with the American Baptist Home Missionary Society and support the newly formed Southern Convention.

The major alteration in Kentucky's religious demography before the Civil War, however, came with the massive German and Irish Catholic migration to Louisville and Covington (greater Cincinnati) in the 1840s and 1850s. While the foreign-born constituted only four percent of the Kentucky population in 1850, almost one third of Louisville's 43,000 residents were of foreign birth, a large percentage of these Catholic. The importance of Louisville as a center of Catholicism was recognized in 1843 when, at the request of Bishop Benedict Flaget, the see was removed from Bardstown to that city. With the leadership of Bishop Flaget and his successor, Martin J. Spalding, Kentucky Catholicism prospered. In 1843 the French Sisters of the Institute of the Good Shepherd came to Louisville and in 1848 the Trappists established Gethsemani in Nelson County. (It was here that Kentucky's best known religious figure of the twentieth century, Thomas Merton, lived and wrote.) The following year construction started on the magnificent Louisville Cathedral of the Assumption. By 1835 Catholicism in Kentucky had grown so much that a second diocese was established at Covington.

This rapid growth of German and Irish Catholicism stirred fear among the predominantly Protestant Kentucky population and formed the backdrop of the ugliest episode in Kentucky history. The extremely nativistic Know-Nothing party came to power in Louisville in April of 1855. Previous to the election of August 6 that year, they determined to prevent the foreign born from voting. Riots broke out in both the German and Irish sections of town and a large number of buildings were burned. At least nineteen people were killed. Bishop Spalding and Mayor Barbee prevented damage to the Cathedral. Largely because of the immense popularity of Bishop Spalding and the service of the Sisters in caring for the wounded during the Civil War, this form of violent anti-Catholicism subsided in Kentucky.

The coming of the Civil War brought even greater divisions to the state's major denominations. Many Kentucky churchmen who were satisfied with the arrangements forged in the 1840s found themselves faced with the new and more difficult issue of loyalty. Kentucky had the third largest slave-owning population in the nation and this group dominated Kentucky society and politics. Then, too, the mass of poor whites feared loss of status to freed blacks. Strongly proslavery, the citizens of the Commonwealth were also staunchly prounion. Thus torn, the state attempted to avoid choosing sides by declaring neutrality. Many would have preferred to secede from both North and South. While prounion victories in the congressional election of 1861 kept Kentucky officially in the Union, every Kentuckian was forced to choose sides in a way generally unknown either to the North or South. Families—and their churches— were divided.

In some instances these tensions resulted in the realignment of ecclesiastical allegiances, but the chronicling of these does little justice to the nature and extent of the anguish. Many congregations that did not participate in any of these larger movements struggled through the conflict with their membership divided. The Baptists and the Christian churches, again largely because of their strong congregationalism, experienced the least disruption. The Baptist General Association in 1861 urged an official position of neutrality. Military operations in western Kentucky forced the closing of Bethel College in Russellville in 1861 and the following year Georgetown College suspended its theological school. Methodists were not so fortunate. A number of churches along the northern border of Kentucky were divided and some others joined the Kentucky Conference of the Methodist Episcopal Church, North. The largest confrontation occurred in 1865 when the Kentucky Conference, South voted 35 to 25 to oppose reunion. Fifteen of those ministers were admitted to the Northern branch, which grew to a membership of over 16,000 in Kentucky by 1876.

Kentucky Presbyterians also preferred a course of neutrality. When the national Old School General Assembly declared its allegiance to the Union in 1861, ten Synods in the Confederacy formed the Presbyterian Church in the Confederate States of America. The Kentucky Presbyterians led by the antislavery Breckinridge and proslavery Stuart Robinson, vehemently opposed the action of the Assembly but remained in the Presbyterian Church, USA. As in the case of their Methodist counterparts, the major changes came after the war. When the majority of the Synod of Kentucky was excluded by the Northern body, they joined with the South. The Cumberland Presbyterians, aided by the effective statesmanship of Milton Bird and Richard Beard, managed to avoid formal divisions during the war. Although the southern delegates were not able to attend the General Assembly during the war, they were enrolled without hesitation in 1866.

Although the Diocese of Kentucky of the Protestant Episcopal Church was relatively unscathed during the war, several churches and ministers in western Kentucky found themselves in an extremely uncomfortable position during periods of Confederate occupation. For which government would one pray during the liturgy? It was perhaps his Kentucky experience, however, that enabled James Crick, President of the House of Deputies in both 1862 and 1865, to lead the Anglicans to a speedy reunion after the war. Thus, except for the Presbyterians and Methodists, most Kentucky denominations passed through the war without further permanent fragmentation. Nevertheless the war promoted the process of denominational diversity amidst religious homogeneity.

The major impact of the Civil War on the religious configuration of Kentucky came with the rapid emergence of independent black churches after the war. (Formal emancipation did not come to Kentucky until 18 December, 1865.) The expectations of the two races were quite different. In politics the legislature of 1866 adopted a provision for black public education and a code of civil rights which was somewhat paternalistic. It also denied black people the right to vote or sit on juries or testify in trials involving whites. A similar view obtained among white religious leadership. The General Association of Baptists in 1866 saw that body's role as one of providing instruction. Viewing the blacks as essentially children, the white Baptists envisioned Sunday schools, day schools, and theological schools for blacks, but concluded that "this work must be done mainly by ourselves." Black Baptists, however, had a different vision. In August of 1865, representatives from 12 of the existing 17 independent Black Baptist churches met in Louisville and formed the State Convention of Colored Baptists in Kentucky. Black Baptists throughout the state began organizing new congregations. By 1869 there were already four black Baptist associations. That same year the State Convention became the General Association of Baptists in Kentucky and claimed 55 churches and

12,620 members. The Association continued to grow rapidly. In 1879 it established a school in Louisville which was ultimately called Simmons University in honor of William J. Simmons, who guided the school from 1880 to 1890. By 1913 the General Association had 371 churches with a membership of over 75,000. Black Methodists, though not so numerous as Baptists, also moved rapidly to form their own churches. The African Methodist Episcopal Church, initially formed in Philadelphia in 1816, grew rapidly in Kentucky after the war and by 1876 claimed 55 churches and 5,226 members. The African Methodist Episcopal Zion Church sent missionaries to Kentucky and organized a conference in 1863. By 1876 the church had 34 churches and 3,000 members. At this time the Kentucky Conference of the Methodist Episcopal Church, South, had fewer than 200 black members.

By the 1870s, Kentucky churchgoers were members of over 25 denominations, but most of these were of the Baptist, Methodist, Christian, or Presbyterian variety and there was a growing Catholic minority. Even while denominations proliferated, however, there was an ongoing process of religious and cultural homogenization. Kentucky religionists, even of creedal denominations, claimed the Bible to be authoritative. They exposed a general atonement but were fatalistic about the affairs of this life. They were (sometimes militantly) anti-intellectual, dogmatic, and moralistic. Even though petty differences may have at times been exaggerated, they tended to respond more to the personalities of religious leaders than to their particular theologies. While they were intensely concerned about their communities, they were prone to analyze social problems in terms of individual salvation.

Space permits only a few examples of movements in this direction. Baptists had largely abandoned the Philadelphia Confession and Calvinism remained pronounced only in Appalachia. Presbyterian ministers, although still the best educated of the Kentucky clergy, were forced by their congregations to abandon written sermons and were expected to be able to preach at any place on any topic at a moment's notice. Kentucky Episcopalians were strongly evangelical and resisted "formalism." Perhaps of greater significance, however, was the fact that religious controversy was most often among members of a single denomination rather than between denominations.

In the years after 1870, the process of denominational proliferation continued at an even greater rate, but the basic characteristics were only altered slightly. The major intellectual currents of the late nineteenth century, particularly biblical higher criticism and Darwinian evolution, made but little impact on the religious leadership and virtually none on the masses of members. The state's Baptists, who continued to be the dominant religious group, secured the location of the Southern Baptist Theological Seminary in Louisville in 1877 when the young institution moved there from Greenville, South Carolina. The small number of Baptists who supported the General Association welcomed the seminary as a means to establish, at least in the county seat towns, a full time educated professional ministry. In this way they could extend their influence and further their emphasis on expansion, or "progress," which had become virtually an article of faith.

Some of the things that came with the seminary, however, were not so welcome. The seminary faculty, led by President James P. Boyce, was representative of the Southern Baptist aristocracy. They were scholarly, dedicated, and conscientious leaders, but socially and theologically conservative, expressing their creativity in the safe realms of homiletics, organization and administration, or grammar. Crawford H. Toy was an exception to this rule. His thinking, and his teaching, was influenced by the theory of evolution and by Pentateuchal criticism. Although irenic of disposition and well loved by his colleagues of a decade and many of his students, Toy was unable to accommodate the requests that he desist in introducing these ideas. As a result he was forced to resign. A major consideration of those critical of Toy was that he would alienate the wealthy supporters of the struggling seminary. While Toy went on to a brilliant career at Harvard, where he became a leading scholar in Old Testament and Semitic studies, Kentucky Baptists had established an enduring pattern which confined their scholars to modes of culturally acceptable thinking. This was emphasized from 1896 to 1899 when William H. Whitsitt was forced to resign the presidency of Southern Seminary because of his published studies of Baptist history. The majority of Baptists had come to believe that Baptist churches accurately reflected the New Testament model and some held that there had been a historical succession of such churches from Christ to the present. Whitsitt argued that baptism by immersion emerged in mid-seventeenth century England. This created a controversy that shook not only Kentucky but the entire Southern Baptist Convention. Although a loyal member of the seminary faculty since 1872, Whitsitt was forced to resign in 1899.

This rejection of intellectual and scientific inquiry was not confined to Baptists in Kentucky but reflected accurately the stance of the overwhelming majority in the state. The Presbyterian seminary, relocated from Danville to Louisville in 1853, followed the norm established by the majority of Presbyterians both North and South, and taught Bible and theology without reference to higher criticism and evolution. The same was true of the Disciples' College of the Bible in Lexington, which was dominated by the conservative president J. W. McGarvey. This institution began to teach aspects of biblical criticism in the early 1920s, however, after the withdrawal of the more conservative Churches of Christ in 1906.

Of far greater impact than scientific discoveries on religion in Kentucky was the popular Holiness movement. The early Holiness movement was of Northern and Midwestern origin but it found a ready constituency in Kentucky. The doctrine of entire sanctification featured the belief that one could experience a second work of the Holy Spirit which could be dated as occurring at a precise moment. While the Holiness movement spread primarily among Methodists, this doctrine was especially appealing to many rural Kentuckians of other denominations. The leaders of the Kentucky phase of the movement were John Wesley Hughes, who in 1890 established Asbury College at Wilmore, and his successor at Asbury, Henry Clay Morrison. Holiness preaching directly attacked the spiritual coldness and formality of the established churches. Combined with various pentecostal doctrines, especially the premillennial notion of Jesus' imminent return to crush the forces of darkness and install the saints to power, this movement created the most significant changes in the religious configuration of Kentucky in the twentieth century.

This was particularly the case in the eastern Kentucky mountains. The Appalachian region of Kentucky had been the bulwark of Calvinism. Whether direct descendants of the strongly antimission Regular or Particular Baptists or members of one of the more exotic snake-handling sects, Kentucky mountain folk staunchly resisted the gradual theological changes taking place in other areas of the state. Notwithstanding their Calvinistic theology, eastern Kentuckians were also fervently emotional in their religious services. They were responsive to holiness and pentecostal emotionalism and their churches grew rapidly in that region. Today one may find a great variety of Churches of God, Holiness, or Nazarene congregations in the same community alongside Primitive, Old School, or Hard Shell Baptist churches. Of whatever sect or denomination, however, the people of this region express a religion which is both pessimistic and fatalistic about the affairs of this world and points to salvation and the world to come as the only hope. They tend to have a significantly higher religiosity than persons from other areas of the state although their participation in formal religious services is significantly lower. They are considerably more tolerant of human weakness and sin, especially among those with kinship or friendship ties, than are the religious of other parts of the state. With variation for regional distinctiveness, however, Appalachia exemplifies the denominational diversity and religious homogenity characteristic of the commonwealth.

The development of religion in Kentucky in the twentieth century is more reflective of its nineteenth century heritage than it is of major twentieth century movements. One cannot define a Kentucky social gospel movement, a fundamentalist-modernist controversy, or a dramatic turn to Neo-Orthodoxy. What is often described inaccurately as Fundamentalism in Kentucky was nothing more than the persisting moderate folk evangelicalism which was well defined by 1870. Having nurtured no modernists within its borders, the Commonwealth had no need of an aggressive leadership to lead its citizens back to the fundamentals. Division of opinion among members of all denominations in Kentucky has been along what may more accurately be described as conservative-moderate lines. Actual schisms, reflected in both the Disciples and Cumberland Presbyterian divisions in 1906, were interjected not by new but by very old issues.

This absence of a hard and fast division of Kentucky religions into a "two party system" allowed for the venting of different opinions which did not necessarily further fragment a particular denomination. This was especially the case in the controversy in the 1920s over proposed legislation to ban the teaching of evolution in the public schools. All the state's major denominations—Baptist, Methodist, Presbyterian, and Disciples of Christ—had advocates both for and against the bill. Those opposing the bill, however, rarely defended the truth of evolution. E. Y. Mullins, president of the Baptist seminary in Louisville, was a leading opponent of the legislation but did not personally espouse evolution. The bill was defeated in the 1922 General Assembly by a single vote. Since the religious opinion had not been divided into polar opposites, the issue soon subsided.

In other areas the homogeneity of the state's religious leadership was clearly discernible. In Kentucky the drive for good government, sometimes labeled "the Progressive Movement," was rather clearly an attempt

by upper middle class businessmen and professionals to enforce traditionally Protestant virtues. The two major issues were ultimately prohibition and pari-mutuel gambling. Since Louisville was the largest urban
area and most threatened, it quite naturally provided the leadership in
these matters. The Louisville Churchmen's Federation, the most significant organization, attracted support from the entire spectrum of religious
opinion. Episcopal, Presbyterian, Baptist, Methodist, and Disciples clergy
of all leanings cooperated. Among Baptists, for example, everyone from
the genteel professors of Southern Seminary to M. P. Hunt, the closest
thing to a fundamentalist firebrand to be found in the state, supported the
Federation's projects. One of the most active leaders was Patrick H.
Callahan, the "dry" Catholic who was president of the Louisville Varnish
Company. Strangely enough, Callahan paid one fourth of Hunt's salary,
even though the latter was outspoken in his anti-Catholicism. The Federation used a diversity of tactics, which included everything from politics
to the bringing of Gypsy Smith and Billy Sunday to Louisville for revivalistic crusades. In conjunction with the Anti-Saloon League, these Louisville churchmen were joined by religious leaders around the state, and
together they led Kentucky to support the Prohibition Amendment. In
1922 they turned their attention against pari-mutuel gambling. In 1923
Alben W. Barkley, later United States Senator and Vice President, picked
up this issue and campaigned under the slogan, "Christianity, Morality,
and Clean Government."

The pattern of denominational diversity and religious homogeneity
and the persistence of conservative Evangelicalism has also influenced
more recent twentieth century developments. Kentucky has not been the
prolific producer of new denominations nor the location of numerous
schisms. If dissension exists, it is usually expressed by the formation of a
new congregation of the same denomination. Therefore, an almost infi-
nite variety of churches, often reflecting minute sociological differences,
exist in the same denomination. Although in recent decades conservative
churches have continued to grow, Kentucky has not been altogether
fruitful soil for ultra-rightists, as it has never been for the left. Moreover,
this heritage has been particularly suited to promote a limited ecumenism. Kentucky Methodists supported the reunion of 1939. Kentucky
Baptists are more prone to associate with Northern Baptists than are
their brethren to the south and southwest, and Kentucky Presbyterians,
most of whom are dually aligned, may yet hold the key to a long sought
Presbyterian merger.

The period of widespread religious revivalism in the 1950s created a national ethos that could be shared by most of the religious people of Kentucky. Billy Graham and evangelists of a similar nature held particular appeal for Kentuckians. Churches of the Southern Baptist Convention, which sponsored a campaign for a "Million More in Fifty-four," grew rapidly during the decade. At the same time, Kentucky became the location of choice for a number of new industrial ventures of corporations whose core of operations was located in the northeast and midwest. The transfer to Kentucky of managerial employees, a significant number of whom were Catholic, added both numbers and leadership to Catholicism in Kentucky, especially in growing towns other than the traditional urban Catholic centers of Louisville and Covington.

The "exotic" religions of the 1960s, however, made little impact on the religious demography of Kentucky. To be sure, small congregations of Black Muslims, Satanists, and various cults of varying Near and Far Eastern rootage were formed in the urban and university environs of Louisville, Lexington, and Covington. With the exception of a few Muslim temples, however, these never flourished and have not survived. Likewise, the strong national religious anti-war movement of the late sixties and early seventies was but a ripple in the pond of Kentucky's basically conservative evangelical religions.

The latest survey (1971) of Kentucky's religious population confirms the persistence of Kentucky's heritage of denominational diversity and religious homogeneity. The fact that less than 60 percent of Kentuckians, which is somewhat under the national average, are adherents of a particular religion is largely explainable by the reluctance of Appalachian Kentuckians to join even those churches with whom they agree. In several counties in this region, for example, the number of church members is less than ten percent of the population. The state as a whole remains overwhelmingly Southern Baptist, who make up nearly 50 percent of the religious membership. In the urban centers of Louisville and Covington, and in the traditionally Catholic centers around Bardstown, however, Catholicism is the religion of the majority. For the entire state, the Catholic church has the second largest membership with about 20 percent of the religious population. As a percentage of the church related population, Methodists have fallen from their strong position of a century ago to a current 12 percent. The various branches of the Christian movement claim about 10 percent, with that being about equally divided between the Disciples and the more conservative Christian Churches and Churches of Christ. Presbyterians and Episcopalians combined number only about five percent. The real strength of various Pentecostal-Holiness denominations is underrepresented in published statistics. Even so, the Church of God (Anderson, Indiana), Church of God (Cleveland, Tennessee), Church of the Nazarene, and Assemblies of God also represent approximately five percent of the religious membership in Kentucky. While there are over 50 other Christian denominations or organized religions in Kentucky, these groups each represent less than one percent of the population.

Bibliography

W. E. Arnold. *A History of Methodism in Kentucky.*

Ann B. Bevins. "Sisters of the Visitation: One Hundred Years in Scott County, Mt. Admirabilis and Cardome," *The Register of the Kentucky Historical Society* 74: 1 (1976): 30-39.

John B Boles *Religion in AnteBellum Kentucky.*

J. W. Cooke "Stoney Point, 1866-1969," *The Filson Club Historical Quarterly* 50: 4 (1976): 337-52.

Hoke S. Dickinson, ed. *The Cane Ridge Reader.*

William E. Ellis. "The Fundamentalist-Moderate Schism over Evolution in the 1920s," *The Register of the Kentucky Historical Society* 74: 2 (April 1976): 112-23.

Winfred Ernest Garrison and Alfred T. DeGroot. *The Disciples of Christ: A History.*

Fred J. Hood, ed. *Kentucky: Its History and Heritage.*

Lester G. McAllister and William E. Tucker. *Journey in Faith: A History of the Christian Church (Disciples of Christ).*

Frank M. Masters. *A History of Baptists in Kentucky.*

George Voiers Moore. *Interchurch Cooperation in Kentucky, 1865-1965.*

William A. Mueller. *A History of Southern Baptist Theological Seminary.*

A. H. Redford. *The History of Methodism in Kentucky.*

P. E. Ryan. *History of the Diocese of Covington, Kentucky.*

Robert F. Sexton. "The Crusade Against Pari-Mutuel Gambling in Kentucky: A Study of Southern Progressivism in the 1920s," *The Filson Club Historical Quarterly* 50: 1 (Jan. 1976): 47-57.

J. H. Spencer. *A History of Kentucky Baptists.*

M. J. Spalding. *Sketches of the Early Catholic Missions of Kentucky, 1787-1827.*

Bill L. Weaver. "Kentucky Baptists' Reaction to the National Evolution Controversy 1922-1926," *The Filson Club Historical Quarterly* 49: 3 (July 1975): 266-75.

B. J. Webb. *The Centenary of Catholicity in Kentucky.*

LOUISIANA

PENROSE ST. AMANT
SOUTHERN BAPTIST THEOLOGICAL SEMINARY

Beginnings

The territory now making up the state of Louisiana was once a section of the vast Mississippi Valley claimed by Robert Cavalier de La Salle for France (1682) and named Louisiana in honor of King Louis XIV. It was controlled successively by Antoine Crozat (1712-1717), John Law's Company on the West (1717-1731), the French (1731-1763) and Spanish (1763-1800) Crowns. Returned to France (1800-1803), it was sold to the United States as a territory (1803-1812). The extreme southern part of the Louisiana Purchase became the eighteenth state admitted to the Union (April 30, 1812).

The Mississippi River, discovered in 1541 by Hernando De Soto, a Spanish explorer, was the major artery used in the settlement and colonization of what became Louisiana. In 1699 Pierre Le Moyne Sieur d'Iberville proceeded from the Gulf of Mexico up the river beyond the site of the later state capital Baton Rouge. In 1718, Jean Baptiste Le Moyne Sieur d'Bienville, a younger brother of Iberville, founded a city on the banks of the Mississippi and named it New Orleans in honor of the Duke of Orleans. In 1722, he moved the capital of French Louisiana from Biloxi on the Gulf Coast to New Orleans, located on a crescent-shaped bend in the River, hence its sobriquet of "Crescent City."

Franciscan missionaries Zeno Membré and Anastase Douay accompanied La Salle on his historic voyage down the Mississippi River to its mouth. Priests were sent by the Quebec Seminary in Canada to evangelize the Indians in lower Louisiana at the beginning of the eighteenth century.

Jean Francois Buisson de St. Cosme, possibly the first American-born missionary martyr, was slain by Chitimacha Indians near the late site of Donaldsonville on the Mississippi River in 1706. Jesuits, Capuchines, Carmelites, and other pioneer missionaries made their way up and down the river, moving downstream to its mouth and upstream as far as Pointe Coupée organizing missions, out of which came parishes at a later time. They also traveled extensively on winding bayous and picturesque lakes in search of converts among the Indians. Probably the first chapel in the Lower Mississippi Valley was built by the Bayagoula Indians under the direction of a Jesuit missionary, Paul du Ru, in 1700 at what is now Bayou Goula in Iberville Parish. It was named in honor of St. Francis Xavier. The first Mass celebrated in Natchitoches, the oldest town (1715) in later Louisiana, was offered by Antonio Margil. New Orleans had a "substantial church building" in 1727, the same year the Ursuline Nuns opened an academy that has the longest uninterrupted history of any catholic School in America.

Perspective

One glance at a map depicting the religious bodies in the state of Louisiana discloses the sharp division between Protestantism in the North and Roman Catholicism in the South. The difference is not merely a matter of religion but also of culture. The northern part of the state is characterized by a Puritan ethos and a strong pietistic strain, whereas south Louisiana, except in the southeast (once known as "West Florida"), exhibits a French and Spanish Catholic mentality, in which the Anglo Saxon, Puritan, and pietistic heritage of Protestantism is quite subordinate.

There are some subtle and some sharp differences in the life styles of the regions. North Louisiana is characterized by a conservative and rather traditional pattern, with strong legalistic and moralistic elements, a viewpoint that puts a large premium upon personal behavior in conformity with church and community standards. In South Louisiana, the relationship between religious teaching and life style is less clear. The Catholic conception of culture is more concerned with basic moral issues as seen by the Church and less with specific codes of conduct. For example, *Mardi Gras*, the last day before Lent, which is celebrated wildly in New Orleans, is a significant holiday for only a few in Shreveport.

Generalizations about sectionalism in Louisiana in recent years, however, must take into account the homogenizing impact of the mass media,

especially television, and tendencies toward conformity to a secular outlook in the state as well as increasing penetration of Protestantism
throughout South Louisiana and some Roman Catholic growth in the
central and northern parts of the state, largely in Avoyelles, Rapides, and
Natchitoches paishes. Nevertheless, the predominantly Anglo-Saxon
Protestant north and the strong Catholic south represent different view-
points. An additional element in the religious and cultural schism is
Anglo-Saxon versus immigrant values, the culture of the south being
more open to the latter.

Cosmopolitan New Orleans, a mixture of Creole, Acadian (Cajun),
and "American" cultures, is distinguishable from a triangular shaped
section of the state that runs from Lake Charles in the Southwest, to the
"Crescent City" in the East, to Alexandria in central Louisiana. The
Acadian French people who were expelled from Nova Scotia by the
English in the mid-eighteenth century predominate in this area and
constitute a culture that differs from the more syncretistic community in
New Orleans.

Roman Catholic Expansion

Acadian settlements were formed at St. Martinville on Bayou Teche,
in the Opelousas region, and along the Mississippi River above and below
Baton Rouge, notably in Iberville Parish at St. Gabriel, where the historically important Parish Registers of St. Charles Church were deposited at
Grand Pré (1688-1755). Despite a shortage of priests and churches, the
Cajuns retained their Catholic religion and established a cluster of parishes in St. Martinville (1765), Opelousas (1777), Grand Coteau (1819),
Lafayette, formerly Vermillionville (1821), and New Iberia (1838). They
continue their devotion to a colorful and traditional Catholicism, in which
veneration of the Virgin Mary and invocation of the saints are fused with
"the sacred heart of Jesus," pictures of which can be seen on the walls of
many a cottage in south Louisiana. The Blessing of the Shrimp Fleet just
before it sails out into the Gulf of Mexico for the first catch of the season
by priests in elaborate vestments is for them both a social occasion and a
deeply felt religious experience. The Blessing of the Sugar Cane also
carries a profound religious meaning for these faithful Catholics. The
priest begins his walk between the rows of sugar cane just before work
begins in the fields accompanied by acolytes, choristers, and a crucifer.
"As he progresses," Frances Parkinson Keyes once wrote, "the Cleric
bestows his blessing on everyone and everything he passes. He prays that

the workers may be industrious, the mules patient and enduring, the knives sharp, the carts strong, the harvest plentiful." The Sugar Cane Festival in New Iberia, the Rice Festival in Crowley, the Dairy Festival in Abbeyville, and the Jambalaya Festival in Gonzales are begun with solemn Masses.

The Cajun expresses his love of life by staging big Saturday night dances (*fais-dodos*) and pirogue races on Bayou Barataria, by cooking a delectable concoction called gumbo and a mysterious and highly seasoned mixture of crawfish, rice, and "what have you" called jambalaya, by brewing strong black coffee (French-drip) and making much of family ties (*la famille*). His church teaches him that life can be lived in a "state of grace," sustained by contrition and then confession to his friendly priest, who provides penances to counterbalance his moral lapses and offers the serene certainty of absolution. He does not brood about the mysteries of life and death, mortal and venial sins, which he leaves to his church. His conversation is sprinkled with stories passed down to him by his fore-bears. He speaks in a delightful French dialect or equally captivating English with a Cajun accent. He laughs a lot, enjoys his distinctive culture, and does not take himself too seriously. In other words, for the Cajun the sacred and the secular tend to merge into a single way of life.

The Cajuns have been called country folk in contrast to Creoles, who have been described as city folk. This geographic distinction, which had a certain validity in the past, has been tempered by population mobility and intermarriage. Strictly speaking, the Creoles are the white descendants of the French and Spanish settlers of the Colonial period. The Cajuns, as already indicated, came to Louisiana in the mid-eighteenth century, largely from Canada. Both groups and the Italians who settled in the state during the last century are predominantly Roman Catholic.

The French and Spanish cultures from which Catholicism in New Orleans is derived are reflected in place (French Quarter) and street (Almonaster) names, in colorful celebrations (All Saints' Day), in historic buildings (the Cabildo), even in the menus of restaurants (crawfish *étouffé*, shrimp Arnaud). The St. Louis Cathedral (named for Louis IX, the crusading King of France), founded in 1793, is one of the genuinely historic buildings in the nation. Another carryover of Catholicism is the designation of the civil subdivisions of the state as "parishes" instead of "counties". Also, many parishes are named for Saints.

The concentration of Roman Catholics in South Louisiana, mainly along the Mississippi River, Bayou Lafourche, and other streams, posed serious problems. Inundations, tropical hurricanes, yellow fever epidemics, and the toll of typhoid fever resulted in shifts and depletion of population. After the Civil War, heavy debt created a precarious situation. Pew rentals and revenue from parish fairs were insufficient supplements to the depleted resources of the church. Nevertheless, the faithful labor of obscure priests and nuns stabilized the church and, after the stresses of the Reconstruction period (1865-1877) had passed, Catholicism moved forward again. In 1918, the Diocese of Lafayette was established, giving the state three jurisdictions: the Archdiocese of New Orleans (1850), the Diocese of Alexandria (formerly Natchitoches, 1853), and Lafayette. The Diocese of Baton Rouge was created in 1961. More than one million Catholics are concentrated in south Louisiana and constitute about 33% of the total population of the state. Lafayette has a higher proportion of Catholics (61%) and more black Catholic adherents than any other diocese in the United States (80,500). There are 72,000 black Catholics in the Archdiocese of New Orleans. The large number of blacks who adhere to the Catholic faith grows out of the fact that most slave owners who supervised sugar plantations in south Louisiana were Roman Catholics. Another reason for the concentration of black Catholics in the state comes out of the *Code Noir*, formulated by Bienville in 1724, whose prescriptions required that slaves be baptized into the Catholic Church. Separate Catholic for blacks are rather recent: St. Katherine's (1895) in New Orleans was the first congregation of this kind. In 1981, there were more than 100 separate black Catholic churches in the state.

Education has occupied an important place in the policy of the Catholic Church in Louisiana since 1725, when a school for boys was established by Capuchin Raphael de Luxembourg. There are two Catholic universities in New Orleans—Loyola of the South (Jesuit) and Xavier of Louisiana, the latter being the only Catholic university in the United States specifically designed for blacks. St. Mary's Dominican College, also in New Orleans, is a school for women. Each diocese has a school board supervising Catholic elementary and secondary education, the earliest of which was organized in Alexandria in 1889. Joseph F. Rummel, for whom a Catholic high school in New Orleans was named, served as Archbishop of New Orleans from 1935 until his death in 1964. He was succeeded by John Cody, who after a brief tenure became archbishop of Chicago. Philip Hannan was appointed Archbishop of New Orleans in 1965.

Protestant Episcopal Church

Roman Catholicism was the only organized Christian community in New Orleans until the founding of Christ's Church, a predominantly Episcopal congregation also called the New Orleans Protestant Church, whose first service was held in the Cabildo in November, 1805. Philander Chase, who later became rector of the church, described attendants at this service as "numerous and of the most respectable Americans, and very decorous in their deportment." It is possible, though unlikely, that on this occasion Chase preached the first Protestant sermon to an organized congregation in the whole area purchased by the United States in 1803. This church, now Christ Church Cathedral, was not only the first non-Roman Catholic Church in the city but probably in what became the state of Louisiana in 1812. Six years before that it had become officially a Protestant Episcopal congregation.

Three of the leading Episcopal churches of New Orleans were organized within a period of ten years beginning with St. Paul's in 1838 and followed by Annunciation in 1844 and Trinity in 1848. Leonidas Polk, the first Bishop of Louisiana, was also Rector of Trinity Church from 1856 to 1861. He had served as a Missionary Bishop of the Southwest from the time of that diocese's formation in 1838. The Episcopal Church in Louisiana was part of this jurisdiction. Under his guidance, churches were organized in Shreveport, Plaquemine, Opelousas, Thibodaux, Napoleonville, Donaldsonville, along Red River, and Bayous Lafourche and Teche. He spent his energies unstintingly, "gathering congregations, holding services, preaching, baptizing, confirming, and celebrating the sacrament wherever and whenever he could find an opportunity," as his son wrote. A specific example of his courage was an occurrence at Shreveport, where on Sunday March 24, 1839 he led what has been called "the first religious service ever held in that primitive settlement of rivermen" despite the fact he was told "we have never had any preaching here, and we don't want any." He rented a house, borrowed a table to serve as a pulpit, secured a hand-bell which he rang to advertise the service, and proceeded to preach anyway.

Polk became bishop of Louisiana in 1841. He and Bishop Stephen Elliott of Georgia initiated a movement that eventuated in the organization of the University of the South at Sewanee, Tennessee. Known as the "Fighting Bishop," Polk served as a Lieutenant Colonel in the Confederate Army and lost his life at Pine Mountain, Marietta, Georgia in 1864.

William Thomas Leacock became rector of Christ Church in 1852 and served with uncommon devotion for 32 years. An Englishman and a gradute of Queen's College, Oxford, he was familiar with the formalism of the Church of England and yet he was equally aware of the rather informal church life in the Mississippi Valley, where he had served pioneer congregations prior to his ministry in New Orleans. His varied background as a churchman enabled him to strike a balance between high and low church tendencies. For this and other reasons he was greatly loved.

Christ Church in New Orleans, built in 1886, became Christ Church Cathedral in 1892. This change was brought about despite opposition by the older parish churches in the diocese, especially in New Orleans, and in the face of a negative attitude on the part of some low churchmen toward the increase in Episcopal prestige symbolized by the creation of the Cathedral. Davis Sessums, who had become rector of Christ Church in 1887, was elevated to the Episcopate in 1891. Believing "a Bishop needed a church," as he expressed it, he was chiefly responsible for changing the oldest parish church in the diocese into a cathedral.

During the early years of his episcopacy, Bishop Sessums provided vigorous leadership, especially in the areas of missions, the involvement of laymen in the life of the church, and the bearing of the Gospel upon society. A serious illness, from which he never recovered completely, cast its shadow over the last two decades of his episcopacy. The Davis Sessums Memorial Student Center, constructed by the Diocese of Louisiana on the campus of Louisiana State University in 1929, was one of the first facilities of this kind established by any church in the United States and probably the first by any denomination in Louisiana.

When James Craik Morris became Bishop in 1930, the diocese counted 12,592 communicants, about half of whom lived in New Orleans where there were eight churches. Bishop Morris struggled with staggering financial problems during the depression of the 1930s. Though his energies were devoted largely to administrative affairs, he found "nothing disconcerting in the process" by which Christ Church Cathedral was brought in eight years from "the lowest low churchmanship to what earlier would have been rejected as impossibly high." Dean William H. Nes (1927-1947) was chiefly responsible for transforming "Low Church Protestantism" into what was probably the first large Anglo-Catholic Parish in the South. Dean Nes sought "to make the Cathedral authentically Anglican," as he put it. He instituted daily Eucharists, replaced the communion table with an altar, introduced eucharistic vestments, reserved Holy Communion so that it could be taken into sickrooms, and heard confessions on Saturday afternoons.

Communicants in the Episcopal Church in Louisiana in 1955 amounted to 20,622, organized into 45 parishes. In 1980, the Western Diocese of Louisiana was formed with 13,000 communicants and Willis R. Henton was elected Bishop. The Diocese of Louisiana retained 16,000 communicants. No single factor accounts for the slow rate of growth of Episcopalianism in the state. Few Episcopalians migrated to Louisiana because they belonged to the upper economic bracket and were, therefore, not inclined to move from the Atlantic seaboard in search of a better life. Those who came were not of strong missionary and evangelistic inclination. The present bishop is James B. Brown, who was elected in 1977.

The Presbyterian Church

Sylvester Larned, a young Presbyterian minister from Massachusetts, found one Protestant church when he arrived in New Orleans in 1818. It was Christ Church (Episcopal), which worked harmoniously with a small group of Presbyterians led by Larned, who built a house of worship in 1819 and solidified the Presbyterian witness. This community formed the nucleus of the First Presbyterian Church in the city, organized in November, 1823.

Larned's untimely death in 1820 left the young congregation without clerical leadership at a time of serious financial crisis. The church's debt was substantial, $45,000. Theodore Clapp, a Congregationalist, who arrived in New Orleans in 1822 when the Plan of Union bound the two denominations, agreed to become pastor of the church provided the financial problem could be solved. A lottery, legal at that time, raised $25,000 and the rest of the debt was absorbed by Judah Touro, a Jewish philanthropist and merchant, who thereby assumed ownership of the church. As a consequence of these circumstances, a Jew came into possession of a Presbyterian church with a Congregational minister in a predominantly Roman Catholic city!

Clapp's ministry was a stormy one from the beginning owing to personal conflicts between the pastor and some of his parishioners and his growing inability to support biblically what he called "the distinguishing tenets of Calvinism." It is not surprising that Clapp was deposed from the ministry by the Presbytery of Mississippi in 1833 and became the founder of the "First Congregational Church in the City and Parish of

New Orleans," which continued to worship in the edifice Larned had constructed in 1819. Clapp's church was Unitarian from the outset of his new ministry in 1833, though the designation "First Congregational Unitarian Church" was not used until 1853. The first Unitarian Church of New Orleans, a descendant of this congregation, celebrated its 125th anniversary in 1958. It has been said that for more than three decades New Orleans was noted for "the American Theatre, the French Opera, and Parson Clapp's Church."

In spite of difficulties associated with the Presbyterian Church in New Orleans and a paucity of preachers, "no more than seven or eight" in the state, Presbyterianism expanded steadily if not spectacularly throughout Louisiana. Churches were organized in Baton Rouge (1827), Alexandria (1844), and Shreveport (1845). The Second and Third Presbyterian Churches in New Orleans were established in 1845 and 1847, respectively. The Presbytery of New Orleans (1844-1845) was renewed in 1855. A year earlier, the Red River Presbytery in north Louisiana had been formed.

The famous Benjamin Morgan Palmer, who served as pastor of the First Presbyterian Church in New Orleans from 1856 until his death in 1902, became the outstanding figure in Louisiana Presbyterianism and a leader of his church in the South. He shared with James Henley Thornwell leadership in crystallizing the influence of *antebellum* southern Presbyterianism in favor of the Confederacy. At the formation of the Presbyterian Church of the Confederate States of America in Augusta, Georgia, on December 4, 1861, he was unanimously chosen to preach the opening sermon and elected moderator. Someone has remarked that he did "more for the Confederate cause than a regiment of soldiers."

The Synod of Louisiana, which resulted from the division of the Synod of Mississippi into two synods in 1901, is one of the smaller synods, numerically and geographically, of the Presbyterian Church in the United States. There were 105 churches in the synod with about 6,000 members in 1901. In 1959, there were 123 churches with over 30,000 communicants. Though the increase in total number of churches has been minimal, total membership increased five times in the 1901-1959 period. Since then membership has increased modestly.

It should be said that, although size is hardly unimportant, the impact of a church upon the culture in which it functions cannot be calculated adequately in quantitative terms. Judged by the quality of its influence, the

Presbyterian Church in Louisiana has wrought well. Early Presbyterian ministers and churches played a major role in civilizing the Louisiana frontier. Presbyterian policy, always insistent upon an educated ministry and the importance of Christian culture, has provided a significant counterpoise to the anti-intellectualism that has sometimes passed for theology in some sectors of southern religion. (What has been said here about Presbyterianism can be said equally concerning the Episcopal Church in Louisiana.)

Baptists

Baptists first appeared in Louisiana toward the end of the eighteenth century. The first known Baptist in the area was John Coulter, who arrived with his family at Ft. Miro, later named Monroe, in April 1797. Nothing is known of his activities as a Baptist until he moved to Wilkinson County, Mississippi, in 1807, where he served as treasurer of the Mississippi Association for several years.

Bailey E. Chaney, a member of the Salem Church in Mississippi and a licensed minister, probably preached the first Baptist sermon in what is now East Feliciana Parish of the state of Louisiana. That event may have occurred in 1798 but more likely it took place early in the nineteenth century. There is no evidence that he organized a church.

The initial Baptist church in Louisiana was founded on a bluff overlooking the Bogue Chitto River in present day Washington Parish. It bore the name of Half Moon Bluff Baptist Church and was accepted for membership in the Mississippi Association on 17 October 1812.

Edmund J. Reis, a Frenchman from Nova Scotia, was probably the first Baptist missionary to enter New Orleans. He arrived in late 1812 and remained for about six months, during which he distributed Bibles and preached with little success. Without question, he was the first French-speaking Baptist minister to visit Louisiana. Benjamin Davis served as an agent of the Louisiana Bible Society in New Orleans from December 1815 to March 1816. He returned to the Crescent City in 1818 and was chiefly responsible for organizing a church, which also affiliated with the Mississippi Association. Davis was probably the first Baptist to administer the ordinance of baptism in the city. It was also the first baptism by immersion ever witnessed by most of the curious crowd gathered on the banks of the Mississippi River in front of the Custom House. James A. Ronaldson arrived in New Orleans in 1816, finding a few Baptists already on the scene, Cornelius Paulding among them. In a commodious house owned by Paulding, a place to hold services was provided. Ronaldson left New Orleans in 1817 and later (1830s) was accused of adopting the restorationist views of Campbellism.

William B. Johnson, a South Carolinian who subsequently achieved the distinction of serving as president of both the Triennial Convention and the Southern Baptist Convention, was invited to visit New Orleans by Paulding early in 1817. During his brief visit to the city, Johnson preached in Paulding's house and on board a ship. By permission of Antonio de Sella (known also as Father Antoine), he gave an address in the St. Louis Cathedral in behalf of the Poydras Orphan Asylum. In 1980, this writer (a Baptist) preached in the Cathedral to the participants in a national meeting of the Association of Clinical Pastoral Education, evidence of an ecumenical spirit that characterizes the major Christian bodies in the state today.

Several efforts to establish Baptist churches in New Orleans (1818, 1826, 1841) did not succeed. The scattered Baptists were eventually unified by Russell Holman, a missionary sent by the American Baptist Home Mission Society, and T. J. Fisher, an evangelist from Kentucky. The church known now as the First Baptist Church, organized on 28 December 1843, was the result. After an unsuccessful effort to establish a church in Baton Rouge (1838), what is now the First Baptist Church of that City was founded in 1874. It is now the largest church cooperating with the Louisiana Baptist Convention.

Penetration of Baptists into central and north Louisiana came about in the 1816-1820 period. In 1816, the Beulah Baptist Church was organized in Cheneyville in central Louisiana. Two years later, the Louisiana Association, the first in the state, was formed in the Cheneyville church. Joseph Willis, who had been instrumental in the formation of the first Baptist church west of the Mississippi River, Calvary, on Bayou Chicot near Opelousas on 13 November 1812, was deeply involved in the formation of the Beulah Church and the Louisiana Association.

James Brinson, who came to Louisiana from Tennessee in 1820, was probably the first Baptist minister to settle in north Louisiana west of the Ouachita River. He was chiefly responsible for the organization in 1821 of the Pine Hills Baptist Church, which within a year joined the Louisiana Association. Assisted by John Impson, Brinson extended the Baptist witness westward into what was then the northern section of Natchitoches Parish. Near what is now Minden, they discovered a group of

Baptists, including Newitt Drew, son of the Governor of Arkansas. Black Lake Baptist Church was established in 1823. A Baptist church was organized in Shreveport on 14 February 1845. The pastor was John Bryce, former associate pastor of the First Baptist Church in Richmond, Virginia, who had come to Louisiana to serve as collector of taxes on imports from the Republic of Texas.

In 1837 a colony made up mostly of Baptists from South Carolina settled in the Mt. Lebanon community in present day Bienville Parish. The Rehoboth Church which was founded almost immediately, became the center of Baptist work in central and north Louisiana. The Louisiana Baptist Convention was organized there in 1848 and a college was begun in 1856.

J. R. Graves (1820-1893), leader of the "Landmark" movement, exercised a significant influence upon Louisiana Baptist life as editor of the *Tennessee Baptist*, which for some years after 1869 served as the official paper for Louisiana as well as for Tennessee. Also he traveled throughout the South, including Louisiana, and cultivated loyal followers who occupied strategic positions among the state's Baptists. For example, A. J. Rutherford could write after the Civil War that the "[Baptist] Churches of Louisiana . . . are standing on the fore and aft line of Landmarkism, contending earnestly for one Lord, one Faith, one Baptism, and the only true and evangelical *church* and *ministry*." The impact of the Landmark view was confirmed by Hanson Lee: "The churches . . . in Louisiana . . . are a unit on the communion question. [They] reject Campbellite and Pedobaptist immersions and would not commune with a church which would tolerate them. We never knew an 'open communion' Baptist or a Pedobaptist or Campbellite immersion to be recognized, though exceptionable cases . . . may have existed." After the death of Graves and the challenge of the Landmark ecclesiology and methodology by Baptist historians like W. H. Whitsitt, Landmarkism split off from the Southern and the Louisiana Baptist Conventions and became a separate historical entity. In 1905 Landmark churches formed the General Association, which became the American Baptist Association in 1924. It divided (1950) to form the North American Baptist Association, which since 1969 has been called the Baptist Missionary Association of America. The Landmark ideology lingered among Louisiana Baptists but ceased to be dominant. There were approximately 135 Landmark (also called "Missionary") Baptist churches in Louisiana in 1981.

Recovery from the ravages of the Civil War was a slow but steady process for Louisiana Baptists. There were times of deep despair as suggested by the report in 1869 of the "Domestic Missions Committee" of the State Convention that "nothing has been done, nothing is being done, nor do we see that much can be done without means." But such notes of discouragement were not typical. In retrospect, the growing unity of Baptists in the state is evident. The three Baptist churches in New Orleans, which were oriented toward Mississippi until the early 1890s, became actively involved in the Louisiana Baptist Convention and entered the twentieth century in full cooperation with Baptists in central and north Louisiana. It is not surprising that Louisiana College was founded in this period of consolidation. The school grew out of a resolution offered by E. O. Ware in 1898 and opened its doors in Pineville in 1906. Ware, who served briefly as the first president of the College, also led Louisiana Baptists as State Secretary for two periods, 1892-1906 and 1910-1912. Claybrook Cottingham, a member of the original faculty, became head of the college in 1910, a position he filled with distinction for 31 years. Mention must be made of H. M. Weathersby who was Dean of the college for over forty years. The solidity and strength of Louisiana Baptists are rooted as much in this institution as in the State Convention itself.

Sporadic efforts to provide a state Baptist paper go back to 1847, when the short-lived *Southwestern Baptist Chronicle* was first published. In 1919, the Louisiana Baptist Convention purchased the *Chronicle* from E. O. Ware and the name was changed to the *Baptist Message*, which continues to serve as a unifying factor in Louisiana Baptist life.

Three Louisiana Baptists have served as presidents of the Southern Baptist Convention: M. E. Dodd (1934-1936), Pastor of the First Baptist Church in Shreveport; W. W. Hamilton, Sr. (1941-1944), President of the Baptist Bible Institute (founded in 1916 and since 1946 the New Orleans Baptist Theological Seminary); and J. D. Grey (1952-1954), pastor of the First Baptist Church in New Orleans. Grey, widely known as "Mr. Baptist" in the Crescent City, serves as a symbol of the significant growth and influence of Baptists in South Louisiana in recent decades.

The Southern Baptist Hospital in New Orleans, though no longer under the auspices of the Southern Baptist Convention, was proposed at a meeting of the Orleans-Tammany Association in New Orleans in 1919. Louis J. Bristow, the first "Superintendent" (1924), laid the foundations for what has become one of the leading private hospitals of the nation.

A small group of Baptists entered what became Louisiana at the beginning of the nineteenth century. By 1860, Baptists in the state numbered about 10,000 and by 1900 they had grown to 35,000. In 1948, the figure reached 260,000. In 1981, there were more than 500,000 members of about 1300 churches associated with the Louisiana Baptist Convention, which has headquarters in Alexandria. Black Baptists numbered about 600,000 and were related to several conventions.

Methodist Church

Methodist beginnings in Louisiana are associated with several colorful figures. Lorenzo Dow, "an eccentric evangelist," was probably the first Methodist to preach in the territory. Early in 1803, he crossed the Mississippi River from Natchez in order to hold "religious meetings." Leander Blackman, presiding elder at Natchez (1805-1807), was apparently the first itinerant Methodist minister to visit Louisiana. Elisha Bowman sought unsuccessfully to organize a church in New Orleans, which he described as an "ungodly city" where he preached to a few "straggling people in the open street," but managed to establish a congregation in Opelousas in 1806. James Axley, whose "pet aversions were Masonry, slavery, whiskey, tobacco, and [what he called] the fashions," was a preacher of unusual power and a person of rare versatility. He erected with his own hands probably the first Protestant church building in Louisiana in 1808 near Catahoula Lake.

In 1815 New Orleans was visited for the first time by a Methodist bishop, William McKendree. But it was not until 1825 that a Methodist church was finally organized by Benjamin M. Drake. In the next two decades Methodism manifested increasing vigor. By 1847 there were 13 churches with 1,328 white and 1,280 black members in the Crescent City.

The General Conference of the (national) Methodist Church in 1844 voted 111 to 60 to ask Bishop James O. Andrew of Georgia to desist from his episcopal labors until he should divest himself of several household slaves he acquired by a second marriage. The Southerners refused to accept this judgment and submitted a plan of separation that was implemented in a Convention of the Southern Churches at Louisville, Kentucky, on May 1, 1845. In this manner the Methodist Episcopal Church, South, was born.

Until 1846, Methodist work in Louisiana was under the jurisdiction of the Mississippi Conference except for a short period when the churches west of the Mississippi River were part of the Arkansas Conference. The

Louisiana Conference of the Methodist Episcopal Church, South, was created in 1845 and included 8,101 members, of whom 3,329 were black. It covered the territory west of the Mississippi River and the cities of Baton Rouge and New Orleans on the east side. In 1849 the remainder of the churches east of the river affiliated with the Louisiana Conference. During the 1853 session, the Louisiana Conference adopted a resolution supporting representation by laymen in Methodist conferences, one of the first steps in this direction in Southern Methodism.

Centenary College was founded by the Mississippi Conference at Brandon Springs in 1841. It was moved to a more suitable site in Jackson, Louisiana, in 1845 on property purchased from the College of Louisiana by Judge Edward McGhee, an ardent Methodist, who then gave the buildings and grounds, which he greatly improved, to Centenary College. During the Civil War, the College was closed and served as a Confederate Hospital; later during the conflict it was occupied by Federal troops. The school reopened in 1865. Centenary was moved to Shreveport in 1908 and continues as a strong Methodist liberal arts college.

The Louisiana Conference also operates Glenwood Hospital (West Monroe), Methodist Hospital (New Orleans), and a Children's Home (Ruston). *The New Orleans Christian Advocate*, established in 1850, continued publication until 1946 when Mississippi Methodists terminated support of it in order to publish their own paper. *The Louisiana Methodist* has been issued in conjunction with *The Arkansas Methodist* in Little Rock since 1949. Wesley Foundations are maintained at eight colleges and universities.

In 1939, when the northern and southern branches of Methodism were unified, the Louisiana Conference that belonged to the Methodist Episcopal Church, South, brought into The Methodist Church 189 ministers and 70,787 members. A second Louisiana Conference, associated with the northern wing of Methodism, was organized in Wesley Chapel in New Orleans in 1869. It was composed of black and white ministers and churches. In 1939, it shared in the merger movement by bringing 18 ministers and 3,278 members into the unified church. A third Louisiana Conference, which supervised the Methodist Protestant Church, was formed in 1846. It brought 48 ministers and 3,529 members into The Methodist Church in 1939. At that time membership in The Methodist Church in Louisiana amounted to 77,594. In 1981, there were 137,077 members and 550 churches in The United Methodist Church—its name since 1968—in the state.

Disciples of Christ

The first sermon preached in Louisiana for the Disciples of Christ was by Jacob Creath near Bayou Sara on the Mississippi River in October, 1826. Creath was a resident of Mississippi but visited Louisiana frequently as the pioneer missionary of a new movement on the frontier started by Thomas and Alexander Campbell.

Jackson was the site of the first congregation in the state formed in April of 1836. James Shannon, president of the College of Louisiana there (and later president of the University of Missouri), presided at this historic meeting of a little band of five members and thereby elicited interest and curiosity on the part of people in Louisiana in the Disciples movement and conferred a certain prestige upon the teachings of the Campbells. During a tour in 1839, Alexander Campbell delivered eight lectures in Jackson.

A second congregation was formed at Cheneyville in 1843 made up of 20 members who withdrew from the Beulah Baptist Church largely as a consequence of reading Campbell's periodical, the *Millennial Harbinger*. Through the medium of his paper, as well as in his preaching, lectures, and debates, Campbell attacked every denominational belief and practice for which he found no authority in the New Testament: "missionary societies, Bible societies, associations, synods, presbyteries, creeds, confessions, church constitutions, bishops, reverends, doctors of divinity," Calvinistic theology, the use of instrumental music in public worship, quarterly rather than weekly observance of the Lord's Supper, baptism as a symbol of salvation already received rather than "for the remission of sins," and a host of other "innovations." Because of certain superficial similarities between Baptists and the Disciples, especially in the beginning, Baptist churches were uniquely vulnerable to Campbell's attacks, of which the split in the Beulah Church is an example.

A strange and curious feature of the Disciples congregation at Cheneyville was the baptistry, which "consisted of a dry compartment for the minister along side the one filled with water for the candidate." This could be the first compartmentalized baptistry for immersion in the history of Christianity! The pulpit used by Alexander Campbell when he preached at Cheneyville has been preserved and was installed in the new church building.

The Disciples church at Cheneyville, supported by wealthy planters, had slave members, who as the custom was in most churches before the

Civil War sat on a balcony especially designed for them. One of the slaves, William "O'Neil," a barrelmaker, accumulated $1,000 toward the price of his freedom by working far beyond what was required of him by his owners. A friend, C. G. McCormick, who hired O'Neil and his wife, Ellen, from their owners to work with blacks in religious matters, provided an additional $2,000 and took the required legal steps to secure his freedom. Then he earned enough to buy liberty for his wife. William and Ellen were among only several blacks who continued in the Cheneyville Church after the Civil War, when most former slaves formed their own separate churches.

A congregation (which did not survive the Civil War) was organized in New Orleans in 1845. Alexander Campbell, an inveterate traveler in his tireless efforts to propagate his restorationist faith, lectured in a brick building housing the church in 1857. He continued his journey to Baton Rouge, where he was the guest of Governor Wickliffe, and lectured in the church that had been organized in 1848. By 1860, there were approximately 600 members of Disciples of Christ congregations in Louisiana.

After the Civil War, growing tensions in the Disciples of Christ movement developed. This was predictable in the light of the fact that "all Disciples, conservatives and progressives alike, . . . aimed to restore New Testament Christianity in order to unite the church for the purpose of winning the world to Jesus Christ." The effort "to restore New Testament Christianity" clashed with the ideal "to unite the church." In other words, the effort to restore primitive Christianity tended to militate against the ideal of unity in the church and the ideal of church unity tended to militate against the effort to restore the "pure" Christianity of the past. Ecumenism and restorationism tended to pull people in opposite directions and the result was growing discord within the Disciples movement that led to division at the turn of the century. The split, which was formally accepted in 1906, was officially confirmed on 22 June 1907 by David Lipscomb, who responding to an inquiry by the United States Census Bureau wrote: "There is a distinct people taking the word of God as their only and sufficient rule of faith, calling their churches 'Churches of Christ', . . . distinct and separate in name, work, and rule of faith from all other bodies and peoples."

At the time of the schism, Churches of Christ were made up of 159,658 members, about two-thirds of whom came from the eleven states that had formed the Confederacy. "The sectional bifurcation of the

Disciples of Christ," suggests one historian, "is one of the most vivid American examples of the bending of the Christian ethos to fit the presupposition of the community."

In 1981, the Churches of Christ showed their greatest strength, numerically and geographically, in the northern and western parts of the state. Accurate statistics are difficult to secure for these churches, a fact which is due largely to the emphasis placed upon the independence of the local congregation by the Churches of Christ and a corresponding lack of intercongregational organization. According to a rough estimate, there were in 1981 about 250 churches with 15,000 members in Louisiana. At that time, the Disciples of Christ ("Christian Churches") had 25 congregations and 5,800 members in the state.

Lutheran Church

Before the Louisiana Purchase (1803), Protestantism had no legal existence in this region. A few German immigrants in the colony sought to sustain their Lutheran heritage through informal organizations, out of which came some of the later Lutheran churches.

After the War of 1812 large numbers of German immigrants came to New Orleans by ship, most of whom continued their trips north by river steamboats to various western and northern destinations. Some of them remained in New Orleans. In the absence of a Lutheran church, many settlers worshipped in German Protestant Church (now the First Evangelical Church) founded in 1826.

A glimpse of the early history of Lutheranism in Louisiana is provided by a report made by Jacob Zinck to the Tennessee Synod soon after he made a missionary tour of the state, on which tour he baptized 28 infants and adults. St. Paul's Lutheran Church was organized in New Orleans in 1840, perhaps partly as a result of Zinck's efforts. The Zion congregation was started in 1847. The St. John's Church, formed in 1852, was the first Lutheran church in the city to become affiliated with the Missouri Synod. At this time, there were three Lutheran churches in the Crescent City.

The Missouri Synod reported 58 churches and 19,713 members in Louisiana in 1964, and a slight increase in membership took place in the 1970s. In 1981 twenty-five congregations, some of which were black, were located in New Orleans. The Missouri Synod supported the Bethlehem Lutheran Welfare Association and the Bethlehem Orphan's Home in New Orleans. In 1964, the American Lutheran Church had seven congregations with 2,011 members and the Lutheran Church in America had five congregations with 892 members in Louisiana. In 1981, membership in Lutheran Churches in Louisiana reached about 24,000.

United Pentecostal Church

Pentecostalism is a movement of considerable variety and, therefore, cannot be treated fully in this article. One expression of this faith, which is reasonably strong in Louisiana, is the United Pentecostal Church, formed in 1945 through a merger of the Pentecostal Church, Inc. and the Pentecostal Assemblies of Jesus Christ.

This form of Pentecostalism is the largest "unitarian" or "Oneness" group within the Pentecostal movement. Pentecostals in the United Church believe that "there is only one person in the Godhead—Jesus Christ." "Baptism in water by immersion [is, therefore] in the name of the Lord Jesus Christ for the remission of sins." They are sometimes called "Jesus Only" Pentecostals and in this respect differ from the so-called normative Pentecostal denominations. The United Pentecostal Church shares in the general Pentecostal movement in most other respects, including baptism of the Holy Spirit and glossolalia.

In 1981, there were 272 United Pentecostal Churches and 600 pastors, missionaries, and evangelists in the state; Sunday School attendance reached about 30,000. The Louisiana District headquarters are located in Tioga.

Mennonites

The first Mennonites to arrive in Louisiana were probably immigrants from Alsace-Lorraine, who landed in New Orleans. In 1839, for example, Christian Reeser, his two brothers and a sister settled in that city. A few Mennonites, with whom John F. Funk had correspondence, were residents of New Orleans in 1874.

In 1898, a Mennonite church was organized in Lake Charles in southwest Louisiana, made up of 40 members at one time. Only one family was left in 1955 because of a decline in rice farming in which they were engaged. In 1918, a Mennonite congregation that did not survive was formed at Des Allemands, west of New Orleans. However, in 1936, three Mennonite families reestablished a church at Des Allemands, which now has 45 members. An outgrowth of this church is a congregation at Akers, north of New Orleans, organized in 1942. In 1955, there were 20 members of this church, largely French-speaking.

Judaism

Jews appeared first in what became the state of Louisiana in the late 1750s. By January 1779, there were six Jews in New Orleans. One of these was Isaac Rodriguez Monsanto, a Dutch merchant, who moved his headquarters from Curacao to New Orleans. A gifted entrepreneur, Monsanto and his entourage, including three brothers, conducted business operations with merchants throughout the boundaries of the later state of Louisiana and beyond. Though they were known to be Jews, they shared in Catholic worship without baptism.

Judah Touro settled in New Orleans in 1801 or 1802 and through his industrious attitude and frugal living became a wealthy man. Indifferent to Judaism until his later years, he was persuaded by Gershom Kursheedt to build a synagogue for the second New Orleans congregation in 1845. Touro's attitude toward Judaism was typical of the early Jewish settlers, who were for the most part equally indifferent to the cultivation of Jewish identity. There is a story about a rabbi who unable to find a Jewish maiden to his fancy married a Catholic lady. When the rabbi died, much persuasion was required to restrain the weeping widow from putting a crucifix into her husband's coffin.

The first congregation, Shaarei Chassed, was established in New Orleans in 1827. It was not only the first synagogue in Louisiana but probably in the Gulf Coast region and in the Mississippi Valley south of Cincinnati. Manis Jacobs was its first president. What is now Touro Synagogue was organized in 1847. In 1850, Sharbay Tefilah Congregation was formed in New Orleans. Judaism, however, did not prosper owing to lukewarm support by people of wealth and extensive intermarriage which occurred "perhaps more [frequently] than in any [other] major city in the United States," it has been stated.

German Jews especially fanned out from New Orleans into small towns and rural areas. They served as artisans, merchants, and traders. Benevolent societies, cemeteries, and congregations in Alexandria (1854), Donaldsonville (1856), and Monroe (1861) resulted from their labors. Except for New Orleans, Shreveport had the largest Jewish community in the state by mid-century. Synagogues were established there in 1859 and 1892. B'nai Brith, Zionist, and other groups were formed to further Jewish interests and embody the culture as well as the religion of Judaism. Though Jews settled in Baton Rouge around 1800, a congregation was not formed until 1858; it became B'nai Israel in 1879.

Jewish communities were also organized in Bogalusa, Lafayette, Lake Charles, Morgan City, Natchitoches, New Iberia, and Opelousas.

The most important Jewish institution created in the state was the Association for the Relief of Jewish Widows and Orphans of New Orleans (1854), probably the first agency of this sort in the United States. Frequent deaths due to recurring yellow fever epidemics in the New Orleans area made this association essential. It was supported by assimilated Jews, "who demonstrated no other concern with their Jewish identity."

Until the late nineteenth century, the full participation and integration of Jews in the life of New Orleans were encouraged by the cosmopolitan spirit of the city and furthered by widespread intermarriage of Jews and Christians. The first King (Rex) of Mardi Gras, in 1872, was a Jew, Louis J. Salomon. Other distinguished Jews were Judah P. Benjamin, United States Senator (1853-1861), Henry W. Hyams, Lieutenant Governor of Louisiana (1859), and Edward Warren Moise, Speaker of the Louisiana Legislature in the 1850s and later Attorney General, all of them assimilationists.

Rabbi James K. Gutheim was the major Jewish leader in New Orleans after the Civil War. Initially discouraged by the poor prospects of Jewry in the city after the war, he moved to New York City in 1868. A group of his friends who founded a Reform Congregation, Temple Sinai, encouraged him to return to New Orleans in 1872. By 1885, Reform Judaism was a significant force in the city. Rabbi Julian B. Feibelman served Temple Sinai for over forty years (1935-1980).

The total Jewish population in Louisiana declined after 1940 when the number of Jews peaked at about 16,000, of whom about 10,000 lived in New Orleans and 2,000 in Shreveport. But Jews have continued to exhibit leadership far beyond what their small proportion of the population would suggest. For example, Jewish mayors have served in New Orleans, Alexandria, Monroe, Crowley, Donaldsonville, and Morgan City. In the twentieth century, assimilationist tendencies have abated and, though Jews still share widely in the social and political life of the state, there is now a deeper sense of historical and psychological identity in the Jewish community than was the case in the nineteenth century.

Voodooism

Though Voodooism in and of itself would hardly qualify for inclusion in this article, justification for including it lies in the fact that it became intertwined with a broad spectrum of religious cults and exerted some influence upon Catholic and Protestant Christianity, especially but not exclusively among blacks in New Orleans. Catholic ritual, incense, and flickering candles that cast an eerie glow in subdued light characterize most of the Temples, led by a usually self-appointed "Mother" or "Father" who wields unusual power. Sometimes Protestant hymns but more frequently gospel songs are sung to the accompaniment of vigorous hand clapping and foot stamping. There is a good deal of "falling out," talking in "unknown tongues," alleged communion with the spirits of departed relatives, and belief in demons poised to do their deadly work unless they are properly placated. These phenomena, of course, have a multiplicity of sources, of which Voodooism is only one. Nevertheless, Voodooism provides a distinctive quality to what it touches and must be taken into account in any estimate of the more spontaneous expressions of religion in the area of which New Orleans is the center. Marie Laveau, a free mulatto, who served as Queen of the Voodoos for more than three decades in the mid-nineteenth century, revised the ceremony of her cult to bring in veneration of the Virgin Mary and adoration of the saints "so that Voodooism became a curious mixture of West Indian fetish-worship and perverted Catholicism."

Voodooism derives from an African cult in which cosmic powers, usually powers of evil, were symbolized, placated, and "worshipped in the form of a large snake." For almost two centuries, most blacks and many whites in south Louisiana felt the influence of this strange practice. Voodoo rites seem to have been especially attractive to slaves. Emotional excesses and occasional violence drove the movement underground and it is difficult to witness a Voodoo ceremony now. However, Voodoo charms are still available. There are sources from which one can secure "Love Powders, Get-Together Drops, Boss-Fix-Powder, Easy Life Powder, Come to Me Powder, Devil Oil, Controlling Oil, and Dice Special" and the celebrated gris-gris, a small bag filled with bits of reptile skin, cayenne pepper, and other exotic elements, the most feared and costliest of Voodoo magic.

Bibliography

H. C. Bezou. "Louisiana," *New Catholic Encyclopedia,* vol. 7.

J. H. Bowdon and F. E. Maser. "Louisiana," *The Encyclopedia of World Methodism,* vol. 2.

Hodding Carter and Betty Werlein Carter. *So Great a Good: A History of the Episcopal Church in Louisiana and of Christ Church Cathedral.*

John T. Christian. *A History of the Baptists in Louisiana.*

John Duffy, ed. *Parson Clapp of the Strangers' Church of New Orleans.*

Winfred Ernest Garrison and Alfred T. DeGroot. *The Disciples of Christ: A History.*

Melvin Gingerich. "Louisiana," *The Mennonite Encyclopedia,* vol. 3

Glen Lee Greene. *House Upon a Rock: About Southern Baptists in Louisiana.*

R. H. Harper. *Louisiana Methodism.*

Frances Parkinson Keyes. *All This Is Louisiana.*

Bertram W. Korn and Edward L. Greenstein. "Louisiana," *Encyclopedia Judaica,* vol. 11.

Lester G. McAllister and William E. Tucker. *Journey in Faith: A History of the Christian Church (Disciples of Christ).*

Benjamin H. Pershing. "Louisiana," *The Encyclopedia of the Lutheran Church,* vol. 2.

Penrose C. St. Amant, *A History of the Presbyterian Church in Louisiana.*

————. *A Short History of Louisiana Baptists.*

Lyle Saxon, State Supervisor, Louisiana. *A Guide to the State.*

MARYLAND

GLENN T. MILLER
SOUTHEASTERN BAPTIST THEOLOGICAL SEMINARY

Geography

Geography has been significant in the religious history of Maryland. Located between Pennsylvania and Virginia, Maryland has been influenced by religious developments in the middle states and in the South. Although small—only 10,577 square miles—Maryland has four regions: the Eastern Shore's lowlands, the Western Shore's rolling hills, the mountains, and the Baltimore area. Baltimore is located at the intersection of the deep waters of the Chesapeake Bay and the fall line of the Piedmont.

Early Development

Maryland was planned by George Calvert (1580-1632), an English convert to Catholicism, who had participated in the Virginia Company and in the ill-fated experiment at Avalon. The charter was granted to his son, Cecil Calvert (1604-1675), the Second Lord Baltimore. The Calverts believed in the ordered society of the medieval period and envisioned a land of country manors supporting a feudal order in which different classes had different obligations. The colony was named for Charles I's queen, Henrietta Maria.

The colony was to be partially a refuge for wealthy Catholics. When the *Ark* and the *Dove* sailed in 1633, the ships had 128 passengers who had taken the Test Oath; however, an additional 72 persons joined the expedition at Crews, Isle of Wight. These included three Jesuits: Father Andrew White, Father John Altham, and Brother Thomas Gervase. On 25 March 1634, the ships landed at St. Clement's Island, and Father White celebrated Maryland's first Mass. White, the leader of the Jesuits until his deportation to England, conducted an active ministry to the Piscataway, Patuxent, and Anacosta Indians. He wrote two works about the colony: *Declaratio coloniae Domini Baronis de Baltimore* and *Relatio Itinerio in Marylandus* as well as a grammar, dictionary, and catechism in the Indian language.

Religious conflict was a mark of the colony from its founding to the American Revolution. The colonists on Kent Island, led by William Claiborne, resented the presence of Catholics in the new colony as well as their own inclusion in Baltimore's domains. In 1635 and 1638, force had to be used to incorporate the earlier settlement into Maryland, and the Kent Islanders invaded Maryland in 1645, forcing the governor into temporary exile.

Some of Maryland's early problems can be attributed to the lack of a definite policy on religion. The Charter, which reserved ecclesiastical patronage to the Baltimores, implied that the colony was to be Anglican, but Baltimore supported a policy of toleration. In 1636, an oath was imposed on the governor that prohibited interference with any Christian on account of religion. During the English Civil War, perhaps to forestall more radical action, Baltimore instructed his governor, William Stone, to secure a toleration act which would protect his coreligionists. In 1649, the law, "An Act Concerning Religion," was passed. It provided for the toleration of all trinitarian Christian groups and imposed heavy penalties for disturbing the religious peace.

The Act was ineffective. The Puritans who had settled "Providence"—the region near Annapolis on the Patuxent River—supported Cromwell's government, and when William Stone supported the claims of Charles II, they revolted and joined the Kent Islanders in an armed force which defeated Stone at the Battle of the Severn, on 25 May 1655. From 1655 to 1658, when Baltimore regained control, Catholics were persecuted and some of their priests forced to leave the colony.

Although such Jesuits as Thomas Copley (d. 1652) secured a strong financial base for the church by purchasing such lands as St. Thomas Manor, seventeenth century Maryland had a chronic shortage of priests. In 1669, Lord Baltimore complained to Rome about the problem, and in 1673, Father Thomas Massey established a Franciscan mission that grew to four priests in 1677. Additional Jesuits were also sent to the colony.

The problem of providing Catholic education was pressing. Maryland's pattern of large farms and plantations scattered the population, and priests taught the catechism by traveling house to house. In 1677, Father Michael Foster, S.J., established a classical academy at New Town which would have been the second oldest college in the United States had it survived the Glorious Revolution.

Anglicanism had been in Maryland before Baltimore's colony. The Rev. Richard Stone served Kent Island from 1631 to 1638, and the chapel at St. Mary's was shared by Catholics and Anglicans until 1638. The growth of the Church of England, however, dates from the Restoration when Anglicanism began to replace Puritanism on the Western Shore. By 1676, there were four Anglican congregations in Maryland: Trinity Creek, St. George's, St. Paul's, and Kent Island, and such laymen as Jeremiah Eaton and Roger Coger had begun to leave property for glebes to support the ministry.

Seventeenth century Anglicanism, lacking wealth and government support, did not have the means to support an active ministry. The few priests who came to the colony came more for secular than religious reasons. Another deleterious factor was the scattered location of such churches as there were. The faith was carried primarily by the family, although anti-Catholicism does seem to have strengthened some people's determination to remain Anglican.

In 1657, the Quaker Elizabeth Harris began to preach in the area around Annapolis and on Kent Island. Although Maryland passed laws against Quakers in 1657 and 1658, the movement made progress and by 1665, Quakers were beginning to attain positions in local government. In 1668, the legislature passed a bill permitting affirmation to replace the oath. The community was strengthened by visits from John Burnyeat, William Edmundson, and George Fox in the 1670s.

Lord Baltimore, who owned sizable property in Ireland, encouraged immigration from that land to Maryland. In the seventeenth century, these Scotch-Irish pioneers began to settle on the Eastern Shore and in the Annapolis area. The Rev. Thomas Wilson and the Rev. Robert Lawson worked as itinerant preachers in the area, but the first permanent Presbyterian ministry was on the lands of Ninian Beall, a Scot, who made his fortune in the colonial trade. On his landed estate, located between Patuxent and Washington City, two hundred Scots and Scotch-Irish were gathered into a church by the Rev. Matthew Hill (d. 1679). Francis Makamie (c. 1658-1708), who was appointed as a missionary to the new world by the Presbytery of Laggan, Ireland, began his ministry in 1683 on the Eastern Shore where he established the Snow Hill congregation among others. In 1706, these churches joined with other Presbyterian churches in Delaware and Pennsylvania in the first presbytery in the United States.

Judaism was not tolerated under Maryland's laws. Dr. Jacob Lumbrozo, the first Jew in Maryland, was tried on 23 February 1658 for denying the divinity of Christ. Although he was acquitted of the capital charge, he wisely left the colony.

In England, the period from the Restoration (1660) to the Glorious Revolution (1688) was a time of increasing religious conflict as the royal family drifted toward the open Catholicism of James II. Louis XIV of France revoked the Edict of Nantes in 1685, raising fears about similar acts in England. Finally, James II was deposed by the Glorious Revolution and William and Mary assumed the throne.

In Maryland, these tensions were magnified by Protestant dislike of the Catholic proprietor and by prejudice against the local Catholic minority. Anti-Catholic agitation increased the local Catholic minority. Because of its growing strength throughout the period, in 1681 John Coode attempted a Protestant revolution. When news of the overthrow of James II arrived in the colony, another army, led by Coode, expelled Baltimore's governor. On 26 August 1691, Lionel Capley was appointed as the royal governor of Maryland with instructions to see that the Book of Common Prayer was used in the colony.

The Age of Establishment

From 1692 to 1701, the Maryland legislature passed laws establishing the Church of England. The laws of 1692, 1694 and 1696 were disallowed, because their wording was ambiguous. Largely through the efforts of Thomas Bray (1656-1730), the Commissary for Maryland, the bill of 1701 was approved. The law created thirty parishes to be served by an elected vestry of six members, two church wardens, a clerk, a registrar, and a minister. The priest was supported by a poll tax of 40 pounds of tobacco from which he was to pay the clerk 1000 pounds. Marriage was regulated, and the minister was to be paid a set fee for every service performed. Significantly, the law made no provision for clerical discipline or for the education of future pastors.

Bray was the most important figure in the early history of the establishment. In 1696, he was appointed commissary by Bishop Campton of London. Although there was no colonial chapter, a Commissary did the work of a Dean in the Established Church: visitations, supervision of the clergy, and administration of diocesan affairs. There was some hope in 1697 that Bray might be appointed as suffragan allowing the church to have confirmations and ordinations, but King William, who depended on the non-conformists politically, vetoed the promotion. Bray spent less than a year in his charge and conducted only one visitation. In part, his role was ceremonial. When Annapolis was designated as the capital, Bray represented the crown in the gift of communion silver to the new parish of St. Anne's. His efforts were largely unsuccessful, however, in the area of church discipline and administration where his good intentions were largely ignored by the local clergy.

Bray's primary contributions to Maryland's establishment were made in London. He recruited clergy for the new church, and in 1699, he established The Society for Promoting Christian Knowledge to supply parishes with ministerial libraries. These libraries included works in classics, divinity, philosophy, and natural science. With their help, a local minister could establish a school or prepare a candidate for Holy Orders.

After Bray, the commissary system disintegrated. Although in 1716 Jacob Henderson and Christopher Wilkenson were appointed as commissaries for the eastern and western shores, neither was able to discipline the clergy. After their deaths, no further commissaries were appointed. As a result of the failure of the commissary system, the Church of Maryland became little more than a federation of churches sharing a common liturgy and having rights at law.

The Church of Maryland was a success in the area of evangelism. After establishment, it acquired a popular base on the western shore and displaced the Puritans in the Annapolis area. The parishes of the church maintained a more lively sacramental life than was customary among southern Anglicans. Four parishes observed Holy Communion three times a year; four celebrated four times a year; three celebrated eight times a year as well as on major festivals, and seven had monthly communion as well as celebrations on all major festivals.

Throughout the eighteenth century, complaints were lodged against the quality or morals of the Maryland clergy. In the absence of any form of church discipline, it is impossible to pass judgment on those charges. Colonial ministers, whose parishes covered vast areas and who were isolated from other clergy, may have used alcohol to help ease the pains of settlement—as other colonists did—and the link between the establishment and the aristocracy could encourage the hurting parson. Yet, some of the worse abuses in the Church of England were avoided in the New World. The incomes of clergy were adequate, and there were no poor parishes where a priest might be impoverished. Non-residence, the most serious problem in England, was prohibited in Maryland by law.

The return of the Baltimore family to power in the colony in 1713 created additional problems for Maryland's Anglicans. Under the charter, the proprietor had the right to all ecclesiastical patronage. During the era of Frederick Calvert, 1731-1771, Fourth Lord Baltimore, this right was abused. Frederick was a rake who continually bombarded the governor with requests for the appointment of his companions to sinecures. His most notorious appointment was Richard Allen who had written a pamphlet defending his Lordship from a charge of rape in 1768. Allen was rewarded with St. Anne's parish, Annapolis, as well as other positions..

Unlike other Southern Anglicans, Maryland's priests supported the appointment of a colonial bishop. However, the colony's political leaders, especially William Paca and Samuel Chase, put together a coalition that blocked the proposed office in 1773.

Although Maryland granted complete toleration to Protestant dissenters in 1702, Catholics were not granted civil rights in the eighteenth century. The new government imposed the Test Oath in 1692, and despite the efforts of the former Attorney General, Charles Carroll, the law was allowed in London. In 1704, Father William Hunter and Father Robert Brooke, the latter the first Marylander ordained as a priest, were tried for violating the establishment acts and ordered to cease their priestly activities. In the same year, the legislature passed its "Act to Prevent the Growth of Popery." Catholic worship was prohibited in the state as was the baptism of a non-Catholic child, and Catholics were prohibited from establishing or teaching in schools. In 1707, under pressure from England, laws were passed permitting private masses, but laws were added against the importation of Irish Catholics as servants. In 1708, a census of the Catholic population was ordered as a protection for the province. The last anti-Catholic legislation was passed during the French and Indian Wars when a double tax was imposed on Catholics in lieu of military service. Wealthy Catholics such as the Carroll family threatened to leave the colony unless such laws were changed.

The penal laws affected Catholic religious life. Catholic chapels were closed, and services were held in rooms attached to private homes. Naturally, such services were extremely plain. The absence of a bishop or vicar apostolic limited sacramental life since neither confirmation nor Holy Orders could be received. In 1720, the Franciscans were withdrawn, and the mission placed entirely in the hands of the Jesuits. The Jesuits were stationed at various manors and farms throughout the state, and they would say Mass twice a month at their stations and then ride a circuit to bring the sacraments to their flocks. Often a priest served an area of more than five hundred square miles. The missionary priests were very effective as evangelists of the slave population, with the result that Afro-Americans made up a third of the communicants.

Persecution forced the Jesuits to establish for their order a center that was geographically distant from most of Maryland's population. In 1706, they purchased St. Xavier's Manor on the Little and Great Bohemian Rivers. By 1745, the Jesuits had established a classical school at the Manor which was equivalent to a modern high school or junior college. Among its students were Robert and Edward Neale, James Heath, Robert Brent, Charles Carroll of Carrollton, and John Carroll, later to be Bishop of Baltimore.

In 1748, after driving the French from the Canadian coast, the English deported the Acadian population. About 900 refugees were assigned to Maryland, and their presence caused a wave of anti-Catholic hysteria and a law prohibiting local Catholics from aiding their settlement was passed. About 40 French families settled in Baltimore Town where Father John Ashton, chaplain to Carroll of Carrollton, gathered them into a small congregation.

In 1773, Pope Clement XIV issued *Dominus ac Redemptor* suppressing the Jesuits everywhere except Russia, and on 6 October 1773, the American Jesuits were ordered to present their written submission to the decree. The future of the Church was in doubt since the Jesuits had supplied the financial support as well as priests for the Church.

The Denominational State

In 1776, the legislature passed the Declaration of Rights which disestablished the Anglican church and declared all Christian churches equal before the law. The act was hardly hostile to religion: the legislature reserved the right to tax citizens for the support of the church of their choice and protected the property of the Anglican churches from confiscation. It further assumed that the Christian churches were public corporations entitled to support from the state. This favorable attitude promoted the growth of various denominations whose individual congregations were incorporated by the legislature.

The Episcopal Church. During the Revolution, Episcopal (from 1785) ministers were required to take an oath of allegiance to the state. Since the new oath conflicted with an earlier ordination vow to be loyal to the King, many Church of Maryland pastors were caught in an ethical dilemma. Some, such as Hugh Neill of St. Paul's, Queen Anne, refused the oath without abandoning their posts; others, like John Scott of Stepney, Sommerset, refused the oath and went into exile. While we cannot determine how many of the 14 Anglican clergy who left the state or how many of the five who retired did so because of the oath, it may have been a factor in their decisions.

The War demoralized and disorganized the Episcopal churches. The Rev. William Smith (1727-1803), first provost of the College of Philadelphia, became rector of St. Paul's and Chester parishes, Kent County, in 1779 and used his position to direct an Anglican recovery. In 1780, he called a clerical convention to settle the affairs of the church; it adopted a new name, Protestant Episcopal Church. In the same year, he helped organize Washington College to train a native ministry. In 1783, he led the clergy to secure the right from the legislature to change the Book of Common Prayer. These activities culminated in his election as bishop of Maryland and in instruction to seek consecration in England.

The revision of the Prayer Book caused controversy and weakened Smith's position. Proposed by William White and Charles Warton, in collaboration with Smith, it showed the influence of the Enlightenment understanding of faith and modified many customary practices. In 1786, Thomas Cradock and Samuel Johnson accused Smith of public drunkenness, and while the charge was never established, the Episcopal General Convention of 1789 failed to approve his consecration. By the time that Smith left the state to resume his duties in Philadelphia in 1789, the Protestant Episcopal Church had weathered the storm of the Revolution and was organized as a free church. In 1792, Thomas Claggett, a less colorful man, was consecrated as the first Bishop of Maryland.

While the Eastern Shore churches (which were to be organized as the Diocese of Easton in 1861) have tended toward a more evangelical nature, the churches on the Western Shore and in Baltimore have manifested a more high church orientation. The leader in the high church development was St. Paul's, Baltimore. By 1790, the Rev. Joseph Bent had introduced liturgical changes, and the Rev. Edward Watt, rector from

1827-1864, was the first Episcopal priest to wear Eucharistic garments in the United States; he also practiced the reservation of the Sacrament. The Rt. Rev. William Robinson Whittingham, bishop from 1840 to 1879—the longest term in Maryland's episcopal history—was firmly committed to a high church policy. Although his tenure was marked by controversies over liturgy and theology, these did not inhibit the growth of the church. Nine new parishes were formed in Baltimore alone during the 1850s.

Maryland's Episcopal parishes have been centers of benevolence. In 1789, St. Paul's, Baltimore, led in the establishment of the Maryland Society for the Abolition of Slavery and the Relief of Free Negroes. During the 1820s, individual parishes created local missionary societies and Sunday Schools. A number of churches established in the late nineteenth century offered a broad range of services to their communities. English influence was seen in such special organizations as the choir school at St. Paul's that were directly related to Oxford Movement concerns. In both World Wars, Maryland Anglicans led in providing religious and social services for the troops stationed in the state.

Establishment religious values have continued into the twentieth century in the form of a strong sense of the role of place in religious life. In the 1960s, as racial and urban tensions mounted in Baltimore, St. Paul's had to decide whether it would join the flight to the suburbs. The church decided to remain in the central city and to adapt its style of ministry to the changed conditions. St. Paul's response was typical of many Maryland Episcopal institutions which decided to stay in difficult, but traditional, locations.

Lutherans. Although Lutherans entered Maryland in 1649 when Swedes established a colony in Cecil County, the largest numbers of Lutheran settlers began to enter the colony in the late eighteenth century. German settlers used Western Maryland as a highway from Pennsylvania to the Valley of Virginia, and Lord Baltimore, who needed people to fill his Western claims, offered them attractive terms to establish residence there. Western Maryland assumed many of the social characteristics of German Pennsylvania.

There were few pastors among the German settlers, and many who claimed that title had little or no religious training. These irregular pastors caused serious disruptions, and appeals for help to Henry Muhlenberg in Philadelphia were common. In the absence of regular ministers, school teachers often preserved Lutheran traditions by conducting services of morning prayer and by encouraging the reading of the Luther Bible. As in the case of many other immigrant groups, cemeteries were often founded before churches could be erected.

Early Lutherans in the West were often served by itinerants. John Casper Stoever, whose circuit reached from New Holland to York, Pennsylvania, came to Monocracy in 1733 to baptize the children; in the next year, a congregation agreed to share its pulpit with any Reformed pastor in the area. When Stoever resigned from his circuit, he ordained David Chandler, a teacher from Conewego, to serve the charge.

One of the most important centers of Lutheranism in the West was the town of Frederick where a church was established in 1745. Two years later Muhlenberg visited there to attempt to correct problems caused by the irregular ministers, Carl Rudolph and Empiricus Schmidt. Muhlenberg led the congregation in the making of a covenant in which they agreed to support Lutheran doctrine and to exclude the Moravians from fellowship. Such covenants were common in the formative period. In 1752, the Rev. Bernhard Hausihl, who arrived in the area with a company of Palatine Germans, became pastor of the congregation. The broad church type of Lutheranism that was characteristic of the Palatinate was to have considerable influence on that denomination's life in Maryland.

From 1750 to 1794, a score of Lutheran churches was founded in Washington, Frederick, and Carroll counties. By this time, most new German settlers were entering Maryland through Baltimore and pushing west from there. One of the significant churches founded by these immigrants was the Evangelical Lutheran Congregation in Cumberland established by Frederick Lange, an itinerant clergyman, and which served as a missionary center for the far western part of the state.

In 1750, after Baltimore began its growth as a port, Germans established a joint Lutheran and Reformed Congregation. The union did not last. In 1756, under the leadership of John Christian Faber, the Reformed members were able to erect a meeting house of their own. The High German Evangelical Lutheran Congregation, established in 1755, was unable to secure a meeting house until 1762.

Pastor John Daniel Kurtz (1763-1856) was the first full time minister to serve the Baltimore congregation. Kurtz had been born in America, and he studied divinity at the school of the prophets maintained by Henry Ernst Muhlenberg at Lancaster, Pennsylvania. Strongly influenced by the theology of the Awakenings, Kurtz led in the establishment of the

Maryland Bible Society and of the seminary at Gettysburg. In 1820, he was one of the leaders in the establishment of the Synod of Maryland and Virginia and served four terms as its president.

The establishment of the Synod provided Maryland's older Lutheran communities with stability. Maryland's practice of incorporating congregations rather than denominations meant that the synod was a voluntary society that pastors and churches might join, if they chose. It had no doctrinal requirements before 1829, when the Augsburg Confession was adopted, and in its first half century, the synod functioned more as a coordinating agency for church benevolences than as an ecclesiastical body. Liturgically, the synod tended toward a German service somewhat similar to the Book of Common Prayer. At the same time revivalism was practiced, though not as commonly as among other Protestant groups.

In the 1820s a new wave of German immigration began to enter Baltimore which made the city one of the most heavily teutonic in the East. Language problems among Lutherans became acute as the newer immigrants entered the older German churches. In 1828, the First English Lutheran Congregation was established in Baltimore, and in 1840, the Second English Lutheran church was formed in response to the revival of 1839-1840.

The clash between older and newer Germans, however, was more than a "language dispute." Maryland's older Lutherans were committed to a different style of faith. Conscious of their own frontier roots, Maryland Lutherans sent circuit riders, such as C. F. Heyer, Jacob Medtart, and N. B. Little, deep into Ohio and Indiana. Debates were held over the continued use of wine in the communion services, and strong support was given to the temperance movement. Theologically, Maryland's older Lutherans tended to follow the American Lutheranism popularized by Samuel Schmucker at Gettysburg Seminary where many of Maryland's pastors were trained.

The newer immigrants were not drawn to the frontier kind of life and tended to settle in urban ghettos in Baltimore. For them, the church was one of the primary supports of their culture. Theologically, the immigrant pastors brought the German disputes between rationalists, confessionalists, and mediators with them into their new environment. In 1845, F. C. D. Wynken led his congregation into the confessional Missouri Synod which was popular with conservative immigrants. Even more typical was St. Stephen's Lutheran, Baltimore, established by the Rev.

Charles A. Meister in 1849. The parish church was complemented by a host of German organizations as well as a strongly confessional parochial school.

The Rev. Henry Scheib (1801-1897) represented the more radical form of immigrant Lutheranism. Scheib was called to Zion Lutheran Church in 1835. Deeply influenced by rationalism and biblical criticism, he led the congregation to a virtual German Unitarianism. During his pastorate, the church maintained no synodical connections. Scheib was perhaps the most creative religious educator of his day. His parochial school allowed students and a faculty to share in the formulation of policy, and from 1838 had an active P.T.A. The program of studies was based on a developmental understanding of childhood. Scheib's successor, Julius Hofmann, who came in 1889, also represented European theology. An admirer of the German theologian Schleiermacher, Hofmann led the church back into the synod. World War I presented the great crisis of Hofmann's ministry, and he was able to convince his church to be active in support of the American position in the conflict.

The Civil War had little impact on Maryland's Lutherans who were more concerned with the problems of the immigrants than they were with national politics. Local congregations, while occasionally disturbed by individuals with strong views, maintained a steady course.

Maryland Lutheranism's social concern grew out of both a frontier setting and its German background. Such charities as the Lutheran Pastor's Fund, established in 1839, Sunday Schools, and Women's Sewing and Missionary Societies, were rooted in American Evangelicalism. Two very successful charities, the Deaconesses, whose Mother House was established in Baltimore in 1895, and the Inner Mission, founded in 1913, were based on German understanding of home missions; these have remained active in the innner city.

The rapid growth of the Washington-Baltimore corridor has produced a significant growth among Lutherans. As new job opportunities have drawn Lutherans of different synodical, theological, and geographical backgrounds, the state's Lutheran bodies have assumed a more rational character. In architecture, many of the new churches have abandoned the gothic so common in the past in favor of modern and ultra-modern styles.

The Catholic Church. The Catholic Church in Maryland emerged from the Revolution in an unsettled condition. John Carroll (1735-1815), an ex-Jesuit missionary at Rock Creek, took the lead in reorganizing the Church. In 1782, he formed the remaining priests into the Select Body of Clergy that was incorporated by the state as the legal successor to the property of the Jesuit order, and in 1784, Carroll was appointed as Vicar Apostolic for the United States. Five years later, the clergy elected him as Bishop. Significantly, he elected to reside in Baltimore rather than the more heavily Catholic, rural St. Mary's.

Carroll was deeply concerned with Catholic education. In 1791, Georgetown College was opened in the District of Columbia, and in that same year, the Sulpician Fathers opened the first major seminary in the United States, St. Mary's, at the Nine Mile Tavern in Baltimore. A French order of priests dedicated to theological education, this group made considerable impact. Unlike some other orders, the Sulpicians historically have concentrated their efforts on the religious formation of the seminarian. Accordingly, they gave Maryland's Catholics much of their intellectual leadership in the early nineteenth century, and two from their number, Ambrose Marechal (served 1817-1834) and Samuel Eccleston (served 1834-51), became Archbishops of Baltimore.

Maryland became a center for many American religious orders. In 1790, Carmelite nuns established a contemplative convent at Port Tobacco, and in 1808, the restored Jesuit order made Maryland its headquarters. But the most significant religious order founded in the state was the Sisters of Charity of St. Joseph. Elizabeth Ann Seton (1774-1815), a Catholic convert, came to Baltimore in 1808, and in 1809, she and a small group of women opened a school in Emmitsburg. Officially recognized in 1812, the Sisters of Charity have been a major teaching order in Maryland, and their schools have contributed much to the character of Catholic Maryland.

John Carroll's cathedral in Baltimore was old St. Peter's Church. In this church, the first ordination to the priesthood (Stephen Badin in 1793) took place, also the first episcopal consecration (Leonard Neall in 1800). In 1806, Archbishop Carroll laid the cornerstone for the new Cathedral of the Assumption of the Blessed Virgin Mary, a basilica designed by the prominent church architect, Henry Latrobe. However, the poverty of the archdiocese kept the new church in debt and unconsecrated until 1876. The Plenary Councils of the American Catholic Church met here in 1852, 1866, and 1884. In 1959, the Cathedral of Mary Our Queen was opened in a more residential section of the city.

The diocese that elected John Carroll bishop was largely composed of old American stock; by the time of Archbishop Neale's era, the archbishopric was in the midst of a social revolution. Immigrants were pouring into Baltimore. The Irish, who were the largest group, quickly assimilated themselves to the American church; however, the Germans insisted on separate ethnic parishes such as St. Alphonsus, built in 1842. Later, Italian, Polish, and Ukranian parishes were founded. Maryland became a polyglot of different Catholic traditions sustained by the parochial schools which taught the immigrants' language as well as English.

In the 1850s, Baltimore was the center of Know-Nothing agitation in the state. Mobs roved the streets attacking the immigrants and often beating priests. Every effort was made to keep the new citizens from the polls. James (to be Cardinal) Gibbons experienced this terror as a young priest in an immigrant parish, and his later attempts to provide an American foundation for the Church may have stemmed from these experiences.

Although sectional feeling ran high in Maryland, the Catholic community maintained an official policy of neutrality. The only disruption of church services that occurred was at St. Ignatius, Baltimore. When Union troops arrived in 1861 during Father Charles King's Solemn High Mass, the entire congregation as well as the deacon, subdeacon, and altarboy fled. Father King finished the service as a low Mass.

Catholic parishes in Maryland have been complex organizations housing a variety of benevolent and social activities, Confraternities of Christian Doctrine, Holy Name Societies, St. Vincent de Paul Societies, Legions of Mary, and the Knights of Columbus have been widespread. These societies have not only provided opportunities for fellowship and spiritual growth; they have often been the backbone of the financial programs of their parishes. A yearly "bull roast" to help support the school, sponsored by the various groups in the parish, is an abiding tradition.

The rural parishes in St. Mary's county and on the Eastern Shore have their own traditions. Many of them were served by missionary priests who rode a circuit until the twentieth century. Often the priest would leave his parish church with his missionary kit and deliver the sacraments to those too far from the church for regular attendance. Religious education was conducted by individual catechetical sessions at different homes on the circuit. In St. John's, Hollywood, such visitations did not cease until

1935, and priestly ministry continued to have a traveling component until the 1950s.

Twentieth century developments changed the patterns of Eastern Shore Catholicism much as immigration had changed Western Shore Catholicism in an earlier epoch. The advent of the automobile made possible the growth of parochial schools in the 1920s and helped to introduce the complex organizational patterns of urban Catholics to a hitherto rural society.

Vatican II has hastened changes. Notwithstanding their immigrant heritage, Maryland's Catholics have been in the forefront of efforts to Americanize the Church. James Cardinal Gibbons, archbishop from 1877 to 1921, established Catholic University in Washington to open the Church to modern culture, and James Courtney Murray, the great Catholic theorist of Church-State relations, taught at Woodstock. In one sense, the Council simply affirmed the direction that the state's Catholics had been taking. The most visible changes in the Church have been in the area of worship. Not only are Masses in English, often with modern music, but new churches tend to be simple in their construction. In many older parishes, the old statues and side altars have been replaced by plain iconographic presentations.

Although the archdiocese lost many priests in the aftermath of the Council, the introduction of new associations of priests has strengthened the vocations of those who have remained. The most striking changes have been in theological education. The Jesuits moved their training center from Woodstock to New York, and the Sulpician Fathers have appointed Protestants to their faculty at St. Mary's. In addition, St. Mary's has been accredited by the American Association of Theological Schools and has experimented with a new curriculum that stresses scriptural studies and field education. The Catholic Church in Maryland continues to change as the full implications of the new directions in theology and ministry are drawn out on the parish level.

The Methodists. In Maryland, the evangelical impulse of American Protestant life was expressed primarily through the Methodist movement. Although George Whitefield visited the colony in 1740 and 1746, there was little response to his preaching. The first Methodist preacher in the colony was Robert Strawbridge (d. 1781), an Irish convert. He arrived between 1760 and 1766 and purchased a farm in Frederick County to use as a base for his evangelistic tours. Strawbridge traveled throughout the colony, including the Eastern Shore, establishing chapels and winning converts. The areas visited by him were the heart of the great Methodist revivals of 1780-1781 on the Eastern Shore and 1789-1793 on the Western Shore. Strawbridge was unconcerned with church order and insisted on celebrating the sacraments. Largely as a result of his labors, almost half of the Methodists in the colonies in 1773 were Marylanders.

Early Maryland Methodism depended on the class leader and local preacher who conducted extensive programs of lay witness and education. These men kept the Methodist revival alive during the long periods of absence of the traveling ministry and provided much of the pastoral care for the newly awakened converts. When the representatives of British Methodism, such as Joseph Pilmoor, Thomas Coke, and Francis Asbury arrived, they stressed the role of the itinerant minister who was to admit new members to classes, regularize societies, and supervise the local ministry.

The Methodist revival was closely connected to the resurgence of pietism among the German Reformed. The Reformed were strongly influenced by the Dutch precisionist movement and by the work of Spener. Most Reformed immigrants brought a belief in the religion of the heart with them from Germany. Benedict Schwobe, pastor of the German Reformed Church in Baltimore, was a warm friend of Robert Strawbridge and Francis Asbury.

Philip William Otterbein (1726-1813) was another important Methodist ally among the Reformed. In 1754, Otterbein had an experience of conversion that opened his heart to new forms of ministry, and when he came to Baltimore in 1774, his preaching led to a major revival among the German Protestants. The congregation outgrew its small building, and a new church, symbolically constructed from the bricks used as ballast in ships bringing immigrants from Germany, was constructed for him. The bells of the new church were to be rung whenever a ship from Germany arrived in the harbor, although Otterbein prohibited their use on Good Friday. In 1800, Otterbein and Martin Boehm, a former Mennonite, founded the United Brethren to spread revival among the Germans.

Although many itinerants were imprisoned or beaten because of their refusal to take the loyalty oath from 1776 to 1781, the Methodists were gradually displacing the Church of England in many counties. The latter was more seriously disrupted by the movement for independence than the Methodists, and many Christians, especially on the Eastern Shore, turned to the chapel in the absence of their regular clergy. Maryland, curiously enough, recognized the denominational independence of Methodism before official action was taken: in 1781, a law was passed exempting Methodists, but not Anglicans, from the loyalty oath.

In 1784, the famous Christmas Conference held at Lovely Lane Chapel in Baltimore recognized the independence of American Methodism. John Wesley had appointed Dr. Thomas Coke and Francis Asbury superintendents of the new church, and they were formally elected. Asbury was ordained and, following the adoption of the Discipline and a liturgy, assignments to circuits were made. John Andrews and William West, Episcopal rectors in Baltimore, met with Asbury and Coke to attempt to persuade them to remain within the Anglican church but their pleas were in vain.

The Christmas Conference also authorized the founding of Cokesbury College. When the school opened in 1787 at Abingdon under Levi Heath, it was clear that the new denomination had overextended itself. Money was not available for such a venture. When the original buildings burned, the school was reopened as an academy in Baltimore in 1796; when those buildings were destroyed as well, the venture was abandoned. The experiment had cost between $710,000 and $720,000. It was not until 1832, when the Baltimore Conference purchased Dickinson College in Pennsylvania, that Methodists in Maryland had a center for higher education.

The Great Methodist Revival of 1780-1820 began on the Eastern Shore and gradually moved west. At its height in 1789-1792, the churches were adding 1,000 members annually. The smallpox epidemic of 1792-1793 slowed the rate of growth, but the movement was not to be contained. In 1800, 1,232 converts were made in Baltimore; 382 in Frederick County; 330 in Montgomery; and 60 in Harford. In the same year, black membership in Calvert County went from 814 to 1,664.

In 1803, the camp meeting was introduced by Henry Smith on the Winchester circuit. This new technique spread rapidly, with Nicholas Snethen attracting between 1,000 and 2,000 to his 1803 meeting in Reisterstown. In 1806, 579 were converted and 118 sanctified at a Baltimore County camp. The new style of evangelism, however, was harder to discipline than the older techniques, and in 1811, the Conference agreed that camp meetings had to be approved by the presiding elder. Symptomatic of the problem was a Maryland law, passed in 1812, that prohibited the sale of liquor within two miles of a camp meeting. In 1820, Snethen and Alexander McCaine demanded lay representation in the Conference and were opposed by the bishops and presiding elders. Through the *Wesleyan Repository* and its successor, *Mutual Rights*, the dispute was carried into the congregations where Union Societies of itinerants, local preachers, and laypeople were formed. After the expulsion of the Baltimore Union Society in 1828, schism was inevitable. In 1830, the resultant new denomination took the name the Methodist Protestant Church.

Although polity was the stated reason for the split, the need for the new church was occasioned by other social factors. The Methodist Protestant people favored a warmer style of evangelism than the Methodist Episcopal Church, especially the expanded use of the camp meeting, and they were strongest in the west and on the Eastern Shore—areas that were removed from the growth of the Western Shore and the City of Baltimore. By 1867, the new church was strong enough to establish Western Methodist College in Westminster and, in 1887, to create Westminster Theological Seminary. Following the reunion of the two churches, the Protestant Methodist and the Methodist Episcopal in 1939, the seminary was taken over by the newly united body and in 1958 relocated in Washington, acquiring the name Wesley Seminary.

The Civil War disrupted Maryland's Methodists more than it did the other religious groups in the state. Although Maryland had remained with the North in 1844, the "new chapter" on slavery which was added to the Discipline in 1860 created an uproar. Rival conferences were created, and several independent Methodist societies were formed. After the War, the church extension boards of the northern and southern churches stole members from each other and founded competing churches in the area of the other denomination's strength. The Methodist Episcopal Church, South, won many of these battles, and when the two were reunited in 1939, it was able to bring almost 100,000 members into the new body.

The most important change in the state's Methodism after the Civil War was the gradual but steady increase in the number of seminary trained pastors. As a result, the churches moved in the direction of a more liberal theology and of a transformation of the older holiness ideal into modern concepts of social service. Harris Franklin Rall, pastor of First Methodist (Lovely Lane) from 1905 to 1910, was an organizer of the Methodist Federation for Social Service in 1907, and an important spokesman for the Social Creed, adopted by the northern church in 1908. The Baltimore Conference opposed Negro disenfranchisement in 1915, and the work of the Conference was one of the primary reasons for the defeat of a referendum on Afro-American voting in 1910.

The greatest period of post-Civil growth was 1945-1965 when a national religious revival coincided with the expansion of the Washington-Baltimore suburbs. This was also a period of rising ecumenical interest. In 1966, the Baltimore Conference merged with the Washington Conference (Black), and in 1969, union was effected with the United Brethren. In 1970, a joint ordination service was held in Washington Cathedral in which William F. Creighton, the Episcopal Bishop of Washington, joined with Bishops Love, Lord, and Leddin of the United Methodist Church in ordaining new elders for the Baltimore Conference. Methodism remains the largest Protestant denomination in the state; on the Eastern Shore it continues to comprise more than half the total population.

The Baptists. Despite strong missionary efforts, Baptists have never been as numerous in Maryland as in other southern and border states. The First Great Awakening, which laid the foundations of Baptist growth further south, did not occur in the state, and Methodism dominated the Second Great Awakening. Further, the moderate form of aristocracy in Maryland did not spark the sharp Baptist democratic reaction that other forms of aristocracy, such as Virginia's, provoked.

The first Baptist church in Maryland was a General Baptist congregation established at Chestnut Ridge, Baltimore County, in 1742. By 1754 this congregation had divided, and a Particular Baptist church was gathered and admitted into the Philadelphia Association. Elder John Davis (1712-1808) served this Chestnut Ridge congregation for 60 years; he traveled as an itinerant throughout the Western Shore region, and his labors resulted in the establishment of many churches in the area. The First Church in Baltimore was one of these. Established about 1773, the church called Lewis Richards, a graduate of Lady Huntington's school at Trevecca, as its first full time pastor. The Second Baptist Church in the city migrated as a body from England under the leadership of John Heally, a new connection Baptist. This church may have had the first Sunday School in the state. In 1793, the churches on the Western Shore united to form the Baltimore Association.

Elijah Baker and Philip Hughes, itinerants from Virginia, established the first Baptist churches on the Eastern Shore at Salisbury, Broad Creek, Fowling Creek, and Fishing Creek. In 1782, these churches formed the Salisbury Association.

The anti-missionary movement sharply divided Maryland Baptists from 1820 to 1836. The issue was particularly heated on the Western Shore, and in 1836 the Baptist Union of Maryland was formed from those churches that supported missions and evangelism. There were fewer than 2,000 Baptists in the state at the time of the schism. Maryland was the only state where Baptists with a strong alliance with the Philadelphia Association resisted the new movements in missions and benevolence.

After the schism, Baptist efforts in Maryland turned towards the new city evangelism that had been developed in the North. In 1834, William F. Broadus, William T. Brantley, Sr., and J. O. Choules conducted a protracted meeting at First Baptist, Baltimore, and in 1834, 1839, and 1856 Baptists invited Jacob Knapp, an evangelist who modelled his ministry on that of Charles Finney, to conduct revivals in the city. In 1879, Baptists were among the leaders in extending an invitation to D. L. Moody to conduct a revival in the city. Although these city-wide efforts benefitted other denominations as much or more than they benefitted the Baptists, they did establish a strong Baptist presence in the city. In 1905, the Baltimore Baptist Training School was organized to help evangelize the city through lay witness and religious surveys.

The other approach to evangelism taken by Maryland Baptists was to invite prominent Baptists from other states to serve Maryland churches. William Crane (1790-1866), a wealthy Baptist layman from Virginia, moved to Baltimore in 1834 to help bolster Baptist fortunes. In 1847, Richard Fuller, the popular pastor of First Baptist, Beaufort, South Carolina, accepted a call to Seventh Baptist, Baltimore, as a missionary duty and through energetic evangelism increased the membership from 87 to 1200. The socially prominent Eutaw Street Baptist Church was formed by Richard Fuller and members of Seventh who had moved into that area in 1871. W. T. Brantley, Jr., (1816-1852) came to Seventh Church in 1871 for reasons similar to those that had brought Fuller there earlier. Under his leadership, the Young Men's City Mission began the Sunday School that would later become the Brantley Baptist Church. Rising young Baptists leaders, such as E. Y. Mullins and Curtis Lee Laws also felt drawn to the city that presented such a challenge.

Despite their small size, Maryland Baptists have played important roles in Southern Baptist history. During the Civil War, when Southern Baptists were cut off from their missions abroad, Baltimore Baptists provided money and leadership to sustain the enterprise. After the war,

Maryland women led by Anne Graves, Alice Armstrong, Annie Armstrong, and Mrs. A. J. Rowland, helped to establish the Women's Missionary Union to support Southern Baptist work. The Week of Prayer for Foreign Missions and the Christmas Offering, now convention-wide endeavors, originated in their work. Joshua Levering (1845-1935), layman and philanthropist, helped to restore financial order to the Southern Convention in the dark days of the late nineteenth century when it appeared that the enterprise would go bankrupt. He served as President of the Convention and as chairman of the Trustees of Southern Seminary, Louisville.

Although Maryland Baptists made modest gains in the thriving suburbs of Washington after the Second World War, social changes in the Baltimore area in that same period have weakened the heart of Maryland Baptist work. Efforts have been made to establish new churches in Baltimore's suburbs, and some congregations, such as Seventh, have decided to stay in the inner city and experiment with multiracial forms of congregational life.

The Presbyterians. Despite firm colonial foundations, Presbyterianism in Maryland has remained relatively small. The heavy Scotch-Irish immigration of the late eighteenth and early nineteenth centuries tended to settle north or south of the state where more western lands were available, and few of the nineteenth century German immigrants had a Reformed background. The identification of revivalism and Methodism in Maryland further weakened Presbyterian efforts at growth.

In 1763, Patrick Allison, a Princeton graduate, became the first Presbyterian pastor in Baltimore. John Glendy, a Scotch-Irish immigrant trained at the University of Glasgow, was the first pastor at Second Presbyterian. Apparently, Glendy's preaching had unitarian overtones. In 1817, the presbytery warned against the denial of the trinity, and when John Breckinridge, another Princeton graduate, became associate pastor in 1826, the church had to dismiss half its membership for non-trinitarianism.

Maryland Presbyterian life was conservative. Although Sunday Schools were added to the churches, the first in 1802, denominational societies were strongly preferred. The only non-presbyterian organization to have widespread support was the American Colonization Society. It was introduced at Second Presbyterian by that church's third pastor, Robert Breckinridge. Maryland's Presbyterians adhered to the Old School in 1837, and, although four pastors supported the southern church during the Civil War, remained loyal to that position until the merger of Old and New School in 1869. By and large, pastors in the state have been drawn from Princeton Seminary and have reflected its style of leadership.

Maryland Presbyterianism has been prosperous and stable. The most controversial product of the church was J. Gresham Machen, the son of an old Baltimore family, who led the conservative forces against modernism in the 1920s. Significantly, J. Ross Stevenson, whose reforms at Princeton contributed to Machen's withdrawal from Presbyterianism, came to the presidency of the Seminary from the pulpit of Brown Memorial Church in Baltimore. Today, three presbyteries serve the state: Baltimore, New Castle (Eastern Shore), and the National Capitol Union, which is a joint effort with the southern church.

Afro-American Religion. In Maryland, slavery rarely involved the large commerical plantation, and blacks and whites lived more intimately than in the deep South. Further, some religious traditions served to ameliorate the conditions of the slaves. The Quakers maintained a strong anti-slavery tradition, and many Methodists were opposed to slave holding on principle. Roman Catholicism, while not campaigning against slavery, insisted that slavery was only an economic condition and did not affect the slave's relationship to God. Further, Maryland had a large free black population in the nineteenth century that was numerically equal to the slave population at the time of emancipation. This older free black community, which was intensely interested in education and social advancement, tended to set the standards for the Afro-American community in religious as well as social matters.

Catholic missionary work among the slaves began as soon as they arrived in the colony. The Jesuits saw the Africans as a natural extension of their charter to conduct Indian missions, and Catholic planters, unlike many Protestants, recognized an obligation to convert their servants. Although massive immigration from Europe deflected Catholic energies, concern with the religious needs of black Catholics continued. In 1829, the Oblate Sisters, the Church's first black religious order, arrived from Santo Domingo and established St. Francis School for Colored Girls. Their mission quickly expanded to include Sunday Schools and catechetical instruction for those Negro children who could not attend parochial schools. As the parish school became a mark of Maryland's Catholics, the Oblates established new schools in predominantly black parishes.

Although blacks were rarely as segregated from whites in Catholicism as in Protestantism, the Catholic Church in the nineteenth century moved toward the establishment of black ethnic churches. In 1859, Father Peter Miller, S. J., was appointed as a missionary to the blacks of Baltimore. His church, St. Francis Xavier, originally met in the basement of St. Ignatius' Church, but in 1863, Archbishop Spalding dedicated a new building for the congregation. In 1871, the Afro-American mission was transferred from the Jesuits to the newly formed Josephites.

In addition to launching St. Francis Xavier, the Josephites, who had been founded in England to work with the freedmen, established a minor seminary at Walbrook and a major seminary in Washington, D.C. Although Afro-Americans had been ordained earlier in Europe, Charles Uncles (1859-1933) was the first black priest ordained in the United States. He attended the Oblate Sisters' School at St. Francis Xavier and the Baltimore Normal School before his baptism in 1879. When he decided to enter the priesthood four years later, he followed other Afro-American candidates to St. Hyacinthe's College in Quebec. In 1888 he applied to St. Mary's Seminary, and after a meeting of the student body to vote on his admission, was the first Negro admitted to the school. In 1891, he was ordained and began a teaching ministry with the Josephites at Walbrook; when the school moved to New York in 1920, he left Maryland to continue his duties there.

One of the crusaders for justice among black Catholics was Father John Henry Dorsey, S. S. J. (1873-1926). He served as an altar boy at St. Francis Xavier, and was educated at St. Thomas (Minneapolis), Walbrook, and St. Mary's, Baltimore. Following his ordination in 1902, he became a missionary to poor whites and blacks in Alabama. When his work there became too controversial in 1923, he was made pastor of St. Monnica's, a poor black parish in Baltimore. In 1926, he was killed by a parishioner whose apparent motive was robbery.

The Methodist revival attacked large numbers of Afro-Americans, especially in the city of Baltimore which had approximately 9,000 free black residents in 1800. In 1802, Lovely Lane Methodist Church helped to establish Sharp Street Methodist for its black members. Sharp Street was an early center of black activism: money was raised to purchase the freedom of slaves; reading and writing were taught in the Sunday School; the Liberian colonization plan was studied, and abolitionist speakers, especially those active among Maryland's Methodists, were invited to speak. Since Maryland had no laws prohibiting the education of free blacks, the church was able to establish an influential private school.

More racially conscious Afro-Americans had founded a Colored Methodist Society in 1782, and in 1802, the African Methodist Bethel Society, as it was then known, called Daniel Coker as their pastor. Coker had been a slave on the Eastern Shore and was a convert of Robert Strawbridge. He had escaped to New York, and with the aid of Francis Asbury had earned enough to purchase his freedom. Under his leadership, Bethel left the parent Methodist organization. The church was a center for the publication of attacks on slavery and for the education of free blacks. Coker himself became disillusioned with the changes for racial improvement in Maryland and emigrated to Africa. Bethel has remained a key Afro-American pulpit, and fourteen of its pastors, including Daniel Payne, the historian, have served the African Methodist Episcopal Church as bishops.

The third early Afro-American pastor in Baltimore was William Livingston. Born in New York, he was ordained by Bishop William White of Philadelphia, and in 1824, established St. James' First African Episcopal Church. Although related to the Church of England, St. James' maintained a style of ministry that was similar to that of the black Methodists in the city.

In 1848 Sharp Street and Asbury Station Methodist churches petitioned the General Conference for a separate Negro Conference, but this request was denied until after emancipation in 1864. In that year, the Methodist established the Washington Conference which united black Methodists in Maryland and the District of Columbia. In 1940, A. P. Shaw became the first Afro-American to serve the conference as its bishop, and in 1956, Mrs. Emma Birrell was ordained by the Washington Conference. She was the first woman ordained as a Methodist elder in the state. In 1965, after a century of leadership among black Marylanders, the Washington Conference was merged with the formerly all white Baltimore Conference, and Afro-Americans and whites shared the positions of leadership in the new body.

The period after 1864 was the beginning of a half century of steady growth. By 1890, the Methodist Episcopal Church had expanded to include 7,000 black members and black Methodist owned property valued at $225,000. In that same period, the African Methodist Episcopal Church grew to 5,000 members and owned property valued at $200,000. Since both denominations had strict membership requirements, average attendance was probably twice the reported membership. Afro-American Methodists were more than twice the size of their nearest Protestant rival, the Baptists, who reported only 5,700 members at the same date.

Higher education was a major concern of Maryland's Afro-American Methodist community. In 1867, the Centenary Biblical Institute was opened to train black pastors. The growth of the segregated public school system offered new opportunities for educated blacks, and in 1876 a normal department was opened. Many Methodist ministers appear to have combined ministry with school teaching. In 1890, the name of the school was changed to Morgan College, and in 1939 the school was purchased by the state. Afro-American Methodists, however, were allowed to retain facilities on the campus.

Black Baptists, like their white counterparts, have not been as influential in Maryland as in other southern states. In part, this has been due to the pattern of white evangelization. The areas of heaviest slave owning in Maryland were in the southern counties and on the Eastern Shore where Catholics, Episcopalians, and Methodists were dominant.

In 1834, Moses Clayton formed the First Colored Baptist Church, and in 1836, the church was admitted to the Maryland Baptist Union. In that same year, William Crane purchased the freedom of Noah Davis, a slave preacher, and he traveled the state preaching to slave and free. In 1848, Seventh Baptist dismissed its black members to form the Second Colored Baptist Church. Both First and Second Colored Churches were active in the Maryland Baptist Union until 1864 when they withdrew to establish the Maryland State Convention.

The most remarkable of Baltimore's black Baptists churches was Union Baptist which was formed by the merger of two small congregations in 1866. The congregation purchased the old Disciples' Meeting House, and in 1872 called the Rev. Harvey Johnson as its pastor. Johnson, a graduate of Wayland, made the church a center of black education and evangelism. By 1885, Union had 2,000 members who formed the base of the Brotherhood of Liberty which fought discriminatory legislation in the state. The outreach of Union resulted in the formation of Macedonian, Calvary, Perkins Square, Frederick, Winfield, and Westminster Baptist churches. Significantly, Union refused to ordain a candidate for the ministry who had not acquired some formal education, and the congregation provided money and other forms of support for students at Wayland and Howard Colleges.

Afro-American Christians in Maryland were active participants in the civil rights struggles of the 1960s. In the 1970s, however, the black denominations began to face two different problems. On the one hand, there was a new Afro-American immigration into Baltimore that put increased pressure on very limited resources. On the other hand, the new opportunities for blacks which they had done so much to create were producing a middle class that was moving to the suburbs. Whether the black denominations will be able to meet the demands of this exodus or whether these newly established people will turn to the mainstream denominations is not clear.

Unitarians. Unitarianism has not played a significant role in Maryland's religious history. First Unitarian Church, Baltimore, was constructed in 1817 to serve the needs of immigrants from New England to the city. In 1819, William Ellery Channing preached his famous sermon, "Unitarian Christianity," at the ordination of Jared Sparks there. The sermon made almost no impression on Baltimore. The most successful Unitarian minister to serve in Maryland was the Rev. John Ware who preached to crowds of 2,000 at Ford's Opera House during the Civil War. The spread of liberalism, however, among other Protestant churches, especially the Methodist, prevented those gains from becoming permanent. Enoch Pratt (d. 1896) was the leading nineteenth century Unitarian layman. His gift of $1,200,000 to the city established the Enoch Pratt Library, one of the leading public libraries in the United States.

Judaism. Judaism grew slowly in Maryland in the years immediately folowing the American Revolution. The state's constitution and laws assumed that Maryland was a Christian state and, although a cemetery was purchased in Baltimore, it was not clear whether a Jewish organization could be incorporated. From 1818 to 1826, bills were introduced in the legislature to extend civil rights to Jews. Thomas Kennedy (1776-1832), a Presbyterian immigrant from Ireland, led the battle, and the final law allowed Jews to be admitted to the courts and to vote on an oath of belief in God. The last civil rights bill for Jews was passed in 1847 when the state's prohibition against black suits of "white Christians" was changed simply to "whites."

Baltimore's early Jewish community was largely composed of immigrants from Bavaria and in 1830, *Nidlei Israel,* later Baltimore Hebrew Congregation, was established. Abraham Rice (1800-1862), who came in 1840 as rabbi, was the first person with full rabbinic training to settle in the United States. From the beginning of his ministry, Rice faced the problem of Americanization in his congregation. Despite a heavy program of fines and an attempt to exclude Sabbath breakers from the reading of the Torah in the services, Rice was unable to bring his congregation into line with his convictions. In 1849 he resigned and was followed by Dr. Henry Hochheimer, a graduate of the University of Munich, who continued to attempt to maintain orthodoxy. In 1870, however, the congregation formally acknowledged the Reform position of many of its members, and the Chizuk Emunah Congregation was formed in reaction to the changes.

The first Reform Synagogue in Baltimore was *Har Sinai* which was established after Rabbi Abraham Rice protested the use of Masonic rites at the funeral of Jacob Ahrens in 1842. David Einhorn (1809-1879) was called to the synagogue as rabbi in 1855. Einhorn, one of the founders of Reform Judaism in Europe and a radical on secular as well as religious subjects, was forced to flee from Baltimore in 1861 because of his uncompromising position on slavery.

Oheb Shalom Congregation was established in 1853 as an alternative to the orthodoxy of Baltimore Hebrew and to the radicalism of *Har Sinai*. In 1859, the synagogue secured the services of Rabbi Benjamin Szold (1829-1902) who had been trained both in European rabbinical schools and at the University of Breslau. Szold was one of the leading advocates of Conservative Judaism in America.

The renewal of persecution in Eastern Europe radically changed Baltimore's Jewish community. The newcomers were not comfortable in German speaking congregations, and they tended to form small Orthodox synagogues composed of their fellow countrymen. In 1909, for example, there were 25 congregations of Russian Jews within the city. The new immigrants were poor, and the pattern of German Jewish owners and Eastern European Jewish workers quickly developed in Baltimore's garment industry. Further, the Eastern Jews created a different culture composed of night schools, unions, Zionist organizations, and cultural activities that made East Baltimore the scene of countless, unending debates. Despite their differences from either the older Jewish or the Gentile communities, Eastern immigrants in Baltimore made rapid social progress, and by the early 1920s they had begun to leave the ghetto.

Although Judaism in Maryland has often seemed to function like one of the Christian denominations, there have been significant differences.

As important as the synagogues have been, especially for the German Jews, Jewish charities and organizations have provided more of the cement that has held the community together than has worship. The first charity had the improbable name, Irish *Chevra*, and it was followed by a long list of organizations that included the Hebrew Benevolence Society (1856), the Hebrew Orphanage Society (1872), the Free Burial Society (1869), the Jewish Consumptive Hospital (1909), and the Jewish Educational Alliance (1890). In 1920, the Associated Jewish Charities was formed to coordinate the work of German and Jewish charities.

The need of Jewish education has also united the community. Early Jewish education was conducted in the synagogue where the rabbi taught secular and religious subjects. In 1856, the small Sephardic congregation experimented with a Sunday School for those students attending public schools, and the institution spread. In 1900, Samson Benderly (1876-1944) came to Baltimore as the principal of the Hebrew school maintained by the Hebrew Educational Society. Under his leadership, the school adopted progressive education and stressed the integration of play and learning. Benderly's school highlighted the need for trained teachers and in 1902 Hebrew College was established to train men and women to work in Jewish education. In 1910, Benderly left Baltimore to take a similar position in New York, and Hebrew College was temporarily closed. The school reopened in 1919 with a broader curriculum designed to train people in all areas of Jewish life and history.

Baltimore Jews supported fellow Jews in Israel before the modern Zionist movement. In 1847, Jehiel Cohen collected funds for the Jewish settlements there, and in that same year, Rabbi Rice organized a group to provide regular aid. Although few Jews from Maryland had immigrated to the Holy Land, Zionist organizations of all types have been supported. In 1897, Rabbi Schepel Schafer attended the First Zionist Congress, and Henrietta Szold (1860-1945), the founder of Hadassah, was the daughter of one of Baltimore's leading rabbis. The rise of Nazism and the subsequent establishment of the state of Israel have intensified the Baltimore community's commitment to Israel and have had the effect of creating a deeper appreciation of Jewish faith and customs. Like the charities and Jewish education, Israel is a major object of the support of Jews in Maryland.

Summary
Maryland's religious patterns have remained stable over a significant period of time. The primary changes in that pattern have come from

immigration into the state; however, immigration has often changed particular denominations more than it has changed the pattern of denominational loyalty. Even the rapid expansion of the Washington suburbs has had less influence than one might have supposed. Maryland appears to be basically content with its patterns of religious diversity. Although the ecumenical movement has had some impact, especially among Methodists, denominationalism will probably continue to dominate the state's religion in the future. Maryland's denominations serve many social functions: religious, ethnic, educational, and charitable. And these functions have built for the churches a firm foundation in the life of the state.

Bibliography

Patrick Allison. *First Presbyterian Church, Baltimore, Maryland.*

Gordon P. Baker. *Those Incredible Methodists: A History of the Baltimore Conference of the United Methodist Church.*

Thomas Beaenkoph et al. *Moody in Baltimore.*

L. P. Bowen. *The Days of Makemie.*

Isaac M. Fein. *The Making of An American Jewish Community: The History of Baltimore Jewry from 1773 to 1920.*

Theodore Gambrall. *Church Life in Colonial Maryland.*

Rufus Jones. *The Quakers in the American Colonies.*

J. J. Johnson. *Historical Summary of the Shrines, Churches, Chapels, and Homes of the Priests in St. Mary's County since 1634.*

Charles G. Herbermann. *The Sulpicians in the United States.*

Julius Hofman. *A History of Zion Church of the City of Baltimore, 1755-1897.*

Anabelle M. Melville. *John Carroll of Baltimore.*

Nelson Rightmeyer. *Maryland's Established Church.*

Joseph Watts. *The Rise and Progress of Maryland Baptists.*

Adel Ross Wentz. *History of the Evangelical Lutheran Synod of Maryland of the United Lutheran Church in America, 1820-1920.*

Albert Werline. *Problems of Church and State in Maryland.*

Blanche Sydnor White. *Our Heritage: History of the Women's Missionary Union, Auxiliary to the Maryland Baptist Union, 1742-1958.*

MISSISSIPPI

EDWARD NELSON AKIN
MISSISSIPPI COLLEGE

Religious folks in the community shunned him. After all, everybody knew of his fondness for whiskey, the many hours he spent swapping tall tales around checker games on the town square, and his inability to hold down a steady job. But when Bill Faulkner won the Nobel Prize, he became interpreter by default of Mississippi culture—including religion. When a University of Virginia student asked him if the tall convict in *Old Man* believed in God, Faulkner must have smiled quizzically as he replied, "His background would be the bucolic, provincial, Southern Baptist; and it may be a debatable question whether that sort of Baptist believes in God or not."

A bucolic, provincial Southern Baptist, committing the fallacy of generalizing from the particular, might roundly criticize William Faulkner for such an unorthodox statement; but few knowledgeable persons would challenge Faulkner's understanding and use of Mississippi religion in his works. Faulkner himself was well aware of the role religion had on his writing. Replying to another Virginia inquisitor, he stated, "Remember, the writer must write out of his background. He must write out of what he knows and the Christian legend is part of any Christian's background, especially the background of a country boy, a Southern country boy." Academicians often lament that Southern Christianity is more Southern than Christian. But just as religion permeates the narrative and symbols of William Faulkner and Walker Percy, so it permeates the lives and touchstones of black and white Mississippians. Mississippi culture and religion have been so interwoven that an effort to extract the thread of religion from the fabric cannot avoid incompleteness and falsification of social reality. Even so the effort must be undertaken.

An unstated assumption in Faulkner's Virginia dialogue was that whenever a people search for meaning in life, religion becomes a part of, often directs, that search. Therefore, religion in Mississippi began with the first human beings to inhabit the area, the American Indians. Admittedly, little is known of their culture. The writings of archaeologists and anthropologists indicate that the Mississippi Indian groups, especially the Muskogean speaking peoples, were a part of what is known as the Southern Ceremonial Complex. The complex consisted of a set of natural and abstract symbols based on an understanding of nature. In their worship, the sun, the Great Holy Fire Above, played a crucial role. Each household was able to share its warmth and power with a ceremonial fire. Rites of passage, especially birth and burial, were events which emphasized both man's relationship to the larger cosmos and his dependence on its rhythm and flow.

This culture was challenged by the entrance of the European into the area in 1540, with the De Soto expedition. Although the Catholic nations of France and Spain were to dominate the area for the next two and a half centuries, there is little evidence that religion gained any more than a toehold in what would become Mississippi. Natchez, the center of economic and governmental activity, had a Catholic church, but that outpost of civilization had the only Christian religious edifice in the area. The conquistadors were interested in power and wealth; they had no time for spiritual dialogue with savages. The inadvertent introduction of European diseases, resulting in epidemics among the Indians, had a greater impact on the tragic fate of the Mississippi Indian than either the presence of the sword or the absence of the cross.

Christians largely ignored the Indian until the Protestant evangelical efforts of the Jeffersonian Era. The ancient cultural practices of the Indian, religious and otherwise, had largely crumbled because of a decline in the network of clan society. There are many explanations for the disintegration of a viable Indian culture: disease, warfare, mixed-marriages, Europeanization, and other cultural and demographic forces both within and without the Indian society. The first Protestant missionary among the Indians was Joseph Bullen. Vermont bred and Yale educated, he came to the Mississippi frontier in 1799. Over the next four years he made several tours through the Choctaw and Chickasaw nations.

Bullen was followed in his efforts by the work of Presbyterian, Baptist, and Methodist groups during the first three decades of the nineteenth century. Presbyterian missionaries Cyrus Byington and Cyrus Kingsbury translated hymnals and other religious material into the Choctaw language during the 1820s. With the Indian removals of the 1830s and the attendant attitudes of alienation, Protestant activity among the Indians lost its former fervor. Although sporadic efforts continued, especially in the frontier camp meeting tradition, the Indian became generally an object of white derision.

During the period from 1763 to 1798 Mississippi was a Spanish colony. The colonial authorities relaxed their pro-Catholic qualifications for citizenship and worship in order to attract more Americans to the Natchez area. Protestants were allowed to worship as they chose, but they were not to hold public meetings or proselytize. Although Spanish Catholics considered this to be a fair compromise, evangelical Protestants were not disposed to cater to such constraints. In 1791 a Baptist minister named Richard Curtis began his ministry at Coles Creek, north of Natchez. Four years later, following a series of violations of local religious rules, the Spanish authorities sought to arrest him after he performed a Protestant marriage ceremony. He went into self-exile until the United States acquired the territory in 1798. The following year the first Protestant missionary activity began in the area with the arrival of a minister, Tobias Gibson, who had been sent by South Carolina Methodists to evangelize the frontier. First, he established a church at Washington, north of Natchez; within a year Gibson had established the Natchez Circuit with as many as nine churches.

The Presbyterians began their missionary activity in the Mississippi territory in 1800 with the sending of three missionaries, the impetus again coming from the Carolinas. During their eight-month stay in Mississippi they were able to establish nine preaching stations, five of which eventually became churches. It should be noted that these sporadic mission activities were neither the beginning of Protestantism in the area since Protestants had already moved into Mississippi nor did they produce the permanent establishment of ecclesiastical institutions.

During the first decades of the nineteenth century Mississippi was a part of frontier, known (along with Alabama) as the Old Southwest. For most if not all of the antebellum period, Mississippi remained a rough and tumble place, the saw-toothed cutting edge for an expanding society.

Religious observances were sporadic: a circuit rider coming through every four weeks or so; a fall camp meeting that the people could attend or ignore; or the bi-weekly visitations of a rural farmer-minister, that is, provided a local church had been established. For the most part, the preachers arose from the folk. To use the term "clergy" for "the frontier parson" broadens—and distorts—the traditional image of both.

There were two basic types of ministers in Mississippi, the educated and the uneducated. The Episcopal and Presbyterian denominations required a trained clergy, a condition that hindered these groups on the frontier. The generation of a trained clergy took time, money, and patience, three necessities in short supply on the frontier. The predominant Baptist and Methodist denominations made no educational requirement of their ministers. In fact, there was a strong anti-intellectual attitude on the frontier, a value that was sometimes expressed openly. One Primitive Baptist gathering in Mississippi was so adamantly opposed to an educated ministry that it officially challenged "the learned world to show any divine authority for sending a man to school after God called him to enter the ministry. If He wants a learned Moses or Saul of Tarsus, He will have them qualified before He calls them into his work." Although other groups were not so dogmatic in their attitudes, the basic motive of Evangelicals on the frontier was the conversion of the sinner, not the intellectual cultivation of the saint.

In rural Mississippi, laymen have often stated with good humor that more preachers are called *from* the field than *to* the ministry. In frontier Mississippi, that joke would not have possessed enough realism to elicit a smile. The life of the frontier preacher was anything but a life of ease. In 1816 the standard salary of a Methodist circuit rider was $100 a year, plus his expenses. Owing to the hardships incurred, he was expected to remain single. Baptists, and other groups without an hierarchy, decided on a church-by-church basis how a pastor was to be paid. Since most of these pastors were also farmers and usually served more than one congregation, churches were often able to rationalize inadequate compensation or even, at times, to pay nothing at all. During the antebellum period Baptist churches voted annually on the calling of a pastor. Since he was in God's service, it was considered bad form to ask about compensation. Therefore, for many, service in the ministry stood as a financial liability. Of all religious groups, only Presbyterians and Episcopalians paid their clergymen an adequate salary. But financial compensation was not why these men were in the ministry; the hardships of the Methodist circuit riders attest to that most dramatically.

On the American frontier, there were several ways denominational leaders could choose to minister to their flocks. The method most representative of the frontier style is that of the Methodist circuit rider—other denominations, especially the Cumberland Presbyterian, used the same system. The basic pattern was to designate a group of churches as a circuit, thereby allowing a single minister to visit with each congregation at least once every six weeks.

The circuit rider daily contended with the ruggedness of life on the frontier. When Milton H. Jones was riding the Carroll Circuit in 1836, his horse had to outrun a panther on a ridge between the Big Black and Yalobusha rivers. There being few roads and bridges, a rider had to be resourceful. John D. Shaw spent a portion of his ministry in the lowlands of the Mississippi Delta where at times "he would mount his canoe instead of a horse" as he threaded through the many rivers, lakes, bayous, and swamps in the area of his circuit. Once he finally arrived at his destination, the preacher would find the accommodations to be meager. Sometimes with the onset of dusk, he would prevail upon a frontiersman to allow him to spend a night in a half-finished cabin. As George Shaeffer discovered, even the finished cabins of host families could be difficult to adjust to. For in the standard one-room cabins, all the family and any guests slept in the same area. Shaeffer recalled that "I felt considerably embarrassed the first time I had to retire under such circumstances, but I soon adapted myself to the usages of the people."

Not all single Methodist circuit riders were willing to adapt to all the rigors of the circuit, however. By 1825, the conference was accepting married ministers. Some of these married clergymen boarded their wives during their journeys; others took their wives with them. Arrangements made did not always meet with acclaim within the circuit. The Louisville Circuit complained of the 1838 appointment of Lorenzo Langford: "Mr. Langford had a family; and they lived a considerable distance from the circuit, how was he to render the circuit full service?" Just as basic was the question as to how these men were to provide financial support for their families. By the 1850s, a married circuit rider received only $150 a year plus a supplement of $100 if he had children at home.

As mentioned before, to the Evangelical the winning of people's souls was the first duty of the preacher on the Mississippi frontier. For many churchmen, the best method to attain that goal was through camp meetings. Although the excesses of the Cane Ridge (Kentucky) revival period beginning in 1801 had largely passed by the time Protestantism became established in Mississippi, the camp meetings offered preachers opportunities to evangelize the dispersed population of the state quickly—or so it seemed. These events, at least in the beginning, were community-wide with most denominations participating, and with as many as 20 preachers present at a single event. Presbyterians had started the tradition in Mississippi, but by 1810 they had turned over that promising strategem to others. The Methodists reaped the greatest numerical harvests, with Baptists not far behind.

The camp meetings of the late summer and early fall were as much social affairs as religious gatherings. They perpetuated the myth of the leveling effect of the frontier by often making it a reality. Prevailing social and economic divisions were eroded by the tides of emotion. Within the context of revivalism, some continued to be "more equal" than others: blacks and Indians were not only allowed to participate but were actively encouraged to do so—so long as Indians worshipped away from whites and blacks worshipped only in the presence of whites.

The boundaries between races were frequently violated during periods of revivalism. The first revival meeting in Yalobusha County had only one preacher, a black man. Pompey, a slave of the Rawls family of Marion County, exhorted throughout the state. One white participant in the Yalobusha meeting reported that Pompey was the best praying preacher he had ever heard. When the black preacher had gotten the audience's emotion to a fever pitch, he sat down, exclaiming (as the white observer stated), "When de Lord preaches, Pompey stops."

The first decade of the nineteenth century witnessed the introduction of hierarchical structures for the major Evangelical Protestant groups. Because Baptist "hierarchies" are grassroots organizations, it is no surprise that the people of that denomination were able to organize at the associational level at an early date. In 1806 six local churches banded together to form the Mississippi Baptist Association. As with other religious activity in the territory at the time, the association was located in the Natchez District, that being Adams and surrounding counties. By 1819, two other Baptist associations, Union and Pearl River, had been organized as the edge of the frontier pushed eastward from the Mississippi River.

In 1813 the Mississippi Conference of the Methodist Church officially met for the first time in Spring Hill; it comprised a few churches from Louisiana as well. Not until 1816, however, was a bishop able to be in attendance for the annual conference. That conference ordained William Winans as a local preacher, marking the beginning of his long and notable career as a frontier spokesman. The next year after Mississippi attained statehood (1817), there were six Mississippi circuits with 2,235 members, one-fifth of the membership being black.

Presbyterians were able to organize a Mississippi presbytery in 1816, under the sponsorship of the Kentucky synod. The particular style of Presbyterian organization is immediately apparent when one notes that the seven congregations with a total membership of only 200 persons had five full-time resident ministers. Throughout the antebellum period Presbyterians, along with Episcopalians, were to remain smaller but at the same time better organized than their Baptist and Methodist counter-parts. Much of this was due to the emphasis on a trained clergy. But organization and education were not highly sought religious goals on the Mississippi frontier. Frederick Law Olmstead, in his travels along the Southern frontier, recorded overhearing the following conversation:

"Uncle John's an Episcopalian, ain't he?"
"Yes."
"Well, there ain't no religion in that no how."
"No, there ain't."

Frontier religion preferred a more emotional expression.

An American stereotype of today has the rural preacher breathing fire against personal morality's sinful triplets: drinking, dancing, and gambling. The preachers of the Mississippi frontier graphically depicted these vices before their audiences, but with varying degrees of enthusiasm. For example, the subject of alcohol consumption was not a well-defined issue on the American frontier. Not to offer a guest a dram of your favorite whiskey was downright inhospitable. The frontier minister was as likely as not to be a regular if moderate imbiber.

Thus, it should come as no surprise that most pastoral sermonizing against drinking during the antebellum period was directed toward a call for moderation rather than for abstinence. A brief survey of changing Baptist attitudes is instructive. The Mississippi Association, at its gathering in 1827 resolved:

> That this Convention considers drunkeness one of the most
> injurious and worst of vices in the community, and we deeply
> deplore the destructive ravages made in our country and
> churches by the excessive and improper use of ardent spirits.

Three years later, the Pearl River Association indicated that the
problem was rather close to home when it declared: "Resolved, that the
church and friends in general provide no ardent spirits for the association
when she may hereafter meet, as we do not want it." The following year
the host church acceded to the request. As civilization challenged the
Mississippi frontier, the pronouncements of Baptist groups became
bolder. The chairman of the Baptist Committee on Temperance stated in
1847, "The fashionable and inordinate use of intoxicating drinks is a great
evil—a curse in the land—the bane of society, morals, and religion." But it
was not until 1853 that Southern Baptists in Mississippi called for
prohibition as the proper remedy for the problem of drink. Even then,
the flexible mind of the frontier Christian was able to condemn the seller
of liquor while having little to say concerning the consumer.

The campaigns for the soul and against personal sin paid numerical
dividends for Evangelical Protestantism. Methodists reaped the greatest
harvests during the antebellum period. From their 1818 membership of
2,235 members, the Methodists grew to 10,949 by 1846, almost a thousand of them black. Owing to the continued success of the circuit riders
and camp meetings, by the eve of the Civil War there were 50,000 whites
and over 11,000 blacks in the denomination. Much of this phenomenal
growth was due to the ability of Methodism to attract Mississippians
from every class of society. In many ways, the Methodist churches came to
mirror the society around them.

Baptist growth was not far behind. By 1824 Baptists in the state were
able to organize their first state convention; it was disbanded in 1829,
however, because of internal opposition to so "hierarchical" a body.
Baptists were divided along mission/anti-mission and other lines. Also,
the appearance of the primitive Christian, or restoration, movement cut
into Baptist numerical strength as Primitive Baptists and the Disciples of
Christ (also called Christians or Churches of Christ) gained a following in
the state.

Offsetting some of the losses due to this factionalism was the opening
of new territory to white settlement when the Choctaw and Chickasaw
cessions were made in 1830 and 1832. With the northern half of the state

available for white relocation, Baptists exhibited tremendous growth. In 1835 there were 10 Baptist associations with 107 churches having almost 5,000 members. Ten years later, the number of associations had doubled, the number of churches and membership had increased almost fourfold. By 1860 there were 41,482 Baptists with 305 ordained ministers and 596 churches.

The established denominations began to have new competition in the 1830s when, as just mentioned, the Campbellite movement entered the state. Actually some work had been done in the 1820s by these followers of Alexander Campbell. They were seen by other Protestants, especially the Baptists and Methodists, as troubling the Mississippi calm with "seeds of heresy, discord and disaffection." Although it is true that there were many debates and some tract writing among the various groups involved, much of the fight against Campbellism was simply for power and prestige. In fact, a number of Baptists, including William E. Matthews, became Disciples during the course of the period. Matthews had come from Alabama as a Baptist minister in 1828, but within a year had become a Disciple and had convinced three Baptist churches to follow Campbell's teaching. By 1860, there were almost 2,500 Disciples in the state in 24 churches.

Presbyterians and Episcopalians represented the high-church Protestant tradition in Mississippi. By 1829, the Mississippi Presbytery had grown enough to justify the creation of the Synod of Mississippi and South Alabama. This was followed six years later with the creation of the Synod of Mississippi with 24 churches having 800 to 900 members. Although the Presbyterians did not have the tremendous numerical increase of the Baptists and Methodists, by 1860 there were 148 Presbyterian churches, excluding those of the Cumberland Presbyterian movement.

Reaching out from the hills of Tennessee, the first Mississippi presbytery among the Cumberlands was organized in 1832. In many ways, Cumberland Presbyterians were more similar to Baptists and Methodists than to their fellow Presbyterians. They used a circuit riding system and eschewed a trained ministry. By 1860, there were 60 Cumberland Presbyterian churches in Mississippi.

Much closer to regular Presbyterians in class and order were the Episcopalians. Their work in Mississippi had begun in 1790 with the work of Adam Cloud in Natchez. Even he came into conflict with the

Catholic authorities for "preaching, baptizing, and marrying people contrary to the laws of the existing Government." Therefore, in 1795 his property was confiscated, and he was arrested and sent to New Orleans. There is no recording of further Episcopal work in Mississippi until 1820, when Christ Church at Church Hill in Jefferson County was organized by Cloud. Six years later the Episcopal Diocese of Mississippi was organized with four churches, five clergymen, and 100 communicants. The diocese became self-governing in 1849. Although never large in number, the Episcopal Church, under the able leadership of William Mercer Green, steadily grew during the last decade before the Civil War. By 1855 there were 30 clergymen, 33 parishes, and 941 communicants.

From the beginning of the nineteenth century until the 1840s, Mississippi Catholics were few in number. When Mississippi became a state in 1817, there was only one Catholic church in the state. The clergymen of the Church were poorly compensated; usually foreign-born, few of them were able to speak English well enough to minister to the needs of their parishioners. As the Irish migration of the 1840s and 1850s took place, the Catholic population in Mississippi also began to increase. By the mid-1850s there were at least six Catholic churches in the state. Although the times continued to be difficult, Mississippi was beginning to attract some American-born priests. By 1852 there were 6,000 Catholics in Mississippi and 11 priests.

The institutions of religion and slavery were in constant tension on the Mississippi frontier. The white Christian's "responsibility" for the slave's soul posed a vexing problem. There was little debate that the black person should be made aware of the Word of God, but the issue was how to present this message selectively. For the most part, masters encouraged their slaves to attend church with them in order to learn about God's admonition that servants should be obedient to their masters. Since by 1840 blacks made up a majority of Mississippi's population, this practice led to some rather one-sided statistics. In 1846 a Natchez Baptist church had only 62 whites out of 442 members and at Grand Gulf the comparable numbers were eight and 113.

At an early date blacks in towns began to seek acceptable alternatives to the repression the white churches imposed upon them. One of the most successful movements occurred in Natchez. There blacks attending the Wall Street Baptist Church first began to meet as a part of the church, but in a separate building with white observers present. A little later they established the Rose Hill Baptist Church and began worshipping without white intrusion.

The Rose Hill story was not typical, however. Legal measures were taken to insure that blacks did not become too independent. The Poindexter Code of 1821 provided that blacks could only assemble to worship with their master's written permission and at least two white persons present. The Code also forbade free blacks and mulattoes from serving as ministers. In practice, however, its provisions regarding slavery were seldom honored until abolitionist attacks on slavery began in the 1830s.

Throughout the antebellum era, white urban churches manifested quite a bit of flexibility in their dealings with blacks. One story coming from the period concerned the conversion of Prior Lee, a prominent white member of the Jackson community who was converted at a black revival meeting. He was so grateful that he had his slaves make bricks which he then donated for the erection of a white church. He made sure that blacks were allowed to use the basement for their worship services. Other communities had similar arrangements for black worship. In urban areas to some extent, but especially in the more prevalent rural churches, blacks had their most meaningful worship experiences in "prayer meetings," at some remove from the glances of prying whites. As one former slave in Simpson County recalled during the 1930s, blacks would often slip away to an arbor for their religious gatherings so that "we could sing praises and shout all us wanted to." There can be little doubt that they also added to the selective biblical canon which whites had given them.

In spite of white efforts to control the type of Christianity practiced by blacks, by the Civil War period black Christianity was far different from the white version. As Eugene Genovese indicates in *Roll, Jordan, Roll*, blacks throughout the South had taken Christianity, merged it with African antecedents, and made a religion which served their purposes and needs. Whites misinterpreted what had happened. In 1860 Southern Baptists in Mississippi officially acclaimed separate black worship— supervised by whites—as a laudable goal. This concern sprang from the failure of masters to instruct their slaves in the mere rudiments of Christianity. What the Baptists failed to understand was that *blacks* were instructing blacks in the type of Christianity they needed to understand in order to survive in this world.

When Northern abolitionists began to attack the institution of slavery during the 1830s some southern churchmen immediately came to its defense. James Smylie, a Mississippi Presbyterian, was one of the earliest defenders of the institution. He published his pamphlet on the subject in 1836, probably prompted by the fact that he was the owner of 53 persons, making him the third largest slaveholder in Amite County. The positive-good theories of Smylie gained widespread acceptance in Mississippi religious circles. In 1837 the Mississippi Baptist Convention declared that abolitionism was an attempt "to detract from the social, civil, and religious privileges of the slave population." As abolitionist attacks continued, however, others began to express doubts about the amount of "positive good" which had been exercised. In 1847 the Choctaw Baptist Association accepted a committee report which stated: "We feel that we cannot too earnestly recommend the utmost attention on the part of the ministers, churches, and christian owners to the *religious improvement of their servants.*" This direct reaction to abolitionist statements also called for plantation owners with at least 10 adult slaves to build houses of worship for them.

The most prevalent reaction to abolitionism was to distance the church from the problem. William Winans argued that ideally slavery should be done away with; but he added that man should not interfere with the workings of God who in his own time would end it. Jesus would destroy slavery at the Second Coming, which Winans estimated would occur around the year 2,000. Another Methodist minister made much the same point, arguing "that with the abstract subject of slavery, we have nothing to do, nor do we regard it as a subject on which the church has the right to legislate."

The period of the Civil War and Reconstruction caused a basic shift in Mississippi religion. Institutionally, southern churches formally separated from their national groups. Baptists and Methodists parted company with their kinsmen during the 1840s; Presbyterians had their break in 1861. Although other groups did not experience formal rupture, either because of regionalism (Cumberland Presbyterians) or universalism (Catholics), regional loyalty took precedence over religious ties. Although exceptions can be mentioned, members of the clergy seldom took part in political affairs. Once the Civil War did begin, however, churchmen wholeheartedly supported the southern cause. At Mississippi College, a Baptist school for young men, the entire student body became privates and the professors officers as they organized the Mississippi College Rifles. Clergymen often became infantry officers. Mark P. Lowery, founder of Blue Mountain College and father of a family of Baptist pastors, was a general during the conflict.

With the ending of the conflict, whites returned home determined that the church would be one aspect of Southern life which would not be reconstructed along Northern lines. Although some black membership continued in white churches, blacks were not given any authority in church governance. In some cases, blacks were evicted from white churches. But in most instances blacks were more concerned with independence in their religious worship than they were in taking over white edifices. Whites and blacks alike contributed to the formation of racially separate congregations and denominations.

Northern religious organizations were helpful in assisting black institutions during the Reconstruction era. In the field of eduction, Northern Methodists organized Shaw University (later changed to Rust College) in Holly Springs and a number of academies throughout the state at both elementary and secondary levels. The American Missionary Association founded Tougaloo College just north of Jackson; it became a nationally renowned liberal arts institution.

Northern Methodist organizations also assisted in the establishment of black local churches in Mississippi. The African Methodist Episcopal Church sent organizers to the South. The Colored Episcopal Church was organized with support from both Northern and Southern church organizations, although financial support was almost exclusively from Northern groups. Some church organizers, such as Thomas Stringer in Vicksburg, adroitly combined their religious functions with successful Reconstruction political careers.

One group of Mississippi black Baptists organized the General Baptist Missionary Convention. Most of the churches in this convention were small; Mt. Horeb in Greenville having 810 members and Rose Hill in Natchez with 400 members became the largest congregations. The proceedings of the annual meetings of the convention did not show evidence of any great distinction being made between urban and rural churches. All black churches were struggling, despite the aid provided by northern friends. The greatest problem faced by black churches during the post-Civil War era was an uneducated ministry. Churches were often warned to be wary of unlicensed ministers. Educational institutions for ministerial training such as Natchez College, Jackson College, and Roger Williams University (in Memphis) were supported insofar as a poor constituency could manage with the assistance of subsidies from the American Baptist Home Mission Society throughout the late nineteenth century.

There were frequent conflicts within the black Baptist churches during these decades. An item from the 1884 convention report is indicative of the problems black churches faced during this trying period: "The missionaries made good reports this year, financial and otherwise. No 'bogus conventions,' church troubles or 'imposters' were reported." In 1890 the General Baptist Missionary Convention, which by then included portions of Louisiana and Arkansas, united with the General Baptist Convention of Mississippi to form the General Baptist Missionary Convention of Mississippi. The newly consolidated convention consisted of 900 churches with 79,732 members.

In the post-Civil War period, white ethnic groups added to the changing religious complexion of the state. Aside from ethnic Catholics, Jews were the largest white minority ethnic group. French governor Bienville's Black Code of 1724 had prohibited Jewish settlement in the Mississippi area and the Spanish authorities later pursued similar policies. But the relative religious tolerance of the United States enabled Jewish merchants and peddlers to move into Mississippi during the early decades of the nineteenth century. By 1820, 100 Jews lived in the state. Anti-Semitism, which seems to surface during crises, occurred during the Union occupation of Mississippi. General U. S. Grant, noting the speculation and black marketing of cotton in the area under his control, promulgated an order demanding that all Jews leave the area. This singling out of an ethnic group was done in spite of a general knowledge that many businessmen were involved in the trade, and further that not all Jews who were businessmen were so involved. After the War conditions improved for the Jewish communities in Mississippi, congregations being established in Jackson, Vicksburg, Columbus, and other urban areas. The congregations being quite small, usually both Reform and Orthodox services would be performed at the same synagogue.

Other ethnic groups playing a role in Mississippi religion were Greeks and Syrians, both embracing the Eastern Orthodox faith. Their organizational development was similar to that of the Jews in that they first organized social and cultural clubs. When the group became financially strong enough to build an edifice and support a priest, a church would be organized. Depending on the size of the ethnic community,

Greeks would sometimes worship at the Syrian Orthodox Church, as they did in Vicksburg, or the Syrians at the Greek church, as in Jackson.

Mississippi never achieved the heterogeneous religious environment of Florida, Louisiana, or even Alabama. This was due partly to the state's continued reliance on an agricultural economy among white and black Protestant farmers and small businessmen. Even the numerous sectarian divisions prevalent in contiguous areas of Alabama, Tennessee, and Arkansas were lacking in Mississippi. The state continued to be a remarkably homogeneous Baptist/Methodist state.

The subject of "demon rum" tended to unite all the white Evangelical Protestants of Mississippi. Because their attitude toward drinking changed after the Civil War, they saw drinking as a sin in and of itself rather than seeing drink as an activity which could lead to the sin of drunkenness. Baptists led the fight. In 1882 a prohibition convention was held in Jackson, presided over by W. S. Webb, the president of Mississippi College. Frances E. Willard visited Corinth the same year, organizing the Mississippi Woman's Christian Temperance Union. Roderic Gambrell, son of *Baptist Record* editor J. B. Gambrell, edited *The Sword and Shield*, a prohibitionist journal. These efforts successfully led to the passage of a local option law in 1886. Since Mississippi was still a semicivilized frontier in the 1880s, feuds being settled by violent means, an anti-prohibitionist assassinated Roderic Gambrell in 1887. This influenced his uncle, J. H. Gambrell, to become a fervent evangelist on the temperance circuit.

Prohibitionists thought they were on the side of the angels, for by 1890 it was apparent that "a war between rum and righteousness raged, with the general movement in favor of the prohibition cause." While the counties of Mississippi's interior quickly voted "dry," the Mississippi River counties and those along the Gulf Coast remained "wet." This made hill country whites increasingly suspicious of blacks and white ethnics whose votes thwarted prohibition in those areas.

Possibly because of a hierarchical structure which tended to hold in check ministers intent on division, Methodists did not seem to have the internal division of Southern Baptists, Primitive Baptists, and the Christian Church. But these last three had to contend with two areas of friction throughout the nineteenth century; one was local church order, the other primacy of local organization over centralizing tendencies. The first of these, although causing some local churches to split, rarely became the source of major controversy; but it did indicate the need of decentralized church structures to avoid anarchistic tendencies.

Primitive Baptists adhered to strict church discipline long after other organizations had loosened most formal procedures. Letters from sister Baptist churches were not always honored; investigations of belief systems were sometimes made. Disfellowship of persons found to be in violation of the church's stands occurred most often in cases where personal moral codes were involved. In 1879, a member of a black Primitive Baptist church was disfellowshipped when he overstepped the bounds of his newly-found freedom: he had two wives. In the New Chapel Church in 1880, one of the sisters in the congregation stood up during a service, pointed her finger at a prominent man of the community, and stated she had accepted his offer to live in adultery. They were both excluded from fellowship. Merely charging someone with evil deeds did not mean that a kangaroo court was immediately formed, however. In 1877 at the Middletown Creek Church a young lady accused a young man of "horsing around" on a horseback date. The witnesses she had identified were not forthcoming at the hearing and charges were dismissed.

Moral grounds were not always the reason for disfellowship. The Elam Church at Water Valley excluded a female member in 1898 for "getting malicious with the church." A woman was excluded from the Middleton Creek Church in 1882 for "slandering her husband." Often family rifts were repaired through the intervention of the church.

Primitive Baptists, along with other groups, had taken stands against secret orders during the anti-Masonic period before the Civil War. Therefore, many members of secret labor unions and farm protest movements of the 1870s and 1880s were disfellowshipped. Once the secretive organizations either dissolved or came into the open, their members were not discriminated against in church membership.

The great theological struggle among Primitive Baptists late in the century was the Absolutist versus Conditionalist controversy. This had been an undercurrent in the church since its beginnings in the 1830s and 1840s; but it did not surface until the 1890s. Although referred to by other groups as "hardshells" because of their predestinarian views, Primitive Baptists came out of this period as Conditionalists. This meant that they allowed persons a greater role in their own salvation; this placed greater responsibility for personal actions on every individual.

Because of its decentralized structure, the Disciples of Christ movement does not lend itself to easy analysis. By 1891 there were 60 Disciples churches meeting in Mississippi, one-half with their own houses of worship. There were between 5,000 and 6,000 whites and 3,000 blacks in the denomination, with 32 white and 32 black ministers. But around the turn of the century a schism occurred over the issues of centralization and musical instruments. The former issue revolved around how best to marshal resources for missionary activities. The cooperationists argued that churches should band together for such activities but not through the use of missionary societies, since the societies tended to acquire a centralizing tendency of their own. Many people saw the use of musical instruments as another example of the modern church's apostasy from the purity of the New Testament church. During this period most antimission and anti-instrument forces joined under the banner of the Churches of Christ, with those of more liberal persuasion in the Christian Church (or Disciples of Christ). The 1906 religious census shows that more in Mississippi—again unlike the mountainous neighboring states—were members of the Christian Church than of the Churches of Christ.

Mississippi was a crossroads for Southern Baptist controversies of the nineteenth century. From the 1850s forward, Mississippi was one of the three states, along with Tennessee and Alabama, strongly influenced by the Landmark Movement. Its leading proponent, J. R. Graves, was personally popular throughout Mississippi Baptist circles, often preaching in revivals or debating spokesmen from other denominations concerning his exclusivistic doctrines of church polity. During the post-Civil War era, J. B. Gambrell, a much more moderate leader, became the most active spokesman for Baptist causes. As editor of *The Baptist Record*, Gambrell was able to sound the alarm on issues ranging from prohibition to centralization. His opposition to centralizing tendencies did not reach full fruition until later in the Texas phase of his career when he became prominent during the convention-wide debate over the formation of a Sunday School Board.

"Martinism" was the great controversy among Mississippi Baptists during the 1890s, riveting their attention for at least five years. They had been a party to a convention-wide struggle during that decade, having refused financial support to the Southern Baptist Theological Seminary in Louisville when its president, W. H. Whitsitt, would not "admit" that Baptists preceded the Protestant Reformation. Maybe because Whitsitt attended the 1897 Mississippi Baptist Convention at Grenada, there was no official talk of the controversy surrounding him. A person's presence at the particular gathering, however, was not a guarantee of reconciliation. M. T. Martin was indeed there, sitting quietly while a storm erupted around his doctrinal views. Referred to as "Professor," Martin had been a mathematics teacher at Mississippi College during the 1870s. Beginning in 1893, he preached throughout the state of a need for persons to be "re-baptized," since their earlier professions of faith may have been "inaccurate." This doctrine of "re-baptism," which was to become known as "Martinism," smacked of the Methodist belief in backsliding.

The "Martinism" controversy had been spread across the pages of *The Baptist Record* and associational minutes since 1895. Orthodox opponents of this doctrine were determined to stop the heresy in Grenada. A committee presented an unanimous report to the convention: "Resolved, that this Convention does not endorse, but condemns, the doctrinal views of Prof. M. T. Martin, as these views are set forth by himself and published over his own name in his pamphlet entitled 'The Doctrinal Views of M. T. Martin.' " Although this statement seems to have been the climax of the controversy, delegates to the 1905 meeting of the convention still heard faint echoes of the "Martinism" period. As for Whitsitt, he resigned his presidency in 1898, and Mississippi renewed its support of the seminary.

The anti-intellectual attitude of many Mississippians did not always translate into an anti-institutional bias. Churches were responsible for establishing the first viable institutions of higher education in Mississippi. In general, the earliest efforts were intended for the elevation of young women in female institutes, which were usually secondary schools or finishing schools. Both Baptists and Methodists were prominent in this phase of educational life.

In 1826, Hampstead Academy was founded in Clinton. By 1830 it had become Mississippi College, functioning under Presbybterian auspices. In order to help the struggling school financially, Presbyterians organized a lottery. This device did not solve long term problems, however, and Clinton gave the school to Mississippi Baptists in 1850.

Methodists had established Centenary College at Brandon Springs in 1841; but four years later it moved to Jackson, Louisiana. Although it was still a part of the Mississippi Conference, those ties loosened over time until Millsaps College was established in Jackson in 1892. Under the guidance of its founder, Harvard Law School educated Major Reuben

Millsaps, the school quickly established itself as one of the outstanding Methodist colleges in the South. Before the founding of Emory University and Southern Methodist University, Millsaps ranked second to Trinity (Duke) among Southern Methodist colleges in the size of endowment.

Although academies and colleges of all types were established by church groups, female colleges continued to be especially popular among the denominations down into the twentieth century. Baptists were given Blue Mountain College in 1920; it had been a private college since 1873. In 1912 Baptists also opened Mississippi Woman's College of Hattiesburg. It eventually became William Carey College, a co-educational institution. Among Methodists, Whitworth College (1859) in Brookhaven continued to be their largest post-secondary institution until financial problems during the Great Depression forced it to close. The state's Presbyterians relied on Southwestern College (1875) in Memphis for male education, since that institution was supported by the synods of five Southern states, including Mississippi. Belhaven College was established in 1893 in Jackson as a Presbyterian female college; it became co-educational in 1954. All of these institutions—male, female, and co-educational—offered both religious training for people going into church-related vocations and liberal arts instruction in a Christian setting.

The beginnings of the twentieth century marked the maturation of Protestantism in Mississippi. It is true that Protestant denominations continued to grow numerically, at times phenomenally, during the course of the century; but the last vestiges of the frontier were disappearing. Although the camp meeting tradition continued, it was now more of a social than a religious event. One participant at the Seashore camp meeting of 1900 stated, "It looks to us as if Methodist preachers have well nigh forgotten, or are fast forgetting, how to say 'Amen.' The responses we heard were few and feeble." The reports of the results of the round of camp meetings in 1902 were not encouraging: "They were not having success at conversions as they had formerly experienced." By the eve of World War I, denominational walls that had surrounded camp meetings were disintegrating as union meetings, usually sponsored by Presbyterians, Methodists, and "Campbellites," became the standard of the day.

This did not herald the beginnings of modernism in Mississippi churches, let it be noted emphatically. During the Progressive Era, Mississippi religious groups rarely enlisted in the cause for social better-

196 / Religion in the Southern States

ment. Not only did they not support crucial social legislation with general social purposes, they were not even able to get a statewide prohibition law until 1918. But social concern was being shown outside the political arena. Baptists in the state supported the building of a hospital in Jackson and a tri-state facility in Memphis; Methodists were engaged in similar building programs during the era. Both groups upgraded the orphanages they had long supported. The major efforts of Evangelical Protestants continued to be on evangelism and numerical growth.

The rallying cries of Evangelical Protestantism in twentieth century Mississippi were the three "E's": Expansion, Enlistment, and Enlargement. The religious census from 1906 through 1936 showed Southern Baptists winning the numbers game over Methodists. Trends within the decentralized black religious community were not as readily apparent since the religious statistics were unreliable. Almost certainly, the growth of black denominational institutions was at a standstill.

During recent years, Southern Baptists have so dominated the growth within white denominations as to claim an uncontested victory. A 1971 religious survey indicated that Southern Baptists were a majority of the religious adherents in 68 of the state's 82 counties. In only three counties, two predominantly black and the third on the Gulf Coast, did Southern Baptists fail to place first among denominational bodies.

Race relations continued to be the Achilles heel of Mississippi's religious bodies. During the 1960s, a white culture which had failed to wrestle with Christian social ethics all along, began under the stress of crisis to dictate its own terms. The leadership of black churches, with its relative freedom from the oppression of the segregated society, began to exercise its role as the catalyst of a freedom movement. As a result, black churches were often bombed or burned. Meanwhile, many well-meaning white ministers were either quiet or left the state. The White Citizens Councils were proving to be rather adept at silencing the men of God in their pulpits. Many promising ministerial careers were shattered—from the fertile fields of the Delta to the state's large urban churches. As Jewish leaders spoke out in favor of human rights, the anti-Semitism of the Ku Klux Klan gave rise to the bombing of a rabbi's home and temples in Jackson and Meridian. Although the civil rights movement in Mississippi had begun with a strong religious underpinning, young blacks were especially frustrated by the reaction of white churchmen and began to turn to alternative worldviews, such as black separatism and Marxism. In white churches, the world was so out of kilter that moderation was seen as a sign of courage.

Both Mississippi culture, black and white, and Mississippi religion survived the tumult of the 1960s. The exact nature of the survival is more difficult to determine. Sunday morning church services are still the most segregated events in the state. There is still a strong current of religious conservatism, as exemplified several years ago when five Episcopal priests, having become disenchanted with the liberalization of the church, took vows in the Eastern Orthodox tradition and entered a Mississippi monastery for instruction. But there also seems to be a new tolerance for diverging religious views in Mississippi—pluralism, if you will. During the 1970s many Baptists supported the conservative television evangelism of James Robison while others listened attentively to John Claypool, liberal minister of the Northminster Church in Jackson. Pentecostal groups, one of the fastest growing movements in the state, received implicit establishment recognition with the election of one of their own, Cliff Finch, as governor in 1975. For the most part, the 1970s were years of quiet introspection.

The story of religion in Mississippi has been one full of faith—and fatalism; brotherhood—and bigotry; peace—and platitudes; kindness—and the Klan. The tragedies of the past, especially the recent past, lead one to search for a prophetic voice which may give hope for the future. What Mississippians need now is reconciliation. A native son, Will Campbell, has been in such a "business" for many years. He grew up in Amite County, but not in the same world as that of that antebellum slaveholding Presbyterian James Smylie. Campbell has been at the forefront of the human rights struggle while at the same time attempting to heal the wounds of divisiveness. He recently recounted many of his experiences in *Brother to a Dragonfly*. To many, the allegory of his friend P. D. East is appropriate for the religious condition of Mississippi. According to East's story, an Easter chicken was born different from the other chicks in the barnyard; but over time it became just like everyone else. East, an atheist, was rather fond of jesting Campbell concerning his Christian beliefs. Finally, East asked him to state the essence of the Christian message—in 10 words or less! After thinking for a moment, Will replied, "We're all bastards but God loves us anyway." Man is the leveler; God is the elevator. Godless humanism is not what Mississippi, the buckle of the Bible belt, should fear most, but unChristlike Christianity. If Campbell's prophetic voice is heeded, Mississippi will not only endure, it will prevail.

Bibliography

Jessie L. Boyd. *A Popular History of the Baptists in Mississippi.*

Janice Byrd. "A History of the Jews in Mississippi," M.A. thesis, Mississippi College, 1979.

J. B. Cain. *Methodism in the Mississippi Conference, 1846-1870.*

Edward Riley Crowther. "Mississippi Baptists, Slavery and Secession: A Study in Religious Ideology," M.A. thesis, Mississippi College, 1981.

Charles Conrad Di Michele. "The History of the Eastern Orthodox Church in Mississippi," M.A. thesis, Mississippi College, 1968.

Fred R. Graves, compiler. *The Presbyterian Work in Mississippi.*

W. L. Hamrick. *The Mississippi Conference of the Methodist Protestant Church, 1829-1939.*

John G. Jones. *A Complete History of Methodism as Connected With the Mississippi Conference,* vols. 1 & 2 (1799-1845).

W. B. Jones. *Methodism in the Mississippi Conference, 1870-1894.*

Lewis G. Jordan. *Negro Baptist History, U.S.A., 1750-1930.*

J. Allen Lindsey. *Methodism in the Mississippi Conference (1894-1919).*

Charles Howard Lucas. "History of the Church of Christ in Mississippi," M.A. thesis, Mississippi College, 1964.

B. W. McDonald. *History of the Cumberland Presbyterian Church.*

Richard Aubrey McLemore. *A History of Mississippi Baptists, 1780-1970.*

Gene Ramsey Miller. *A History of North Mississippi Methodism, 1820-1900.*

James J. Pillar. *The Catholic Church in Mississippi, 1837-1865.*

_____. "Religious and Cultural Life, 1817-1860," in Richard A. McLemore, ed., *A History of Mississippi*, vol. 1.

Patrick H. Thompson. *The History of Negro Baptists in Mississippi.*

Ernest Trice Thompson. *Presbyterians in the South* (3 vols.).

MISSOURI

RICHARD M. POPE
LEXINGTON THEOLOGICAL SEMINARY

I

Missouri is strategically located at the heart of the North American continent and near the confluence of three great rivers. It has thus been historically shaped by cultural influences from both the North and the South.

The first human inhabitants were Indians. They hunted its great forests and fertile plains, fished its clear streams, cultivated its productive soil, and fought for possession of its land. Since they left no written records, our knowledge of their religion is limited. But through archeological investigation, oral tradition, and the reports of early travelers and traders we can know something.

While there were differences among the various tribes that lived in this area, in general it may be said that in their view, the world was inhabited by invisible spirits. They could be good, bad, or simply mischievous. These spirits could be controlled to some extent by the secret lore of medicine men. There were fetishes which could ward off evil or promote good, and there were signs and omens which should be followed. From time to time prophets emerged who could predict the future. They marked with religious rites the great moments in each individual's life, birth, puberty, marriage, and death. At death it was believed that the soul of the individual entered into the life of another world. Their worship was more danced out than thought out. They observed certain taboos in accordance with sacred tradition. There were also sacred times, such as the corn harvest, sacred places, such as a high hill, and sacred objects, such as a curiously shaped stone. In the world around them they sensed the power of a tremendous, mysterious force or excellence known in some tribes as "orenda" or "wakenda"—the "power that moves." This sense of the Holy, or the numinous, as it has been called, aroused in them over-powering feelings of both fascination and fear, as well as awe and wonder. Closely related to this sense of the Holy was their belief in a high god, generally known as the Great Spirit, and called Wah'kon-tah by the Osages, who ruled over all.

The religion of these earliest inhabitants of Missouri had in it a great deal of magic, superstition and fear, and lacked a coherent view of the world. But whatever may have been the weaknesses or failures of their faith, it enabled them to live harmoniously with nature, and there was much that was beautiful in their view of the land, the sky and the Great Spirit.

II

Missouri enters into the full light of history with the coming of French explorers, traders and missionaries in the last half of the seventeenth century. These intrepid men were motivated to endure the hardships and dangers of the wilderness by a desire to claim the vast Mississippi valley for France, by a drive for personal adventure and wealth, and last, but not necessarily least, by a concern for the conversion of the Indians to Christianity.

Among these adventurers were a number of missionary priests, such as Father Jacques Marquette (1637-1675), who in 1673 explored the Mississippi, and Father Louis Hennepin (1640-1701) of the Recollets who in 1679 further explored the region. From about 1700 to 1703 a Jesuit mission station near what is now St. Louis was in operation, and the first church in Missouri was built. About 1735 the first permanent settlement was made at St. Genevieve. In 1764 St. Louis was established and it quickly became the dominant town in the French territory of Louisiana, which included most of the area drained by the Mississippi River.

Thus the first settlements in what is now Missouri were founded by Roman Catholics and the influence of French culture was strong. But though the Louisiana territory was under the rule of France which recognized the Catholic church as the only approved faith, and though Protestants were by law prohibited from conducting public worship, marriages and funerals, in actual practice the French authorities pursued a rather tolerant policy in matters of religion. The founders of St. Louis—Pierre Laclede and Auguste Chouteau— for example, read and enjoyed the works of Rousseau, Diderot, and Voltaire, and other writings which reflected the secular, humanist influence of the Enlightenment. Further, settlers were needed if the Territory was to grow and flourish. So Protestant settlers entered the area in growing numbers and freely followed their faith.

In 1762 France ceded the Louisiana territory to Spain, gave it back to France in 1800, and then in 1803 Napoleon sold this magnificent realm to the United States. In accordance with the United States constitution and the Bill of Rights, religious freedom for all was then officially established, though in practice this ideal was not always faithfully followed. In any event, the population grew and in 1821, after much controversy, Missouri was admitted to the Union as a state and, further, as a slave state.

At about this time Roman Catholic immigrants—mostly from Ireland and Germany—began to settle in Missouri in large numbers. Earlier, Bishop DuBourg formed the first diocese in the State, built a cathedral (now a familiar landmark in St. Louis), and led in a renewal of Catholic life. Schools were established, usually under the rule of nuns, who also founded orphanages and hospitals. St. Louis University was chartered in 1832 under the leadership of the Jesuits. Missions to the Indians, seminaries, monasteries and convents were also brought into being. As it developed into one of the strongly Catholic cities in America, the diocese of St. Louis in time became an archdiocese. Throughout this time of steady growth the hierarchy and priesthood of the Catholic Church deserve great credit for the ways in which they ministered to their immigrant people as they struggled through the trauma of leaving their homeland and adjusting to life in a new and different world. Thus the Roman Catholic church became the largest religious body in Missouri, as well as the first.

III

Through most of the nineteenth century, wave after wave of Americans also poured into Missouri. The first great wave was made up largely of settlers from the states of the upper South—Kentucky, Tennessee, Virginia and North Carolina, and they gave to the state a definite southern character. They were also mainly Protestant in background, and of the denominations that evangelized, among them the Baptists, Methodists, Presbyterians, and Disciples were especially effective.

Baptists began to come into Missouri late in the eighteenth century, and it was a Baptist preacher from Kentucky who preached in February of 1794 what was probably the first Protestant sermon in what is now Missouri. But it was not until 1805 that a Baptist preacher from Virginia, David Green, formed near Cape Girardeau the first Protestant church.

Though some of their preachers, such as John Mason Peck, were well educated men, most of them were "farmer preachers" who largely supported themselves and had only a minimal education. They shared the hard life of their people. They labored during the week at clearing the land, plowing, planting and cultivating their corn patch, splitting rails and, if need be, helping a neighbor build a cabin or barn. Then on Sundays or during "protracted meetings," they travelled on horseback to preach the Gospel. They preached with fervent conviction that Jesus Christ brings to penitent believers forgiveness and new and everlasting life. The congregations they formed were covenant communities in which the members agreed to walk together and help one another live the Christian life. Errant members were subject to exclusion from their fellowship if they failed to reform their lives. Many, like the preachers Abraham Lincoln heard as a boy in Kentucky and Indiana, were inclined to believe the Calvinistic doctrine of predestination. But such dogma did not keep them from being aggressive evangelists and the Baptists (most of whom are now Southern Baptists) became in time the largest Protestant body in Missouri. They were also instrumental in founding several colleges, including William Jewell, Hannibal-La Grange, and Southwest Baptist College.

The Methodists, led by their circuit-riding preachers, also grew rapidly under the difficult and demanding conditions of the Missouri frontier. Their ministers are famed for their courage and hardihood in braving the elements and the many dangers of the wilderness in order to bring the Gospel to a rough and undisciplined folk. These preachers too, many of them, had been converted from a rough and turbulent life; they too, often had very little formal education, but they had the Bible, the Hymn Book, and the Book of Discipline in their saddlebags, whose contents they taught and used, and in addition they encouraged the reading of books from the Methodist Book Concern. Appointed by their Bishops to serve a circuit of churches and to form new ones, they preached as opportunity afforded—in cabins, in taverns, under brush arbors, or wherever a group could be gathered. Many of their converts came from camp meetings in which people camped together for a week or so to socialize, to sing and pray, and to listen to the heart-felt preaching that sought to celebrate the grace of God and to move the unregenerate to find pardon and new life in Christ. The doctrine they taught was Arminian—God's grace is freely available to all through Christ for all humanity. Perhaps their doctrine was best communicated through the great hymns they sang. Both Methodists and Baptists have established substantial seminaries in Kansas City. Today they constitute the second largest Protestant body in Missouri.

The people of the Christian Church (Disciples of Christ) also came into Missouri with the tide of immigrants from the East and South early in the nineteenth century. Theirs was a non-creedal faith which sought to bring about the unity of all Christians through a return to "simple New Testament Christianity." Like the Baptists they were led mainly by lay preachers, with little distinction being made between clergy and laity.

Elders Thomas McBride, T. M. Allen, and Joel Haden, all from Kentucky, were among the earliest Disciples preachers in Missouri. McBride founded what was probably the first Disciples church on Salt Creek in the "little Dixie" area of central Missouri in 1817.

Along with their commitment to the restoration of New Testament Christianity as the way to Christian unity, they developed the idea that salvation is not so much an event as a process—a process of logical steps that included faith, repentance, believer's baptism by immersion and growth in Christ through regular worship and the celebration of the Lord's Supper each Lord's Day.

Although led by lay preachers, Disciples ministers were frequently men who respected learning, and so it was natural that they should found colleges as well as churches. Among the schools that they founded which have survived are Culver Stockton, William Woods, Columbia, and the Missouri School of Religion, and since 1909 they have shared with the United Church of Christ in the support of Drury College.

But among the Protestants it has been the Presbyterians who have provided the most distinguished intellectual leadership to the churches and the culture of Missouri, and this from an early date. In 1816 one of the first Presbyterian churches in the state was formed by Salman Giddings near Potosi with the help of four elders who had moved there from North Carolina. Additional congregations were soon established and in 1819 the first presbytery was formed, and, ten years later the first synod.

Many of these Presbyterian ministers were commissioned and sup-ported by missionary societies back east. Well educated, they tended to be young and idealistic and were shocked by the crudity and squalor of frontier life. In time, however, they came to understand and appreciate the good qualities of the people whom they sought to serve. Timothy Flint, for example, a Harvard graduate, came to the St. Louis area and found it to be a godless place in which swearing, drunkenness, sabbath-breaking, slovenliness, and violence abounded. But ten years later his attitude had changed: without ceasing to deplore the drudgery and crudity of their lives, he could now see, and warmly praise, their hardihood, courage, generosity, and honesty.

With their insistence upon a learned ministry and their concern for education, the Presbyterians founded numerous colleges. Among those that have survived are Westminster, Park, Tarkio, Missouri Valley, the School of the Ozarks, and Lindenwood. They also shared with the Dutch Reformed and Associate Reformed Presbyterian churches in the estab-lishment of a mission school—Harmony Mission—for the Osage Indians.

In the nineteenth century the Congregationalists, working mostly through the American Home Missionary Society, founded a considerable number of congregations in Missouri. But they remained small and in the nineteenth century most of them faded away, perhaps because there was not a heavy migration of people from New England and the upper middle west into Missouri.

There was, however, some migration from the Northeast, and it tended to be made up largely of teachers, merchants, and other profes-sional people. Among these sons and daughters of the Puritans were some Unitarians. William Greenleaf Eliot, grandfather of the poet, T. S. Eliot, came out to St. Louis shortly after his graduation from the Harvard Divinity School and organized the first Unitarian church in the state in 1834. Then, a little later, he founded a school that developed into Washington University.

Another influential New Englander was W. T. Harris, a Connecticut school master, who came to St. Louis where in time he became superin-tendent of schools. Enamoured of the Idealist tradition in philosophy, especially as manifested in the thought of Hegel, he led in forming the Saint Louis Philosophical Society and in publishing the *Journal of Specul-ative Philosophy,* whose first issue came out in 1867. It was the first philosophical periodical in the English language.

Harris was especially attracted to Hegel's idea that history is a process of development, through struggle, towards a better human society. In this struggle the individual is gradually being liberated from the control of the group to which he belongs. Back of this progressive advance is the World Spirit and this Spirit is imminent in all things. From this Harris concluded that America, with its freedom and individualism and other democratic principles, represents the culmination of history. Against the atheism of Marx, and the agnosticism of Spencer, Harris thus posited a power that works for good. He found in Hegel what he believed to be an essentially religious view of the world's meaning. To Americans, at least, it could also mean that this is the best of all possible worlds.

It was in St. Louis that the first Episcopal parish, Christ Church, was formed in 1819. Its rector was Jackson Kemper who would later become the first Missionary Bishop of the Episcopal Church in America. In 1844 the first diocese was formed with Cicero Hawks as its Bishop, and in 1859 a beautiful cathedral was built. Eventually Episcopal parishes were established in every part of the state, though not so much in rural areas. With its strong sense of history, its concern for order and beauty in worship, and its leadership in the quest for Christian unity, the Episcopal Church exercised considerable influence on the religious life of the state.

Another religious group with a strong and poignant sense of history is Judaism. Jews were not allowed to enter the Louisiana Territory while it was under French and Spanish rule, but after it became a part of the United States a growing Jewish community came into being which was made up largely of immigrants from Germany and Poland. It was not until 1836, however, that regular services of worship were conducted. Three years later these services led to the organization of the first synagogue in Missouri—Acduth Israel. In the course of the nineteenth and twentieth centuries other synogogues were formed, in St. Louis, Kansas City, St. Joseph, Sedalia, Springfield, and elsewhere. Like their Christian counterparts, the Jewish religious community has divided along Orthodox (conservative), Conservative (moderate), and Reform (liberal) lines.

German settlers from the east and from abroad came into Missouri very early in its history. Indeed, the first resident Protestant minister in the state was probably Samuel Weyburg, a German Reformed pastor from North Carolina, who settled near Cape Girardeau in the 1800s. The settlers from the east were mainly the descendants of Germans who had settled in Pennsylvania and then in succeeding generations had moved to Ohio and Indiana or the Carolinas and then to Missouri. This migration included Lutheran, German Reformed, Evangelical (a union in Germany of Reformed and Lutheran churches), Moravian, Mennonite, and Church of the Brethren traditions. Then, through much of the nineteenth century there was a great wave of immigrants from Germany into Missouri. In religion, they included Roman Catholics (destined to become the largest religious group in Missouri), liberal intellectuals who were leaving what they believed to be oppressive conditions in their homeland, moderate members of the Evangelical church, Lutherans, and an ultra-conservative group from Saxony which in this country developed into the Lutheran Church Missouri Synod. This latter church is not confined to Missouri—it is to be found in most parts of the country as well as abroad—but its great strength is in the Midwest.

Influenced by pietism, its members have also sought to maintain strict fidelity to traditional Lutheran doctrine. Where liberals had left Germany because they felt it was too much bound by ecclesiastical and political despotism, the Missouri Synod Lutherans had left their homeland because of what they believed to be its growing drift towards rationalism and liberalism.

Arriving in the St. Louis area in 1839, their first years were difficult. But they found a strong leader in Carl Walther, and they became in time a growing and dynamic church.

With their concern for scholarship and for purity of doctrine, they quickly devoted themselves to founding educational institutions. In the same year as their arrival, 1839, they established Concordia Theological Seminary in St. Louis for the training of their ministers. Colleges and parochial schools for the proper education of their people soon followed. From these schools have come some of the outstanding scholars in the fields of biblical and historical studies.

Traditionally, they have held themselves aloof from other denominations. The central theological issue for them has been the nature of the inspiration and authority of the Bible, and it was over this issue, primarily, that they have in recent years suffered through a division that grew out of repeated clashes between conservatives and moderates.

The great immigration from Germany in the early and middle years of the nineteenth century made St. Louis a national center of Lutheran education, scholarship, and publication. But it is also true that many of these immigrants were farmers who sought and settled on land in every part of the state, although the spires and towers of their churches are especially to be seen on the prairies of western Missouri and in the villages and towns in the central part of the state. They frequently created communities known for their stability, and strong family ties, with the church as the center of their life. The Missouri Synod church at Freistatt, for example, has won national recognition for its effectiveness in creating a wholesome community in which religion and life are meaningfully joined together.

In all of this movement of diverse peoples into Missouri, we can see that a rich diversity is becoming a hallmark of its religious life. No one form of religion dominates the scene. And learning to live with this diversity did not come easily for those who were involved in it. There were denominational rivalries that at times became heated and bitter. This was especially true in the case of the Mormons.

As a young man of 18 living in upstate New York in an area known for its revivals and religious excitement, Joseph Smith, Jr. began to report visions of an angel who directed him to a place in a field where he dug up some writings on golden plates which he translated—with divine help—into the Book of Mormon. This was in 1827. He and some friends began to sell the book from door to door. The next step was the formation of a religious organization—The Church of Jesus Christ of Latter Day Saints, with Smith as the leader. As they grew they experienced the hostility of neighbors so they moved to Kirtland, Ohio. Here also they encountered suspicion and threats so that in the early 1830s they moved again, this time to Independence, Missouri, which Smith declared to be the "promised land," the "new Zion." But relations between "the saints" and the "gentiles" soon soured. The Mormons were accused of practicing polygamy and committing sacrilege. As they continued to grow they aroused the fear that they would eventually gain control of the area. Further, they were abolitionists, and this aroused the ire of the pro-slavery people who feared that they would incite slaves to rebellion.

Threats and some violence caused the Mormons to move out of the Independence area to Clay and Caldwell counties, and from there to Illinois where the familiar pattern of suspicion and hatred repeated itself. Smith was jailed, and then shot to death by a mob. After this, most of the Mormons, led by Brigham Young made a heroic trek in 1846 across the plains and mountains to their new Zion in the desert country of what is now Utah. However, the Reorganized Church of Jesus Christ, a smaller body produced by a division over leadership, has a number of churches in Missouri and continues to make Independence its national headquarters.

The history of black people in Missouri is, in an even more profound way, a story of suffering. For they came as slaves, first during the French and Spanish eras, and then in much greater numbers with the tide of immigration from the South. They worked in the lead and zinc mines, they labored to clear, plow, plant, and harvest the fields, they built fences, loaded and unloaded the steamboats and in general provided much of the labor that was needed to transform a wilderness into thriving farms, towns and cities. In 1821 Missouri was, after much controversy, admitted into the Union as a slave state. In 1860, on the eve of the Civil War, blacks constituted about 10 percent of the population.

Most of the slaves in Missouri did not work in gangs under an overseer, but rather worked with their owners, who typically owned only two or three slaves. This made for a more human and personal relationship. But in spite of the intention of many white masters to be just and good masters, the fact remains that families were separated and black people were subjected to the degradation of the slave system with its trade in human flesh.

For these reasons, and many others as well, the institution of slavery was a source of controversy among white church people almost from its beginning, and this controversy increased in intensity and violence—especially as slaves became more valuable. In Missouri, as in other border states, families, churches, and society in general were torn by dissension.

An ominous sign of the gathering storm may be seen in the murder of Elijah Lovejoy, a Presbyterian minister and editor. His strong anti-slavery articles in a paper he published in St. Louis so enraged proslavery sentiment that a mob destroyed his printing shop in 1836. Undaunted, he moved across the river to the free-soil of Alton, Illinois, from which he continued his attack on slavery. Again a mob destroyed his presses and this time murdered him as well.

Other signs followed. Church people opposed to slavery were increasingly willing to defy laws that established or perpetuated slavery. So, in the name of what they believed to be a higher law, they organized to help slaves escape to Canada and freedom via the "underground railroad." In 1841 two ministerial students and a young friend were tried, convicted, and sentenced to from three to five years for encouraging and helping blacks to escape from slavery.

In the 1850s a vicious border warfare broke out along the Missouri-Kansas line, with proslavery partisans making raids into Kansas to kill and burn, and equally bloody raids into Missouri by abolitionists. John Brown became nationally known as a violent abolitionist, and received guns and other support from church people in the north and east.

In this explosive atmosphere churches were torn apart. The Presbyterian, Methodist,and Baptist churches divided over the issue of slavery and so far only the Methodists have been able to find their way back to unity.

The controversy in the churches was by no means a simple matter of being for or against slavery. There was in it a tangle of other issues—such as the preservation of the Union—and in the churches several categories of people might be found. There were fire-eaters like James Shannon who defended slavery on arguments drawn from nature and the Bible; there were moderates who sought to find a gradual way by which slavery might be abolished without recourse to war; and there were abolitionists who in the name of God demanded an immediate end to slavery whatever the cost.

The rising tide of anger and conflict finally erupted into civil war in the spring of 1861. It continued for four long years, and Missouri endured her share of violence and disruption.

In their travail the black people of Missouri learned how to cope and how to endure. In this process they sometimes developed an inner strength and compassion that is impressive. Mark Twain (Samuel Clemens) knew blacks as he grew up in Hannibal, and when he worked with them as a riverboat pilot on the Mississippi. There is good reason to believe that his sympathetic portrayal of Jim, the friend and companion of Huckleberry Finn in his novel of that name, was drawn from life. A further illustration is that of George Washington Carver, who was born a slave in southwestern Missouri, but overcame severe handicaps to become an outstanding scientist, committed to helping poor farmers grow better crops.

In their years of bondage many black people became Christians, and after the Civil War they left the churches of their former masters and formed their own churches (mostly Baptist and Methodist) led by black preachers. These churches provided consolation and faith in times of adversity as well as a sense of dignity and worth. Their preachers were frequently men of natural ability who found in the church a place where they could exercise their talents and leadership. Indeed, the church offered not only spiritual guidance, but also music, some opportunity and incentive to learn to read and write, and support and counselling in time of crisis.

In the twentieth century secularism has bit deeply into the religious faith and practice of both blacks and whites, especially as they left farm and village to live in crowded city ghettos. But in these cities, such as Kansas City and St. Louis, black musicians created a new form of music—jazz, especially the blues—which sometimes expresses a religious dimension—a feeling of loneliness, abandonment, and sadness, in powerful ways.

IV

The Civil War represents a kind of continental divide in American history in the sense that after 1865 the United States became a rather different kind of nation. The frontier faded and in increasing numbers Americans lived in cities. New waves of immigration from central and eastern Europe helped to fill the burgeoning urban areas. The rise of universities with their humanistic and scientific point of view, the historical and critical study of the Bible, the Darwinian theory of evolution, the growing encounter with other religions, the technological revolution which annhilated space and time and made the world a neighborhood—these are only some of the forces that were creating a new kind of world with new problems and challenges to religion.

One of the leading characteristics of this post-Civil War era was the increasing pluralism of American religious life. Although this diversity was often due to ethnic and cultural differences, there were also, in many instances, theological conflicts, especially those which might be broadly categorized as a clash between liberal and conservative points of view. For example, in the late nineteenth century the holiness issue was a major factor in some splits away from the Methodist church. The Holiness movement was made up largely of people who believed that the Methodist church had become too worldly and liberal and had departed too much from the teachings of the founder, John Wesley. They were especially concerned to keep his doctrine of holiness, or Christian perfection, in which it was taught that a Christian should seek to receive a second blessing of entire sanctification, a state of being in which one's whole life might be centered on the love of God. A number of Holiness churches were formed out of this controversy, but in Missouri the Church of the

Nazarene has been especially strong, its international headquarters being in Kansas City.

The Pentecostal movement generally held to the doctrine of holiness, but in addition advocated the experience of Glossolalia, or speaking in tongues. They further believed in faith healing and, like most Fundamentalists, held to the inerrancy of Scripture. The Pentecostal movement has divided over various issues, but one of the largest of these divisions is that of the Assemblies of God. It makes Springfield its world headquarters, and in addition maintains there a publishing house, a graduate seminary, a training school called Central Bible Institute, and Evangel, a liberal arts college. Other Pentecostal bodies have headquarters in St. Louis and Joplin.

Missouri, like the rest of the nation, has also experienced an upsurge of interest in religious movements influenced by Asian religions, particularly forms of Hinduism and Buddhism. In some instances this influence has been mediated by the Transcendentalist ideas of Emerson and Thoreau. Some aspects of this strain of thought may be seen in the teachings of the Church of Christ, Scientist, which founded congregations in Missouri. This movement in turn influenced the founders of the Unity School of Christianity begun in 1889 in Kansas City by Charles and Myrtle Fillmore. The movement they launched grew and prospered, and a 1300 acre farm near Lees Summit, in the Kansas City area, was purchased and beautifully developed into a publishing, learning, and worship center. Unity accepts the reality of the physical world, and holds to a belief in reincarnation, but its aims are not so much theoretical as practical: it seeks to show people through the power of constructive thought the way to more abundant living.

If Missouri's growing religious pluralism has been due to some basic theological differences—as well as ethnic and social differences—then much of this conflict may be reduced to the fundamental conflict between liberalism and conservatism. These terms are notoriously difficult to define. That they are also relative terms is indicated by the fact that Southern Baptists are generally regarded as conservative by liberal Protestants, but to the independent Bible Baptists, who have built some of the largest congregations in the state, the Southern Baptist Convention is regarded as tainted with liberalism, or as harboring "modernists."

But these slippery terms may have some usefulness in considering the differing ways in which religious people reacted to the modern world.

Liberals, for example, have tended to be more open to the culture of the twentieth century, more willing to accept the scientific world view, while conservatives have been more resistant to change, more critical of science—especially Darwinian evolution—and more loyal to the traditional beliefs and practices of their faith.

Conflicts over these and other issues troubled nearly all forms of religion in the post-Civil War era, and these conflicts have continued right up to the present. In 1889, for example, a Disciples minister in St. Louis, R. L. Cave, preached a series of sermons in which he stated that he could no longer believe in the virgin birth or physical resurrection of Jesus. Forced to resign by a majority of the church members, he led a minority in founding one of the first community churches in America. A little later, another Disciples minister, Burris Jenkins, developed a community church which became one of the most controversial congregations in the state.

In some cases liberal-conservative tensions led to disruption, as when the Disciples divided into the Churches of Christ, the Independent Christian churches, and the Christian Church (Disciples of Christ), or, most recently, when the Lutheran Church (Missouri Synod), the Presbyterian Church U.S. and the Episcopal Church, suffered through the trauma of division (the last two in less major ways).

It should be remembered, however, that these and other divisions are counterbalanced by a strong and sometimes dramatic surge towards Christian unity in which Roman Catholics, Episcopalians, Methodists, Presbyterians, and Disciples have given conspicuous leadership. The cause of Christian unity has also been served by the Missouri School of Religion in Columbia, which has offered courses in religion at the University of Missouri, and for awhile won national recognition for its efforts to bring small churches in rural communities together to form one strong church which could more effectively serve the needs of the people.

But by and large Missouri remains a rather conservative state and is generally considered to be a part of the Bible Belt that reaches across much of the South. This conservatism is especially marked in the Ozark hill country, as is illustrated by the extreme case of the small town of Liberal, Missouri. Founded in 1880 by G. H. Walser to be a refuge for free-thinkers, the founder boasted that the village had no priests, preachers or peace officers, no churches or saloons, and no loafers or beggars. When some Protestants tried to settle at the edge of his town

Walser built a fence to try to keep them out. But in the course of time the enterprise began to fail financially, the founder became a convert to spiritualism, several Protestant churches moved in, and the whole episode is largely forgotten except as it may appear in sermon illustrations.

On a more significant level, Missouri was the birthplace of one of the nation's greatest theologians, Reinhold Niebuhr. Born in Wright City, where his father was the pastor of the local Evangelical and Reformed church, Niebuhr studied at Elmhurst College, Eden Theological Seminary, and the Yale Divinity School, and then became pastor of a small mission church in Detroit. There he became aware of the plight of the industrial worker whose cause he subsequently championed. He became nationally known as a prophetic speaker and writer. In the late 1920s Niebuhr became a member of the faculty of Union Theological Seminary in New York where he lived out the busy years of his distinguished career.

In his early years Niebuhr had been a liberal, a socialist, and a pacifist, but the rise of the Nazis to power in Germany led him to a new consciousness of the inherent and inescapable sinfulness of human nature. There was for him no possibility that a utopia might be established on earth. Yet man must act and shoulder the responsibilities that must be borne. The Bible, which he took seriously but not literally, provides a more realistic and profound view of human existence than did other religions and ideologies. At the end, he believed that the Bible also offered hope and the promise of forgiveness through a God who is the transcendent Lord of all life and history. Thus he found both liberalism and conservatism inadequate, and found in biblical religion that Word of God which brings both judgment and mercy.

In retrospect, we can see that the history of religion in Missouri is one in which, as Niebuhr might have taught, there is a mingling of vision, courage, pride, tragedy, and new beginnings. It is also, as this sampler might suggest, a history in which there is constant change and elaboration. As to the future, of only one thing can we be sure: like one of the clear, fast flowing streams of the Ozark hill country, movement and some surprising turns will continue to mark the history of this state and its people.

Bibliography

Ahlstrom, Sydney. *A Religious History of the American People.*

Everett Dick. *The Dixie Frontier.*

William E. Foley. *A History of Missouri, 1673-1820.*

Samuel S. Hill, Jr. *Southern Churches in Crisis.*

John Joseph Matthews. *The Osages: Children of the Middle Border.*

Duane Meyer. *The Heritage of Missouri: A History.*

Missouri: A Guide to the "Show Me State." Compiled by Workers of the Writers' Program of the Works Project Administration in the State of Missouri.

Perry McCandless. *A History of Missouri, 1820-1860.*

Edwin C. McReynolds. *Missouri: A History of the Cross-Roads State.*

Paul C. Nagel. *Missouri.*

William E. Parrish. *A History of Missouri, 1860-1875.*

Henry A. Pochman. *German Culture in America.*

Reinhold Niebuhr: His Religious, Social and Political Thought. Edited by Charles W. Kegley and Robert W. Bretall.

Earl T. Sechler. *Our Religious Heritage: Church History of the Ozarks, 1806-1906.*

NORTH CAROLINA

JOHN R. WOODARD
WAKE FOREST UNIVERSITY

Religious activity in colonial North Carolina dates from the Ralph Lane Colony that sailed from Plymouth, England, in 1585. A clergyman accompanied this and subsequent groups. The Lane Colony returned to England with Sir Francis Drake in 1586. The next year another colony was sent out under John White; they returned to Roanoke Island in July 1587. Within two weeks the first recorded Protestant baptism in the New World took place when a friendly Croatan Indian, Manteo, was baptized. This has come to be known as the famous "Lost Colony" because it disappeared.

The first permanent settlers in the state followed the streams in southeastern Virginia that emptied into the Albemarle Sound in north-eastern North Carolina. There were already well-established settlers in this area when Charles II granted a charter to the eight Lords Proprietors in 1663. The proprietors were to have "the advowsons and patronage of churches" and were authorized to grant liberty of conscience to all persons who should conform to the practices and beliefs of the Anglican Church.

Although the intent of the Royal Charter and subsequent instructions to the Royal governors were for the Church of England to be the established church in North Carolina, its inaction and neglect played into the hands of dissenting groups, notably the Quakers. This group had become very influential in political affairs in the Albemarle region. According to one history, they constituted only about one-seventh of the total population but were better organized than any other religious body.

In 1704, John Blair, an Anglican missionary, described the religious sentiment in the colony when he wrote:

> The country may be divided into four sorts of people: first the Quakers, who are the most powerful enemies to church government, but a people very ignorant of what they profess. The second sort are a great many who have no religion, but would be Quakers, if by that they were not obliged to lead a more moral life than they are willing to comply to. A third sort, something like the Presbyterians which sort is upheld by some idle fellows who have left their lawful employment, and preach and baptize through the country without any manner of orders from any sect or pretended Church. A fourth sort, who are really zealous for the interest of the Church are the fewest in number, but the better sort of people. And would do very much for the settlement of the Church government there, if not opposed by these three precedent sects: and though they be all three of different pretensions, yet they all concur together in one common cause to prevent any thing that will be chargable to them, as they allege Church government will be, if once established by law.

In 1701 the colony's first church law, the Vestry Act, was passed. This legislation provided for the laying out of parishes, the organization of vestries, the erection of churches, and a poll tax on all tithables for the support of the clergy. In 1703 an act provided that an oath be taken by members of the General Assembly that they were communicants of the Church of England, which repealed the right of affirmation that the Quakers had enjoyed for years. The dissenters continued to be opposed to these various acts, but the government continued to pass laws and vestry acts in 1758, 1760, 1761, and 1762. Finally in 1765 a Vestry Act was agreed upon. William Tryon, Royal governor and zealous churchman, kept requesting that clergy be sent from England to assist the Established Church.

In 1776 North Carolina adopted a new constitution. There would be no established church, no compulsory attendance at religious worship, or compulsory support of any religious organization. All citizens would be at liberty to exercise their own "mode of worship." Clergymen could not serve in the General Assembly while still exercising their pastoral functions. No person "who should deny the being of God or the truth of the

Protestant Religion, or the Divine Authority of the Old or New Testament, or who shall hold Religious Principles incompatible with the Freedom and Safety of the State" would be eligible for public office.

These provisions caused some problems in later years. John Culpeper and William Taylor in 1801 and Joshuah Crudup in 1820 were expelled from the legislature because they were practicing ministers. This was an unpopular cause since both Culpeper and Crudup were elected to the national Congress. An effort to expel Joseph Henry, a Jew from Carteret County, failed in 1809. In 1833 William Gaston, a Roman Catholic, was elected to the Supreme Court of North Carolina. The Constitutional Convention of 1835 met to redress this problem and others. Despite a two-day address by William Gaston against religious tests for office, the convention only substituted "Christian" for Protestant in the clause, thus removing the test for Roman Catholics but not for Jews. It was not until the Constitution of 1868 that this was changed and then only atheists were barred from holding public office.

Despite governmental support for the Anglican Church the Society of Friends (Quakers) was the most important religious group in the colony before 1700. The earliest recorded missionary to North Carolina was the Quaker William Edmundson, the founder of the Quaker faith in Ireland. He first came to America in 1672 with George Fox, founder of the Society. By May 1672, Edmundson was preaching his first sermon near present-day Hertford in Perquimans County. If his observations were correct, the settlers of the Albemarle Sound area at that time had "little or no religion." They did attend his preaching and he won two converts. Later in November of the same year George Fox visited the area and did evangelistic work for eighteen days. Fox came again in 1676-77 and found the Friends to be "finely settled."

According to William P. Johnson the signing of the Carolina Charter in 1663 probably served as an impetus to migration, and hundreds of settlers began to pour into the northeast in the 1660s and 1670s. A large number came from lower Virginia into the Albemarle area. In the western part of the state New Garden meeting in Guilford County was established in 1754 and populated largely by New England Quakers from Nantucket. This became the most important Quaker settlement in North Carolina.

By the end of the American Revolution, the Friends' opposition to the war had cost them in both numbers and growth. They had also retired from public life; as a result their political influence declined. They did continue to pioneer in prison reform and the care of the insane. From the beginning North Carolina Friends were deeply involved in the anti-slavery movements. It was this last fact that caused many families to leave the state and its slave-holding society for the lure of fertile farm land and greater freedom in the Northwest Territory. They migrated to Indiana and other midwestern states.

The state's Quakers were organized in a series of meetings. The first day meetings for worship; the Monthly Meetings for congregational business; Quarterly Meetings combined worship and business for a group of congregations in a specific geographical area; Yearly Meetings were and are the units of Quaker jurisdiction over a given geographic area. The North Carolina Yearly Meeting of the Religious Society of Friends dates from 1698. By the 1860s there were twenty-five monthly meetings established in North Carolina.

The Friends suffered further during the Civil War because of their opposition to war and their antislavery sentiments. Many were conscripted to work in the state salt works on the coast. Others paid substitutes in lieu of military service. After the Civil War they received financial support and other materials from coreligionists from other states.

The Friends had a deep interest in the support of education. Guilford College was chartered in 1833 as New Garden Boarding School. It opened in 1837 and unlike the state university and other denominational schools Guilford was coeducational from its beginning. After the Civil War concern was shown for the emancipated blacks. Schools were established to serve them, these often being operated by volunteers.

Return migration from the midwest helped the Friends to grow. Former North Carolinians and their families came back from southern Ohio and Indiana. By 1876 membership had climbed to 5,500. Clothing and encouragement had been sent by Baltimore Friends to assist people devastated by war. With outside assistance, schools were established and schoolhouses rebuilt. Then in 1874 the Society of Friends experienced a great revival. Eleven years later the first Woman's Missionary Society met at New Garden. Publication of a newspaper, *The Friends Messenger* began in 1904 and lasted until 1932, to be replaced by *The Friends News Letter*, now the chief means of communication for North Carolina Friends. According to 1971 statistics the Friends have 73 churches with a total membership of 12,511, most of them concentrated in the central Piedmont.

The first missionary sent to North Carolina by England's Society for the Propagation of the Gospel (S.P.G.) was Daniel Brett, who probably arrived in the year 1700. Little is known of his work. Following Brett the Reverend John Blair came by way of Virginia, arriving among the people of the Albemarle in 1704. The S.P.G. that sent these missionaries was the missionary arm of the Church of England. It provided financial and moral support for some thirty-seven missionaries who served in North Carolina between 1701 and 1775. The most promising young men, however, did not come to the wilderness of North Carolina. The Reverend C. E. Taylor wrote of his parish and predecessor: "I have therefore settled myself for a while in St. George's Parish, Northampton County, void by the Resignation of Mr. Barnet, one of the Society's Missionaries who I am informed has fled into Virginia being charged with crimes too base to be mentioned."

Despite being the state religion, encouraged and supported by government officials, the Church of England did not enjoy the favor of a majority of the inhabitants of North Carolina. The people of this province and colony were more concerned with conquering a frontier and having ample provisions in store than with supporting an established clergy.

By the close of the Proprietary period in 1729, the S.P.G. had sent a few missionaries, and provided a library. Also several chapels had been erected but little else had been done. In 1739 Governor Gabriel Johnston called the Assembly's attention to the fact that there were only two places in the Province where divine services of the Established Church were regularly performed. By the end of Governor Tryon's term in 1770 there were ministers in 18 of the 22 parishes.

The American Revolution ended any influence that the Church of England may have had in North Carolina. The 1776 State Constitution did away with the idea of an established church. Many of the ministers left the state because of their understanding of the oath they had taken to the king. Chapels and meeting places were abandoned or taken over by other denominations. It was many years before the Protestant Episcopal Church with any significant effect was to take the place of the Church of England.

Baptists were among the first permanent settlers of North Carolina. The first record of their presence in the colony was contained in a letter written by John Urmstone, an Anglican minister, on 12 June 1714 in which he complained that two of his vestrymen in the Chowan Precinct were "professed Anabaptists." The first Baptist minister of record was Paul Palmer, a native of Maryland, who was living in Perquimans Precinct in 1720. His missionary endeavors led to the formation of North Carolina's first Baptist church in 1727 in Chowan County. This church existed for several years and then disappeared. Palmer was also the founder two years later of Shiloh Church in Camden County. This church is the oldest extant Baptist church in the state.

Seventeen General Baptist churches had been formed in the eastern part of the state by 1754, according to one historian. The next year many of these churches transferred to the Particular Baptist persuasion, largely through the efforts of Benjamin Miller and Peter P. Vanhorn, evangelists from the Philadelphia Baptist Association. The Jersey Settlement and Baptist Church under the leadership of Benjamin Miller and John Gano was the Particular Baptist enterprise that influenced the piedmont section of the state.

The same year, 1755, saw the founding of Sandy Creek Baptist Church south of Greensboro by Shubal Stearns and Daniel Marshall. The coming of the "New Lights" or Separate Baptists, and the formation of Sandy Creek was to prove the most significant event in North Carolina Baptist history. This congregation was to become not only the mother of other local churches but the mother of all Separate Baptists in the Southern states. In the first 17 years of the church's existence, Morgan Edwards wrote, 42 churches and 125 ministers had "sprung from the parent church." They were called "New Lights" because of their belief in the possibility of individual inspiration and enlightenment through the Holy Spirit. They were called "Separates" because of their desire to separate themselves from the Congregational Church and organize independent societies.

In the eastern part of the state the Particular Baptists began to call themselves "Regular Baptists" to emphasize the distinctiveness from Separates. Most of the eastern North Carolina Baptist churches had been members of the Charleston (SC) Baptist Association from its beginning in 1751 but the distance from the main body made this affiliation impractical. Therefore, on 6 November 1769, the delegates from five churches formed the Kehukee Baptist Associaton, the second oldest association in North Carolina, and the first in which the Separate and Regular Baptist churches united. Distinctions between the two soon were obliterated. The Kehukee Association included all the Baptist churches in eastern North Carolina with the exception of two or three of the Free Will order.

During the seventy-five years immediately following the organization of Shiloh in 1729, Baptists had spread from the Atlantic Ocean to the Tennessee border and had organized these churches into associations for cooperative activities. According to David Benedict there were 11 associations, about 200 churches, and some 13,000 Baptists in North Carolina by 1812.

By 1805 Baptists under the leadership of Martin Ross began to take an interest in the support of missionary activities. A "Baptist Philanthropic Missionary Society" was organized in 1805. In 1811 a corresponding body called the "General Meeting of Correspondence" was organized. This body lasted until 1821 when it was supplanted by the North Carolina Baptist Society for Foreign Missions (later Foreign and Domestic Missions) that had been formed in 1814. Again Martin Ross took the initiative and introduced a resolution in the 1826 annual meeting of the Chowan Baptist Association, calling for the formation of a Baptist state convention. Unfortunately he died before plans could be completed for this state-wide unification of Baptists.

In 1820 Joshua Lawrence presented a document entitled "Declaration of the Reformed Baptists in North Carolina" to the Kehukee Association. A year later the majority of the thirty-five churches in the Kehukee had endorsed Lawrence's proposal to "discard all Missionary Societies, Bible Societies, and Theological Seminaries, and the products heretofore resorted to for their support, in begging from the public." The mission-minded churches began to withdraw from the Kehukee Association. Several churches in the Kehukee and other associations split over the issue of supporting missions. Shortly thereafter the anti-mission elements adopted the name of Kehukee Primitive Baptists.

The friends of Martin Ross and of missions sought to revive organized Baptist work in the state. On 10 February 1829, several ministers and laymen met in Greenville and formed the North Carolina Baptist Benevolent Society. When they convened the next year they adopted the following resolution: "That this Society be transformed into a State Convention." At this time there were 14 Baptist associations, 272 churches, and "upwards of 15,360 members," according to Thomas Meredith. They were interested in supporting state missions and soon realized that this involved the development of a state newspaper, a college, and Sunday schools.

Early in 1835, Thomas Meredith's new periodical, the *Biblical Recorder,* was issued after a trial issue the year before. This became the voice of the missionary Baptists in the state; except for the year 1842 and a short suspension in 1865 the *Biblical Recorder* has been published continuously.

In 1833 Wake Forest Manual Labor Institute was chartered. Its doors were opened for the education of young ministers in 1834, with 72 students attending the first session. The institute was rechartered as a college in 1838. In 1956 it moved from its first location in Wake County to Winston-Salem and ten years later it became Wake Forest University.

Delegates from west of the Blue Ridge Mountains found it difficult to participate because of the difficulties of travel. That largely accounts for the formation of the Western Baptist Convention in 1845. It organized three boards and supported Judson College and Mars Hill College as educational institutions, and several newspapers as well. When travel became easier these Baptists of the West sought to reunite with the state convention, accomplishing that goal in 1898.

Sunday school activities were not neglected. In 1845 the North Carolina Baptist Sunday School and Publication Society was organized to promote the work. The state convention organized a Sunday School Board in 1863 that took over the Society's work.

In 1860 North Carolina Baptists had 780 congregations with a total of some 65,000 members—already the largest denomination in the state. During the Civil War Baptists were very active in supplying tracts and Bibles to the Confederate soldiers.

During the 1870s the Convention began to show an interest in new fields of activity, among which were the care of orphans and the work of women's missionary societies. The Thomasville Orphanage was finally opened in 1894 under John H. Mills. The scattered woman's societies came together in a state organization in 1877 as the Central Committee, later the Woman's Missionary Union. Fannie Exile Scudder Heck, its first president (1886-1887) later became president of the Woman's Missionary Union of the Southern Baptist Convention. In this same period, the education of women became a concern of the Convention when the Baptist Female University was chartered in 1891. This became Meredith College, located in Raleigh, in 1909. In 1899 the former Chowan Baptist Female Academy (now Chowan College) joined the Convention's other schools.

After World War I a cooperative endeavor with the Southern Baptist Convention to raise 75 million dollars led to the formation of the Unified Program, that became the Cooperative Program. Another result was the establishment of the North Carolina Baptist Hospital in Winston-Salem, which opened its doors to patients in 1923.

The Convention took over the operation of Mars Hill College in 1911; Campbell College (now University) in 1925; Gardner-Webb College in 1948; and Wingate College in 1949.

The Baptist Children's Homes and the Baptist Homes for the Aging have also expanded their activities and presence over the state. A new headquarters building was completed in Raleigh in 1955 and at present plans are being made for an expanded state headquarters complex on the outskirts of Raleigh.

North Carolina Baptists continue to be the largest Protestant denomination in the state. In 1981 that body reported 3,452 churches and a total membership of 1,129,735.

After the Civil War black Baptists generally withdrew to form their own churches, associations, and even denominations. The American Baptist Home Mission Society (northern) sent workers and financial assistance into the state. Shaw University was established in Raleigh, largely through the efforts of H. M. Tupper. Other Baptist schools and academies for blacks were supported. The Baptist Educational and Missionary Convention of North Carolina (now the General Baptist Convention) was organized in Goldsboro in 1867. A century later, in the 1970s and 1980s, both the General Baptist Convention and the Baptist State Convention of North Carolina had joint annual meetings. A few black churches have affiliated with white associations. Black Baptists have established the *Baptist Informer* as their state newspaper.

Free Will Baptists in North Carolina began their history with the work of Paul Palmer (1692-1763), a General Baptist preacher, whose threefold doctrine consisted of free grace, free will, and free salvation. He first organized the "church in Chowan" in 1727, and then Shiloh in 1729. Both Missionary and Free Will Baptists trace their beginnings to this church. By 1750 other churches had been organized in eastern North Carolina and northeastern South Carolina. Some of these churches were those that Benjamin Miller and Peter P. Vanhorn could not convert from General to Particular in 1755. Joseph and William Parker are given the credit for saving these five churches for the Free Will Baptists.

By 1800 total membership was reported at 25,000. Eastern North Carolina was and remains the stronghold of the denomination. The General Conference of Free Will Baptists was meeting as early as 1807 according to one historian. This conference divided into the Bethel and Shiloh Conferences that met until 1842 when they reunited into the

General Conference. In 1886 they split into the Eastern and Western Conferences. Cape Fear Conference was formed in 1855, the Pee Dee in 1869, and Central in 1895. In 1839 the General Conference listed 2,006 members and 32 preachers. The Conference of 1884 listed 7,649 members and 82 ministers in 111 churches. In 1913 the State Conference was organized. They began the Free Will Baptist Press (dating to 1873); an orphanage at Middlesex (1920); Cragmont Assembly at Black Mountain; a seminary (founded in 1896); Eureka College (founded in 1925); and Mount Olive College (1952). A split came in the North Carolina Free Will Baptist ranks in 1958 over the recognition of a minority by the Western Conference. As a result the General Conference of Original Free Will Baptists was organized in 1961, and the North Carolina Association of Free Will Baptists came into being in June of 1962.

In the colonial period the Presbyterian Church in North Carolina, like the Episcopal Church, enjoyed a prestige far out of proportion to the number of its followers. Its ministers had the reputation for education and leadership and its layman for sobriety and industry that made Presbyterianism a term of approbation. Organized Presbyterian work came into the piedmont areas of North Carolina from the 1730s to 1770s when the Scotch-Irish swarmed into the piedmont from Pennsylvania, then down the Valley of Virginia to settle on the edge of the North Carolina frontier. They quickly appealed to the synods of New York and Philadelphia for missionaries and ministers, and these synods responded to their call.

In the eastern part of the state there were Scotch-Irish Presbyterians on the Henry McCulloh grants in Duplin and New Hanover counties as early as 1736. The first large group of Highlanders from Scotland made their way up the Cape Fear River and settled in the Cross Creek area (now Fayetteville) in 1746. They scattered themselves over an area that now includes Bladen, Cumberland, Sampson, Moore, Robeson, Richmond, and Anson counties; a section which to this day is a stronghold of Presbyterianism. These Scottish Highlanders spoke only Gaelic, a fact which protected them from nearby Baptists and others, and kept them faithful to the Calvinist tradition even when they had no pastors.

In 1770 the Orange Presbytery held its first meeting at Hawfields. By 1788 the Synod of the Carolinas was composed of three presbyteries, namely Orange, South Carolina, and Abingdon. In 1795 Concord Presbytery was set off from Orange. Then in 1812 the General Assembly of the Presbyterian Church was petitioned to establish the Synod of North Carolina, the new synod boasting 31 ministers, 85 churches, and about 4,000 communicants the next year.

According to one historian "a coldness and want of energy" had pervaded the Presbyterian Church in North Carolina. There had been ruptures in the denomination, of which the 1837 split was felt the most, involving the Old School and the New School. Between 1838 and 1849 Presbyterians were increasing at the rate of less than one hundred per year, but in the 1850s a new spirit arose in the church. As a result the denomination increased its interest and support in contributions, foreign and domestic missions, and evangelism. This last activity came too late for the Presbyterians to compete with the Baptist and Methodist denominations, however. From 1813 to 1860 the number of churches had increased by only 99. They were generally in the principal towns and villages of the piedmont and Cape Fear sections of the state. In the west there were churches at Wilkesboro, Lenoir, Asheville, Morganton, Marion, and Statesville, but the denomination had scarcely penetrated the Northeast.

On 1 November 1861, the Synod of North Carolina meeting in Raleigh, voted to join the formation of the General Assembly of the Presbyterian Church in the Confederate States. During the Civil War chaplains were supplied to the soldiers, and collections were taken for the benefit of orphans, and the education of children of deceased soldiers. In this four-year period the Presbyterian Church in North Carolina gained only eight ministers and five churches, and lost more than 2,000 communicants.

The 1870s and later decades saw the denomination turning to evangelizing as the country became more settled. The denomination even had a "Committee on Aggressiveness" to further its evangelizing efforts but synodical Home Mission endeavors did not begin until 1887. One of the immediate results was the establishment of a home for orphans, now at Barium Springs.

The Presbyterians were the first denomination in the state to attempt the establishment of a college with the founding of short-lived Queen's College in the 1770s in Charlotte. Individual Presbyterians had been prominent in the early history of the University of North Carolina, but they were not successful in founding a permanent college until 1837 when Davidson College opened its doors to young men; it was chartered by the state legislature late in 1838.

The North Carolina Synod of the Presbyterian Church in the United States was composed of seven presbyteries in 1975, with 677 churches and 821 ministers. Most of the black churches, located primarily in the

Cape Fear area, belonged to the northern branch of the Presbyterian Church.

The interpretation has been offered that "the fact that Presbyterians considered it a mark of vulgarity not to be able to read or repeat the Shorter Catechism in a time when half the people of the State were illiterate was sufficient to set them apart from the adherents of other denominations." The gentry and middle class dominated the membership at a time when the other denominations in the state were making great numerical gains. The discipline within the family and the church's continued efforts to educate its youth has been a significant contribution to the state through the years.

The first Lutherans in the original colony of North Carolina were wiped out by the Indians in 1711. Permanent Lutheran congregational life in the state can be said to date from the mid-eighteenth century flow of German immigrants from Pennsylvania. They came down the Shenandoah Valley into piedmont North Carolina bringing their German language and customs. This movement is reflected today in the large concentration of Lutheran churches in the central and western parts of the state.

A congregation was reported on the Haw River as early as 1745. This early congregation and others that were soon established needed pastors. Pastor Adolph Nussmann was sent from Germany, along with John Arends as teacher, to assist the early congregations. During the American Revolution there were only two Lutheran pastors in the state. After the war other denominations began making inroads into the Lutheran congregations. Paul Henkel made this report in 1802: "There were many immersionists (Baptists) in the audience . . . . These found my sermon so contrary to their taste that they strongly disapproved . . . one of the company who carried a large club in his hand stepped up to the pulpit and interrupted my sermon."

The Lutherans also distrusted the revivalistic methods that appealed to North Carolinians in the frontier area. The dominant trend among them was toward a stricter orthodoxy. This led to the establishment of a synodical organization, the North Carolina Synod being formed in Salisbury in 1803. Most of the Lutheran synods in the South have derived from this body. Its constitution did not contain any references to the confessional writings of the Lutheran Church. This fact, and the new synod's control over the licensing and other requirements, led to its first crisis. David Henkel was placed on probation and his license was withdrawn in

1819. His father Paul Henkel and others withdrew and organized the Tennessee Synod in 1820. This new synod covered the same area as the North Carolina Synod. The two synods existed side-by-side until 1921 when they merged to form the United Evangelical Synod of North Carolina.

The Civil War deeply affected North Carolina Lutherans. Southern Lutherans met in Concord in 1863 and formed the General Synod of the Evangelical Lutheran Church in the Confederate States of America, later altered to the United Synod of the South. It took a half century, until 1918, for the state's Lutherans and other Southern Lutherans to join in a national organization. As a result of the Civil War the small number of blacks withdrew to found the Alpha Synod of the Evangelical Lutheran Church of Freedmen in America in 1889. It dissolved a few years later. A rival Lutheran denomination, the Missouri Synod Church, began to assist the black congregations in the state. Immanuel College, founded in Concord in 1903, later moved to Greensboro where it continued to educate blacks for about fifty years.

After several educational institutions had failed, Lenoir-Rhyne College in Hickory was organized in 1891 (as Lenoir College), and it continues as the state's only Lutheran school. The Women's Missionary Society was organized in 1885. In 1923 the *North Carolina Lutheran* was founded as the denominational newspapers. The ALC and LCA both recognize Sipes Orchard Home (boys) at Conover. The LCA owns the North Carolina Homes, Inc. at Hickory.

In 1860 Lutherans were the fourth largest denomination in North Carolina with 3,942 members and 38 congregations. Today Lutheran churches in North Carolina are divided among three national bodies: the American Lutheran Church (ALC), the Lutheran Church-Missouri Synod (LC-MS), and the Lutheran Church in America (LCA). The LCA embraces the North Carolina Synod of seven districts. In 1971 the total membership was 98,184 in 265 congregations. The largest membership is in the Central District with congregations in China Grove, Salisbury, and Statesville.

The first members of the Reformed tradition of Protestantism came into the Pamlico section of North Carolina from Virginia in 1690. They had no minister and no organized congregation. They were members of the Reformed Church of France. Other Swiss and Palatine Reformed members settled in the New Bern area in 1710, but the majority of this group were killed by the Indians in 1711 and the survivors went into the Presbyterian Church.

The high tide of German immigration into North Carolina was from 1745 to 1755, these representing the Reformed, Lutheran, and Moravian churches. All three groups settled in the piedmont area of the state. Often the Lutheran and Reformed members built union churches. The greatest problem experienced by these ethnic churches was lack of ministers, but several made their way into the colony from South Carolina and Europe.

The Reverend Samuel Suther began his ministry in North Carolina in June 1768, and served Reformed churches until 1786. He was credited with organizing most of the Reformed congregations still in existence where the North Carolina Classis was organized in 1831. From brush arbors to substantial churches the Reformed churches developed their ministry among the German settlers. The need for more ministers persisted, however, there being only one pastor left in the state by 1812. The German Reformed Synod meeting in Pennsylvania responded to the need in North Carolina by sending ministers on several occasions.

After the Civil War blacks began to form their own Reformed congregations. A black congregation was admitted to the classis in 1868 but was not listed after two years. The classis went on record as favoring Sunday schools and prayer meetings. They were against the evils of intemperance and in 1858 took an advanced stand for that time, when they resolved "that the making or distillation for the purpose of indiscriminate sale of intoxicating liquers, its use as a beverage, the practice of giving it to hands invited to log-rollings, huskings, raisings, etc., is immoral in its tendencies and justifies the exercise of discipline."

Most denominations in the South divided with their Northern counterparts over the question of slavery but not the Reformed Church. The Classis of North Carolina did secede, however, but over the "Mercersburg Theology," a question of the soundness of theology taught in that Pennsylvania seminary. The regional factions were reconciled in 1866.

The Classis of North Carolina's involvement in education saw its culmination with the founding of Catawba College in 1851. Benevolent activities resulted in the formation of the Nazareth Orphan's Home in 1906. The Woman's Missionary Society was organized in 1897. Beginning in March 1894, J. L. Murphy and T. C. Leonard began publishing the *Corinthian*, that was subsequently endorsed by the Classis and became the *Reformed Church Standard*.

After several years of preliminary meetings the Evangelical Synod of North America and the Reformed Church in the United States united in 1934 as the General Synod of the Evangelical and Reformed Church. A committee met in 1939 at First Church, Salisbury, and organized the Southern Synod of the Evangelical and Reformed Church.

The German Reformed denomination in North Carolina has never been large. In 1860 it consisted of 15 congregations. In 1971, after merging with the Congregational Christian Churches to form the United Church of Christ, 255 congregations were reported with 53,839 adherents.

Better organized than the other German religious groups that came to North Carolina and smaller in numbers than the Lutherans, the Unitas Fratrum (United Brethren), or Moravians, purchased the huge Wachovia tract (almost 99,000 acres) in what is now Forsyth County. Bethabara was first settled in 1753, nearby Bethania was begun in 1759, and the construction of Salem (now Winston-Salem) was underway by 1766. During the early years, the Wachovia settlement was governed by Moravian church boards abroad, although the state's Brethren also maintained close ties with the Pennsylvania settlements.

From the beginning Salem was a planned community organized on a communal basis with the congregation's governing boards controlling the civil, business, and religious matters. The lease system was installed to keep undesirable citizens and businesses out of the community. It is worth remembering that congregational and business records were kept in German. In 1849 the congregation gave up its supervision of businesses and in 1856 the lease system was abolished.

Moravianism was more than a religion—it was also a way of life. The community was organized into a choir system, individuals grouped according to their age, sex, and marital status. The various groups lived in separate quarters with their own separate officers. When a member died he or she was buried in a cemetery site set aside for the choir of which he or she was a member.

The Brethren did not emphasize conversion to Moravian tenets, but were interested in preaching the Gospel to all, a practice pursued by hardly any other denomination. From earliest years, the Brethren were sending missionaries to the Indians. Records that they carefully preserved give present-day historians a glimpse of their life and activities as well as information on other denominations and ministers in piedmont North Carolina with which the Moravians came into contact.

During times of war this company of hardy Christians suffered greatly, particularly during the American Revolution. Their refusal to bear arms for either side led to raids on their communities and farms by both Loyalists and American forces interested in locating foodstuff and livestock. They took a strong stand to help everyone and to fight no one. By the time of the Civil War ideas had changed so much that the Salem congregation band became the regimental band of the 26th North Carolina Infantry, CSA; it still exists and enjoys wide popularity. The Moravian Music Foundation of Winston-Salem is the principal repository for music scores used by Moravians world-wide.

The Academy for Girls was established in Salem in 1772 with one teacher and two pupils. It continued to grow and was opened to non-Moravians in 1802. This early school is continued at present in the work done by Salem College and Salem Academy. Moravians were also interested in foreign missions and spreading the faith to non-Moravian areas. In 1825 the state's Moravians established work in Indiana and then in Illinois. In 1850 another group left for Iowa. Congregations also were established in the larger communities and cities: Raleigh in 1903, Greensboro in 1908, Charlotte in 1920, and Mt. Airy in 1925. Their congregations are still confined largely to the piedmont area of the state, however. The Southern Province of the Moravian Church in America, founded in 1771, has its headquarters in Winston-Salem. In 1971 there were 43 congregations with 2,000 members.

Methodists were the last major Protestant body to appear in colonial North Carolina. Preaching had begun in 1772 when Joseph Pilmoor preached in the eastern area of the state. The first permanent foothold of Methodism in the colony, however, resulted from the preaching of Robert Williams of Brunswick County, Virginia, leading to the formation of the first North Carolina circuit in 1776 with 683 members. Methodists began to spread rapidly over the state; only three years later there were three circuits with 1,467 members. Other circuits were formed and ministers came on horseback from Virginia mostly and went as far west as the Blue Ridge. Thus, with few areas excepted Methodists had succeeded in covering the entire state of North Carolina in little less than a decade.

The Methodist Episcopal Church in the United States was organized in Baltimore in 1784. The first annual meeting in the state was held in the home of Green Hill, near Louisburg, the next year, conducted by Francis Asbury and Thomas Coke, the two major figures in early American Methodism. In 1836 the North Carolina Conference was formed by dividing the Virginia Conference. The Methodist ranks have experienced several divisions. The first came in 1792 when James O'Kelly and his associates left the General Conference and formed the Christian Church, now a part of the United Church of Christ. In the 1820s the Methodist Protestant Church was formed from dissidents within the Methodist Episcopal Church. They created a separate conference in 1828. Strains created by the approach of the Civil War resulted in the formation of the Methodist Episcopal Church, South in 1844. Three national branches, the Methodist Episcopal Church (Northern), the Methodist Episcopal Church, South, and the Methodist Protestant Church effected unification in 1939 as The Methodist Church. In 1968 another merger, this one with the Evangelical United Brethren (EUB), occasioned the changing of its name to the United Methodist Church. The vast majority of North Carolina Methodist churches are United Methodist.

By the end of the 1850s Methodists had established a newspaper, the *North Carolina Christian Advocate.* Trinity College (now Duke University) had been founded a few years earlier. Commitment to higher education was continued in the 1950s with the establishment of Methodist College at Fayetteville and North Carolina Wesleyan College at Rocky Mount. Homes for the orphans and elderly have been part of Methodist life for over a century.

However, smaller groups of Methodists have also split away over the years. The Wesleyan Methodist Church was formed in the 1840s, as was the Primitive Methodist Church; the Free Methodists came into being in the 1860s. In 1968 the Wesleyan Methodists merged with the Pilgrim Holiness Church to form the Wesleyan Church. After the Civil War, the Methodist Episcopal Church (northern) organized many black congregations in North Carolina. But other black congregations were organized independently at black initiative: the African Methodist Episcopal Zion Church (AME-Zion) as early as 1865; the African Methodist Episcopal Church (AME) by 1868; and the Colored Methodist Episcopal Church (CME) which became the Christian Methodist Episcopal Church in 1956.

Figures for 1971 for all Methodists in North Carolina credit the denomination with 2,018 churches and 534,721 total adherents, making it the second largest denomination in the state.

The Christian Church in North Carolina was founded largely through the efforts of James O'Kelly, a Methodist lay preacher and later elder. He was assigned to the Tar River Circuit on the Virginia-North Carolina border. O'Kelly and his followers withdrew from the Methodist Episcopal Church in 1792, desiring to have "a free constitution and a pure church." Prior to 1831 some of the churches practiced baptism by immersion only, and rejected infant baptism, a practice that led to a split in the denomination in 1810. The followers of William Guirey, with the majority of the Virginia churches, withdrew and formed the Independent Christian Baptist Church. O'Kelly and the North Carolina churches formed the Old North State Conference. By this time his followers were also known as O'Kellyites; the North Carolina churches that did not join the O'Kellyites were known as Christian Baptists.

After preliminary planning the Virginia and North Carolina Christians were united in 1825. O'Kelly, the founder, died the next year and was buried in Chatham County. In 1844 the denomination began publishing the *Christian Sun*, in Raleigh and Pittsboro, until the Civil War years. Several reorganizations took place in the nineteenth century. Then in July 1961 the Congregational Christian Churches merged with the Evangelical and Reformed Church to form the United Church of Christ. In 1971 that body reported 255 congregations and 53,839 adherents in North Carolina.

What of the Established Church of the colonial period? The American Revolution intensified predjudices against the Church of England that persisted for many decades. Episcopal clergymen continued to preach after the Revolution but it was not until 5 June 1790 that the Reverend Charles Pettigrew, the Reverend James L. Wilson, and two laymen, Dr. John Leigh and William Clements, met in Tarboro to provide some organization for the Episcopal Church in North Carolina. In 1817 the state's Diocese was organized. By 1830 there were only eleven ministers and thirty-one congregations, most of them concentrated in the East, with two in Orange County, and two others farther west in Rowan County.

When the North Carolina convention was held in Salisbury in 1823 the clerical deputies unanimously elected John Stark Ravenscroft of Virginia as the first Episcopal bishop of the diocese. One historian wrote:

> Thus at last, after years of struggle the church in North Carolina was firmly established—not on the old basis of state support, in which it had failed, but on a new basis of an independent, voluntary church supported by the desires, energy, and labors of its clergy and its congregations.

The clergy that served the scattered congregations in the state were also very active in preaching and ministering to the blacks prior to the Civil War. Several plantations had separate services for their slaves. A mission school was established at Valle Crucis in the northwestern mountains in 1844. Bishop Levi S. Ives, who served from 1831 to 1851, was torn by conflicting religious beliefs. He was first a Presbyterian, then an Episcopalian, and then a Roman Catholic.

North Carolina Episcopalians were members of the Protestant Episcopal Church in the Confederate States during the Civil War period. Twelve Episcopal chaplains served with the soldiers and one served the military post at Wilmington. Losses in church membership and wartime damages to churches had to be repaired, and Bishop Thomas Atkinson gave leadership. His endeavors increased the clergy from thirty-six to sixty-six, and the number of communicants from 1,778 to 5,889 by 1881.

A Missionary District of Asheville was formed in 1895. The Diocese of Western North Carolina was formed in 1922. In 1883 the Diocese of East Carolina was established—both of these dioceses coming out of the Diocese of North Carolina. The Rt. Rev. Henry Beard Delaney was consecrated Bishop Suffragan of the Diocese of North Carolina in 1918, with the responsibility of working with blacks in North and South Carolina.

Saint Mary's College was founded in Raleigh in 1842 by Albert Smedes as an Episcopal school for girls. Saint Augustine's College was founded there in 1867 to educate blacks. Christ School, Arden, began its work in 1900. Patterson School, Lenoir, is the only preparatory school for boys owned by the Episcopal Church in the state of North Carolina.

The 1971 statistics list 223 churches and 65,665 adherents in the three dioceses that now cover the state. Comments made by an ante-bellum historian on the Episcopal Church in the pre-Civil War era could probably still apply today. He wrote: "The Episcopal Church was far more influential in the state that its small number of adherents would indicate. Most of the church buildings were located in the towns, substantial buildings supported by substantial citizens, merchants, planters, professional men, [and] government officials." The church was not popular with the common people and "its real influence had scarcely stirred beyond the coastal plain, its chief field during Colonial times."

The Disciples of Christ began their work in North Carolina largely through the efforts of some former Presbyterians. Barton Warren Stone, while serving in Kentucky, began to advocate that the various denominations discard all formal discipline and return to the Bible as the all-sufficient rule of faith, so that all Christians might unite in brotherly love. Alexander Campbell was also advocating much the same position. David

Purviance, a former Presbyterian from Iredell County, was the first to preach the faith of the "Restoration Movement" in North Carolina.

Alexander Campbell first visited North Carolina in 1833. During his stay in the state for some six months, entire Baptist congregations went over to the "Campbellites," as his followers were then being called. Later visits in 1838 and 1845 were also productive in winning adherents.

The Bethel Free-Will Baptist Conference of the Disciples of Christ was organized in 1841. They soon became the Annual Conference of the Disciples of Christ in North Carolina. Because of the exceedingly democratic and individualistic polity of the church it is difficult to estimate the numbers of the Disciples in North Carolina during the formative years. Their strength prior to the Civil War appeared to be in the East. After the Civil War most of the Union Baptists, an Open-Communion group numbering more than three thousand, were largely absorbed by the Disciples.

The 1870s were marked by an aggressive expansion of the North Carolina Disciples of Christ. Women's work began to be recognized and in 1871 "Sisters' Beneficent Societies" began to be formed. By 1892 there were twenty auxiliaries in the state. In 1877 the North Carolina Christian Missionary Society was formed to spread the Gospel within the state. In 1878 a State Evangelist was selected and began his work. In 1902 Atlantic Christian College was incorporated in Wilson. *The North Carolina Christian* began publication in 1920.

Growth came slowly to the Disciples but they were increasing their ranks in a methodical manner. In 1971 they reported 334 congregations and 46,310 adherents.

Catholic immigrants first settled in the Pamlico Sound region in eastern North Carolina as early as 1737. But Catholics were few in number and their organizational life limited. From 1790 until 1829 they were under the jurisdiction of the Diocese/Archdiocese of Baltimore. In 1820 the Diocese of Charleston was formed and North Carolina Catholics were served by clergy from South Carolina. Its bishop, John England, made many visits into the state from Charleston between 1821 and 1824.

By 1830 Catholics in New Bern had a church building. In 1832 the first Mass was celebrated in Raleigh. In 1838 the Very Rev. Thomas Murphy was stationed in Fayetteville, the first Catholic pastor in North Carolina, and served in the eastern part of the state until 1844. After a year in Georgia he returned to Wilmington, where he continued to serve until his death in 1863.

Catholic missionary endeavors in the western part of the state began with the opening of the gold mines in the Mecklenburg County area around 1830. Churches were built in Gaston County in 1843, in Charlotte in 1852, in Asheville in 1869, and in Concord in 1870. These stations were largely served by clergy from South Carolina and Georgia until the 1850s. On the eve of the Civil War there were seven congregations containing 350 members in the state.

In 1868 the state of North Carolina became a separate vicariate, the famous Bishop James Gibbons being the first Vicar Apostolic of North Carolina. In 1868, according to his biographer, "He found only two or three priests, about the same number of humble churches, and a thousand Catholics scattered at different points all over North Carolina." He "traveled night and day, and by all modes of conveyance, new and obsolete." Gibbons administered the sacraments in such secret places as garrets and basements, and knew all the adult Catholics in North Carolina personally. He established the Benedictine Order at Belmont Abbey, the Sisters of Mercy in Wilmington, ordained some dozen priests, erected a half-dozen new churches, and opened several schools.

The state's Catholic population amounted to 1,700 in 1878. In 1924 the Diocese of North Carolina was formed. It was later divided into the Raleigh Diocese, serving the eastern portion of the state and the Charlotte Diocese, serving the western portion of the state. By 1971 North Carolina Catholics were reporting 157 churches with a membership of 69,133.

The Seventh-Day Adventists denomination was organized 21 May 1863, with 125 churches and 3,500 members into a General Conference. The states of North and South Carolina are in the Carolinas Conference, first organized in 1901, and reorganized in 1918. In 1971 North Carolina Adventists had 71 churches and 8,739 total adherents.

North Carolina was among the first of the original 13 colonies to welcome Jewish settlement explicitly. The Fundamental Constitutions for the Carolinas stated that the colony was open to settlement by "Jews, heathens, and other dissenters." The first Jewish settlers came into the state from Barbados, and were of Spanish-Portuguese origin. Wilmington seems to have had a Jewish community as early as 1738. The earliest Jewish name on record appears to be Aaron Moses who witnessed a will in 1740. Others came into the state with some becoming quite prominent. Jacob Henry was elected to the state legislature in 1808. He successfully kept his challenged seat but it was not until 1868 that the state constitution officially gave Jews the right to hold public office in the state.

The Jews who came into the state in the second half of the nineteenth century were mostly immigrants from Germany. They turned to the one profession universally open to them, peddling. (The Cherokee Indians referred to such Jews as "egg-eaters." The probable reason for this term was the strict adherence to the Jewish dietary laws. The peddlers avoided meat of any kind until they returned home on Friday evening in time to observe the Sabbath.) "Way Stations" were established in Wilmington, Albemarle, and Yanceyville where they could resupply and where they could be "home for the Sabbath." Isaac Harby estimated that there were 44 Jews in the state in 1826. In 1860 the Jews of Wilmington were advertising for a cantor to serve them.

It was not until 1867 that North Carolina's first congregation was established in Wilmington. This was formally incorporated as Temple of Israel in 1873. Other towns and communities began to organize their resident Jews in the post-Civil War years. Asheville had two congregations, Durham one; Goldsboro established a congregation in 1883; New Bern had a congregation, Tarboro had a congregation by 1872; and in 1883 Statesville formed a congregation. After 1880 the East-European Jews began to settle in the state—principally in the mill towns and the larger cities and communities. The largest group of Jews settled in the piedmont area with the largest congregation in Greensboro. In 1970 there were 27 synagogues in the state. North Carolina could also boast of having the only "circuit rider," a Jewish lay-leader who visited the scattered communities unable to maintain a synagogue or a rabbi on their own. *The American Jewish Time-Outlook* began publishing in Greensboro in 1935 and the late Harry Golden founded the *Carolina Israelite* in Charlotte in 1940.

In any brief resumé of religion in North Carolina a number of extant and extinct denominations alike must be omitted, owing largely to the lack of information sources. These groups, too, have made contributions to the religious life of the state.

Religion has played a very important role in the history of the state of North Carolina from the Colonial era to the present. The various strands of denominationalism have been tightly interwoven with the secular history of the state. Denominations provided the stability on the frontier before civil and judicial authorities arrived. They were in the forefront, often being the first to provide educational opportunities, orphanages for the children, and homes for the aging. Leaders in denominational life have often been the leaders in political, social, and public arenas as well. Most of the surviving denominations in our state have suffered one or more splits in their ranks but in most circumstances this division has led to larger memberships and greater growth for all concerned. Religion and denominationalism continue to exert a wholesome and much-needed influence on North Carolinians of today.

Bibliography

George H. Anderson. *The North Carolina Synod Through 175 Years (1803-1978)*.

Francis C. Anscombe. *I Have Called You Friend: The Story of Quakerism in North Carolina*.

Lawrence F. Brewster. *A Short History of the Diocese of East Carolina, 1883-1972, With Its Background In the History of the Anglican Church in the Colony and The Protestant Episcopal Church in North Carolina*.

Elmer T. Clark. *Methodism in Western North Carolina*.

Wallace R. Draughan. *History of the Church of Jesus Christ of Latter-Day Saints in North Carolina*.

Adelaide Fries, J. J. Hamilton, D. L. Rights, and M. J. Smith, eds. *The Records of The Moravians in North Carolina*, 11 vols.

Cardinal James Gibbons. *Reminiscenses of Catholicity in North Carolina*.

Harry Golden. *Jewish Roots in The Carolinas*.

Thaddeus F. Harrison and J. M. Barfield. *History of the Free Will Baptists of North Carolina*, 2 vols.

Cushing B. Hassell. *History of the Church of God From The Creation to AD 1885: Including Especially the History of the Kehukee Primitive Baptist Association*.

Guion Johnson. "Religious Denominations," *Antebellum North Carolina: A Social History*.

Donald Keyser, ed. Abstracts and index of articles in *The North Carolina Historical Review* related to a study of North Carolina church history.

Jacob C. Leonard. *The Southern Synod of the Evangelical and Reformed Church*.

George W. Paschal. *History of North Carolina Baptists*, 2 vols.

Jethro Rumple. *The History of Presbyterianism in North Carolina*.

Durwood T. Stokes and William T. Scott. *A History of The Christian Church in the South*.

Robert H. Stone, *A History of the Orange Presbytery, 1770-1970*.

Charles C. Ware. *North Carolina Disciples of Christ: A History of Their Rise and Progress*.

OKLAHOMA

JAMES K. ZINK
SOUTHEAST MISSOURI STATE UNIVERSITY

Oklahoma was one of the latest areas to be identified with the South, an action which came about more by accident than by plan. Before 1820 the area was populated by the Plains Indians. The picture began to change after 1820 when the Choctaw Indians purchased land in what was to become Oklahoma; these were the first Eastern Indians to acquire land in the region. Between 1820 and 1842 the Five Civilized Tribes (Cherokees, Choctaws, Chickasaws, Creeks, and Seminoles) were mostly removed from the Southeastern states into Indian Territory. Following the Civil War, during which the Indian Nations were aligned with the Southern cause, the population pattern began to change again with the intrusion of white settlers. Eventually the Indian Nations were dissolved and the state of Oklahoma was established. For almost a century Oklahoma served as an Indian colonization zone; nearly 60 tribes were settled within its borders in that time. Much of Oklahoma history is Indian history.

Early History of Oklahoma: 1541—1817

European influence in Oklahoma began with the Spanish explorers. Francisco Vásquez de Coronado started his expedition northward from Mexico in 1541 and crossed western Oklahoma during his journey. Possibly Hernando de Soto traveled across northeastern Oklahoma during his three year expedition in North America (1539-1542). Juan de Oñate entered Oklahoma in 1601. Claims of the lands explored were made for Spain, but no permanent settlements were established.

Oklahoma was also claimed by the English and French. English charters extending all the way from the Atlantic to the Pacific were granted to commercial companies as a result of their exploration of the Atlantic coast. René Robert Cavelier, Sieur de la Salle, laid claim to all the territory drained by the Mississippi River for France. The region was awarded to Spain as a part of Louisiana by the treaties of 1762-1763 culminating the Seven Years War.

French traders settled among the Indians and frequently intermarried. Lively trade was carried on between the French and the Caddoans before 1700. Trade villages were established, and Ferdinandina, a trading post west of the Arkansas River in what is now Kay County, has been called the first white settlement in Oklahoma.

After Louisiana was retroceded to France by Spain in 1800, President Thomas Jefferson offered to purchase the Isle of Orleans. A counter-offer was made by the French to sell the entire province of Louisiana. Louisiana was transferred to the United States on 3 November 1803. All of Louisiana north of the 33rd parallel was designated the District of Louisiana and placed under the administration of Indiana Territory in 1804. The next year the Territory of Louisiana was organized with the seat of government at St. Louis.

American exploration of Oklahoma took place during the years 1806-1821 beginning with James B. Wilkinson. Seven expeditions were conducted to explore the region. One of the notable explorers was Thomas Nuttall, the English botanist whose journal describes the flora and fauna of the region as well as the Indians encountered. Six more explorations were conducted in the period 1832-1853.

Soon after Louisiana was purchased from France, President Jefferson drew up a proposal to exchange land occupied by Indians in the eastern states for "equivalent portions" in Louisiana, and Indian removal became a policy of the United States government. Some voluntary migrations occurred between 1817, when the Cherokees signed a removal treaty and obtained land in Arkansas, and the passage of the Indian Removal Act in 1830. The removal of Choctaws from Arkansas led to the establishment of a permanent border between Arkansas and Oklahoma in 1825. Arkansas Territory was created in 1819 and included all that is now Oklahoma with the exception of a strip between 36° and 36° 30' south latitudes.

The removal of the Five Civilized Tribes to Oklahoma was a process which lasted more than 20 years, beginning in 1825 and ending with efforts to comb the Seminoles out of the Florida swamps in the 1840s. For all the Indians involved in the removal the experience entailed great hardship and suffering, as the term "Trail of Tears" indicates. Many people, especially infants and the elderly, died along the trails. In the case of the Creeks and Seminoles warfare occurred because of the resistance of some to removal. The most costly of these was to the Seminoles whose numbers were reduced by one-third as a result of war and the hardships of journey from Florida to Indian Territory.

Establishment of the Indian Nations: 1817-1890

The first substantial formal Indian colonization of the trans-Mississippi West occurred among the Cherokees. They originally occupied an area extending over western North Carolina, eastern Tennessee and Kentucky, northern Georgia, and northeastern Alabama. Very early they came under the influence of traders from the coastal English settlements. Many, especially the mixed-bloods, adopted the ways of their white neighbors. Two factions arose among the Cherokees when the question of removal was posed: some favored relocation in order to continue the old ways of life, and others were opposed to relocation, preferring to remain on their ancestral land as planters and stock raisers.

The first Cherokee removal occurred in 1817 on a voluntary basis when the tribe ceded about one-third of its lands in the East for equal acreage between the White and Arkansas Rivers in Arkansas. This territory was traded for land in northeastern Oklahoma in 1828.

The treaty of 1828 provided for the removal of white persons resident in the new Cherokee Nation, compensation of the Cherokees for the improvements they had made on their Arkansas lands, payment of the sum of $50,000 for the inconvenience the move caused them, provision of a printing press and type, an annual payment of $2,000 for 10 years for the support of schools, and subsidization of the removal of the remaining eastern Cherokees including the cost of subsistence for one year. The treaty contained the promise: "Under the most solemn guarantee of the United States, [this land shall] be and remain theirs forever—a home that shall never, in all future time, be embarrassed by having extended around it the lines, or placed over it the jurisdiction of a Territory or State, nor be pressed upon by the extension, in any way, of any of the limits of any existing Territory or State."

The Treaty of New Echota (Georgia) in 1835 provided for the removal of all the remaining Cherokees to the assigned Cherokee lands west of Arkansas and Missouri. The treaty also provided for the settlement of friendly tribes, including the Osages, Kaws, Pawnees, Poncas, Nez Percés, and Oto-Missouris on surplus Cherokee lands.

As part of the removal policy, Indian tribes purchased or were assigned land in Indian Territory. The first of the tribes to acquire land was the Choctaws who purchased the area south of the Canadian and Arkansas Rivers. In 1825 the Choctaws ceded their lands in Arkansas to the United States and were promised an annual sum of $6,000 per year "forever," the removal of white settlers from the newly defined Choctaw nation, and no future settlement of United States citizens on Choctaw lands.

Most of the Chickasaws moved into their district in southern Indian Territory by the end of 1840. Their presence was resented by the Kiowas and Comanches who had occupied the land before, and intertribal strife occurred. Intratribal warfare marked the removal of the Creeks. The Seminoles had to be moved by force.

As a consequence of the various removal treaties, Indian Territory contained five semi-autonomous Indian republics. These Indians had been strongly influenced by their white neighbors while in the East and adopted the republican constitutional system of government. The first constitutional government among the Five Civilized Tribes was that of the Choctaws who adopted a written code of laws prior to 1820 and, in 1826, enacted a constitution which provided for the election of their district chiefs and council. After their arrival in Indian Territory, each of the Five Civilized Tribes established a government and four adopted written constitutions. The Seminoles observed an unwritten code.

The tribal constitutions had common features and were a mixture of Indian and Anglo-Saxon usages. Generally the constitutions were characterized by their liberal rules of eligibility for office, the recognition of the fundamental right of people to change their laws, the equality of free citizens, and the separation of governmental powers. The Choctaw and Cherokee constitutions each had a bill of rights. The final forms of the constitutions were adopted by four tribes between 1839 and 1867 in the following order: Cherokee (1839), Chickasaw (1856), Choctaw (1860), and Creek (1867). The capitals of the Indian nations were located in Tahlequah (Cherokee), Tuskahoma (Choctaw), Tishomingo (Chickasaw), Okmulgee (Creek), and Wewoka (Seminole).

The period 1830-1861 may be called the Golden Years for the Five Civilized Tribes. It was a time of respite from the demands of settlers for their lands and progress in taming the wilderness. They organized their governments, and established towns, farms, ranches, and plantations. Newspapers, books, and magazines were published. An extensive school system was established which, in most of the Indian nations, made it possible for every child to attend school through the academy level and, in some cases, the first two years of college.

By 1885 Oklahoma was divided into two large Indian communities. The eastern half was occupied by the Five Civilized Tribes and the western half by more culturally deprived tribes. The Medicine Lodge Council in 1867 set up twenty-one separate reservations administered by eight agencies. Each of the agencies had at least two tribes under its jurisdiction, and several had five tribes or more.

All of Oklahoma except the Panhandle remained Indian Territory until 1889 after which successive areas in western Oklahoma were opened to homesteaders. By means of the Organic Act of 2 May 1890 Oklahoma Territory was formed out of the Unassigned Lands and No Man's Land (the Panhandle) plus lands which were added by land openings. The Organic Act divided Oklahoma into two areas: Oklahoma Territory, being the western portion, and Indian Territory, the eastern. The federal census of 1890 showed the population of the Twin Territories to be 78,475 in Oklahoma Territory and 180,182 in Indian Territory. In 1907 the Twin Territories were fused into the state of Oklahoma.

Education and Missions in Indian Territory

Efforts to achieve social and religious progress in Indian Territory were a part of the settlement of the Indians in Oklahoma. Missionaries had been active among the Five Civilized Tribes while they were in the southeastern United States, and those efforts continued after the removal.

The earliest organized missionary efforts among the Five Civilized Tribes were undertaken by the Moravians, who established a school and mission for the Cherokees at Spring Place, Georgia, in 1801. When the Cherokees moved west the Moravian missionaries went with them and constructed a mission center called New Spring Place.

The United Foreign Missionary Society was organized on 25 July 1817 by the General Assembly of the Presbyterian Church, the General Assembly of the Dutch Reformed Presbyterian Church, and the General Synod of the Associate Reformed Church. The Society was responsible for organizing schools and missions in the Indian Territory. In 1826 the American Board of Commissioners for Foreign Missions, an ecumenical board supported by the Presbyterians and Congregationalists, absorbed the United Foreign Missionary Society. Work among the Five Civilized Tribes was begun in 1817 in the eastern United States, and teachers and missionaries accompanied the Indians on their journey to Indian Territory.

The UFMS sent two Presbyterian missionaries, Epaphras Chapman and John P. Vinal, to explore the possibility of establishing a mission among the Cherokees of Arkansas in 1819. However, because the American Board had already made plans for a station among the Cherokees, Chapman and Vinal travelled further west into the Osage country and selected a site for a mission. After Vinal died on the return trip to New York, Chapman organized a missionary party and, along with William F. Vaill, led a group of 17 adults and four children to Indian Territory where Union Mission was established in 1821. The missionaries organized a church in May 1821 and erected a school building. They admitted four Osage students in August of the same year. Union Mission was the first Indian School in Oklahoma.

The Creek removal to the Indian Territory began in 1827, and 3,000 Creeks were living in their designated national boundaries by 1830. The Creeks wanted a mission and a school, and Union was the mission that could serve them. Later the Creeks asked for their own school for their children.

Union Mission closed early in 1833 and remained closed until the summer of 1835 when Samuel Austin Worcester, a Congregational missionary sent out by the American Board, installed a printing press at Union. Worcester had established a newspaper, the *Cherokee Phoenix*, at New Echota in 1828 and printed the newspaper and other Cherokee items in the syllabary composed by George Guess (also known as Sequoyah). Worcester was forced to leave Georgia in 1834, and the American Board decided to continue his work in the West. Worcester installed his printing press which he moved from New Echota at Union Mission in 1835. In 1837 Worcester chose Park Hill as the permanent location for his press because of its more favorable location.

The missionaries in the Creek Nation faced growing hostility and were forced out in late 1836. During the time the missionaries were banned from the Creek Nation, the Presbyterian Church divided into the "old school" and "new school" factions. The "old school" renewed its mission work, and in 1841 the Board of Foreign Missions sent Robert M. Loughridge to visit leaders in the Creek Nation. He was granted permission to establish a school and to preach, but in the school only. Loughridge returned to his home in Alabama to raise money for the new mission and established the Kowetah Manual Labor Boarding School for Creek Indians in 1843.

A new treaty between the United States and the Creeks in 1845 included a provision for the education of Creek children; the monies were referred to as the Creek National School Fund. An agreement was made between the Presbyterian board and the Creek government for the expansion of the Kowetah Mission, the allocation of $75 a year for each student, and a new school of manual labor. The new school opened in 1848 as the Tullahassee Manual Labor School with Loughridge as its superintendent.

The Tullahassee school enjoyed the advantage of a good location and the educational program was successful for 10 years. The Civil War, however, divided the Creek Nation into two factions, and both the Tullahassee and Kowetah Missions were seized by the Creek government in 1861.

The Tullahassee Mission reopened in 1868 upon the return of William Robertson, who had been principal at the school under Loughridge. The school burned in 1880, but neither the Creek government nor the Board of Missions encouraged Robertson to rebuild because of a shift in population. The mission came to an end after Robertson's death on 26 June 1881.

Robertson's daughter Alice went to the East to raise money for a new mission. She was successful and began Nuyaka Mission near Okmulgee, the Creek capital, in 1884. Later Alice Robertson was appointed head of the Presbyterian School for Indian Girls in Muskogee.

The Methodists carried on mission work among the Five Civilized Tribes before the removal. Their work was conducted through Methodist Conferences adjacent to the nations rather than a missions board. The Missouri Methodist Conference and later the Arkansas Methodist Conference assumed the responsibility for serving the Indians in Indian Territory. The Methodists relied on house-to-house visitation and circuit-rider preachers rather than fixed religious centers and schools. The Methodists gave little attention to schools among the Five Civilized Tribes until the 1840s.

Methodist preaching to the Indians in the Oklahoma-Arkansas area is first recorded as taking place about 1820 by the Rev. William Stevenson. The Asbury Manual Labor School near North Fork Town was established in 1850.

The Baptists worked among the Five Civilized Tribes before removal beginning in 1817, and several missionaries accompanied the Indians to Oklahoma. The first Cherokee Baptists in Oklahoma arrived in 1832 when 80 families led by Duncan O'Briant established a settlement 70 miles north of Fort Smith. Evan Jones, an immigrant from Wales, and Jesse Bushyhead, a Cherokee, each led a party of Cherokees to Indian Territory where they settled at Pleasant Hill, also known as Baptist Mission. In 1845, Jones was furnished with a press and type by the Baptist Mission Board of Boston. The Baptist Mission Press was responsible for some important imprints including the *Cherokee Messenger*, the first magazine published in Oklahoma. The paper was devoted to religious and temperance topics printed almost entirely in Cherokee characters. The Baptist Mission Press also printed the book of Genesis, about half of the New Testament, and English and Creek hymnals, among other publications.

Roman Catholic work among the Indians in Oklahoma on a continuing basis did not begin until 1840 when some Jesuit Fathers began to establish mission stations in Indian Territory and built the first church at Atoka in 1874. Some Spanish missionaries who accompanied the first explorers reached some Indians. French trappers and traders also came into contact with them, but no permanent missions resulted from those efforts.

The first permanent resident priest was the French Benedictine, Isidore Robot, who was appointed Prefect Apostolic of the Indian Territory in 1876 with his residence at the Benedictine Abbey of the Sacred Heart. He established a college and, in 1880, an academy for girls. Fr. Ignatius Jean followed Robot as the second and only other Prefect Apostolic in 1880. Jean founded the first and only pre-1900 Catholic periodical in Oklahoma, *The Indian Advocate*, in January 1889. After the opening of No Man's Land for settlement, secular priests were needed in addition to the Benedictines already serving. Fr. Theophile Meerschaert was sent to Oklahoma as the first bishop of the newly created diocese of Oklahoma in 1905.

Missionary efforts by the Christian Church first occurred in 1856 when James J. Trott, a missionary appointed by the American Christian

Missionary Society who worked among the Cherokees in North Carolina and Georgia, went on a preaching tour that included the Cherokee Nation in 1856. It was his hope to begin a mission in Indian Territory, but with the prospects of war looming by 1860 the ACMS decided to retrench rather than expand its efforts. There were no permanent congregations established by Trott's efforts in the Cherokee Nation.

Other Christian Church preachers worked among the Indians during the 1870s, but it was not until 1884 that a missionary was engaged by the ACMS to work with them. Isaac Mode began working among the Creeks in 1885 but was transferred to the Cherokee Nation because of language difficulties. A mission among the Choctaws was begun about 1884 by R. W. Officer who received permission to open a mission and training school at Atoka. Officer was the first Christian Church missionary to engage in the training school activities characteristic of most of the other missionary groups.

The greatest influx of Christian Church ministers and the founding of permanent churches did not occur until the opening of Indian lands for white settlement. At that time, for example, J. H. Monroe, a minister, joined the homesteaders and established a church in Guthrie less than two weeks after the opening of the Cheyenne and Arapaho territories. Another minister, E. F. Boggess, staked a claim for a church lot in Perry when the Cherokee Strip was opened. Other preachers and members followed so that before statehood there was a Christian Church in every town with a population of 1,000 and in every county seat except two.

Mission work by the Mennonites began in 1880 when the General Conference Mennonite Mission Board began working among the Arapahos and later the Cheyennes and others. The first missionary was Samuel S. Haury. He was scheduled to begin work in the Indian Territory in April 1878 but was unable to go until September. When he arrived he found that a Quaker missionary had already arrived and the field was no longer open. The next year the Indian agent at Darlington, a Quaker, informed Haury that the Quakers would work only among the Cheyennes and urged the Mennonites to begin work among the Arapahos. The Quakers also turned the Cheyenne work over to the Mennonites in 1884.

The Mennonite mission at Darlington opened in 1880. Word was received that year that the military post at Cantonment, 65 miles northwest of Darlington, would be abandoned, and the buildings were offered for missionary work. Haury went to Cantonment. As the Indians began to scatter after 1890 other stations were occupied. When the government began to build Indian schools to replace the mission schools, Darlington and Cantonment closed, in 1898 and 1901 respectively.

The end of the missionary work among the Indians as carried on in the missions described was brought about by the building of Indian training schools by the government, the break-up of the reservations, the allotment of land which the Indians were required to occupy, and the intrusion of large numbers of white settlers. New approaches were needed to meet the demands of a changing territory.

The earliest formal education in Oklahoma was that provided by the Indian schools. As stated before, some of the schools were established by churches and combined religious teaching with instruction in basic subjects. Among the notable academies that grew out of the missions were Sacred Heart, Asbury, Tullahassee, Wheelock, and Bloomfield.

Congress established an annual fund of $10,000 on 13 March 1819 to be used to "civilize" the American Indians and gave it to missionary organizations to administer. The missionaries were to use the money to employ "persons of good moral character to instruct the Indians in reading, writing, and arithmetic." The funds were insufficient for the task and monies from private sources were raised to build schools in the Indian nations. The tribes also appropriated funds for the support of public schools and to subsidize the mission schools. The theories of manual labor of Johann Heinrich Pestallozzi interested the missionaries, and they applied them to the education of the Indians as schools of manual labor for Indians were established. The missions were a powerful factor in the transformation of the Indian culture, not only because of the religious training given but also the general and manual education provided.

Dwight Mission, established in 1830, was the oldest school in Oklahoma although Union Mission was established earlier. Prior to 1890, 37 missions were established and 13 more during 1890 or after. Most of the earlier missions were in the northeast part of Indian Territory between the Arkansas border and the Grand River and in the southeast near the Texas border. Missions were not established in the central area until later.

The Cherokees supported public schools independent of the missionary schools. Despite the extensive educational activities established by the various missionary societies for the Cherokees, far more Indian children were involved in the Cherokee Nation's public schools than in the mission schools.

The Creeks had no public school system but supported the mission schools. The Creeks tried to ban Christian worship between 1834 and 1842, but rescinded that action, and the Presbyterians were invited to return and reopen the Kowetah Mission.

The Choctaws were among the most enlightened tribes and maintained an excellent educational system. The schools were supported by funds from the sale of their eastern lands. The tribe allowed missionaries to-evangelize only if they furnished qualified teachers equal to the number of preachers. The schools were constructed by tribal funds, but churches were required to supply teachers. The American Board was active in supplying teachers and had as many as 10 schools under their care. The Methodists also assisted in operating Choctaw schools.

After the Chickasaws moved west in 1842, W. H. Duncan of the Indian Methodist Conference established a school at Pleasant Grove. The Chickasaws used money from the sale of their land in Mississippi to establish a system of schools, and Methodist and Presbyterian missionaries served as teachers.

The Seminoles developed educational programs belatedly and had no funds from the United States government for the support of their schools. Not until after 1844 were mission schools established. A mission to the Seminoles was established by the Presbyterians at Oak Ridge after 1848 by John Bemo, a Seminole, and John Lilley, a Presbyterian missionary. Joseph S. Murrow, a Baptist missionary and teacher, arrived in the Seminole Nation in 1857.

Dissolution of the Indian Nations: 1890—1906

The Indian cultures in Oklahoma were quite diverse. Between 1820 and 1880 over 60 tribes were colonized, joining the tribes which had claimed the area as their home before. Some tribes were sedentary, agricultural, and peaceful; others were migratory, hunting and gathering, and warlike. Each tribe was an independent self-contained social unit with its own system of government.

At the outbreak of the Civil War the Five Civilized Tribes found themselves in an unfavorable situation. At an intertribal council held in 1861, John Ross, a chief of the Cherokees, counselled neutrality in the conflict. In fact, many of the tribal leaders favored neutrality; however, most of the United State officials who had been assigned to the Five Civilized Tribes were from the South. A bad impression was made on the Indian Nations by the withdrawal of Federal troops from Indian Territory at the outbreak of war and the hesitation of officials of the Indian Bureau to pay annuities when due, especially through the agents who were southern men. The situation of the Indians is defined by Roy Gittinger in *The Formation of the State of Oklahoma*: "The position of the Five Civilized Tribes on the border, not their sympathy for the Southern Confederacy, caused them to take part in the war between Union and secession. The abandonment of the Indian Territory by the United States and its occupation by the Confederacy made it necessary for the Indians to recognize the authority of the Confederate government or opposed it unaided."

Citizens of the Five Civilized Tribes were sharply divided on the question of support for the Confederacy at the outbreak of the Civil War. Partisan conflict stemming from disputes over westward removal influenced the attitudes of many. Nearly all Choctaws and Chickasaws supported the Confederacy until its destruction; but the Cherokees, Creeks, and Seminoles were divided into hostile parties. Some Indians enlisted in the armies, and eventually the Creeks numbered 1,575 men in the Confederate Army and 1,675 in the Union forces. Union Cherokee soldiers totalled 2,200 in contrast to 1,400 Confederates. Seminoles in the Union army outnumbered those of the Confederacy.

Although there were no great battles in the Indian Territory comparable to those in the East, fierce fighting did occur with the irregular fighting of partisan groups being most destructive. Heavy losses were suffered by the Cherokee, Creek, and Seminole tribes among whom bitter internal strife added to the destruction of large-scale war.

The most costly aspect of the Civil War, however, was the aftermath. Although the citizens of the Indian Nations had not been solidly for the Confederacy, the federal government used the commitment of the tribal governments to alliances with the Confederacy as an excuse to force the tribes into acceptance of the dissolution of their republics. The Indian nations were regarded as having been in rebellion against the Union and the treaties by which they had been formed therefore nullified.

The Reconstruction plan for the Indian territory was worked out by the two Senators from Kansas, James Lane and Samuel Pomeroy. Basically, the Lane-Pomeroy plan authorized the President to suspend treaties with the Five Civilized Tribes, appropriate portions of their domain, and direct removal of the tribes from Kansas to Indian Territory. During 1866 the Five Civilized Tribes submitted to the Reconstruction Treaties which included the cession of tribal lands as proposed by Lane and Pomeroy. These treaties provided for the abolition of slavery, the recognition of citizens' rights for the freedmen of the Indian tribes, and the settlement of tribes from Kansas, Nebraska, and elsewhere in land in the western part of Indian Territory. Land ceded by the Creeks and Seminoles was limited to "such other civilized tribes as the United States may choose to settle thereon."

Between 1865 and 1889 drastic social, economic, and political changes occurred in Indian Territory causing it to become a kaleidoscope of tribal and ethnic cultures. During that period railroad construction brought about a revolution of transportation of people and goods and promoted new enterprises. As the railroads spread across Oklahoma, pressure built up for the opening of Indian Territory to homesteaders. The railroad interests claimed they were entitled to large land subsidies as a reward for their risk in developing the railroads. To their demands were added the voices of mining, lumbering, and ranching interests. A class of professional promoters called "Boomers" appeared in 1879 dedicated to pushing the cause of opening the land to homesteaders.

The pressure for change was increased by the influx of new immigrants. The white population increased steadily in Indian Territory after 1865 in what was referred to as the "Silent Migration."

Between 1879 and 1884 Boomer raids were made into Indian Territory and white settlements established. On 3 March 1889 a rider known as the Springer Amendment was attached to the Indian Appropriations Bill which provided for opening the Unassigned Lands for settlement, and President Benjamin Harrison issued a proclamation that the Unassigned Lands would be opened 22 April 1889. Probably the total of persons who made the run on this date was over 50,000. Other Indian lands were occupied by white settlers through runs or lottery between 1872 and 1901. The Curtis Act passed by Congress in 1898 provided for the compulsory liquidation of the Five Civilized Tribes. Surplus land in the Cheyenne-Arapaho country was made available for homesteaders on 19 April 1892, and on 16 September 1893 the Cherokee Outlet was opened. The last remaining Indian land in western Oklahoma was opened in August 1901. None of the lands in the national territory of the Five Civilized Tribes were opened to runs.

The Dawes Commission began meeting in 1894 and concluded its work in 1905. Through the Dawes Commission's negotiations with the

Five Civilized Tribes it was agreed that all tribal governments were to cease operation during 1906. The territory of the Five Civilized Tribes was allocated to members of the tribes.

The question of single or double statehood was settled by the 58th Congress. Bills were introduced in the House of Representatives and the Senate in 1905 calling for the admission of the state of Sequoyah, the territory of the Five Civilized Tribes, but both were tabled. President Theodore Roosevelt signed the Enabling Act which provided for the creation of a single state from the "Twin Territories" in June 1906. Oklahoma was admitted to the Union as the 46th state on 16 November 1907.

The effect of the "Silent Migration," the Boomer settlements and the land runs is seen in the fact that when Oklahoma Territory and Indian Territory were fused into a single state the population stood at about 1.5 million. Of the 750,000 in Indian Territory the ratio of non-Indians to Indians was at least seven to one. The population of Oklahoma increased dramatically; from 180,182 in Indian Territory and 78,475 in Oklahoma Territory in 1890 to 392,000 in Indian Territory and 398,331 in Oklahoma Territory in 1900.

Developments After Statehood: 1907—1981

After statehood was achieved attention was focused on bringing order to the state and developing industry, exploiting the mineral deposits, expanding agriculture, and stabilizing social customs.

A side-light to the story of the development of the economy, but illustrative of the development of social concern, is seen in the decision of the citizens of the new state to have a prohibition clause in the state constitution. Regulations regarding alcoholic beverages differed in Oklahoma Territory and Indian Territory. When Indian Territory was formed, Congress passed an act which stated: "If any person shall sell, exchange, or give, barter, or dispose of any spirituous liquor or wine to an Indian . . . such person shall pay the sum of five hundred dollars." In Oklahoma Territory licenses for the sale of liquor could be granted by the Board of County Commissioners.

As plans for statehood developed in the 1890s the Women's Christian Temperance Union and the Anti-Saloon League, in alliance with Protestant churches, began to organize and campaign for constitutional prohibition. The Anti-Saloon League was especially influential and prided itself as "the church in action." Carrie Nation visited Guthrie in 1905 and founded a branch of the Prohibition Federation.

Much of the attention of the prohibitionists was directed toward Congress. They reasoned that, since the United States government had a moral responsibility to the Indians and the treaties had guaranteed the tribes protection against alcohol, it would be legal for Congress to outlaw the manufacture and sale of liquor in all parts of the new state.

The Oklahoma Enabling Act passed by Congress in 1906 declared for single statehood and required continuation of prohibition within Indian Territory for 21 years after the admission of the new state. No restriction was placed on Oklahoma Territory except for the former Osage Nation. The state was permitted to establish an agency to supervise the sale of liquor for medical and other prescribed purposes. On 11 September 1907 approval was given to constitutional prohibition for the entire state. Prohibition lasted until 1959 when the state constitution was amended to permit regulated sales of liquor.

The constitutional prohibition on the manufacture and sale of liquor was not considered by some to be strong enough and efforts were made to enact "Bone Dry" legislation. A bill was passed in 1917 which made it "unlawful for any person in the state to possess any liquors received directly or indirectly from a common or other carrier" with the exception of pure grain alcohol intended for scientific or medical purposes. Because the Webb-Kenyon Act of 1913 forbade the interstate shipment of alcohol in violation of state laws, possession was outlawed. A problem arose with the law in that it did not exempt sacramental wine. No effort had been exerted by the Catholics during the formation of the law for an exemption for religious purposes. Some sacramental wine was confiscated in Norman in August 1917, and the Attorney General issued an interpretation of the law that sacramental wine was prohibited. A test case was filed on behalf of the Catholic Church in Guthrie after the MKT Railroad refused to transport eight quarts of sacramental wine from Kansas to Oklahoma, and the court upheld the law. The national attention which this case focused on the plight of the Catholic Church in Oklahoma caused concern on the part of prohibition forces because, even if the Catholics were not numerous in Oklahoma, the Catholic vote would be necessary to pass the Eighteenth Amendment in other states. Some defeats of the prohibition election in New York were attributed to the Oklahoma situation, with the result that even dry leaders attempted to force a change in the Oklahoma ban on sacramental wine. The Oklahoma Supreme Court ruled that sacramental wine was exempted from the law in May 1918. The sale of liquor was finally legalized in 1959 after more than 50 years of prohibition.

The period of World War I produced significant social changes. War-generated urbanization developed rapidly in the greater Southwest, and between 1910 and 1920 the urban population of Oklahoma increased almost 69% as compared to the national average of 29%. During the World War II years more of the population was drawn to the larger communities. The trend has continued so that the 1980 United States Census reports that 58.6% of the total population live in four Standard Metropolitan Statistical Areas (Enid, Lawton, Tulsa, and Oklahoma City). The Tulsa and Oklahoma City SMSA's account for 51% of the total population.

A wide variety of racial and ethnic strains have contributed to the population of Oklahoma. This became especially conspicuous beginning in the 1870s with the mining boom and the influx of Europeans into the Choctaw Nation. The immigrants included Italian, Welsh, Irish, Slavic, Greek, Polish, and Russian miners. Later the land rushes saw homesteaders from Mexico, England, France, Canada, and even China and Japan coming into the region. Farming attracted Czechs and German Mennonites.

Those settlers from abroad did not stream into Oklahoma in such multitudes as they did in other states, but the numbers were significant. At the time of statehood approximately eight percent of the population was composed of foreign-born people and their children. The immigrants brought with them their own languages, social customs, and religious practices. Many of the foreign-born tended to concentrate in certain localities, a fact that gave them disproportionate influence.

Seven European countries sent more than 1,000 immigrants. The Germans were the largest group, numbering about 10,000. They included both those born in Germany and Russian-born Germans. Religiously they consisted of two distinct groups: Mennonites and Lutherans. In the number of immigrants represented, the Poles and Lithuanians were the next largest groups.

The first Jewish settlers entered Indian Territory following the Civil War. They began to come in substantial numbers after the opening of the Unassigned Lands in 1889, which was the year in which the first permanently organized Jewish community was established at Ardmore. The majority of Oklahoma Jews appear to have come from Germany or Austria although some were from Russia.

Negroes were among the earliest settlers in Oklahoma. A large percentage of Oklahoma's Negroes are descendants of slaves who belonged to the Five Civilized Tribes, although there was a limited migration from the South to Indian Territory immediately after the Civil War. Others came to Oklahoma during the land runs beginning in 1889. Today about seven percent of the population of the state is black.

Through this admixture of Indian, European, and non-European immigrants Oklahoma attained a highly diverse set of ethnic cultures and religions. The presence of Roman Catholic, Greek Orthodox, Episcopal, Lutheran, and Mennonite churches attests to the variety of European immigration, and a reflection of the European immigration to the mining camps in the Choctaw Nation is found at Hartshorne where one of the few Russian Orthodox Churches in the entire Trans-Mississippi West is located. But even in the face of the variety of immigration into the state there has been a trend toward uniformity in the religious picture.

The development of oil resources in the state was the cause of much change and the catalyst for new urban troubles. Crime became a sensational and widely noted aspect of life in the boomtowns. The seeming inability of the law enforcement agencies and politicians to arrest social change caused many Oklahomans to turn to the Ku Klux Klan to enforce both laws and moral behavior. The KKK represented for them a force to oppose the perceived threats of Negroes, Catholics, and Jews and sustain old social values. Because the Klan's primary role in Oklahoma seemed to be the restoration of moral authority, the membership even included some non-Protestants and non-whites. By 1922 some 70,000 Oklahomans had joined the Klan. Following Klan-inspired violence in 1922 the Klan lost much of its prestige and faded as a power in the Oklahoma political scene by the close of that decade.

The popularity of the Klan demonstrated a religious and social attitude that has characterized Oklahoma through much of its history as a state. That is, there is a tendency toward uniformity of religious expression, as evidenced by the predominance of a relatively small number of denominations in the state and the conservation of old, or traditional, values. The state presents an overall countenance of religious conservatism and seems to be particularly hospitable to Fundamentalism. Two examples are seen in the prominence of Oral Roberts and Billy James Hargis in the religious scene.

Oral Roberts is one of the best known religious personalities in the United States. His career has included that of an evangelist with a faith-healing ministry, president of an evangelistic organization, founder and president of a university, and founder of a health-care facility of large proportions. Roberts was born in 1918 in Ada, Oklahoma, the son of a Pentecostal preacher. Roberts entered the ministry in 1935 and for the next twelve years served in general evangelistic work and as pastor of churches in Enid and Shawnee, then in Toccoa, Georgia, and Fuquay Springs, North Carolina. He took courses at Oklahoma Baptist University and also attended Phillips University. He holds an honorary doctorate of laws from Centenary College. He began his healing ministry in Tulsa in 1947 and by 1955 was travelling with his "cathedral tent" which, with all the campaign equipment for his crusades, required eight truck trailers to carry it. He established Healing Waters in 1956; later this organization became the Oral Roberts Evangelistic Association. Roberts is now an ordained elder of the United Methodist Church.

Oral Roberts University officially opened in 1965 with a student body of 300 students, and by 1981 the number had risen to 4,000. The university is described as being committed to the "historic Christian faith" and standing for the authority of the Bible as the Word of God. The baptism in the Holy Spirit and the gifts of the Spirit are stated to be the distinctive charismatic dimension of the university. The City of Faith Medical and Research Center, a diagnostic center, hospital, and clinical research center, is located adjacent to the university campus. The hospital opened in 1981 and will provide 777 beds according to plans.

The Christian Crusade was founded in 1948 by Billy James Hargis who was serving at the time as minister of a Christian Church in Sapulpa. The Crusade was organized to safeguard and perserve "conservative Christian ideals," to oppose persons or organizations who endorse socialist or Communist philosophies, and to oppose U.S. participation in the United Nations, among other goals. Hargis had been ordained at the Rose Hill Christian Church in Texarkana and served as a minister for Christian Churches in Sallisaw then Granby, Missouri, before going to Sapulpa in 1946. He was educated at the Ozark Bible College, which was located at Bentonville, Arkansas, at the time, and was the recipient of an honorary doctorate from Bob Jones University in 1961.

Hargis began to devote his full-time efforts to the Christian Crusade in 1950 and became a leader in the right wing political movement of the early to mid-1960s. In 1966 the Church of the Christian Crusade was founded. Also associated with the Christian Crusade were the David Livingstone Missionary Foundation and the American Christian College of Tulsa. The church and its associated ministries suffered a setback in the mid-1970s when Hargis was charged with sexual immorality and the board of the college asked for his resignation as president. In October 1974 Hargis resigned his position with the college and retired from the church and the associated ministries. Six months later, however, Hargis came out of retirement and regained control of the church and the allied ministries except for the college.

A significant exception to this assertion of the Protestant dominance in the religious scene of Oklahoma is the persistence of the primitive Indian religion. Such historic observances as the Sun Dance and Ghost Dance have been vital spiritual forces among the tribes of western Oklahoma, and the Native American Church is a faith recognized by state charter.

The Native American Church dates to 1906 when an intertribal association of peyote groups in Oklahoma and Nebraska was formed. The name Union Church was adopted in 1909. The Bureau of Indian Affairs began a campaign in 1918 to declare peyote illegal, and in reaction the Native American Church was incorporated. The practices of the Native American church vary widely but a common feature is the peyote ritual. Legal battles have surrounded the use of peyote since 1899 when its use was outlawed in Oklahoma. The law was repealed in 1907. When psychedelic drugs were declared illegal by federal law in 1966, peyote and the Native American Church were excluded by the law.

The character of religion in Oklahoma is demonstrated by the religious institutions. Primarily, the institutions of higher education supported by religious bodies and the relative strength of the various denominations provide such a picture. Religious support of higher education dates from 1894 when Henry Kendall College was founded in Muskogee by the Presbyterians. Later the college became Tulsa University. Other colleges and universities supported by religious bodies are:

INSTITUTION	LOCATION	SPONSORING BODY
(FOUNDING NAME AND/OR DATE)		
Bethany Nazarene College (Oklahoma Holiness College, 1899)	Bethany	Church of the Nazarene
Oklahoma City University (Epworth College, 1904)	Oklahoma City	United Methodist
Oklahoma Baptist University (1906)	Shawnee	Southern Baptist
Phillips University (Oklahoma Christian University, 1907)	Enid	Christian Church (Disciples of Christ)
St. Gregory's College (1915)	Shawnee	Roman Catholic
Midwest Christian College (1946)	Oklahoma City	Christian
Southwestern College (1946)	Oklahoma City	Pentecostal Holiness
Oklahoma Christian College (Central Christian College, 1949)	Edmond	Church of Christ
Bartlesville Wesleyan College (Central Pilgrim College, 1959)	Bartlesville	Wesleyan Methodist
Oral Roberts University (1963)	Tulsa	Independent
Hillsdale Free Will Baptist College (1964)	Moore	Baptist General Conference in America
American Christian College (1907)	Tulsa	Independent

Graduate theological programs are offered at Phillips University and Oral Roberts University. Both of these programs are accredited by the Association of Theological Schools.

Maps displaying the distribution of churches in 13 religious denominations or families of denominations are presented in *Religion in America: 1950 to the Present.* The maps indicate the size and concentration of these churches in terms of their respective percentage membership of the total population, based on the 1970 United States census. The census reported 2,559,463 people in 77 counties in the state of Oklahoma.

Twelve of the denominations analyzed are represented in Oklahoma. The percentages of the total population in the seven most heavily populated counties in the state are presented in the following table:

Church Membership in Terms of Percentage of Total Population of the Seven Most Populous Counties

DENOMINATION	COUNTY (Population in 1,000s)						
	Payne	Garfield	Musko-gee	Cleve-land	Coman-che	Tulsa	Okla-homa
	(50)	(56)	(81)	(59)	(108)	(399)	(527)
	%	%	%	%	%	%	%
Baptist	15-24.9	15-24.9	25-49.9	15-24.9	15-24.9	15-24.9	15-24.9
Methodist	5-14.9	5-14.9	5-14.9	5-14.9	5-14.9	5-14.9	5-14.9
Roman Catholic	1-4.9	1-4.9	1-4.9	5-14.9	1-4.9	5-14.9	1-4.9
Presbyterian	1-4.9	1-4.9	1-4.9	1-4.9	1-4.9	1-4.9	1-4.9
Christian*	5-14.9	1-4.9	1-4.9	0-.9	0-.9	1-4.9	1-4.9
Episcopal	0	1-4.9	1-4.9	1-4.9	0-.9	1-4.9	1-4.9
Lutheran	1-4.9	5-14.9	0-.9	1-4.9	0-.9	1-4.9	1-4.9
Pentecostal	0	0-.9	0-.9	0-.9	0-.9	0-.9	0-.9
Adventist	0-.9	0-.9	0-.9	0	0-.9	0-.9	0-.9
United Church of Christ	0	0-.9	0	0	0-.9	0-.9	0-.9
Reformed	0	0	0	0	0-.9	0	0
Mennonite	0	0-.9	0	0	0	0	0

*[Includes Christian Church (Disciples of Christ), Christian Church, and Churches of Christ as a family of denominations.]

The strength of these denominations statewide is indicated by the following tabulation:

Church Membership in Terms of Percentage of Total Population by Number of Counties

DENOMINATION	0%	UNDER 1%	1-4.9 %	5-14.9 %	15-24.9 %	25-49.9 %	OVER 50%
Baptist				4	23	47	3
Methodist			2	51	21	3	
Christian	5	9	41	19	3		
Roman Catholic	2	17	46	12			
Presbyterian	12	16	47	2			
Lutheran	34	16	25	2			
Pentecostal	19	34	24				
Episcopal	34	30	13				
Adventist	37	37	3				
Mennonite	65	3	8	1			
United Church of Christ	65	10	2				
Reformed	75	2					

The preceding tables demonstrate that only the Baptists and Methodists are represented in all counties in the state. The most numerous churches in order are Baptists, Methodists, Christian Churches (denominational family), Roman Catholics, Presbyterians, and Lutherans. The Episcopal, United Church of Christ, Adventist, Reformed, and Pentecostal churches constitute less than five percent of the total population in any county.

The distribution of the churches is important. The northeastern quarter of the state (the area within a line beginning at the southern boundary of Cleveland County and running eastward to Arkansas and a line at the western border of Oklahoma County running northward to

Kansas) contains 29 counties. Thirteen of the counties in this section of the state account for approximately 56% of the total population; and, of these 13 counties, three account for approximately 25% of the state's population. Overall, 68% of the population is urban and 32% rural.

In summary, these statistics demonstrate that in the counties with the highest population, Baptist churches have the largest membership by a significant margin over the other denominations in all parts of the state. Second in size of membership are the Methodists, who show a consistent strength throughout the state. Also, these statistics indicate that the religious picture is dominated by seven denominations, and that the character of religion in the state is mainly conservative.

Bibliography

Thomas E. Brown. *Bible Belt Catholicism: A History of the Roman Catholic Church in Oklahoma, 1905-1945.*

——— . "Oklahoma's 'Bone-Dry Law' and the Roman Catholic Church," *Chronicles of Oklahoma* 52 (Summer 1974): 316.

Jackson W. Carroll et al. *Religion in America, 1950 to the Present.*

Leland Clegg and William B. Oden. *Oklahoma Methodism in the Twentieth Century.*

Herbert M. Dalke, "Seventy-five Years of Missions in Oklahoma," *Mennonite Life* 10 (July 1955): 100.

Stephen J. England. *Oklahoma Christians: A History of Christian Churches and of the Start of the Christian Church (Disciples of Christ) in Oklahoma.*

Grant Foreman. *Beginnings of Protestant Christian Work in Indian Territory.*

——— . *The Five Civilized Tribes.*

Arrell M. Gibson. *Oklahoma: A History of Five Centuries.*

Roy Gittinger. *Formation of the State of Oklahoma, 1803-1906.*

Douglas Hale. "European Immigrants in Oklahoma: A Survey," *Chronicles of Oklahoma* 53 (Summer 1975): 179.

Richard H. Harper. "The Missionary Work of the Reformed (Dutch) Church in America Oklahoma," *Chronicles of Oklahoma* 18 (September 1940): 252.

Charles J. Kappler. *Indian Affairs: Laws and Treaties, II.*

Christian Krehbiel. "The Beginnings of Missions in Oklahoma," *Mennonite Life* 10 (July 1955): 108.

H. Wayne Morgan and Anne H. Morgan. *Oklahoma: A Bicentennial History.*

John W. Morris et al. *Historical Atlas of Oklahoma.*

Jesse Rader and Edward E. Dale. *Readings in Oklahoma History.*

E. C. Routh. "Early Missionaries to the Cherokees," *Chronicles of Oklahoma* 15 (December 1937): 449.

Walter N. Vernon. "Beginnings of Indian Methodism in Oklahoma," *Methodist History* 18 (April 1979): 127.

Fred G. Watts. "A Brief History of Early Higher Education Among the Baptists of Oklahoma," *Chronicles of Oklahoma* 17 (March 1939): 26.

SOUTH CAROLINA

LEWIS P. JONES
WOFFORD COLLEGE

Founded as an English proprietary colony in 1670, South Carolina has had a religious history dominated by Protestants (Baptists, Methodists, Presbyterians, Episcopalians, Lutherans) but marked by religious tolerance. Until the present century, leading churches have usually reflected a conservative theology and supported the views and mores of "the establishment" and of society rather than moulding them or guiding them in new directions. In a state with a black majority for so long, race has been a major factor in church history.

Started as a venture for profit, the seven Proprietors offered religious tolerance as a lure for settlers, and very quickly dissenters constituted a majority. Newcomers were supposed to "acknowledge a God," and any seven persons were authorized to form a church and worship as they pleased. The Church of England was depicted as the "National Religion" and the Carolina parliament was authorized to "establish" it and tax the people for its support, a step not taken until 1706. The large Anglican minority was disproportionately influential, including many colonial leaders in a society marked by an identifiable aristocracy.

The first ten years on the west bank of the Ashley River were difficult and tenuous. Soon after the arrival of the first minister and after the colony had been moved to the peninsula between the Ashley and Cooper Rivers (present Charleston), a church (Anglican) was organized and built (ca. 1681) on the site of the present St. Michael's. As historically significant was the "White Meeting House" begun about 1690 by Calvinists of various sorts—from New England, northern Ireland, and Scotland.

Sometimes called "the Independent Church," from it ultimately sprang Congregationalists, Presbyterians, and Unitarians. The Baptists—today the most numerous group—began with a migration led from New England by William Screven in 1696 and the building by 1701 of their first meeting house in Charles Town. Not numerous but to become very influential in state history were French Huguenots who came following the revocation of the Edict of Nantes (1685) and who had a church in Charles Town by 1687. Often successful in the business community and shrewd in politics, Huguenots soon tended to join the church of King and Proprietors who had given them refuge and thus they helped undergird the special position of Anglicanism.

Particularly important was the 1702 arrival of the first missionaries of the Society for the Propagation of the Gospel in Foreign Parts (SPG), destined to provide about two-fifths of the always understaffed ministry of the Anglican establishment, to spread the Church beyond the confines of Charles Town, to promote education, and to be the first whites to show much humanitarian concern about Indians and Negroes. Planters (many from Barbados, of which Carolina to a degree was an offshoot) were reluctant to have slaves converted lest such would alter their status (based on a theory that one should not own "baptized property"). A statute of 1712 reassured planters (and their consciences?) on that point, but still for many generations planters and other colonial leaders did little to encourage Christianizing blacks.

As an SPG missionary viewed early Carolinians, "Religion was the thing about which they troubled themselves the least." But some Anglican colonists troubled themselves considerably about their dissenter neighbors after 1700—as much over economic and political rivalry as over their theological views. In 1704 an act which would have severely reduced dissenters' political participation and would have subjected Anglican ministers to a lay commission was disallowed in England, but the Church Act of 1706 was both an ecclesiastical and political landmark: Anglicanism was established as the state church to receive fiscal support from government, and parishes were laid out which had civil as well as church functions and were to be the basis of representation in the Low Country until 1865. Non-Anglicans, however, could continue to vote and to serve in the Assembly.

In the parish system, the vestry—called by one scholar "the real seat of power in the establishment"—reflected American distrust of distant tyranny so that the prestigious merchants and planters of the Carolina aristocracy through the vestry dominated the Anglican Church and its ministers with a "congregationalist attitude." It was a latter-day manifestation of "the spirit of the Puritan Revolution."

With no local episcopal authority to restrain strong-willed Anglican clergy, the Bishop of London appointed "commissaries" to represent his office and to exercise jurisdiction where he could not visit in person. The Rev. Gideon Johnson, the first commissary (1708-16), soon described his flocks as "the vilest race of men on earth," though ultimately he saw things less darkly once he reconciled himself to an Anglicanism quite different from that in England. A more famed commissary was the Rev. Alexander Garden, also rector of St. Philip's (the oldest congregation of Charles Town), who in 1740 became embroiled in an acrimonious controversy with George Whitefield whose unconventional and emotional preaching in South Carolina seemed much too radical and irregular to Garden. Nevertheless, Whitefield's emphasis on the salvation of the individual soul by effective evangelism was to be a format and doctrine most widely embraced and preached by those denominations which thereafter became dominant in South Carolina religious history. Whitefield's appeal was such that had he stayed in the colony, the church which contained about 45 percent of the churched might well have been disestablished.

The "White Meeting" (so called from the color of the meeting house) containing Scots, Scotch-Irish, English dissenters, and even French Huguenots was the grandmother church for many congregations. The groups tolerated each other harmoniously, but Scots disposed to presbyterianism left in 1732 to form the "Scots Presbyterian Church" (later called by some the First Presbyterian Church). A group of congregationalist-minded souls moved from Meeting Street to Archdale Street to form the "Second Congregational Church," and then migrated even further philosophically by becoming a strong Unitarian Church in the nineteenth century. In the original church, Congregationalists and Presbyterians stayed together for years (of the first six ministers, four were Congregationalists and two were Presbyterians, including the famed William Tennent). Ultimately the church was the leading Congregationalist group in the state.

The tolerance of the Carolina colony was most evident in its acceptance of Jews who established the second American congregation (Beth

Elohim) in Charles Town in 1750. Not only was this group accepted, but also became proportionately one of the largest communities of Jews in America by 1800, making up about 5 percent of Charleston white population. One scholar has stressed their early right to vote in the colony and states that the first Jew in America, if not in the modern world, to be elected to public office was Francis Salvador, chosen for the Provincial Congress of 1775.

In the 1730s the colonial government sought to populate the inland area by promoting establishment of townships (across the "midlands" of the present state). Although the scheme as envisioned had mixed results, it began a population movement of immigrants from abroad and the North who drastically altered the religious complexion of the colony. Certainly Anglicans shrank proportionately as Welsh Baptists poured down from Delaware to the banks of the Pee Dee, Scotch-Irish Presbyterians to Black River, and Germans and Swiss (both Lutheran and Reform groups) to various areas.

All suffered by not having a supply of pastors to accompany them, perhaps the Germans most of all. Factionalism further plagued the Germans, some—like Huguenots—becoming Anglicans as they followed a remarkable preacher, John Ulrich Giessendanner II. Earliest of these (1732) were the German Swiss on the lower Savannah at Purrysburgh which evaporated after a few trying years. Largest German influx was to the Saxe-Gotha area (modern Lexington County) with a spillover into the "Dutch Fork" between the Broad and Saluda Rivers, all of which is still plainly evident in local names and Lutheran concentration. By the 1750s Germans were settling in Charles Town and there organized the mother Lutheran church of the state, St. John's, in 1755, to be finally stabilized in the 1770s during the pastorate of Henry Melchior Muhlenburg.

The Baptists who came south to the Welsh Neck on the Pee Dee, later moving across the river to Society Hill, built their first meeting house in 1744. Like Puritans, they undertook (as Baptists were to do for a century) to police and punish the morals of their own community. Establishing contacts with English Baptists in Oliver Hart's Charles Town church, they formed the first Baptist "association" in the South. The Charleston Association, to be the model for others and also for the conventions yet to come, stabilized scattered Baptist churches, provided criteria and guidance, and yet was no threat to the independence in congregationalism. At the time when South Carolina had not yet produced a Baptist minister from its own ranks, Hart won into the fold Richard Furman, his disciple and successor who in many respects was the dominant founding father of Southern Baptistism.

After 1750 came the big wave of newcomers to the Back Country. One group, originally moving out of New England, were the "Separate" Baptists, so called because they had separated from Congregationalists as the "New Lights" after coming under the influence of Jonathan Edwards and the Great Awakening. Pouring into the piedmont with the Rev. Philip Mulkey in the vanguard, they appeared to Hart and the Charles Town Baptists as an intense, rigid group—often also rude and unlettered. Gradually the Low Country faction became reconciled to the Separates and their zealous religion.

Among the major "firsts" of South Carolina Baptists was the formation of the first all Negro congregation in America at Silver Bluff (near Augusta) between 1773 and 1775.

After 1750 the largest tide broke upon the piedmont Back Country from Virginia and Pennsylvania. Some were Separate Baptists with a mild Calvinistic flavor, but many were inclined to Presbyterianism. Rude subsistence farmers, unsophisticated and often high-strung, this scattered population above the fall line jumped from 22,000 to 83,000 during 1765-75—to four-fifths of the colony's white population. In 1768 there were 38 Presbyterian settlements in the colony. Like early Lutherans, few Presbyterian groups had ministers and depended on synods of the North for occasional missionaries; there were only three settled Presbyterian pastors in the vast hinterlands when Revolution came. This problem that long plagued Presbyterians stemmed partially from their insistence on an educated ministry—a limited supply amid a growing population, a factor which worked to the benefit of Separate Baptists. Emphasis on liturgy or anything smacking of "Romanism" thwarted the bold SPG missionaries, especially the famed and vitriolic Charles Woodmason, who detested the "Pack of vile levelling common wealth Presbyterians" whose "roving Teachers . . . stir up the Minds of the People . . . " But then he was no more complimentary of his prospective converts, "a Sett of Vile unaccountable Wretches." At least Anglicans had nearly all of their 22 parishes staffed in 1776.

Unlike some colonies, Anglicanism in South Carolina was not a major force for Loyalism in the Revolution; only five of 23 Anglican ministers stuck with Great Britain, and many of the major leaders of the cause came from St. Philip's Church. Until 1780 the Back Country was largely Loyalist or neutralist, resisting a barn-storming 1775 tour by William Tennent and Oliver Hart, leading Presbyterian and Baptist divines of Charles Town, who sought recruits for the Revolutionary cause. After British conquest of the coast in 1780 and oppressive measures of some military leaders, the state became more committed to secession. Dissenters won a victory in 1778 with disestablishment of Anglicanism, equal rights being extended then to all Protestants and in 1790 to Catholics and Jews.

Among late-comers, Methodists had the biggest impact. Although Wesley himself had visited South Carolina (his "Charleston Hymn Book" was printed there in 1737) and Whitefield in 1740, probably the first later Methodist was Joseph Pilmoor in 1773 although no preacher was stationed in South Carolina until a visit by Francis Asbury in 1785, after which Charles Town Baptists let Methodists use their meeting house.

In 1787 South Carolina Methodism formally began with the first annual conference presided over by Bishops Francis Asbury and Thomas Coke at the "Blue Meeting House" (to distinguish it from Congregationalists' "White Meeting") on Cumberland Street. The first conference assigned three presiding elders over seven circuits containing 2,071 white and 141 Negro Methodists. In the state, the church enjoyed meteoric growth (484 churches by 1850) explained by organization and theology. The former was built around an itinerancy based on circuit riders assisted by local preachers, certainty of services at designated places and times, Methodist "classes" under zealous lay leaders, and a firm discipline under an authoritarian system. The theology stressed the gospel of free will and free grace available to all, a view appealing to listeners who sought to be masters of their own destiny. Rather than hoping to establish a church once there was a sufficiently large congregation to call a pastor if one was available, frontier folk might find the Methodist circuit rider there before the population or the congregation, his task being to greet the newcomers and to make Methodists out of them.

As Methodism flourished after 1785, Presbyterians entered a relative decline—still handicapped by a paucity of ministers. They further dissipated their strength by heresies and theological controversies, "the Scotch mind," as D. D. Wallace put it, "seeming to take a mournful pleasure in making itself miserable in that way." One such division produced Associate Reformed Presbyterians (ARP) who organized a separate presbytery in 1790 and in 1803 their own synod with 2,000 members, a conservative psalm-singing band of "seceders" who have remained strong in the state but not numerous.

The post-Revolution years for South Carolina Baptists centered around the Rev. Richard Furman who took the Charleston pulpit in 1787 and did much to shape Southern Baptist life in general. His church had been the first Baptist church in the South; the Charleston Association was the first in the South (preceded only by Philadelphia); the first Baptist state convention was established in the state in 1821, with Furman as president; and the Triennial Convention of all Baptists was formed in Philadelphia in 1814, with Furman as first president. Despite the charge that Baptists had little concern for an educated ministry, its leadership in the state—Oliver Hart, Richard Furman, and John M. Roberts—stressed and encouraged it. Furman had organized the first children's society in the state, the first Baptist college in the South (at Greenville) was to be named after him, and the first general Baptist seminary in the South was to begin there. Long before such institutions, the Charleston Association in 1755 had established a fund and society to assist the education of needy young men seeking ministerial training.

Just as the Baptists' maturing rotated around Richard Furman, so did the Lutherans emerge to order and stability with a notable leader, John Bachman. After decades of too few churches and no strong cohesive organization, the formation of the South Carolina Synod in 1824 with Bachman as its president portended a new day. Coming to St. John's, Charleston, in 1815, he began a ministry that was to last over fifty years; practically defunct in 1815, St. John's was soon one of the most dynamic congregations in the state. Bachman was also a major force in establishment of the seminary that began in 1830.

Just as Bachman was famed as a naturalist, the key personality in Unitarianism was a leading literary figure in Charleston, Samuel Gilman, who presided (1819-58) over what was an influential church.

Catholic history in the state virtually began in 1821 with the arrival of Bishop John England to head the new Diocese of Charleston. During his time the best-known Catholic leader in the nation, this native of Ireland was a controversial figure of great intellect and ability. Although a few tactful Catholics may have settled in the state in earlier days, there was no priest until 1788. When the Bishop arrived, there were only a few small churches with a few communicants (estimates vary from 1,000 to 5,000).

Although the diocese included North Carolina and Georgia, Bishop England concentrated his attention upon the Charleston area where he soon got an academy started, a new convent established, and an orphanage launched. In 1822 he founded the *U. S. Catholic Miscellany*, the first Catholic paper of strictly religious nature in the country. By 1842 there were 7,000 Catholics (mostly Irish in background) in the large diocese scattered among 65 churches which had 21 priests; in 1850 there were 14 South Carolina churches, the strongest area (then as now) being Charleston. Although the colonial doctrine of religious liberty had specifically excluded "papists," the Constitution of 1790 granted them the right to vote.

Church practices and appearances varied greatly. Some stately Anglican churches could almost match the classical eighteenth century London structures on which they were modeled. In the hands of Robert Mills, the Independent Church (Charleston) came to be known as the Circular Church, when "rectangular box" would have been an appropriate label for scores of meeting houses. Music varied from Bach to bedlam. "Singing Billy" Walker's *Southern Harmony*, published in Spartanburg in 1835, not only set publishing records but also shaped the singing habits and tastes of thousands.

Sermons—especially among non-Episcopalians—were long and often loud, with favorite topics repentance, damnation, salvation, and the millennium. Individual humility was supposed to precede salvation of the individual who then expected an experience of grace to be followed by regeneration. The larger and growing denominations maintained strict watch over the conduct of members by frequent discipline and even expulsion—perhaps socially useful where law and government had not kept up with settlement. The object of greatest concern seemed to be drinking, followed by neglect of church. In the region where increasingly religion was more concerned with individual salvation than with improvement of society, at least churches were involved with individual conduct that was detrimental to social order. Fighting, mistreatment of spouses and children, breach of contract—all were fit subjects for churches to punish but also to mediate or arbitrate. Unfortunately, amusements of every variety were viewed as Satan's playground, Methodists even frowning on "idle visits" on the Sabbath. A Welsh Neck church enjoined good Baptists to keep children from "wicked company and vain pleasures, such as playing at cards" because "lovers of pleasure are not lovers of God." In church discipline cases, women were usually expected to remain silent.

Economic distinctions were clearer in 1800-1860: South Carolina Episcopalians were more affluent and perhaps best educated; Presbyterians increasingly spread across a broad spectrum (more affluent along the coast); and Baptists and Methodists the poorest economically. (Methodists complained that if they converted wealthy sinners in the summer by winter they were Episcopalians or Presbyterians.) Preachers in these two had to accept an austere existence (though many Baptist pastors held other jobs). In 1800, Methodist salaries were $80 a year; South Carolina Lutheran pastors were said to be the most poorly paid of that group in the nation in 1849—only two making as much as $250 a year. Average salary for Presbyterian clergy in 1850 was $300. Never at home, Methodist circuit riders almost had to be bachelors and to put much of their meager income into one valuable and necessary possession: a horse.

The rapid growth of Baptists, Methodists, and Presbyterians came from constant evangelism and frequent revivalism that all sponsored and in which they sometimes cooperated. Highlight of the church year was the "protracted meeting" (dubbed by the irreverent "distracted meeting") unless they had a camp meeting in the area—the fruition of the "Second Great Awakening." Emotional extravaganzas, exercises in mass hypnosis, social event of the season, or "the most sublime . . . scenes on this side of eternity": camp meetings were thus variously depicted by South Carolinians who soared off into rhapsody or unconsciousness while "jerking," "wheeling," or "barking" in the holy "exercises" or "under impression." Gradually decorum drew many dour Presbyterians apart and left the excessive joys to shouting Methodists who had dozens of such "camp grounds" and "tabernacles." (One observer lists 42 "prominent" ones.) As one South Carolina Methodist reported to Asbury, "Hell is trembling, and Satan's kingdom falling."

In a state with poor education (no "public schools" in the modern sense), all churches bestirred themselves. Beginning in 1711, Anglicans and successor Episcopalians long had Sunday schools for under-privileged and Negro children, and the Independent Church had two sessions on the Sabbath. Much time went to catechisms and Bible memorizing, but some basic literate skills were also lightly touched. By 1828 Cumberland Street Methodist Church had 400 Negroes in Sunday school (pastor was James O. Andrew, over whom the Methodist Church split in

1844 when he was bishop), and by 1846 there were 265 Methodist Sunday schools in the state. All denominations were thus engaged, the first Baptist convention (1821) having made them a major emphasis.

Comparable to "middle schools" or secondary schools were church academies and "seminaries," both in towns and rural regions, supplemented by many run privately by preachers (especially Presbyterians). A few academies were notable, although most were not. Some examples: Mt. Bethel (Methodist, 1794); Tabernacle (c. 1820), predecessor to Cokesbury Conference School (Methodist, 1834-1918); Willington, most famous one run by the Rev. Moses Waddel, Presbyterian; Lexington Institute (Lutheran); and Reidville Male and Female High Schools (1857), run by a Presbyterian minister.

South Carolina has been birthplace and graveyard for many colleges, many church-related. Several reasons explain denominational efforts in ante-bellum days: the need for an educated ministry; a proper function for the church to render to society; education safe from heretical influences of Dr. Thomas Cooper at South Carolina College; tuition cheaper than state colleges (strange sounding today); means for evangelism and good public relations. Although parents were assured that sons could go to Cokesbury, for example, "without risk to their morals," the danger was perhaps no greater one place than another. Curricula were similar in all types. (S. C. College faculty had its share of Presbyterian and Episcopal ministers.) Unfortunately, most of the denominational colleges prior to 1860 had poor standards, facilities, and libraries. Erskine (ARP) began at Due West in 1839, Furman (Baptist) at Greenville in 1851 (having gone through several metamorphoses beginning at Edgefield in 1827), Wofford (Methodist) at Spartanburg in 1854, and Newberry (Lutheran) at Newberry in 1856. In 1854 Baptists and Methodists both began female colleges in Greenville and Columbia, respectively, and ARPs began one in Due West in 1859. (Omitted are academies and seminaries that called themselves colleges.)

In the history of theological training in the South, however, small South Carolina has played a significant role. Despite Methodist emphasis on education, prior to 1860 they founded no seminary and some leaders staunchly opposed such. In 1827 the first property that the new state Baptist convention acquired was for the training of preachers: The Furman Academy and Theological Institution, to have a checkered and migrant career until the 1850s. Once the Southern Baptist Convention was formed in 1845, the new Furman University served its needs until the formation of the Southern Baptist Seminary in Greenville in 1859—transplanted to Louisville in 1877. The ARP denomination in 1837 planted their seminary in Due West where it has remained. Another still flourishing was the first Lutheran seminary in the South, begun in 1830 peregrinating even more than Furman as it wandered through the wilderness to various places from its start until establishment in Columbia in 1911. Plagued by having to go elsewhere for training, in 1830 Presbyterians opened their seminary in Columbia because there "was concentrated the most wealth, literary advantages, and moral force"—and because it might be a bulwark against "infidel principles" emanating from Thomas Cooper's neighboring institution. Housed in a Robert Mills-designed residence (today a restored showplace), it had a notable faculty before 1860 (including James H. Thornwell, Benjamin N. Palmer, John B. Adger, Charles Colcock Jones, and John L. Girardeau) who stressed the Bible's total infallibility, written by God and being a book of science, history, and astronomy as well as ethics.

After 1830, with the exception of the few Quakers, reactions of South Carolina churches to slavery varied little. Most clergy accepted the system of slavery and raised no serious or discomforting questions about its propriety. In earlier days there were sharp Methodist exceptions: Wesley and Asbury minced no words in condemning the institution, and early Methodism in the state suffered ostracism and resentment because of its "integrated" status (4,529 black members by 1791) and concern for "lower classes" and "the spiritual welfare of the colored people." To many, Methodism was a misfit in South Carolina Low Country society, especially after the 1790 General Conference had held that slaveholding was contrary to the laws of God and man.

Gradually South Carolina Methodists softened such views and thereafter had less difficulty winning converts. By the 1830s because of cotton prosperity, phobias caused by abolitionists' attacks, and fear of slave revolts, all South Carolina hierarchies provided religious rationale to defend the institution which the laity wanted preserved. Planters no longer worried about the propriety of owning a Christian. Partially to salve their own consciences and partially to refute strident Northern voices charging them with sinful ways and unconcern for Negroes' souls, all denominations began doing mission work to bring black converts into a special second-class status within their congregations and to provide

Sunday schools for black children. This South Carolina holier-than-thou counterattack was probably sincere and it certainly was impressively energetic.

Slaveholders encouraged mission work, sometimes claiming that devout slaves were more docile and hence better as workers. The synod directed South Carolina Lutherans to provide facilities so that Negroes would be "prepared and fitted for full acceptance . . ., according to their situation in society." (Bachman's Negro Sunday school had 32 teachers and 150 pupils.) Some churches put their black members in balconies or held separate services for them. Some sent missionaries to plantations, a project most ambitious after 1829 with Methodists who by 1855 had 32 preachers thus assigned and were raising $25,000 for this mission work.

One concern beset whites: their fear of free blacks' association with slaves in churches and it stirring discontent or worse. Especially did this fear arise after the Denmark Vesey Rebellion (1822). Despite this, in 1849 Second Presbyterian Church, Charleston, erected a second building for their Negro members, a step so popular that a separate church soon had to be built, the largest church structure in Charleston for this black flock and their popular white preacher. (They did have a gallery for whites.) Bethel Methodist, Charleston, turned its old building over to its black members; in 1880 the building was moved again by its Negro congregation which today therefore has the oldest Methodist church building (1797) in the state—"Old Bethel." Thus blacks were a part—a separate-but-not-equal part—of white churches. Richard Fuller, distinguished Baptist preacher of Beaufort, had 2,000 Negro members; in 1860 there were 3,166 white Episcopalians and 2,960 black Episcopalians; white Baptists attracted 21,911 blacks into their church by 1858; the "white" Methodist church of 1860 had more blacks than whites—42,469 to 34,357.

Whites saw their church efforts as "moral and spiritual progress without any threat, open or implied, to . . . the established order." But Negro churches run by Negroes they viewed askance. In 1817, Morris Brown, a free Negro affiliated with the African Methodist Episcopal Church, started the Emmanuel Church in Charleston, the mother church of that denomination in the South. Quickly it attracted 1,000 members, but white pressures and intimidation (arrests for "disorderly conduct") threatened it, and after the Vesey affair it was closed down by public authorities. (Brown went north and became the second AME bishop.)

After division in the national church bodies, South Carolina ministers became strident defenders of the peculiar institution as a "positive good" that was blessed by God. Most notable were two Presbyterians: James H. Thornwell and Benjamin M. Palmer. Earlier Richard Furman had defended it as not "contrary to the genius of Christianity," and William Capers, leader of the Methodists' mission work, found it quite harmonious with the Gospel. Most did stress the responsibility of masters to be humane. The rigid South Carolina proslavery position spread by emigration: in 1860, 291,300 whites lived in South Carolina while 470,257 who had been born in the state then lived elsewhere.

Even as disruption of the Union approached, churchmen did not flinch in the regional paranoia. Convinced that it was the unfolding of the work of Divine Providence that would protect the South and its institutions if war came, Thornwell said, "We are prepared to meet it with unshaken confidence in the God of battles." The state Baptist Convention in 1861 asserted that God approved of the South's action and "the wickedness of the wicked will return on their own heads." Perhaps ironically, the Secession Convention held its first session in Columbia's Baptist Church.

Most churches suffered deeply during the Civil War years. Catholics lost their cathedral, two orphanages, two convents; Episcopalians had ten churches burned and twenty-three parishes suspended; Baptist ministers declined from 540 to 302; church schools were defunct or virtually so. The fifty-three Presbyterian congregations had only twenty-eight ministers.

At war's end, churches panicked at the invasion of Northern missionaries who had first come to the sea islands in 1862 and came in larger numbers in 1865. Northern churches sought conversions and new members with mixed success, but they did found and support Negro schools and colleges, including Benedict (Baptist) in Columbia (1871), Claflin (Methodist) in Orangeburg (1869), and Allen (AME) in Columbia (1870).

Proud of their prewar evangelization of Negroes, white churches expected to keep their Negro converts (72,349 in 1860, compared to 70,729 white members)—but still in a secondary status. Whites were disappointed and surprised when blacks departed en masse for new churches of their own: Southern Methodist black enrollment plummeted from 42,469 to 653 between 1860 and 1873. Some went to the South Carolina Missionary Conference set up by the Northern Methodists (43,000 by 1890), a group to enter the "Central Jurisdiction" in 1939 and to merge with the South Carolina Conference in 1972. The Baptist convention invited "their" Negroes to stay but on the old basis of inequality; instead they made a mass exodus and in "congregational bliss" started scores of their own churches with no organization or convention for several years. Presbyterians alienated most of their 1860 black constituency by implying that Negroes were not competent to run their own affairs; many of these became Methodists or Baptists, but in 1906 some 8,000 belonged to the Northern Presbyterian Church. The liturgical Episcopalians watched 2,698 of their 2,960 black members defect, but retained St. Mark's, Charleston, as their "mother church" there, though with a white pastor, a situation which caused lengthy controversy in the diocese.

Ultimately white churches accepted realistically that blacks' new allegiance would be to their own churches under their own leaders—the major institution which they henceforth could control. Some new congregations were blocs of blacks who seceded together from white churches and started their own—easiest to do in the Baptist system. The South Carolina Southern Baptists contained 29,211 Negroes in 1858, but only 1,614 in 1874; by 1886, the new black convention (Baptist Educational Missionary and Sunday-School Convention) had 100,286 members. The new Colored Methodist Episcopal Church (CME), sponsored somewhat as a client by white Southern Methodists, failed to hold the allegiance of blacks, getting only 3,468 members in the state by 1890—perhaps suspect because of its origins.

Particularly effective was the revival of the AME Church in Charleston which Morris Brown had started prior to the Vesey Rebellion. Led by the Rev. Richard H. Cain, charismatic AME Northern preacher, a South Carolina conference was organized in 1865 at a meeting held in Zion Presbyterian Church. As pastor of the restored Emmanuel Church, Cain soon had the largest congregation (about 3,000) of the AME Church in the South. Indication of the lack of bitterness was that Trinity Methodist (white) let Emmanuel meet in their church until the new AME building was completed. Like many Negro preachers—by definition leaders in the race's one large institution, Cain played many roles: member of Constitutional Convention, state senator, and member of Congress. After leaving South Carolina, he was elected an AME bishop.

That oldest black denomination (AME) expanded rapidly: By 1866 it had 22,388 members and 13 ministers; in 1878 it divided the state into two conferences; and by 1898 it had more members in South Carolina than in any other state. (AME membership statistics disconcert: If a communicant does not pay during the year, he is not counted.) The AME, Zion blacks formed a South Carolina conference also in 1867 and within twenty years it had about one hundred churches, mostly along the North Carolina border.

The generation following Reconstruction was the most formative one for "main line" South Carolina churches. Attitudes and habits that were to shape several generations were then fixed—as were political, social, and economic attitudes and outlooks of South Carolinians. To many later, this "Bourbon Era" was made to appear the "good old days."

The era of 1875-1914 was also a paradoxical period: Church bodies seemed bustling and statistics growing, church administration becoming more efficient and effective, new programs and institutions starting, and revivals claiming great conquests. On the other hand, despite such obvious changes, the church was itself not changing greatly in response to the changes and problems of the society that enveloped it. As the major all-Southern institutions remaining after the Confederacy, churches embraced the Bourbon and Lost Cause concept that Utopia lay somewhere in a South now gone, that the "Southern way of life" (whatever that was) was superior and that as much of it as possible should be preserved. (Historians often suggest that "the South" did not die at Appomattox, but was born there.) Hence ecclesiastical organizations that appeared to be bustling and changing were often quite dedicated to maintenance of much of the status quo, to a conservative religious orthodoxy suspicious of innovation or of anyone slightly skeptical. The Southern clergy have been called "the most radical of sectionalists," and the church had become a prisoner of the South which it had done so much to create and now to perpetuate. Religiosity was fused with regionalism. In such cultural isolationism, fear of change and alliance with "the establishment" meant that the church was not disposed to examine that society with critical eye nor to commit the heresy of advocating changes in it. Much that was good was guarded and protected in that stance; much that was bad was tolerated and pickled by that stance. Such was not altogether new: South Carolina churches had long "gone along"—most notably by providing theological defense of slavery when that pleased the lay flock. For decades they had preached against individual sin and promoted individual salvation rather than identifying factors in the environment which shaped or oppressed individuals or suggesting ways of applying Christian principles to social problems. To a large extent, the church continued on that same path in the New South.

During 1875-1914, the "social gospel" came to the North, concerned particularly with problems connected with large-scale industrialization, urbanization, and immigration. South Carolina did not have quite the same problems. But it too had problems: abject poverty in agriculture and share-cropping, drab life in the new cotton mill villages, inhumane evils in the convict-lease system, the demeaning status of the Negro, and the perennial problem of racial tension. On all these, the church spoke—occasionally, discreetly, and in muted tones. In general, the South Carolina church had its old emphasis—"the old time religion" with stress on such sins as card playing and dancing.

Even so, churches did not altogether "pass by on the other side of the road" and they engaged in activities which later could be and were expanded in ways to make for a healthier society and a healthier church.

South Carolina churches had been mission-minded before the war, and although now they virtually ceased their mission work to Negroes (though the South Carolina AME Church sent a missionary to Liberia), "missionary societies" sprang up like onions. After a dormant period, the state's Methodist Conference in 1881 made this a major thrust and ultimately a large number of South Carolinians went abroad to many countries, Brazil and China leading the list. Baptists did the same, but South Carolina Presbyterians lagged behind their fellow Presbyterians elsewhere. Lutherans did home mission work with new German groups arriving in the state, thereby adding new congregations (seven of which were German-speaking).

Two important spin-offs resulted. The first was the establishment of all kinds of "societies" by which enthusiasm could be generated for a "cause" and machinery provided to further it—missions at first, but then temperance, youth work, and other concerns of the church. Second, the missionary societies began the emancipation of women, providing acceptable and available opportunities for involvement outside the household, for self-awareness and self-assertion. The response of South Carolina women in 1868 was described by one as "truly magnificent." In 1878, South Carolina Methodist women in the state had 83 missionary societies—even before the General Conference gave official sanction to such. Baptist women had done missionary work in the sea islands as early as 1811, but in 1881 they organized their first missionary society and soon were supporting a Shanghai hospital.

Sunday schools were not new, but statewide organization of them was, as was affiliation with the American Sunday School Union which standardized procedures, provided a uniform lesson plan, and made literature available. Congregations sometimes coordinated efforts in "union schools" or with teachers' meetings on Saturday night where there was ecumenical study together of the same lesson. The flourishing of this wing of the church brought more lay people than ever—including women—into "church work." South Carolina Lutherans had more Sunday schools than they did churches, discovering that as a good way to incubate new congregations. In 1894 the Baptist Convention put pressure on its churches for the schools, admitting that many earlier efforts had involved "aimless unconcern" and "vague glittering generalities." The Methodist Conference of 1900 reported 705 Sunday schools.

Akin to "societies" was the upsurge of organizations for youth— maybe because of denominational misgivings about such non-church movements as the YMCA and Christian Endeavor. The Luther League started at Newberry in 1895; the Baptist Convention pushed the BYPU beginning in 1894; and the Methodists started the Epworth League in the state in 1891 and had 47 operating by the end of the decade. Episcopalians had many youth involved and organized in the 1920s.

"Spreading the gospel" and keeping the constituency informed involved many publications, organized in various ways. The *Sunday Visitor* of South Carolina Episcopalians claimed to be the first such magazine in the United States (1818), followed by the more ambitious *Gospel Messenger*. John England's *U. S. Catholic Miscellany* initiated such publication among American Catholics. The second Methodist periodical in America was the *Wesleyan Journal* begun in 1825 with William Capers as editor, though it soon merged with the *Christian Advocate* of New York. With the growth of Southern self-consciousness, the *Southern Christian Advocate* began in Charleston in 1837 with Capers as editor—an organ which once served several conferences but ultimately came to be the state's paper. Baptists began their highly successful *Baptist Courier* in 1877—like some of its predecessors, a private venture rather than an official organ but one endorsed by the Convention, which did buy it in 1920 and make it the voice of the denomination. Since 1879 it has been published at Greenville, "the Baptist capital." In 1847 James H. Thornwell founded the *Southern Presbyterian Review*, and in 1831 the *Lutheran Observer* began , but the first journal just for the South Carolina Synod was the *Lutheran Messenger* (1922), renamed later (1938) the *S. C. Lutheran*.

Expansion of church institutions characterized the 1875-1914 period and began with the Presbyterians' opening Thornwell Orphanage at Clinton in 1875 with eight children. Chief founder was Dr. William P. Jacobs, Clinton pastor, who named it for his friend and teacher. The *Baptist Courier* then reminded its readers that they had ignored that field, a gap filled in 1892 when the first child entered their Connie Maxwell Orphanage in Greenwood. In 1894 Methodists did go and do likewise— setting aside talk of a hospital—and opened Epworth Orphanage in Columbia in 1895. (All are today called children's homes.) After 1909, Episcopalians concentrated their efforts of this nature in a Children's Home in York. South Carolina Lutherans support one in Salem, Virginia.

Only Baptists and Catholics have entered the hospital field: The former now have a large one in Columbia, opened in 1914, and another in Easley (1958). Roman Catholics maintain hospitals in Charleston, Columbia, Greenville, York, and Dillon.

The antebellum church maintenance of schools and academies continued into the twentieth century. As public education came following Reconstruction, many still had reservations about it. The *Baptist Courier* in 1882 opposed compulsory education, perhaps in an adverse mood because of the fear and friction then raging between state and denominational colleges. Ministers—both with and without parishes—were still also school teachers, and in the day before public high schools, there were numerous church-related forerunners of such. These varied widely, as did the nature and extent of church control and governance. Samples of some of the long-forgotten citadels of learning that dotted the landscape are Harmony "College" at Bradford Springs and Parochial School of Arsenal Hill Church (both Presbyterian); Six-Mile Academy and Ridgedale Academy (Baptist); Leesville English and Classical Institute, and Summerland College (Lutheran). Church colleges owned or cooperated with "fitting" or preparatory schools to train budding scholars for freshman level. For example, Furman had Spartan Academy (at Landrum) and its own fitting school, and Wofford had Carlisle School (Bamberg), ties with Cokesbury, and its own fitting school in Spartanburg.

The denominational colleges founded before 1860 (see above) survived the war, and in 1880 were joined by Presbyterian College in Clinton, another Jacobs venture. Two common denominators existed: poverty and the goal of providing some ministers. Joining the three women's colleges started before the war were some new but not strong ones that had varying degrees of closeness with their churches: Coker College at Hartsville (1908), Anderson at Anderson (1912), Limestone at Gaffney. (Coker and Limestone are now independent.) The Presbyterian venture at Clinton was a success, unlike their College for Women at Columbia (1893), which was combined with their Chicora (1906) of Greenville in 1916, and then later the combination moved to Charlotte with Queens College. The Wesleyan Church began Central Wesleyan in 1906. The Negro colleges of Reconstruction did survive but not thrive. Other four-year black colleges were also started: Morris (1908) of the Baptist Educational and Missionary Convention and Voorhees (1897), taken over by the Protestant Episcopal Church in the 1920s. Latest college additions have been Baptist College at Charleston (1960) and one that labels itself properly the "world's most unusual university," the large and fundamentalist Bob Jones University, which moved to Greenville in 1947. Also unusual were two that had characteristics of the "manual labor schools" of the nineteenth century: Ferguson-Williams Industrial College, one under Presbyterian auspices (1903-1920) that provided industrial training for Negroes at Abbeville till 1920; and the Textile Industrial Institute (1911) at Spartanburg (now Spartanburg Methodist College), which maintained two student bodies rotating with each other, one in class for a period while the other worked in mills earning school costs.

The seminaries (already noted) were marked by stability at Erskine, great strengthening by the Lutherans once they settled in Columbia (1911), and near-suicide by Presbyterians (also in Columbia) in their controversy over Professor James Woodrow and evolution in the 1880s (a spectacle precipitated by weakness and small enrollment that finally led to reestablishment in Decatur, Georgia, in 1927).

The noisiest theological controversy was the one that roared about evolution, itself tied to the bigger issue of inerrancy of scripture read literally. The Fundamentalists alarmed by Darwin were also usually the same group favoring rigid rules about social conduct. Though widespread, the issue was highlighted by the Woodrow case at Columbia Seminary and the efforts to unseat this professor who had been brought there in 1859 to a new professorship designed to deal with the relations between religion and science. After two decades when this moderate compromiser said the conflicts between the two were "apparent" but "not real," he alarmed the conservatives who were also upset by his statement that the relationship of science and religion was more "one of noncontradiction" than one of harmony. After furious debate during 1883-1888, he was removed not for the fallacy of his statements or interpretation but for discussing these matters at the seminary which were "contrary to our church's interpretation of the Bible, and to her prevailing and recognized views." He was personally respected, and even chosen moderator of the South Carolina Synod in 1901. After the imbroglio, he was elected president of the University of South Carolina, and the commotion was virtually forgotten by the time of his death in 1907.

Another theological row of 1880-1910 centered about the Holiness movement rooted in John Wesley's theology. The Methodist founder had preached justification, or "being saved" by faith at the time of "conversion" and commitment—an "experience" emphasized in revivals. But Wesley also went on to define a "second blessing" in which one may later be purified of his sinful nature and thus surrender his will to God—this conceived of as a transcendent, purifying experience which in effect puts one beyond the reach of sin. Those rare persons who achieved this second step—i.e., sanctification, or holiness of hearts—perceived this as the ultimate goal of religious experience—or holiness. Holiness groups thus sought to stress and reach this "second blessing," or Christian perfection, a sanctification of one's life thereafter free of sin.

With reforming zeal returning to Methodism about 1870, many pietists stressed this doctrine and formed "holiness associations," within the Methodist Conference and sometimes in other churches, usually amid considerable emotionalism. Not surprisingly, factionalism within traditional churches resulted, and from this came over a score of holiness denominations after 1894. One significant group began in Iowa in 1895 but was organized in Anderson in 1898 as a denomination, "The Fire-Baptized Holiness Church." South Carolina had met the Holiness movement not only among troubled Methodists (with the Rev. R. C. Oliver maybe the best known one), but in other forms as well: in Benjamin Hardin Irwin, an evangelist at the Wesleyan Methodist Church in Piedmont in 1896; in a holiness paper, *Way of Faith*, published at the Oliver Gospel Mission in Columbia and circulating all over the nation; in the *Way of Holiness*, published in Spartanburg; and in the career of N. J. Holmes, a Presbyterian preacher. About the turn of the century a number of Holiness adherents moved on to embrace Pentecostalism, which to most involved a third "step" or blessing, that of speaking in tongues as a mark of progression.

With this came a number of additional congregations. Holmes, who received pentecostal baptism in 1907, established a "Bible and Missionary Institute" in 1898 which moved about the state but finally settled in Greenville as the Holmes Theological Seminary where it became—and is—an important force in the pentecostal movement in the nation, exercising a conservative influence and "discouraging extremism and excessive emotionalism." As a seminary, it has produced hundreds of preachers, especially for the Pentecostal Holiness Church, a successor of the Fire-Baptized Holiness Church. Although holiness and pentecostal groups are often considered to be limited to "socially disinherited and economically underprivileged," such stereotyping may be unwise. As one scholar put it, they "rejected a society that they felt wicked and corrupt, and that social order rejected them as unstable, backward, and self-righteous." Some holiness people are probably correct to say that they are closer to Wesley's theology than are many modern Methodists. One might also see in the group of 1890-1910 adumbrations of the charismatic movement of the 1970s.

Interesting was the original absence of racism in the movement: Present and accepted in the 1893 Fire-Baptized Holiness Church was a Negro, W. E. Fuller, of Mountville, who became a leader and brought in others to the new denomination. In Greer in 1908, however, he formed a new black pentecostal denomination, "The Fire-Baptized Church of God of the Americas" which continues with headquarters in Greenville at the Fuller Normal and Industrial Institute.

While the holiness movement was emerging, there was also underway a new "Awakening" marked by nationally known "princes of the pulpit" such as Dwight L. Moody, Billy Sunday, and others who brought to revivalism the tactics of big business: efficient organization, salesmanship, and shrewd public relations. Insofar as revivals can be measured by statistics, they were fabulously successful. Most of these dynamic preachers did not tour the South, perhaps because the region still had its own revivalism in its own "protracted meetings," camp meetings (less numerous now), union services, and its own evangelists—Sam Jones, Mordecai Ham, "Cyclone Mack" McLendon, and others who played the opera houses, tents, and "tabernacles" apart from the regular sanctuaries. Many delighted in it; perhaps many of the dejected got their minds off the ills of this world, even those existing in Henry Grady's much touted New South.

Amid revivals, South Carolina churches could be expected to continue pursuing the old villains of sin—and they did. Baptists noted that the "cardinal sin" (drinking) kept growing. The presbytery blamed the Yankees: "The gloom and despondency caused by the downfall of the Confederacy no doubt tended to lead many young people especially into unusual and excessive dissipation." In this mood, Calvinists also lambasted "promiscuous dancing, card playing and theatrical performances as worldly folly" and charged that "The Lord's Day was desecrated by worldly pursuits, profane swearing and drunkenness." A Baptist paper found itself on the horns of a dilemma since the creation of a third party, the Prohibitionists, "would imperil white supremacy." The Methodists in 1887 called theaters "traveling cess-pools" and one preacher warned against "promiscuously" indulging in the "fascinating art" of dancing which would "lead to dissipation and lasciviousness." Lutherans moved in gingerly fashion, maybe because some of their new Germans were accustomed to a "continental Sabbath." The unfortunate legacy of these "Gloomy Guses" was the stereotype created among the young who long after saw such as the chief characteristics and value system of "the church."

South Carolina reactions to the issues that concerned Northerners involved in the Social Gospel were both positive and negative. On the matters connected with rapid industrialization, Carolinians were ambivalent. Rejecting Darwin on biological evolution, they nevertheless tended to embrace Social Darwinism—the gospel of laissez-faire and the worship of "free enterprise." Echoing Henry Grady and New South boosterism, churchmen welcomed cotton mills, singing hosannas for entrepreneurs, and cooperating with their paternalism. In the mill-built instant communities, here were potential instant-congregations. As mill owners attracted workers with low-rent houses, credit at the company store, subsidies for schools, and other forms of "welfare capitalism," so did they aid with church construction and contributions toward ministerial salaries. All this led one Methodist pastor to see "the hand of God" in the coming of the mills and to "think of Southern industry as a spiritual movement." At least 161 churches were built either entirely or in part by new mill companies. The population explosion on new "mill hills" provided an opportunity for church expansion and also for missionary challenge. Lutherans issued warnings in 1909 lest labor unrest and strife ("ruinous, anarchistic") accompany the transformation. Lutherans and Presbyterians talked about problems to be assuaged, but most of the expansion with mill churches was that of Baptists and Methodists, with holiness and pentecostal groups soon involved.

Still strongly rural, Protestantism showed little concern about urban problems or immigrants, far less than the North did, though the Baptist Convention in 1895 deplored "sinful" cities and immigrants, proclaiming, "We must evangelize them, or they will overcome us," the "they" being foreigners who "bring along with them their anarchy, their Romanism, and their want of morals."

But in the Progressive Era and the early twentieth century, the church was not totally ossified. Although church papers frowned on women's suffrage, the church encouraged education for women more than the state did. Although the church did little to change the basics of a white supremacy society, it did condemn gross injustice and begin to acknowledge that the problems had not been "solved." Women's groups concerned themselves with problems of children (not just in their orphanages), formed organizations for various causes, advocated efforts to improve race relations, and faced "relevant" issues. In 1889, Mrs. Sally Chapin of Charleston in a national convention of the Women's Christian Temperance Union (WCTU) lashed out at the convict-lease system ("a disgrace to the civilization of the nineteenth century") and pled for reducing the work week for men. At the time, the Spartanburg WCTU was running an employment bureau for women needing work.

Maybe the church had not turned society wrong-side-out, but church agencies were beginning to "view with alarm" several vexing conditions. In 1906, a presbytery fumed about the need for the church to work in mill villages, lumber camps, and areas laden with other neglected unfortunates. In 1914, the Baptist Convention established a new committee to encourage interdenominational efforts to solve community problems, particularly those of race and labor relations. Maybe this was talk and not action—but earlier the talk had not noted this direction. In 1928, the Episcopal Department of Christian Social Service set out to awaken the diocese to the problems of interracial relations and continuing child labor problems, and as the Depression came advocated a public welfare program for the state.

While the larger denominations were moving slowly in those directions, newer denominations—many of them offshoots of Wesleyan pietism—grew and flourished as they declaimed the old-time religion of anathemas about personal conduct, fundamentalism, and revivalism. "The church"—in the broadest sense—was embarked simultaneously on two different courses: the larger, older denominations on a new one; the newer denominations on one which the big denominations were beginning to abandon after so many generations.

Some tenuous generalizations about religion in South Carolina since 1914 are, in order:

1. In 1980 the six largest denominational groupings, in order, are Baptist, Methodist, Presbyterian, Catholic, Lutheran, Episcopal. Of these, Catholics were showing fastest growth: 42 percent in 12 years, and 22.8 percent for the last four years, largely from in-migration.

2. Main line churches have not been growing (statistically) as fast as the population has.

3. Most notable recent expansion of institutions has been in the development of homes for the aging by all major denominations.

4. As the "mill village" as a detached, homogeneous community passes from the scene, the future of the "mill church" becomes a challenge and underscores a possible role for an industrial chaplaincy.

5. The problem of rural churches in a rapidly urbanizing society has not been solved. The ARPs present a classic case of the dilemma. A similar problem is that of numerous small and weak churches in a day of easier transportation.

6. Dozens of small churches and sects abound, despite the preceding paragraphs concentrating on six major groups. The "church directory" in a typical Saturday newspaper may include thirty or more varieties.

7. Among the large denominations, church harmony and cooperation have become quite marked. One factor has been Vatican II. Another has been the South Carolina Christian Action Council, formed in 1933 and made up of 17 denominations (Protestant and Catholic). Starting with temperance emphasis, it has gradually broadened to issues of people and society: voting rights, death penalty, race relations, drug problems, and particularly the moral implications of political decisions. In the latter, many state officials have been involved and show sensitive concern.

8. In the era of changing race relations, church leaders have not followed the crowd, as in the nineteenth century, but have sometimes courted unpopularity by supporting social change. Methodists have generally been in the lead; black and white annual conferences merged in 1972; Wofford was the first white college to desegregate voluntarily. The contrast with nineteenth century churches and their defense of slavery as a "positive good" has been a sharp one.

9. Long the leaders of the Negro community, black ministers have declined somewhat in relative influence and status as leaders from other occupations and professions have emerged amid the changes in society.

10. Leadership and many parishioners in major churches have accepted these and other social changes and have deemphasized the old

stress on "individual sin" as the chief concern of religion. Baptists in 1965, for example, shunned efforts to get them to revive the opposition to teaching of evolution. Social justice and public problems have been accepted as proper matters for church concern. In so doing, church voices have not always echoed the "popular" side or the view of powerful vested interests. Maybe this explains why South Carolina churches have not "grown" much in statistics, but they nevertheless may have been growing in other ways.

Bibliography

Hugh George Anderson. *Lutheranism in the Southeastern States, 1860-1886: A Social History.*

Abran V. Goodman. "South Carolina From Shaftesbury to Salvador," *Jews in the South,* ed. Leonard Dinnerstein and Mary D. Palsson.

Ernest M. Lander, Jr. *A History of South Carolina, 1865-1960,* chapter 6.

George C. Rogers, Jr. *Church and State in Eighteenth-Century South Carolina.*

Vinson Synan. *The Holiness-Pentecostal Movement in the United States.*

Francis B. Simkins and Robert H. Woody. *South Carolina During Reconstruction* chapters 14, 15.

Rosser H. Taylor. *Ante-Bellum South Carolina: A Social and Cultural History,* chapter 10.

George B. Tindall. *South Carolina Negroes, 1877-1900,* chapter 10.

David Duncan Wallace. *Historical Background of Religion in South Carolina.*

———. *History of South Carolina,* 3 volumes.

Some of the denominational histories

Albert D. Betts. *History of South Carolina Methodism.*

Barnett A Elzas. *Jews of South Carolina.*

History of the Lutheran Church in South Carolina.

F. D. Jones and W. H. Mills. *History of the Presbyterian Church in South Carolina Since 1850.*

Joe M. King. *History of South Carolina Baptists.*

Loulie Latimer Owens. *Saints of Clay: The Shaping of South Carolina Baptists.*

Albert S. Thomas. *Historical Account of the Protestant Episcopal Church in South Carolina, 1820-1957.*

Leah Townsend. *South Carolina Baptists, 1670-1805.*

Ernest Trice Thompson. *Presbyterians in the South,* 3 volumes.

TENNESSEE

DAVID E. HARRELL, JR.
UNIVERSITY OF ARKANSAS

Early in its history, Tennessee became an important center of denominational headquarters and boards. The Southern Methodist church located its publishing house in Nashville in 1858, and the city is now the home of several agencies of the United Methodist church, including the United Methodist Publishing House, the Board of Education and Ministry, and the Board of Discipleship. Nashville also houses the Executive Offices of the Southern Baptist Convention, along with that church's Sunday School Board, Education Commission, and other major agencies. The city has long been a center of religious education. Among the accredited four-year colleges in Nashville in 1980 were: Belmont College (Baptist), Scarritt College for Christian Workers (Methodist), Trevecca Nazarene College (Nazarene), and David Lipscomb College (Churches of Christ). Vanderbilt University was the pride of Southern Methodism until a majority of the trustees, over the protest of the bishops, dissolved the university's ties with the church in 1914, resulting in a controversial court case.

Not only has Tennessee been important in the history of the major southern churches, it has also been the most prolific breeding ground for new sects in the United States. A recent survey of sects in the United States indicated that Tennessee was the headquarters of more sects per million inhabitants than any other state in the country. The diversity of religion is indicated by a listing of the other major religious colleges in the state: Carson-Newman and Union (Southern Baptist); Lambuth and Tennessee Wesleyan (United Methodist); the University of the South

(Protestant Episcopal); King College and Southwestern at Memphis (Presbyterian in the United States); Knoxville, Maryville, and Tusculum (United Presbyterian Church in the United States of America); Bethel (Cumberland Presbyterian); Covenant (Reformed Presbyterian); Lane (Christian Methodist Episcopal); LeMoyne-Owen (United Church of Christ and Tennessee Baptist Missionary and Educational Convention); Christian Brothers (Roman Catholic); Lee (Church of God, Cleveland, Tennessee); Milligan (Christian Church); Southern Missionary (Seventh Day Adventist); Tennessee Temple (Independent Baptist); and Bryan College (Fundamentalist). Numerous other junior colleges and unaccredited schools represent such churches as the Free Will Baptists, the Church of God of Prophecy, and the United Christian Church and Ministerial Association.

The times were not auspicious for the future of religion when the first Scotch-Irish Presbyterian ministers arrived in Tennessee just before the American Revolution. A few years later, in 1790, the first national census listed only five per cent of the nation's population as church members. Few travelers into the West failed to comment on the moral and spiritual backwardness of the area. The moral laxity of the hardy Celtic and English frontier settlers in East Tennessee shocked and disturbed the early evangelists in the area. One Tennessee minister reported finding his entire congregation so drunk they could not listen to him; another told of repeated encounters with "refugees from justice"; gambling, horse-racing, fighting, and other "popular sins" were constant targets of frontier preaching.

Perhaps the greatest obstacle to establishing organized religion in early Tennessee was the physical isolation of the settlers. Churches were difficult to sustain among the scattered frontiersmen, and few ministers were eager to venture into the wilderness where dangers were real and support uncertain.

Early Tennesseeans also imbibed of the rationalism of their age. The state was settled during the euphoric days of the Revolution and was admitted to the union in 1796, only seven years after ratification of the constitution. Many of the new nation's intellectuals had replaced faith in a personal Christian God with a respect for reason and an adoration of Nature and Nature's God. Rationalism combined with the dissatisfaction of the "dissenting" sects to bring an end to established religion in the South by the end of the Revolution. The Tennessee Constitution was drafted in 1796 when the disestablishment debate was still fresh, and that document not only forbade religious establishment, but also provided that "no minister of the gospel or priest" could be elected to the legislature of the state, a ban which remained in force until struck down by the state Supreme Court in 1978.

In the midst of this hostile environment, however, religion made modest headway in Tennessee's earliest history. Small numbers of church members, infrequent occasions for formal worship, and the apparent immorality on the frontier obscured the residual Christian faith which most of the settlers brought with them across the mountains. Organized religion came close on the heels of the first settlers into the Southwest Territory in the 1770s. From the earliest days, frequent appeals were sent back to the East for ministerial help. In a few instances, entire congregations in North Carolina moved west to Tennessee.

Excluding the likely ministrations of Catholic priests in the company of the De Soto expedition and early French traders, and an Anglican chaplain who accompanied William Byrd into the territory, the first ministers to hold services in Tennessee were Presbyterians. The early religious history of the state was dominated by the three great evangelical churches of the frontier: Presbyterian, Baptist, and Methodist. Each of these churches expanded rapidly in early Tennessee history, and the Methodists became particularly adept at bringing religion to the settlers who fanned out across the state in the antebellum period.

A few hardy and independent Scotch-Irish Presbyterian ministers followed their countrymen down the valleys of the Appalachians into Tennessee in the last quarter of the nineteenth century. As early as 1773 at least two Presbyterian congregations had been formed, and in answer to a request from 130 families, Charles Cummings, the first settled minister in southwest Virginia, visited Tennessee to preach. Another Presbyterian, Samuel Doak, became the first minister to settle permanently in the territory in October 1777. Educated at Princeton and for a time a member of the faculty of Hampden-Sydney College, Doak followed a pattern typical of Presbyterian clergymen in the South when in 1785 he established Martin Academy (later Washington College) in Washington County. The school was reputed to be the first educational institution west of the mountains. Other ministers soon joined Doak, and by the time Tennessee became a state in 1796, 27 congregations had been established stretching as far west as Nashville. The Presbyterian ministers brought with them a respect for education and refinement which earned them a lasting reputation as the cultural leaders of the state.

Baptists were the second important religious group in the early history of Tennessee. Two Baptist congregations were established in the territory as early as 1765, but they did not survive the Indian wars which preceded the Revolution. Among the earliest permanent settlers in the Southwest Territory, however, were Separate Baptists from North Carolina. In 1779 a congregation of North Carolina Baptists migrated along with its minister, Tidence Lane, and built the Buffalo Ridge church near Boone's Creek, probably the first permanent Baptist church in the territory. In 1781 the Holston Association began meeting as a branch of the Sandy Creek Association of North Carolina, and in 1786 it became an independent association with seven member churches. By the time Tennessee was admitted to statehood a second association had been established in the central part of the state.

Early Tennessee Baptists brought with them a missionary zeal inherited from their Separate Baptist heritage in the Great Awakening. In addition, the Baptist belief in independence was well suited to frontier conditions. Most helpful to early Baptist expansion was the system by which each congregation "called" its own minister, generally one of the more energetic and devoted local members. These innovative and self-supporting ministers (early Tennessee Baptists generally disapproved of "hireling" clergymen) placed the church on a firm footing by the time of statehood.

The only other religious body to play a significant role in the early history of the Southwest Territory was the Methodist Episcopal Church. Although the church was not formally founded until the famous Christmas Conference in 1784, Methodist missionaries had been active in forming societies in America since 1766. Most Methodist work had been along the coast, but by 1783 the Holston Conference of Methodist societies had been formed. Jeremiah Lambert became the first traveling preacher in the territory. In 1788, Bishop Francis Asbury made his first trip into the territory, meticulously recording his impressions of the religious life of the area and laying plans for the expansion of the church.

The Methodist circuit riders who worked in the territory before 1796 statehood made slow progress, although in 1790 the Methodists erected in Nashville the first stone meeting house in the territory. In 1796 the church still counted only about 550 members in Tennessee. But the

Methodists were poised for expansion at the turn of the century. The church had completed a period of reorganization after its break from Anglicanism, had an aggressive and dedicated leader in Bishop Asbury, had firmly established the circuit rider system which made possible the supply of ministers to widely scattered congregations, and espoused an Arminian theology which seemed perfectly suited to the intellectual climate of the frontier.

As settlers poured into Tennessee in the wake of statehood, the basic religious structure of the state was shaken and reformed by the eruption of the Great Revival in the West. The revival was triggered by the fervent preaching of Presbyterian James McGready who moved to Logan County, Kentucky, in 1796. In 1799 McGready's churches began to experience fervent revival and a similar stirring broke out in the Presbyterian congregation of William McGee in Sumner County, Tennessee. In 1800, William McGee and his brother John (who was a Methodist minister) visited and participated in a meeting held at one of McGready's congregations. By the fall of 1800, the full revival fervor had been transferred to Tennessee and spread rapidly through the Presbyterian and Methodist churches of the state. In 1801, in an ecumenical fervor which was short-lived, the Baptists joined with the other two churches and revival fires swept across the state. Religious meetings frequently attracted 5,000 listeners.

Tennessee revivals were accompanied by all of the physical manifestations which came to be known as "acrobatic Christianity" in the East. Perhaps the most curious "exercise" was the "jerks." Lorenzo Dow, one of the most famous itinerant evangelists on the frontier, recorded his impressions of the "jerks" while on a tour of East Tennessee in 1801: "I spoke in Knoxville to hundreds more than could get into the courthouse, the Governor being present: about one hundred and fifty appeared to have jerking exercises. . . .I have seen Presbyterians, Methodists, Quakers, Baptists, Church of England, and Independents, exercised with the *jerks*; Gentleman and Lady, black and white, the aged and the young, rich and poor, . . . from which I infer . . . that it is no trifling matter. . . .I passed by a meeting-house where I observed the undergrowth had been cut up for a camp meeting, and from fifty to one hundred saplings, left breast high . . . and left for the people to jerk by. . . .I went over the ground . . . and found where the people had laid hold of them and jerked so powerfully, that they had kicked up the earth as a horse stamping flies."

Perhaps the most important religious innovation connected with the revival was the camp meeting. The first camp meeting in Tennessee was apparently held in August 1800 under the leadership of John McGee, a Smith County Methodist known as "the father of camp meetings in America." The early camp meetings were spontaneous affairs, but within a few years they became regularized. Permanent camp grounds were built, though many still camped in tents and wagons, and a more formal routine was followed. The meetings also became less ecumenical. First the Baptists cooled because of theological reservations and sectarian inhibitions; by the end of the first decade of the nineteenth century, Presbyterians began to question the emotional excesses and the leadership of "lay" ministers often associated with the meetings.

Of the three denominations present in the state at the outbreak of the revival, the Methodists clearly profited most from the new religious enthusiasm. Camp meeting techniques—including emotional appeals to come to the mourner's bench—meshed well with Methodist Arminianism. The revival combined with the efficient circuit rider and class meeting systems to greatly expand the influence of Methodism. In 1800, William McKendree, a Virginia convert to Methodism, came to Tennessee as "presiding elder" over the work in the West. In 1808, McKendree became the first American-born bishop appointed in the young church's history. He continued to live in Nashville and wielded a tremendous influence on Tennessee Methodism until his death in 1835. By 1800 the Methodist church claimed over 10,000 members in the state and had become the largest religious body in the state. In 1824 the state was divided into two conferences, Holston and Tennessee, and in 1840 the Memphis Conference was added. By 1830 the Tennessee Methodist church counted 35,000 members and far outnumbered its nearest competitor.

When the great revival began in Tennessee the Baptists were reluctant participants. Within a few years most Baptists had abandoned the camp meeting, with its alleged excesses, in favor of "protracted meetings." More important in retarding Baptist growth in the first half of the nineteenth century, however, were a series of internal struggles within the denomination. Independent in the extreme, Tennessee Baptists proved to be among the most obstinate critics of an emerging national denomination consciousness which found institutional expression in the formation of the General Missionary Convention in 1814. Although pioneer missionary Luther Rice visited Tennessee several times in the years after 1815, cooperative mission work was seriously retarded in the state by antimission preachers, the most famous of whom was Daniel Parker. Until 1821 Parker preached at the New Hopewell Church in Middle Tennessee. Throughout the 1820s and 1830s the antimission controversy plagued Tennessee; many new Primitive Baptist associations were formed and probably a majority of the state associations tried to take a neutral position in the controversy. In 1840 the West Tennessee Association included the following statement in its articles of belief: "We believe, from experience, the Missionary, Bible, Temperance, Tract, and Masonic Societies, S. S. Unions and theological seminaries to make preachers for the Lord, are destructive to the peace and fellowship of the baptist church. . . . But all almsdeeds any member is at liberty to perform; *Provided* he does not let his *left hand* know what his *right* doeth." In 1833 the Tennessee Baptist Convention was organized by supporters of missions, but it remained weak and disbanded in 1842. Between 1842 and 1874 Baptist churches in the state met in their sectional conventions and went through a period of internal strife described as "the darkest in Tennessee Baptist history."

A second major controversy racked Tennessee Baptists in the 1840s, centering around the personality and teaching of James R. Graves who became editor of the *Tennessee Baptist* in 1847. Graves soon made the paper a stronghold for "Landmarkism," a doctrine which claimed the historical continuity of Baptist churches from Bible times and emphasized the independence of local churches. Graves and Landmarkism were bitterly opposed by respected Nashville minister R. B. C. Howell, but Landmarkism had a powerful conservative influence on the churches of Tennessee and elsewhere in the South.

In spite of this internal strife, and to some degree aided by the expreme independence of the local churches, Tennessee Baptists increased in numbers dramatically during the antebellum years, though not at the same rate as the Methodists. In 1790 Baptists had one association, 18 churches, 21 preachers, and 889 members in the state. By 1814 those numbers had increased to seven associations, 174 churches, 133 preachers, and 12,194 members. By 1845 Tennessee Baptists numbered 32,159; in 1860 the churches reported 46,564 members.

The third major denomination in Tennessee at the time of the great revival, the Presbyterians, suffered a series of crippling setbacks in the years before the Civil War. Presbyterian ministers remained important to the educational system of the state, but the church's emphasis on ministerial training proved to be a hindrance to expansion. When some Presbyterian leaders began to criticize camp meeting revivalism in the second decade of the nineteenth century, open dissension broke out in the church. The major issues were the revival's softening impact on Presbyterian Calvinism and a growing disregard of the traditional educational requirements for ministerial ordination. Accused of wrongdoing on both of the questions, in 1814 the Cumberland Presbytery in West Tennessee became independent, and in 1829 the Cumberland Presbyterian Church was formed. That body quickly became the largest Presbyterian body in the state. In 1830 the *Presbyterian Advocate* reported that the Presbyterian church in Tennessee had only 97 churches, 76 ministers, and 7,374 members.

Presbyterian development was hindered further by continued doctrinal strife after the Cumberland schism. Southern Presbyterians remained strict Calvinists and, as a result of growing theological liberalism and antislavery sentiment in northern Presbyterianism, a national division into Old School and New School churches occurred in 1838. Presbyterian churches in Middle and West Tennessee were overwhelmingly loyal to the Old School General Assembly, but many of the churches in East Tennessee revealed an antislavery disposition by joining the New School. The coming of the Civil War brought a complicated and general reshuffling of the churches. In 1858, the southern New School synods, including Holston Presbytery in Tennessee, withdrew from that church because of its increasingly radical abolitionism and formed the United Synod of the Presbyterian Church in the United States of America. In 1861, the Old School church divided along sectional lines, resulting in the formation of the Presbyterian Church in the Confederate States. The Confederate church courted the United Synod Presbyterians in the South during the war years, and in 1864 a union was negotiated. Outside of Tennessee this merger was completed with little incident, but in East Tennessee confusion and strong passion continued well into the Reconstruction period. Union sympathizers in East Tennessee denounced the union with the Confederate church and voted to unite with the General Assembly of the Presbyterian Church in the United States of America (New School). The struggle for local churches was bitter and sometimes violent; the disposition of numerous church buildings was decided by the courts. The conflicting claims of the two groups made the statistics of the period unreliable, but the churches of East Tennessee were probably divided about equally. One presbytery report sadly noted: "Sad division and bitter alienations among God's people furnish the world an opportunity of taunting and reproaching by saying 'see how these Christians hate one another.' " In 1861 the southern Presbyterians claimed only about 150 churches in Tennessee with around 8,500 members; perhaps 50 congregations were affiliated with the northern church. The 1860 census of "church accommodations" placed the Presbyterian church fourth in the state with 78,655 seats, far behind the Methodists with a reported 288,460 and surpassed also by the Baptists and the Cumberland Presbyterians.

These were years of bitter sectarian competition in Tennessee, marked by vituperative religious journalism and public debate. The most noted Methodist antagonist was "Parson" William Brownlow of Knoxville who was editor of the *Knoxville Whig*, and in 1865 was elected Republican governor of Tennessee. Brownlow's Baptist counterpart was James R. Graves, who in a series of books, as well as through the columns of the *Tennessee Baptist*, regularly scorned Methodism, Presbyterianism, and the "Campbellites." The other two major participants in this rough and tumble struggle for the religious loyalty of antebellum Tennesseeans were the Cumberland Presbyterians and the Disciples of Christ. Both of these new churches were born amidst the revival fervor of the early nineteenth century and both spread rapidly in Tennessee.

The Cumberland Presbyterian schism had begun in 1805 when the Synod of Kentucky questioned the laxity of the Cumberland Presbytery, including James McGready, in the appointment of new ministers. After several abortive attempts at compromise, a dissident group led by minister Finis Ewing formed an independent Presbytery in 1811 and the General Assembly of the Cumberland Presbyterian church in 1825. The Cumberland church was strongly revivalistic and experienced remarkable growth. Cumberland Presbyterians were particularly adept at capturing and establishing churches in rural areas. In 1861, about 35,000 of the Church's 100,000 members were in Tennessee.

The second important new church to enter Tennessee in the wake of the great revival was the Disciples of Christ. The Disciples, generally known at the congregational level as the Christian church or the Church of Christ, grew out of the combined reform of Alexander Campbell of western Virginia and Barton Stone of Kentucky calling for the "restoration of New Testament Christianity." Both Campbell and Stone had been Presbyterian ministers, but more important in Tennessee was Campbell's association with the Baptist cause. Campbell was a Baptist for a number of years before launching an independent movement, and from 1823 to 1830 edited an influential magazine named the *Christian Baptist*. When the Disciples became independent in the 1830s, they ravaged the Baptist church in Tennessee. The Disciples began in Tennessee as a result of the work of Philip Fall. Fall became pastor of the First Baptist Church in Nashville about 1830 and subsequently led nearly the entire congregation into the Christian church. The Concord Baptist Association was reduced from 49 churches with 3,399 members to 11 churches with 805 members as a result of Disciple defections. The dominant figure in early Disciples' history in Tennessee was Tolbert Fanning who edited the *Christian Review* in the 1840s and the *Gospel Advocate* beginning in 1853. By 1860 the Disciples had an estimated membership of over 12,000 in the state in 106 churches.

While these five evangelical churches played dominant roles in the development of religion in antebellum Tennessee, other religious groups slowly established themselves in Tennessee. By 1860 Episcopalianism, Catholicism, Lutheranism, and Judaism had small memberships in the state.

It seems remarkable (in view of its long establishment in the colonial South) that the Episcopal Church did not have a congregation in Tennessee until 1827. But the Episcopal church had been crushed by the events of the Revolution and preoccupied with internal problems in the early nineteenth century. James Hervey Otey, an extraordinarily able and zealous convert to Episcopalianism, established the first church in Franklin in 1827, St. Paul's. Otey was an energetic missionary, and within a few years, preaching to small groups in rented halls, he established Christ Church in Nashville, St. Peter's Church in Columbia, and Trinity Church in Clarksville. In 1834, Otey was consecrated as the first bishop of the Diocese of Tennessee at the age of 34. He was a vigorous bishop, but by 1860 the church still claimed only 26 parishes, 27 clergymen, and about 1,500 communicants in the state.

It is not clear when the first English-speaking Roman Catholics entered Tennessee, but it is likely that some began to spill over from the Catholic settlements in Kentucky around the turn of the century. Between

1808 and 1810 Father Stephen Badin, pioneer Kentucky priest, made four trips into Tennessee to visit Catholics. Kentucky priests continued to make occasional forays into Tennessee, and a church was apparently built in Nashville shortly after 1820, but it was not until 1830 that the first parish was formed in Nashville. In 1837 the Diocese of Tennessee was formed, and the Rt. Rev. Richard Pius Miles, a native American Catholic, was consecrated as the first bishop. Bishop Miles, known as the father of Catholicism in Tennessee, aggressively expanded the church in Tennessee. During the 1850s Catholics endured severe persecution with the outbreak of Know-Nothing enthusiasm. Violence erupted in Knoxville, Nashville, Murfreesboro, Franklin, Pulaski, and other places where Catholics had churches. According to one early estimate, the Nashville diocese still had only 11 churches in 1858.

A few German Lutherans entered Tennessee during the very early years of the state. The first church in the state was organized about 1795, but it was not until 1820 that the Tennessee Synod was formed. The church grew slowly because of its dependence on German immigrants and because of a lack of ministers. In 1860 it claimed only 18 churches, mostly in the eastern counties.

According to one contemporary estimate, the state of Tennessee had about 2,500 "Israelites" in 1858 and two synagogues, one in Nashville and the other in Memphis. The first Jewish settlers were apparently Germans, but the first rabbi in the state was Alexander Iser, a Russian Pole, and both of the early synagogues were Orthodox. In 1862, a Reform congregation was established in Nashville, and by 1867 synagogues had been established in Chattanooga and Knoxville.

Most of the Tennessee churches were active in social and benevolent causes in the antebellum period, supporting Bible, tract, and education societies, and fervently denouncing drinking, dancing, and other "popular sins." But one social issue dominated their attention and that of their fellow southern Christians—the relationship of Christianity to slaveholding. In their earliest days, all three of the evangelical churches in Tennessee were antislavery. Prior to 1830 most Methodists and Baptists were nonslaveholding whites. The churches of East Tennessee remained moderately antislavery throughout the antebellum period. As attitudes hardened in the country after 1830, Tennessee churches followed sectional loyalties. Then the major evangelical churches divided, when most Tennessee churches remained loyal to the South.

To some extent, the peculiar geography of Tennessee, which set East Tennessee apart economically, socially, and politically, complicated the religious divisions within the state. As has already been noted, East Tennessee became a battleground for competing Presbyterian churches. However, most Tennessee churches supported the South prior to the war. When the Southern Baptist Convention was founded in 1845, Tennessee churches uniformly supported the new convention. When the Methodist Episcopal Church, South was formed in the same year, all of the conferences in Tennessee united with the southern church. The Protestant Episcopal Church finally divided under the pressure of war in 1861, and the Tennessee Diocese joined the Confederate church without controversy (unity was restored in 1865). Both the Disciples of Christ and the Cumberland Presbyterian Church escaped division over slavery and Civil War. Most of the members of both churches were in the border states, and the leaders of each body tried to take moderate, non-divisive stands on slavery.

The conversion of blacks to Christianity took place in two spurts in Tennessee. The first, a result of the general evangelical fervor of the great revival and the antislavery sentiment that accompanied it, established the ascendancy of the Methodist and Baptist churches among blacks. In 1836, however, the Methodist Church still reported only 7,500 black members in the state. A second spurt of missionary activity among the slaves followed the establishment of the independent southern churches. Self-conscious about their relation to slavery, southern Baptists and Methodists made extraordinary efforts to convert slaves, and one historian has estimated that 90 percent of the black population of Tennessee was Christian by 1860.

Most blacks worshipped with and held membership in white congregations. Church record books generally noted that they were "colored" and chronicled their achievements and trials alongside those of white members. Sometimes black members had separate Sunday Schools; probably typical was the arrangement in the Christian Church in Nashville: "There are two colored Sunday Schools under the immediate control of colored members; but over which the Church exercises general superintendence." Independent black congregations were less common; however, a few black Baptist churches appear to have existed in the state before the Civil War. An ordained black minister named Nelson Merry presided over the large quasi-independent Spruce Street Colored Church in Nashville beginning in 1853. Methodist black "mission" churches operating under the supervision of a white church were common.

The Civil War had a devastating effect on organized religion throughout the South, but the impact was particulary severe in Tennessee because of the military activity within the state and because of the animosity between the Unionists in East Tennessee and the Confederate majority in the remainder of the state. The Methodists and Baptist churches lost perhaps a third of their members during the Civil War, and other churches suffered similar disruption. Church buildings were frequently seized by the government and used for military purposes. In the early years of the war clergymen who were Union sympathizers were persecuted in a variety of ways and some were expelled by their churches. By 1863 the tide was reversed in Tennessee, and, with Union forces in control of the state, radicals like Brownlow called for retribution against the "rebel church." The only substantial pacifist statement by Tennessee ministers during the war was made by a group of Middle Tennessee Disciples led by David Lipscomb and Tolbert Fanning. Their position was ignored by the civil authorities and apparently was not widely endorsed by the members of their own church in Tennessee.

The occupation of Tennessee by Federal troops also made the state a field for missionary work by the northern churches. Led by Brownlow, the northern Methodists established the Holston Conference in 1865 to compete with the southern conference, and with the support of the army many southern churches were seized. Secretary of War Edwin Stanton ordered all Baptist churches in the state turned over to the American Baptist Home Mission Society if the churches were not presided over by a "loyal" minister. Although President Johnson ordered all buildings returned in 1865, bitter disputes continued.

A third major development during the Civil War and Reconstruction was the separation of blacks into independent churches. Whether mostly at the instigation of the liberated freedmen or of southern whites, blacks quickly moved out of the white churches. Immediately after the war, the two most successful black churches were the African Methodist Episcopal Church and the African Methodist Episcopal Zion Church which had been established in 1816 and 1821 in the North and began organizing churches in Tennessee before the war was over. Southern Methodists apparently gave encouragement to the new churches in order to diminish the influence of the Methodist Episcopal missionaries among the freedmen. By 1863 both of the black churches had sufficient members in Tennessee to organize a conference. Southern Methodists encouraged the segregation of their remaining blacks into separate churches, and in 1870, in a meeting in Jackson, those churches were organized as the Colored Methodist Episcopal Church of America. The Methodist Episcopal Church also made vigorous efforts to attract blacks and probably ten per cent of that church's membership in the state was black at the end of Reconstruction.

The Baptist denomination gained increasing numbers of blacks after the Civil War, many attracted by the congregational independence of the Baptists. While segregation of the races into separate congregations went on rapidly after the Civil War, black Baptists retained an adjunct relationship to the regular associations until the 1890s. In 1865, the Primitive Baptists of the state separated their black congregations into the Negro Primitive Baptist Church, and in 1869 the Cumberland Presbyterians, in a meeting in Murfreesboro, organized the Colored Cumberland Presbyterian Church. Both southern Presbyterians and Disciples of Christ continued to include their black congregations as a part of their denominations, but neither church had a significant number of black members.

Equally as important as the establishment of the black churches was the educational and benevolent work of the northern churches. The Methodist Episcopal Church founded an educational institution in Nashville in 1866 which subsequently became Meharry Medical School. The Congregational Church, through the American Missionary Society, established schools for blacks throughout the South, including Fisk in Nashville and LeMoyne in Memphis. Schools were also operated in Tennessee by the Northern Baptists and the Presbyterian Church in the United States of America.

The dominant white evangelical churches in Tennessee went through a generation of rebuilding in the wake of the Civil War. The Baptist State Convention was finally organized in 1874, and in 1889 the *Baptist and Reflector* became its official organ. The Methodists took a major step forward in 1876 when, under the leadership of Bishop Holland McTyeire, Vanderbilt University was established. Nashville once again became a major publishing center. Competition for new members was keen among the major evangelical churches, and the Baptists and Methodists were extraordinarily successful in rebuilding their memberships by 1900. The intense sectarian rivalry of the late nineteenth century was only slightly less acrimonious than that of earlier years.

At the same time, the post-Civil War years were marked by a powerful southern civil religion. Southern church leaders, including Catholics and Jews, united on countless public occasions to memorialize the "lost cause" and to explain in religious terms the tragedy of southern history. No institution was more central to this religion of the lost cause than the University of the South which opened its doors in 1865 in Sewanee through the efforts of Bishop Charles Quintard of the Protestant Episcopal Church. The school had been planned in 1856 by Bishop Leonidas Polk. When the dream was resurrected in 1867 by Confederate veteran Quintard, the school quickly became the "stronghold of the Southern aristocracy," as well as a distinguished educational institution.

By 1900 the denominational shuffling caused by sectional tensions and the organization of independent black churches had been completed. The most spectacular single development at the turn of the century was the growth of the Baptists. Between 1880 and 1900 the Southern Baptists passed the Methodist Episcopal Church, South, as the leading denomination in the state and surged far into the advance in the twentieth century. Methodist growth slowed, partly as a result of the bitter fight in Tennessee between the northern and southern churches and partly because of a diminishing evangelical zeal. According to the 1906 religious census, the largest denominations in Tennessee were: Southern Baptist, 159,838; Methodist Episcopal Church, South, 140,308; National (Negro) Baptist Convention, 93,303; Methodist Episcopal Church, 46,180; Cumberland Presbyterian Church, 42,464; Churches of Christ, 41,411; African Methodist Episcopal, 23,377; Presbyterian Church in the United States, 21,390; Colored Methodist Episcopal, 20,634; Roman Catholic, 17,252; Disciples of Christ, 14,904; Primitive Baptist, 10,204; Protestant Episcopal Church, 7,874; Presbyterian Church in the United States of America, 6,786; African Methodist Episcopal Zion Church, 6,651; and Colored Cumberland Presbyterian, 6,640.

The major denominations present in Tennessee had changed little since the 1830s (with the exception of the separation of the black churches), although there were variations in the vitality of each group. In the years from 1890 to 1910, however, each of the four largest white churches in the state—the Baptists, Methodists, Disciples, and Cumberland Presbyterians—suffered divisions. Each of the divisions was national in scope, but Tennessee played a central role in all of them. This new religious ferment combined with an increased influx of non-southern churches to bring a new diversity to Tennessee religion. All of the divisions reflected the changing economic and social conditions in the state, particularly the growth of the middle-class and increased rural-urban tensions.

Perhaps the clearest example of social and economic religious tensions was the division within the Disciples of Christ. In the religious census of 1906, the most theologically conservative Disciples churches were separated from the remainder of the movement and listed as Churches of Christ. The doctrinal basis of the division was disagreement over the use of instrumental music in worship and organized missionary societies. At the national level the Churches of Christ captured only 159,658 of the movement's total membership while the more liberal Christian church listed 982,701 members. The South, particularly Tennessee, was the stronghold of the Churches of Christ. Even within Tennessee the division was sectional; a majority of the churches in East Tennessee became Christian churches while in both Middle and West Tennessee an overwhelming majority were Churches of Christ. But the division also had clear rural-urban characteristics. In every major city in the state with the exception of Nashville, the Christian church won far more members than the Churches of Christ. A second division in the Disciples of Christ occurred in the 1920s leading to the establishment of a liberal, ecumenical denomination, the General Assembly of Christian Churches (Disciples of Christ) and the evangelical (but instrumental and cooperative) undenominational Fellowship of Christian Churches and Churches of Christ. This division was also sectional. Most of the urban churches joined the liberal General Assembly, while in East Tennessee the rural congregations which had refused to join the Churches of Christ formed their own fellowship and retained control of Milligan College.

In 1971 the liberal Christian church listed 17,849 members in 88 congregations in Tennessee. The conservative Christian churches listed 22,379 in 148 churches, mostly in East Tennessee. In the twentieth century the Churches of Christ grew rapidly in the state, listing 72,015 members and 978 congregations in the census of 1926. A loose collection of local churches, the Churches of Christ have not reported membership statistics in recent years, but the group's aggressive evangelism has probably made it the second or third largest religious body in the state.

This movement's membership is concentrated heavily in Middle Tennessee. Davidson County listed over 120 Churches of Christ by 1980, and the Madison Church of Christ claimed over 5,300 members. The *Gospel Advocate*, published in Nashville and edited by the minister of the Madison Church, Ira North, probably has the largest circulation of any periodical among the Churches of Christ.

The Cumberland Presbyterian division resulted from the refusal of about one-third of the churches in the denomination to accept union with the Presbyterian Church in the United States of America in 1906. The way opened for union when the northern Presbyterians abandoned Calvinism at the turn of the century. Many of the southern churches, however, reflecting pride in their Cumberland heritage as well as fear of the influence of blacks in the united church, refused to participate. In Tennessee, the Cumberland Presbyterian church reported 536 congregations with 42,464 members in 1906; in 1916, after the merger, those figures declined to 398 congregations and 27,631 members. The division was also sociological. The congregations that remained Cumberland were mostly rural; the church was virtually devoid of urban congregations until well into the twentieth century. In 1980, the Cumberland Presbyterian Church's main denominational offices were in Memphis where the *Cumberland Presbyterian* was published. In 1971, the church listed a membership of 38,246 in Tennessee.

Baptist growth in the late nineteenth and early twentieth centuries was rapid, but the church continued to be troubled by Landmark resistance to organized mission work. James R. Graves's influence remained strong in Tennessee until his death in 1893, and Landmarkism pushed the entire denomination in a conservative direction until the 1960s. Nevertheless, some Landmarkers became so dissatisfied with what they believed to be organizational encroachments on the local churches that they bolted the Southern Baptist Convention in 1905 and formed the American Baptist Association. While this new church was strongest in Arkansas and the Southwest, in 1936 the Landmarkers listed 5,582 members in Tennessee in 37 churches, almost all in rural areas.

More serious were the divisions within southern Methodism around the turn of the century. The Holiness movement erupted first among northern Methodists shortly after the Civil War and had a divisive influence in that section in the late nineteenth century. For the most part, however, southern Methodism captured the Holiness movement, welcoming the reopening of camp grounds and encouraging the renewed emphasis on perfectionism. B. F. Haynes, editor of the *Tennessee Methodist* in the 1890s, was an ardent advocate of Holiness and subsequently left the church over the question. The influence of the separatist Holiness churches did not appear in the census until 1916, and in that year the most influential of them, the Church of the Nazarene, reported only 24 churches with 1,903 members in Tennessee. The Nazarenes grew slowly to a membership of 5,416 in 1936 and 11,767 in 1971.

More important was the growth of Pentecostalism in Tennessee. In the 1890s the Holiness movement developed an increasingly radical extreme wing which urged pushing on to deeper and deeper spiritual experiences. At the same time the Methodist church began to try to control the influence of the movement. The radical Holiness movement became Pentecostal around the turn of the century when the "baptism of the Holy Spirit," accompanied by speaking in tongues, spread across the nation. Cleveland, Tennessee, became one of the centers of Pentecostalism. A. J. Tomlinson was the most prominent leader of a group of Holiness churches in western North Carolina and East Tennessee near the end of the nineteenth century, and from 1903 to 1923 he served as General Overseer of the Church of God. In 1908 the movement turned Pentecostal, adopted the name Church of God, and established its general offices in Cleveland. The Church of God, along with other Pentecostal groups, was extremely schismatic because of its dependence on charismatic leaders and because of its extreme conservatism in matters of doctrine and personal morality. The Church of God suffered a major split in 1923 involving Tomlinson's autocratic management of church affairs, and Tomlinson took about one-third of the membership into the Church of God of Prophecy. In 1957 Grady R. Kent led a small group out of that church to form The Church of God (Jerusalem Acres) based on a prophetic concept of "New Testament Judaism." Also headquartered in Cleveland was the United Christian Church and Ministerial Alliance, formed in 1958 by H. Richard Hall, a tent revivalist and former minister in the Church of God of Prophecy. Jellico, Tennessee, became the headquarters of the Church of God of the Mountain Assembly, Inc., founded in 1906.

Pentecostalism remained a vital movement in Tennessee in modern times. The Church of God had 23,936 members in the state in 1971 and had completed a modern headquarters building in Cleveland. In 1952 the

Church of God of Prophecy reported 3,577 members in the state. In addition, other major Pentecostal groups entered the state and grew during the charismatic boom of the 1970s. At the same time, the creative cutting edge of Pentecostalism continued to generate new sects among the poor of the state, including the Church of God with Signs Following, a group of loosely connected rural churches which continued to arouse the periodic interest of the press with snake-handling services.

In the midst of this sectarian caldron, many of the mainline churches experienced great growth in Tennessee, particularly during the national religious boom in the 1950s. Southern Baptist membership in the state grew from 226,896 in 1936 to 900,743 in 1971. Baptist churches also expanded their social vision in a variety of ways, particularly after the 1950s. Throughout the twentieth century the churches of the state were liberal supporters of such institutions as the Baptist Memorial Hospital in Memphis, the Baptist Hospital in Nashville, and a number of other benevolent institutions. More than anything else, however, Baptists emphasized missions, and state churches liberally supported both the foreign and home mission boards. The state convention underwent a general reorganization in 1957 to bring greater efficiency. In 1980, four Baptist churches in Tennessee—Highland Park in Chattanooga (independent), Park Avenue in Nashville, and Bellevue and Broadway in Memphis—were listed among the 100 largest churches in the nation.

A small but old Baptist group which made significant gains in Tennessee in the post-World War II period was the Free Will Baptist Church. The descendant of Arminian Baptists who came to North Carolina in 1727, the church remained alive in isolated rural congregations throughout the nineteenth century. The church reported only about 3,000 members in Tennessee in 1906, but by 1971 it had grown to 20,801. A conservative evangelical group with a strong sense of its own history, the church has its national headquarters and a Bible College in Nashville.

The Methodist Church in the state grew to a membership of 360,749 in 1971, but most of its increase resulted from the union of the northern and southern Methodist bodies in 1939. In spite of its slowed rate of growth, the Methodist church remained an important influence in the state, and, increasingly, a liberal influence. Southern Methodists were among the founding members of the Federal Council of Churches in America in 1908, and Bishop E. R. Hendrix was the council's first president.

The Presbyterian Church in the United States grew from 34,255 members in 1936 to 63,259 in 1971, obviously profiting from the growth in the mainline churches after World War II. The church became increasingly urban; by 1926 over half of its members lived in Memphis and Nashville. In the 1970s most southern Presbyterians remained theologically conservative and a part of the evangelical establishment of the state. The Cumberland Presbyterian Church during the same years increased its membership from 19,556 to 38,246 and slowly began to establish churches in the major cities of the state. The Presbyterian Church in the United States of America gained from its acquisition of many Cumberland churches and in 1971 reported 18,146 members in the state.

The Protestant Episcopal Church grew from 14,156 members in 1936 to 30,679 in 1971. Like the other moderate Protestant denominations in the state, the Episcopal Church slowed in growth in the 1960s and 1970s and faced yearly budget strains. Along with Methodists and Presbyterians, Tennessee Episcopalians made the boldest social statements in the post-World War II years, especially in their advocacy of the rights of blacks and women.

The appearance of small numbers of Unitarians, Mormons, and Seventh-Day Adventists in recent religious polls in the state reflect the growing heterogeneity of the state's population. More significant, however, was the large growth of the Roman Catholic Church and Jewish synagogues in the twentieth century. The number of Roman Catholics in Tennessee grew from 31,985 in 1936 to 92,577 in 1971. In 1963, the Catholic Church in Tennessee was operating 67 elementary schools, 13 high schools, and three colleges with a total student population of 21,506. In spite of its substantial growth, Roman Catholicism remained largely an urban phenomenon in Tennessee. The growth of the Church in the state led to the establishment of a second diocese in Memphis in 1971.

The growth of Judaism in Tennessee was even more dramatic. The religious census of 1906 reported only 919 Jews in the state, almost all living in the state's four urban centers. By 1936, the Jewish congregations in the state listed 23,275 members. Much of the increase came from a large influx of Orthodox Jews around the turn of the century, but the early twentieth century also witnessed the appearance of important Reform rabbis in Tennessee, including Julian Mark in Nashville, Abraham Feinstein in Chattanooga, and Harry W. Ettelson in Memphis. Jews, as well as Catholics, suffered from nativist agitation in Tennessee, particularly during the 1920s, but they were remarkably visible in the cultural and political life of the state throughout the twentieth century.

By far the most powerful black religious group in Tennessee in the twentieth century was the Baptists. In 1936 the combined membership of black Baptist churches in the state was over 140,000. The National Baptist Convention, U.S.A., Inc., maintained its BTU Board in Nashville and its Educational Board in Memphis. The African Methodist Episcopal Church published its national paper, the *A.M.E. Recorder*, in Nashville where it maintained its Education and Publication Departments. In addition, several black Pentecostal churches grew rapidly in the twentieth century. Perhaps the most important was the Church of God in Christ which was founded in Memphis in 1906 by Bishop Charles Harrison Mason. In 1980 the church reported a national membership of 425,000 and maintained its headquarters in Memphis, the home of Presiding Bishop J. O. Patterson.

The evangelical churches of Tennessee in the twentieth century, in spite of their sectarian competition and splintering, formed a nearly solid conservative Protestant Establishment in the state. While some urban Episcopal, Presbyterian, and Methodist pastors and professors were probably embarrassed by the fundamentalist reputation in Tennessee in the 1920s, most of the Protestants in the state were firm supporters of the antievolution law passed by the state legislature in 1925. The law, introduced by Representative J. W. Butler, a farmer and a Primitive Baptist from Macon County, was tested in the famous trial of John T. Scopes in Dayton in July 1925. When William Jennings Bryan came to Dayton to help prosecute the "infidel" Scopes, he received the unanimous support of the ministers of that small town.

The Protestant Establishment of the state also united in countless conservative social crusades and mass revivals during the 1920s and 1930s. Beginning in the 1920s, the state hosted countless mass revivals conducted by Billy Sunday, Mordecai Ham, and such lesser revivalists as J. C. Bishop, "the Yodeling Cowboy Evangelist." In the 1950s that massive company Establishment reacted enthusiastically to Billy Graham's crusades. The issues most often discussed in such revivals and in most Protestant pulpits and papers were soul-saving, prohibition, the dangers of evolution, dancing, and political radicalism. The nomination of Al Smith for the presidency in 1928 roused the Protestant Establishment to new heights of concerted political action. Smith's opposition to prohibition, in addition to his Roman Catholic faith, set off a religious-political campaign which led Tennessee into the Republican camp for the first time in the twentieth century. The Smith campaign also climaxed a renewed outbreak of anti-Catholicism which put tremendous pressure on the 25,000 Catholics in the state.

Since World War II the evolution of the churches has brought considerably more diversity to Tennessee religion. Not only has the number of Roman Catholics and Jews continued to increase, but also the mainstream Protestant denominations have become increasingly liberal and linked with the mainstream churches outside the South. Southern Episcopalians, Presbyterians, and Methodists spawned important social agencies in the post-World War II period. In Tennessee these three denominations led in the establishment of ministerial alliances and other ecumenical agencies in the state's major cities. Many local churches expanded the role of women and the young in their programs.

Tennessee Baptists remained much more conservative. Nevertheless, many Southern Baptists in the years after World War II became increasingly concerned about the social involvement of such agencies as the Christian Life Commission and the Baptist Joint Committee on Public Affairs. Many feared that liberalism had invaded the church's theological seminaries. When conservative Southern Baptists launched a concerted campaign in 1979 to win the presidency of the Southern Baptist Convention, their candidate was Dr. Adrian Rogers, pastor of the 11,500 member Bellevue Church in Memphis. Many Tennessee Baptists became convinced in the 1950s that the Southern Baptist church was beyond rescue and joined the mushrooming independent Baptist movement. The Southwide Fellowship of Independent Baptist churches, centered around the Highland Park Baptist Church and Tennessee Temple University in Chattanooga, was one of the most important national centers of that movement. Dr. Lee Roberson, pastor of Highland Park, built a church in the postwar years that had a total membership of nearly 55,000 in 1980.

In summary, religion in Tennessee has been influenced by all of the forces which shaped religion in the South: the ethnic homogeneity of the state's early settlers, the heritage of the great revival, the presence of large numbers of blacks, the Civil War, the economic backwardness of the state in the aftermath of the Civil War, and the slow Americanization of the state in the twentieth century. In addition, Tennessee religion has been shaped in some unique ways. The Disciples of Christ and Cumberland Presbyterians were important in Tennessee because they entered the state before 1830; after that date religion in the South tended to freeze along the denominational lines that then existed. Neither church successfully spread to the East or South after 1830, though both moved West. Tennessee was composed of three economically and culturally diverse sections. The presence of the mountain white population in the East greatly complicated the denominational history of the state. Finally, Tennessee's central location in the Upper South and its early reputation as a center of culture and education made it an ideal place to establish denominational headquarters and church colleges.

Bibliography

John Alexander. *The Synod of Tennessee.*

Cullen Carter. *Methodism in the Wilderness, 1786-1836.*

James W. Carty. *Nashville as a World Religious Center.*

J. E. Choate. *Roll Jordan Roll: A Biography of Marshall Keeble.*

J. B. Collins. *Tennessee Snake Handlers.*

Charles W. Conn. *Like a Mighty Army Moves the Church of God, 1886-1955.*

E. Merton Coulter. *William G. Brownlow: Fighting Parson of the Southern Highlands.*

George Flanigan, ed. *Catholicity in Tennessee.*

Thomas O. Fuller. *History of the Negro Baptists of Tennessee.*

Ray Ginger. *Six Days or Forever?*

David E. Harrell, Jr. "The Disciples of Christ and Social Force in Tennessee, 1865-1900," The East Tennessee Historical Society's *Publications* 38 (1966): 48-61.

C. W. Heishell. *Pioneer Presbyterians in Tennessee.*

Robert E. Hooper. *Crying in the Wilderness: A Biography of David Lipscomb.*

Paul Isaac. *Prohibition and Politics: Turbulent Decades in Tennessee, 1885-1920.*

W. Fred Kendall. *A History of the Tennessee Baptist Convention.*

Isaac Martin. *History of Methodism in Holston Conference.*

Herman Norton. *Religion in Tennessee, 1777-1945.*

———. *Tennessee Christians.*

Oury Taylor. *Early Tennessee Baptists, 1769-1832.*

James R. Wilburn. *The Hazard of the Die: Tolbert Fanning and the Restoration Movement.*

William Woodson. *Standing for Their Faith: A History of Churches of Christ in Tennessee, 1900-1950.*

TEXAS

HOWARD MILLER
UNIVERSITY OF TEXAS

In 1807 the American explorer Zebulon Pike, who was being escorted by Spanish officials to the Spanish-American border at Natchitoches, Louisiana, recorded his impressions of the scruffy, scattered settlements in what is now east Texas. He noted, among other things, that the religion of Spanish Texas was Catholic—"but much relaxed." Pike's pithy phrase aptly described the religious life of Texas during the years before 1836 in which it was a province, first of Spain and then, briefly, of Mexico.

The settlements Pike visited originated in the second quarter of the eighteenth century as military outposts to guard against the French and as missions to the region's peaceful Hasinai and Caddo tribes. That missionary impetus had failed, though, by 1807. The white man's diseases eventually decimated the small native populations, and those Indians who survived could not be forced to remain affixed to the several struggling missions in northeast Texas. To the southwest, San Antonio de Bexar, the principal Spanish settlement in Texas, was no more successful. By 1800 only a few dozen converted Indians and a handful of rag-tag clerics could be found at San Antonio. After seventy-five years of colonizing efforts, there were at the turn of the nineteenth century fewer than 3,000 settlers in Spanish Texas. Growth was inhibited by the vast wasteland between the Nueces River and the Rio Grande that separated Spanish Texas from northern Mexico and by the Spanish refusal to allow trade with the French in Louisiana. More important, in the early eighteenth century the awesome Comanches swept southward onto the Llano Estacado, the "Staked Plains" of west Texas. Mounted, these "Lords of the

Plains" were among the most effective warriors in history. They were, in fact, the only American aborigines to halt for any length of time—more than a century—the white man's advance in the New World.

In 1821 the first Anglo-Americans began to appear in the vacuum of Spanish Texas. This vanguard of the boisterous young republic's "manifest destiny" to march to the western sea was led first by Moses Austin, a Connecticut Yankee who came to Texas by way of Virginia and Upper Louisiana, and then by his son, Stephen F. Austin, the "father of Texas." Austin's colonists settled in present-day Austin and Washington counties on the Brazos River, where they were tolerated with guarded suspicion by Spanish and Mexican officials. There for 15 years they lived under an established Catholic Church. Moses Austin had already dealt with the problem of an established church in Upper Louisiana, which from 1764 to 1800 was controlled by the Spanish. Between 1783 and 1798 the Spanish had granted religious toleration to Protestants, whom they actively endeavored to attract to the area. In 1798, the year Austin arrived in Spanish territory from Virginia, the Spanish restricted toleration to the first generation of settlers. Austin, however, found it easy enough to be considered "un bon catholique" by vaguely affirming his adherence to the Church. And when he petitioned the Spanish government in Mexico for permission to bring settlers to Texas in 1820, he stated that he was a Catholic.

His son, the person who actually established the colony, was at great pains to advise prospective settlers of the Catholic establishment in Texas. Between 1821 and 1824 Stephen Austin attempted to comply with the stipulation that colonists certify their Catholicism, and as many as a quarter of the first male settlers may have done so. It is clear, though, that most did not and that no Spanish or Mexican official seemed to mind. The attention of those officials was distracted by the Mexican efforts to achieve independence from Spain, which efforts proved successful in 1824. The constitution framed for Mexico after independence was modeled on the "liberal" Spanish constitution of 1812. It established a republican government, which, in turn, expelled all Spanish priests and confiscated the Church's extensive properties. But the constitution also established the Roman Church and prohibited "the exercise of any other whatsoever." In Texas Stephen Austin was not unduly disturbed. He had informally advised some of the Mexican officials who had framed the constitution, and he was confident that the "natural operations" of republican principles soon would make possible the free exercise of all religions.

In the meantime, while republicanism spread "its fostering arms over the vast domains of Mexico," Austin insisted that his colonists acquiesce in the Catholic establishment—at least publicly. He forbade non-Catholic services, he performed provisional civil marriages himself and then bound the couples to be married by a priest when one arrived, and he urged Mexican officials to send such a priest to Texas. And continually he sought to keep evangelical preachers out of Texas.

Stephen Austin was a late product of the American Enlightenment. He attended between 1808 and 1810 Transylvania University in Lexington, Kentucky, which at the time was arguably the most liberal institution of higher learning in the republic. There he imbibed the religious skepticism currently fashionable in Kentucky, that Jeffersonian Virginia at one remove. He then brought with him to Texas the prejudices of that skepticism—an anti-Catholicism, which he managed usually to conceal, and a loathing of Methodist preachers especially, which he publicly proclaimed. He believed evangelical preachers to be fanatics whose presence would do more harm to the colony "than a dozen horse thieves," no light charge in a society absolutely dependent upon the horse. He denounced in typically Jeffersonian terms the denominational bickering he believed inevitably would follow evangelists to Texas and that would just as surely provoke Mexican officials to enforce ecclesiastical regulations they had been content to ignore. Like Jefferson, Austin believed that no one religious group could demonstrate the superiority of its dogma to any other. Indeed, one suspects that the father of Texas may have welcomed the rather innocuous Catholic establishment because it made impossible the sectarian squabbles Austin so abhorred. (It is perhaps worth noting that most of the Mexican officials with whom Austin dealt were Freemasons who probably shared his religious skepticism and distaste for theological debate.)

Austin was not entirely successful in excluding Protestant ministers from his own colony, and, of course, he had no authority to keep them out of other areas of Texas. Between 1820 and 1836, then, the founders of Protestantism in Texas arrived. By the later date, there were 12 Methodist, 13 Baptist, at least one Disciples of Christ, three Presbyterian, and three Cumberland Presbyterian ministers in the area. The earliest of these settled around Nacogdoches and San Augustine in northeast Texas. The second area of concentration was around the Austin colony on the

Brazos. And the last group of preachers to arrive in the colonial period gravitated toward Houston and the nearby island settlement of Galveston.

Virtually all of these men were itinerants. Some of them organized churches during the colonial period, but public worship in them was quite rare before 1836. Since Mexican officials consistently refused to send priests to the area, there was, in effect, no organized religious activity in Texas before it gained its independence. Ministers—and some lay people—were astounded by the almost complete lack of religious exercises in an area that gave the Sabbath over to "visiting, driving stock, and breaking mustangs," which was what Texans apparently did on the other six days of the week also. One Methodist minister could find nothing in 1834 to cheer him on his Texas circuit, where most Methodists he encountered were either "backslidden," or were going to dancing school, or, worst of all, had "joined the Baptists."

This frustrated comment notwithstanding, there was in fact little proselytizing among the Protestant denominations during the colonial period. Of course, proselytizing would not be expected from groups that officially were proscribed. But it is also true that many of the early Protestant preachers and their followers in Texas tended to be of the "hard-shell" variety. Like, for instance, T. J. Pilgrim's church of Predestinarian Baptists, a surprisingly large number of early Methodist, Presbyterian, Disciples, and Baptist settlers did not believe in organized missionary efforts, were predestinarian, and seemed more interested in maintaining congregational purity than in poaching on other denominational preserves.

Because any preaching efforts threatened always to get them expelled from Texas, these early evangelists tended to emphasize the educational aspects of the ministry. Their first activities often were in founding Sunday Schools and primary schools. Later they would be among the founders of an astounding number and variety of denominational colleges in Texas. Gradually, the reputations of these early evangels improved, even among the secular-minded men emerging as the leaders of the developing Anglo-Texas culture. William B. Travis, soon to die at the Alamo, in 1835 even issued a call for American Methodists to send more ministers to Texas, realizing as he did that the churches they would create were simply essential to the success of that culture. And, by and large, Mexican officials left the Protestant evangelists alone. For instance, in 1832 an official in Nacogdoches complained about a nearby camp meeting to his commandant, a Col. Piedras. "Are they stealing horses?" the colonel inquired. No. "Are they killing anyone?" No, again. "Then let them alone," Piedras wisely concluded.

The Americans in Texas encountered a religious culture very unlike the one that produced them. The young American republic was dominated increasingly by an Evangelical Protestantism that was divided into highly competitive denominational voluntary associations to propagate varying versions of religious truth. And Protestant America was aggressively insistent upon the natural superiority of that denominational voluntaryism to all other forms of religious organization. In Spanish Texas all of those beliefs had to be repressed before 1836. That early repression perhaps explains in part the force with which these ideas suddenly appeared in the Republic of Texas.

The alienation of Texas from Mexico after 1824 was probably as inevitable as historians are allowed to designate any historical development. Like the British after 1763, Mexican officials between 1830 and 1835 attempted to impose controls over colonists too long neglected. And, with self-conscious reference to the eighteenth century crisis of the British empire, the ever-growing number of Americans in Texas resisted those efforts. The events of the Texas Revolution—at least the story of the defense of the Alamo—now inform the nation's mythology and need not be recounted here. Suffice it to say that the dead of the Alamo were avenged in April of 1836 by the Texas victory at the Battle of San Jacinto. Though Mexico continued to contest the point, Texas existed as a sovereign republic until 1845, when, after much controversy, she was admitted into the American union.

Religion seems not to have played a significant role in the crisis of 1835-1836 that led to the Texas Revolution. Protestant Texans fared no worse under Mexican rule after 1824 than they had under previous Spanish regimes, and they apparently understood that. Still, the Declaration of Independence of 1836 indicted Mexico with establishing a "national religion" and with supporting a standing army and a tyrannous priesthood, both equally "the eternal enemies of civil liberty." The Republic's constitution guaranteed complete religious freedom and, moreover, prohibited ecclesiastics of all descriptions from holding public office.

It was axiomatic in eighteenth century republican theory that the essential character of any new nation was set irretrievably by first impressions. In an almost mechanistic sense, the political philosophy of first the American and then the Texas republic held that a society would reflect forever the character of its first citizens and the institutions they created. Protestant ministers in the Republic of Texas were determined to influence in significant ways that process. In language that harked back to the early days of the American republic, the Baptists of Washington-on-the-Brazos, the Republic's birthplace, in 1837 urged their brothers in America, "our mother country," to send missionaries to Texas. The Methodists and Presbyterians had already embraced "the favored hour," the Baptists warned. "They know that society is now being formed. They know that early impressions are the most lasting. . . . " The Baptists must not delay.

The denominations of the "mother country" did not quite know how to respond to appeals from an independent nation populated largely by Americans. The late 1830s was one of the high points of Protestant "home" missionary activities on the western frontier, and it was a period that saw most of the major American denominations enthusiastically embarked on "foreign" missionary endeavors also. An independent Texas presented those Protestants with a dilemma: was the new western republic to be considered a "home" or a "foreign" field? The question was not an idle one. The answer determined the part of the denominational hierarchy that would have charge of Texas missions. The Texans themselves certainly were unsure of their status. The Baptists at Washington-on-the-Brazos directed the appeal mentioned above to the American Baptists' Foreign Mission Society. But the appeal was taken up by the Home Mission Society, which arranged for Georgia Baptists to "adopt" the Texans, thereby creating an important and long-lived connection between Texas and Georgia Baptists. In much the same fashion, Texas Methodists during the Republic were in the charge of Mississippi Methodists, who never quite decided if Texas was a home or a foreign field. During the life of the Republic the House of Bishops of the Episcopal Church debated the issue of mission work in Texas along with plans for evangelizing efforts in China, Africa, and Greece. But those discussions were not resolved until 1844 because canons allowing for the support of missions outside the United States had to be drafted and approved. Consequently, organized Episcopal work in Texas did not begin until after the Republic ended. The Presbyterians, though, had the most difficulty in resolving the issue of Texas' status. The Texas Presbyterians during the Republic would not decide whether to join the American hierarchy, and the Americans, in turn, could not decide the conditions under which such a union might be possible.

Clearly, the uncertainty of Texas' present and future status dampened the enthusiasm of American Protestants for mission efforts in the decade of the Republic. Those efforts were hindered further by floods, by recurring attacks of yellow fever and red men, and, especially, by the alarming if unsuccessful Mexican invasion of 1842. And, finally, one suspects that the appeals for aid from nearby Texas were simply not as enticing to Americans as were the calls from the more exotic fields of Hawaii, the Far East, and darkest Africa.

Still, Texas Protestants established during the Republic the organizational foundations of most of the major denominations: the Cumberland Presbyterians' Texas Presbytery (1839); the Presbyterians' Brazos Presbytery (1840); and the Baptists' Union Association (1840). These pioneer judicatories lay between the Austin colony and Nacogdoches/San Augustine, the area in which Protestantism had germinated during the colonial period. More so than in the colonial period, denominational strife—especially conflict between denominational schools—appeared during the Republic. As early as 1843 the students of the Presbyterian school at San Augustine engaged in sharp theological debates with students at the Methodist institution at Rutersville. And a Methodist circuit rider might rail against "the watery tribe" (the Baptists), while the Baptists would join the Methodists in castigating all "Campbellites." But, as had been true in the colonial period, disagreements *within* denominations over missions, an educated ministry, and central versus local authority were often more intense than disputes among the denominations themselves.

The principal denominations sometimes overcame their differences in efforts to elevate the moral climate of the Texas Republic. Fewer than one-eighth of the 100,000 whites numbered in the first census in 1847 were members of any church. Perhaps even more disturbing to ministers than that statistic, though, was the ease with which unlicensed and uncontrolled preachers circulated in the Republic. One notorious example was one "Daddy Spraggins," a hard-shell Baptist who patronized the saloons of Velasco both before and after haranguing sinners. His unconventional ministrations led Presbyterian, Methodist, and Baptist ministers to establish in Houston in May of 1837 the "Ecclesiastical Committee of Vigilance for Texas," which declared its intention to locate and expose religious imposters. The Episcopalians of Galveston even endeavored to protect their church from undesirable members by resolving in 1843 to admit to communion only those who "enjoy the confidence of the rectors at the time of their emigration" and who brought to Texas "satisfactory testimonials for Christian character . . . " Occasionally the Protestants banded together literally to do battle for the Lord, as when in 1838 the Baptist, Methodist, and Cumberland Presbyterian ministers of Washington-on-the-Brazos joined forces and persuaded reluctant gamblers to allow sacred services in an empty billiards room.

Travelers in the Republic of Texas commented frequently upon the sudden visibility of an ever-growing band of Protestant preachers after 1836. One Josiah Whipple in 1843 observed that "the backwoodsman has gone into the forest, and the panther is scarcely more keen scented for his blood than the Methodist preacher is for his soul." And a young visitor to Houston in 1845 was impressed by the variety of religious services available in the rough bayou settlement. He awoke one Sunday to the bells of a Catholic Mass, went to a Methodist Sunday School before hearing a Baptist sermon, took in a Presbyterian Bible class in the afternoon, and topped the day off with an evening lay sermon back at the Methodist meeting house. But, in fact, the Protestant clergymen in the Republic were a tiny handful of men very much aware of their precarious position in an aggressively impious land. Despite their concerns about its moral condition during the Republic, they did not mount extensive campaigns aimed at reforming Texas and Texans.

An independent Texas presented the Roman Catholic Church with problems quite different from those encountered by the various Protestant denominations. For instance, none of those groups had to wrestle with the question of recognizing the independence of Texas. The Vatican diplomatically avoided explicitly addressing the question until annexation rendered it moot, but Rome did take actions before 1845 that granted *de facto* recognition to the Republic. Soon after San Jacinto, the Vatican began activities that, in effect, severed Texas' historical relationship with the Spanish/Mexican/Franciscan continuum in the Church's missionary activities and, instead, pointed Texas Catholicism toward the French Vincentians in American Louisiana. Unlike the experience of Protestants during the Republic, then, the question of the interaction between Texas and American Catholics was determined by a third party, the Vatican.

In 1838 Rome directed Father John Timon, the Visitor of the American Vincentian Province, to survey the Church's work in Texas. Timon, who was stationed in New Orleans, chose to reach Texas by sea by way of Galveston rather than by going overland through east Texas, which was the route whereby Protestantism, by and large, entered the Republic. In Texas Timon entranced the Republic's legislators with an expansive, genial sermon that went a long way toward defusing the still potent anti-Catholic sentiment among the Republic's leaders. Back in New Orleans Timon prepared nine Vincentians who had been recruited in Europe for work in Texas. That work began in 1840 when he was appointed Prefect-Apostolic of Texas. Supervising an enormous jurisdiction now independent of Monterrey, Timon had effectively all the powers of a resident bishop. He appointed as his Vice-Prefect John Odin, whom he sent to Texas to perform the actual supervision of the new efforts. In 1841 Texas became a full Vicariate, and Odin became Vicar under Timon, who simultaneously became the Bishop of New Orleans. Finally, in 1847, Texas was elevated to a diocese and Odin became its first bishop. Significantly, he was not seated in Spanish San Antonio but in Galveston, a city with so many connections with the United States. Odin was given jurisdiction over the disputed area between the Nueces River and the Rio Grande, but he did not exercise power there until the American victory in the Mexican War settled the question of the southern border of Texas. At the same time he endeavored to recruit from Europe German-speaking priests to serve the growing number of German colonies in Texas. The "father of Texas Catholicism," Bishop Odin reported in 1847 that there were 10,000 Catholics in the new state, located primarily in and around San Antonio and these German colonies.

The growth of that German presence was one of the more important developments in Texas between annexation and secession. From 1840 to 1860 more than 30,000 Europeans arrived in Texas, almost invariably through the port of Galveston. They included virtually no potato-famine Irish and were, for the most part, Germans and Czechs from Bohemia and Moravia. These European settlers usually avoided areas of Anglo concentration. The early "Adelsverein" colonies, for instance, put down German roots in and around New Braunfels. Later settlers pushed into the "Hill Country" of central Texas and there created German communities as far west as the Llano River valley, the first successful white settlements above the Balcones Escarpment. The Europeans who came to Texas were overwhelmingly Catholic. In some early communities the Germans and Czechs shared a single house of worship; later they would be differentiated by language. In response to the growing number of these European Catholics in Texas, Rome in 1859 dispatched members of the Benedictine order into the state and focused their efforts in central Texas.

The antebellum period was also a significant period in the history of Jewry in Texas. Individual Jews had been active in Texas as early as 1821 and were among Austin's original Old Three Hundred colonists. And in the mid 1840s Henry Castro had created a thriving colony on the Medina River, the first successful settlement between San Antonio and the Rio Grande. But the emergence of organized Jewish life in the state awaited the period between annexation and secession. The first Jewish cemetery in Texas was established in 1844 in Houston, where the first synagogue was built a decade later. Other cemeteries and places of worship were created before 1876 in Austin, San Antonio, Waco, and Dallas.

During the antebellum years the attention of Texans appears not to have been concentrated on the sectional crisis and the attendant debate over slavery that dominated politics at the national level. The state was preoccupied with paying its debts, determining its boundary with New Mexico, and defending its frontier. Texas was the only state admitted to the Union with unconquered Indian tribes still living within its border, and that fact was perhaps the most important concern of the state for at least a full generation after annexation. But, finally, even the distracted Texans had to deal with the explosive issues that were tearing at the Union.

Fully one-quarter of the 600,000 people counted in the 1860 Texas census were slaves. There seems to have been nothing unique about slavery in the Lone Star state. The Texans, like Southerners everywhere, used biblical arguments to justify slavery. The 1848 report of the Baptist State Convention on "The Religious Condition of the Colored People" rehearsed the traditional interpretation of slavery as the way in which a wise Deity provided for the eventual redemption of Africa by allowing some of her children to be brought—albeit involuntarily—to the land of light and Christian republicanism. The report directed that all congregations should make the blacks under their care "familiar with the Bible by reading and directing their minds to those simple, plain and important parts which appertain to their soul's eternal welfare and future destiny." As they did throughout the South, slaves in Texas most frequently attended services with their master. Separate services for blacks, under white supervision, were held if numbers warranted them. There are records, for instance, of an Episcopal Sunday School, brush arbor meetings, and baptisms exclusively for blacks in Matagorda in the 1850s. And the Baptist Colorado Association in 1854 even accepted an all-black congregation into its membership. However, the Union Association of the same denomination rejected the application of an all-black group in the next year.

Texas is not usually thought of as a "border" state, but the Red River was, after 1854, part of the northern boundary of slavery. Along that border in 1859 and 1860 occurred several outbreaks of violence between Protestant opponents and supporters of slavery that eventuated in the hanging of a missionary of the Methodist Church. When that denomination divided over the issue of slave-holding bishops in 1844, each side had agreed not to send missionaries into the other's territory. That agreement had broken down as early as 1848. In 1858 Anthony Bewley, an antislavery southern Methodist lay elder, was assigned by the Missouri Conference of the northern branch of the church to do mission work along the Red River in Texas. The Conference sent other preachers to Dallas. North Texas in the 1850s was rife with rumors of fires set and whites murdered by slaves enflamed by abolitionist agitators—like the Methodist missionaries, it was charged. Bewley was attacked in particular, especially after the news of John Brown's raid on Harper's Ferry raced through the increasingly alarmed region in 1859. Applauded by the editor of the Methodist *Texas Christian Advocate*, citizens of Dallas drove two Methodist missionaries from Dallas, severely beating at least one of them in the process. A mob was then raised against Bewley, who fled with his family to Arkansas. A posse pursued them, though, and brought the preacher back to Fort Worth, where he was hanged after a mock trial.

This astounding development notwithstanding, the fact is that the Protestant denominations of Texas rarely contended over the issue of slavery during the antebellum period. The overwhelming majority of Texas Methodists supported the ecclesiastical schism of the 1840s as easily as they would the 1861 political division that it foretold. The Southern Baptist Convention was born in the year Texas entered the Union, and Texas Baptists by and large supported the drive toward secession that at least temporarily ended that union. The fact of the matter is that Texas Methodists and Baptists in the antebellum period were never part of ecclesiastical unions that crossed the Mason-Dixon line; instead what they entered were the regional unions of "southern"

Methodists and "southern" Baptists. The Disciples of Christ were strongest in the border states and had learned how to finesse discussions of slavery, which continually threatened that denomination's emphasis on Christian unity. Alone among the major denominations, the Disciples were able to turn back efforts to make "correct views" on slavery prerequisites for communion. And they survived the sectional crisis and war intact. Indeed, the Episcopal Church was the only major denomination that divided as the union dissolved. Among Texas Episcopalians, there were occasional divisions over slavery, as when Austin's Church of the Epiphany split in 1856, in large measure over the issue. But even in that case, the two parts reunited in 1859 to create the present-day St. David's Parish. After Texas seceded, the state's Episcopal Convention joined the rest of the South in a separate Episcopal Church simply by adopting "a principle of Catholic usage . . . the existence of a National Church in every separate Nation. . . ." That logic, of course, made equally simple the return of the southern Episcopalians to a single American church after the war determined that the South would not be a separate nation.

The debate over slavery, the sectional crisis, and the resulting war involved one religious group in a unique way. The American Catholic Church, of course, did not divide over the issue of slavery. But many of Texas' growing number of German Catholics became increasingly critical of slavery in the fifties. In 1854 Germans attending the annual singing festival at San Antonio adopted a resolution that condemned slavery on moral grounds and called for federal assistance in ending the institution in Texas. Inevitably, the resolution intensified the Anglo-Texans' suspicions about the Germans' loyalty to the South and its "peculiar institution." Early in the Civil War 75 German settlers sympathetic to the Union left Kerr County in west Texas determined to find new homes in Mexico. The band was intercepted by Texas forces and defeated in the Battle of the Nueces in August of 1862. Martial law was then established in the German counties of central Texas, a situation that persisted intermittently through the war. Many German Texans, of course, were loyal to the Confederate cause, and several German priests served as chaplains to Texas troops.

The postwar period in Texas, as in the rest of the defeated South, saw the complete segregation of the races. That process was nowhere as complete as in the state's churches. It is true that a few white churchmen endeavored to preserve antebellum patterns of racially mixed worship, but even they apparently sensed the inevitability of change. The Episcopal Bishop Alexander Gregg urged only that the "principle of separation" should not "have place" any further "than is necessary." Again, the Baptist instance is instructive. Black Baptists began withdrawing from white churches at the war's conclusion. Some of their new congregations, though, did petition for membership in the state's Baptist associations. The petitions drew a mixed response. In 1866 the Union Association recommended that a petitioning black congregation be accepted only if it would select its moderator, clerk, and delegates to the Association from the white members of the First Baptist Church of Houston. In the same year the minority of the Colorado Association advocated black congregations' being admitted to the Association under similar "safeguards." But the Association's majority favored complete separation of black and white Baptists, perhaps because of their own eagerness to be done with the freedmen, perhaps because they realized that no group of blacks would now submit to such limitations.

By 1869 the majority of the state's black Baptists belonged to segregated congregations. In the 1870s and 1880s white Christians gladly allowed the blacks to go their own way, emphasizing at all times the freedmen's desire to worship apart from their former masters. Some denominations, the Disciples for instance, made no effort whatever to minister to blacks. Most, however, undertook at least token efforts at outreach. Catholics, for example, established in 1884 the Catholic Missions for the Colored People and the Indians, which in the eighties and nineties established black congregations in the more settled areas of the state, beginning in 1888 with Houston's Holy Rosary Parish. For their part, blacks went about establishing the Texas branches of the great black denominations that flourished in the postwar period, most importantly the Texas Conference of the African Methodist Episcopal Zion Church, organized in 1883.

As black and white Christians withdrew into segregated fellowships in the late nineteenth century, the United States Army waged a finally successful campaign against the last free-ranging Indians in Texas. With the removal of the Indian threat—and with the coming of the railroads and the windmill—the white man's borders in Texas began to advance to the south, west, and north. Texans thereafter had always to contend with the distance—the vast space—that for most outsiders has been the most memorable thing about the Lone Star state. The state's size has been a constant source of amazement and comment. In the Episcopal General Conference of 1874 Texas' Bishop Gregg used a map of Texas to strengthen his appeal for more bishops for the state. An astonished Bishop Wilmer, from adjacent Louisiana, confessed his ignorance of Texas' size: "I never realized before how big your Diocese was," he said. "You can have all the Bishops you want."

The denominations of Texas responded to the state's vastness in varying ways, but the necessity for that response has been until the very recent past one of the two or three most important variables in the religious life of Texans. The Episcopalians early on devised perhaps the most effective means of dealing with those distances by providing for "missionary districts" for north, south, and west Texas. Those districts facilitated the extension of the denomination's hierarchy throughout the state in an ordered, regular fashion. Equally effective was the work of the Methodists' mission conferences, especially among the German settlements of central Texas and, gradually, among the Mexican-Americans south of the Nueces. Predictably, the mission efforts of the aggressively congregational Baptists were less systematic. But after 1876 even the Baptists supported what was called "home" mission work among the Germans, first, and then in the Catholic strongholds of El Paso, Corpus Christi, and San Antonio. It is easy, however, to give too much weight to these Protestant mission endeavors in north, west, and south Texas. To be reminded of their limits, one need only note that as late as 1888 there was *no* minister—of any description—in the area around the raw Panhandle town of Amarillo.

Like Texas Protestants, Catholics in the late nineteenth century moved west, north, and south of the state's antebellum boundaries of settlement. In the south and southwest of the state Catholic mission endeavors culminated in 1912 in the creation of the huge Diocese of Corpus Christi, at 88,000 square miles larger than either Utah or Minnesota. Of the area's 158,000 inhabitants, 83,000 were Catholic; of those, 70,000 were of Mexican descent. In north and west Texas Catholic incursions produced settlements that in the late twentieth century are still among the least expected features of the Texas landscape. Sometimes organized by the church, but more often led by individual Catholic entrepreneurs, small groups of Catholics, many of them from the Catholic German belt of central Texas, created in the midst of a Protestant sea what one geographer has called Catholic "folk-islands." Muenster in the Blackland Prairie, Windthorst in the Cross Timbers, and Nazareth on the High Plains, among others, remain today almost entirely Catholic, testimony to both the audacity and the perseverance of their nineteenth century Catholic founders.

The distances with which Texans contended threatened at all times to intensify the basically congregational nature of all religions in the state. In the late nineteenth and early twentieth centuries two institutions emerged that were intended to counteract the centrifugal force of all that space: the denominational periodical and college. Each remains in the late twentieth century a crucial element in the life of most Texas denominations. The *Texas Presbyterian*, the *Firm Foundation* (Disciples, later Churches of Christ), *The Texas Catholic*, *The Churchman* (Episcopal), the *Texas Baptist Herald* and the *Baptist Standard*, and perhaps most significantly, the Methodists' *Texas Christian Advocate*, were each established to inform, unify and occasionally mobilize the denominational community that supported it. There appears, in fact, to have been a correlation between the congregational nature of a denominational community and the importance it placed on its periodical. For instance, the intensely congregational Baptists supported the *Texas Baptist Herald* as early as 1855. But apparently the two most hierarchical of the state's denominations did not sense the need for periodicals to augment the unifying force of their hierarchies until the 1890s. The *Texas Catholic* appeared only in 1890, and the Episcopalians' *Diocese of Texas* was first published in the same year, ceased appearing in 1898, and did not surface again—as *The Churchman*—until 1906, a full half-century after the first Baptist publication.

Equally important as prospective instruments of denominational unification were the colleges created by Texas religious groups between 1840 and 1920. During that period Texas Christians established more than three dozen senior denominational colleges that have survived to the present. Denominational colleges, of course, have been important everywhere in American religious culture. But they seem to have played an unusually significant role in the religious history of the Lone Star state. Perhaps the distances that separate the communicants of the supporting denominations explain in part their importance. Some of the state's religious colleges and universities have attained in the twentieth century national reputations—Texas Christian University, Baylor University, Southern Methodist University, the Presbyterians' Austin College in

Sherman, and Trinity University in San Antonio come most readily to mind. Others, such as the Church of Christ's Abilene Christian University, are less well known. A.C.U. is only one of three denominational schools—the Baptists' Hardin-Simmons University and the Methodists' McMurry College are the others—located in the west Texas city of Abilene, a community so thoroughly dominated by the mainline Protestant denominations as to have evolved something of a regional folklore around its rigorously religious atmosphere. The same is true of Waco, home of Baylor University, the largest of the Southern Baptists' institutions of higher learning.

Several of the surviving denominational colleges are institutions established for blacks by both black and white Christians. They include the Methodists' Wiley College in Marshall, the oldest black college west of the Mississippi; Austin's Huston-Tillotson College, now sponsored jointly by the Methodists and the United Church of Christ; the Christian Church's Jarvis College in Hawkins; the AME's Paul Quinn College, now in Waco; the two Baptist schools, Bishop College in Marshall and Butler College in Tyler; and the Christian Methodist Episcopal Church's Texas College, also in Tyler.

The urge to solidify denominational communities was even more evident in the creation of a large number of seminaries that in the late twentieth century remain significant elements in the religious life of Texas. The Roman Catholics support three such institutions: Holy Trinity in Dallas, Assumption in San Antonio, and St. Mary's in Houston. Two of the more important Protestant seminaries, Austin Presbyterian Seminary and the Episcopal Theological Seminary of the Southwest are in the capital. But the "Metroplex" of Dallas-Fort Worth has become the center of theological education in Texas. The Disciples' Brite Divinity School at Fort Worth's Texas Christian University and the Perkins School of Theology at Dallas's Southern Methodist University are both well regarded. Also located in Dallas is the Dallas Theological Seminary and Graduate School of Theology, which remains today the aggressive center of the dispensationalism of its founder, Cyrus I. Scofield. And in Fort Worth the Southern Baptist Convention maintains the largest theological seminary in the world, Southwestern Baptist Theological Seminary.

Ironically, the journalistic and educational institutions created to foster denominational unity have often contributed to intradenominational conflict. The history of three bodies, the Disciples, the Methodists, and the Baptists, in the late nineteenth and early twentieth centuries was marked by seemingly unrelenting internal warfare. The Baptists, for instance, supported between 1845 and 1885 *two* competing colleges, one at Waco and the other at Independence. It is clear now that most of the bitter divisions between two apparently irreconcilable groups of Baptists can be reduced to a dispute between the supporters of the two schools. They were united in Waco in 1886, and the resulting Baylor University was thereafter as effective an instrument of denominational unification as its two predecessors had been sources of contention. That is not to say that the divisions among the state's Baptists ceased; the focus of the divisions simply shifted from the colleges to the denomination's paper. Between 1890 and 1915 the Baptists contested among themselves for control of the *Texas Baptist Herald,* a debate that finally saw the two principal antagonists involved in a gunfight! At the same time the state's Methodists were embroiled in the "holiness" controversy occasioned by the teachings of Dr. Henry Morrison of Kentucky. Partisans of Morrison and their foes each endeavored mightily to win the *Texas Christian Advocate* over to their side and, in the doing, turned the journal into a battlefield. The same was true of the *Firm Foundation* when the Disciples began to debate in the late nineteenth century the scriptural basis of instrumental music in Christian worship and the proper way of supporting mission work.

In the twentieth century an ever-widening gap has developed between a mythical and the real Texas. The myths about the state, of course, have been by and large the creations of Texans, who have acquired over the years a well-deserved reputation—or notoriety—for exaggerating the attributes of their state. The main outlines of the myths are well known: everything is bigger and better in Texas than anywhere else, and no sane person would wish to live elsewhere; all Texans have at least one oil well and live on ranches of baronial dimensions; and so forth. Although it is not quite mythic in proportion, a firm popular perception about the state's religious culture has emerged in the twentieth century also. In that popular view Texas is the buckle of the Bible belt, a homogeneous land of flamboyant fundamentalist preachers who periodically galvanize their huge congregations into remarkably potent instruments of political conservatism and social repression.

But a real Texas has developed in the twentieth century that is considerably more complex than the Texas of myths. Since the Civil War the most important constant in the history of the state has been the steady growth of its population. In each of the years between 1870 and 1880, for instance, 100,000 hard-pressed Southerners—black and white—moved to Texas, some of them simply scrawling "GTT"—"Gone to Texas"—on their dilapidated shacks as they left. After the upheavals in Mexico in the 1910s, the number of immigrants from across the Rio Grande increased dramatically; it has never abated. Hundreds of thousands of Americans in the twentieth century got to know Texas as the sweltering site of their basic military training. After World War II a remarkable number of them returned to retire, in San Antonio and Austin especially, where retired veterans have become significant parts of the population. More recently, the veterans have been joined by the "snowbirds" of the "frostbelt," who are attracted by the state's climate, relatively low tax structures, and employment opportunities. These later migrations have been made possible by perhaps the most significant invention in the state's history: air conditioning. And this immigration into Texas has coincided—especially since 1950—with an important intrastate shift of population from the countryside to the state's major cities. By 1980 Texas, the mythic land of wide open spaces and rugged individualism, was ranked among the three most heavily urbanized states in the nation, and three of its cities—Houston, Dallas, and San Antonio— were ranked among the eleven most populous in the United States.

If the realities of Texas' population are increasingly at odds with the myths about the state, there seems, superficially at least, to be much to support the popular impressions about its religious culture. It is undeniably true that the mainstream Protestant churches in general and the Southern Baptist and Methodist churches specifically are dominant in Texas. And those denominations have been, and remain, politically active. The Methodists and their *Texas Christian Advocate* were the most powerful force in the crusade to "dry up" Texas early in the twentieth century. And Baptist and Methodist voters continue to vote to keep officially dry Texas counties that are in reality awash in liquor obtained just across county lines or in "private clubs." The high point—or the nadir, if one prefers—of religious involvement in politics came in the 1960 crusade led by E. S. James, the courtly editor of the enormously influential *Baptist Standard*, against the presidential candidacy of Catholic John Kennedy. And it is obviously true that some highly visible congregations, such as Dallas' huge First Baptist Church, are dominated by colorful figures like W. A. Criswell, men whose strong personalities reinforce constantly the still basically congregational and individualistic tendency of most Protestant denominations in the state.

But there is much more than this to religion in Texas in the late twentieth century. The stereotype of a homogeneous Protestant culture vastly oversimplifies a society that is becoming as diverse and complex as any in the nation. It most obviously ignores the fact that the Catholics constitute the largest single group in the state. And it overlooks a significant if subtle transformation. By the 1970s virtually all of the Protestant denominations—as well as the Catholics—had institutionalized some form of outreach program that gave social and communal dimensions to endeavors that might remain essentially individualistic in their primary focus. And if those efforts, such as the Baptists' Christian Life Commission, do not yet constitute precisely a "social gospel," they do call into question any view of religion in contemporary Texas that emphasizes exclusively its individualistic essence. Moreover, any description of religion in Texas that stops with the Baptists and Methodists errs in ignoring the phenomenal growth since 1945 of the Churches of Christ in the state. Among the most rigorously congregational of all religious groups in America, since 1906 the Churches of Christ have been counted as a separate denomination that since the Second World War has been among the fastest growing of American denominations. Its greatest growth has been in Texas, where it is strong in the northern and, especially, western areas.

The stereotype of religious homogeneity in Texas has been challenged further by the recent proliferation of exotic religious groups in the state. This has been particularly true in the new frontier of urban Texas that rapidly has replaced the wide open spaces as the scene of opportunity, stimulation, and violence in the state. One of the largest Krishna Consciousness groups in the seventies gathered not in Los Angeles or in New York City but in Dallas. In Houston a bombastic, superpatriotic colonel presided with spiritual close-order drills over the Berachah Church, preaching an astoundingly militaristic gospel that seems a caricature of the nineteenth century Texas gospel of competitive individualism. And everywhere in the state one finds the residue of the revivals of the 1970s. A small group of "messianic" Jews gathered briefly on, of all places, the shores of Possum Kingdom Lake near the small Cross

Timbers town of Graham. Charismatics were to be found in virtually all denominations. The Church of the Redeemer in Houston became an important and controversial center of the movement within the Episcopal Church. Not even the Southern Baptists were immune. In that decade the Baptist General Convention of Texas found it necessary to investigate and then expel from its membership two rather large congregations whose ministers proved receptive to the revival of interest in the "gifts." Perhaps the most impressive result of that revival has been the increase in the number of "independent" and "Bible" churches that draw a growing portion of their members from disaffected communicants of the mainstream denominations. This increase appears particularly strong in the captial city of Austin, where the University of Texas is rapidly becoming one of the national centers of the revival of fundamental religion among young people of college age.

In 1986 Texas will celebrate the sesquicentennial of its independence from Mexico. As the state prepares to mark that milestone in its history, the developments that in the recent past have been transforming its religious landscape continue apace. Its rural and village churches die along with the small farms and ranches to which they were once organically connected. The farm folk who tilled the land and ran a few head of cattle have leased their mineral rights to distant corporations and have moved to the county seat, there to die in one of the "old folks' homes" that are becoming one of the most important businesses in those towns. The churches of those centers are growing in numbers, sophistication, and complexity. The towns near the booming major cities find that, virtually overnight, they are suburbs with most of the problems of the city and none of the solaces of the countryside. "First" churches accustomed to serving stable communities of 20,000 find themselves struggling to even comprehend—much less serve—the needs of an ever changing population of 100,000. And the great cities themselves continue to grow more rapidly than almost any others in the nation. And as Dallas and Fort Worth, Houston, San Antonio, and Austin approach the populations of America's nineteenth century metropolises, they begin to behave as those earlier cities did. The great downtown churches and synagogues abandon the inner cities first to black and brown people and then to gentrification and follow their congregations to the suburbs. There they erect physical plants on a true Texas scale and in them attempt to develop programs that will provide for those communicants a spiritual center, a place of fixity in the midst of what has become in the last 25 years one of the most arresting cultural transformations in the history of the American republic, the passing of the great Southwest from one frontier into another.

Bibliography

Carter Boren. *Religion on the Texas Frontier.*

R. Douglas Brackenridge. *Voice in the Wilderness: A History of the Cumberland Presbyterian Church in Texas.*

Lawrence L. Brown. *The Episcopal Church in Texas, 1838-1874.*

J. M. Carroll. *A History of Texas Baptists.*

Carlos E. Castañeda. *Our Catholic Heritage in Texas, 1519-1950.* 7 vols.

Henry Cohen et al. *One Hundred Years of Jewry in Texas.*

Joseph M. Dawson. *A Century with Texas Baptists.*

———. *The Spiritual Conquest of the Southwest.*

Stephen Eckstein. *A History of the Churches of Christ in Texas.*

William Ransom Hogan. *The Texas Republic: A Social and Economic History.*

Richard B. Hughes. "Old School Presbyterians in Texas, 1830-1861," unpublished Ph.D. dissertation, University of Texas at Austin, 1963.

R. E. Ledbetter, "The Planting and Growth of Protestant Denominations in Texas Prior to 1850," unpublished Ph.D. dissertation, University of Chicago, 1950.

DuBose Murphy. *A Short History of the Protestant Episcopal Church in Texas.*

Olin W. Nail, ed. *Texas Methodism, 1900-1960.*

George H. Paschal, Jr., and Judith A. Besmer. *One Hundred Years of the Synod of Texas of the United Presbyterian Church in the U.S.A.*

Macum Phelan. *A History of Early Methodism in Texas, 1817-1866.*

William Stuart Red. *A History of the Presbyterian Church in Texas.*

———. *The Texas Colonists and Religion, 1821-1836.*

Jesse Guy Smith. *Heroes of the Saddle Bags: A History of Christian Denominations in the Republic of Texas.*

Walter Prescott Webb, editor-in-chief. *The Handbook of Texas.* 3 vols.

VIRGINIA

W. HARRISON DANIEL
UNIVERSITY OF RICHMOND

From the founding of the colony at Jamestown in 1607 until the closing decades of the eighteenth century the Anglican Church was the established church in Virginia. Throughout the colonial period it occupied a privileged status in Virginia society; there were statutes requiring attendance at its services, the public provided its clergymen with parsonages and farms, and the salaries of its ministers were paid from tax assessments.

At the time of the American Revolution there were more than 90 Anglican parishes in Virginia and the church operated the only college in the colony (College of William and Mary). Authority in the established church resided in the lay vestry of each parish; this self-perpetuating body conducted all parish affairs, selected the clergyman for the congregation, and determined the type of tenure he received. There was never a resident bishop in Virginia and the authority of the commissary was minimal.

Although the Anglican Church was the established church throughout the colonial era, it was not the only denomination in the colony. Virginia authorities and English laws of religious toleration helped to provide an environment which made religious dissent acceptable. From the late seventeenth century Quakers, Roman Catholics, and Presbyterians were in the area. Thomas Story, a Quaker itinerant, moved freely through the countryside and won converts for the Society of Friends; George Brent, a Roman Catholic planter, was elected to the legislature, and Francis Makemie was engaged in promoting the Presbyterian church from the 1690s.

In the eighteenth century the religious composition of Virginia became highly diversified. The migration of Scotch-Irish and Germans into the colony together with the Great Awakening had a profound effect on the religious structure of Virginia, and by the time of the American Revolution the dissenters outnumbered the Anglicans. The Presbyterians were scattered from the Tidewater throughout the Piedmont area and into the Blue Ridge Mountains and valley regions. They were the new side or evangelical faction of this church and their chief spokesman was Samuel Davies. The Germans, who settled mainly in the Valley, were predominantly Lutheran or members of the German Reformed Church; however, some were Mennonites, Dunkers, and Moravians. All were welcomed to the colonial frontier and were permitted to worship according to their pleasure.

The Great Awakening, which came to Virginia in the 1740s, 1750s, and 1760s, witnessed the growth of Presbyterianism in the area, the emergence of the Baptists as a significant religious and political force, and the weakening of the established church. Although Baptists had been in the colony since the 1690s they were a small and passive group until the decades immediately preceding the American Revolution. In the 1750s "new light" or Separate Baptists from New England came to Virginia and stimulated the growth of this denomination. Their religious fervor and missionary zeal together with their criticism of the Establishment struck a responsive chord with the inhabitants and resulted in the rapid growth of Baptist churches.

John Wesley's Methodist movement came to Virginia in the 1760s when he sent his first preachers to America. Although this was a movement within the Anglican Church few Anglican clergymen in the colony affiliated with it. Nonchurchmen, however, were more sympathetic and by the close of the eighteenth century the Methodist movement had become an independent organization, had established "societies" in all regions of the state, and claimed a membership in excess of 13,000.

The Great Awakening in Virginia not only resulted in greater religious diversity in the area, it also stimulated religious activism, promoted political awareness, and prompted increased criticism of the Anglican Church. The attention of some churchmen was directed to the need for additional educational facilities. The College of William and Mary, established under Anglican auspices in 1693, was the only institution of higher learning in the colony. However, in 1749 Presbyterians founded Augusta

Academy (Washington and Lee) and in 1774 Prince Edward Academy (Hampden-Sydney).

Another interest of churchmen which received attention at the time of the Great Awakening was the spiritual care of the Negroes. Africans had been in the colony since 1619 and by 1750 they constituted approximately 45 percent of the population, but meager efforts had been made to convert them to Christianity. In the 1750s Samuel Davies preached to the blacks and instructed the Presbyterians of their responsibilities to minister to the spiritual needs of these people and to bring them into the church. Baptist and Methodist ministers also sought to convert the Negroes, and by 1800 these two denominations embraced most of the Negroes who had professed Christianity.

During the American Revolution most church members in Virginia, whether Anglicans or dissenters, were ardent supporters of the colonial cause. The political independence which was achieved by the Revolution also ended the religious Establishment in Virginia. The Anglican Church was reorganized as the Protestant Episcopal Church and Establishment was replaced by the separation of church and state. The privileged status which one denomination had held since 1607 was ended; from now on the response of the people to the concepts of religious voluntarism and religious pluralism would determine the religious structure of Virginia. Although these concepts had been championed by Presbyterian and Baptist spokesmen they were a part of the intellectual climate of the Enlightenment and received the support of many Virginia Anglicans.

From the closing decades of the eighteenth century the popular churches—the Baptist, Methodist, and Presbyterian—experienced a steady growth and development. By the 1780s the Hanover Presbytery was sending missionaries to settlers in the trans-Allegheny region of the state, and in this same decade Francis Asbury outlined circuits for Methodist itinerants which reached to the Ohio River. The various Baptist groups in the commonwealth were united in 1801 and ten years later local associations were formed which embraced all regions of the state. The Protestant Episcopal Church experienced a decline of influence following the American Revolution but began a phase of recovery and revival under the leadership of Bishop Richard Channing Moore (1812-1841).

All of the principal Protestant groups in the state were evangelical. Their approach to religion was pietistic and emphasized revivalism and a personal religious experience which the individual could relate to others.

Although the service of worship in the Protestant Episcopal Church was more formal than that found in Baptist, Methodist, and Presbyterian churches, the message "of salvation" was essentially the same in all of them and a period of annual revivals was common to churches of all denominations. The High Church movement which emerged in the Protestant Episcopal Church in the early nineteenth century found few adherents in Virginia. On one occasion Bishop Moore declared that the movement was an attempt to revive the worst evils of the Roman Catholic system.

The opening decades of the nineteenth century witnessed a considerable degree of cooperation between Virginia churches and churches of other states in a number of national agencies. Baptists, Episcopalians, Methodists, Presbyterians, and other denominational spokesmen espoused and urged their fellow members to support such agencies as the American Bible Society and they were active in forming an auxiliary of this Society in the state. Denominational leaders also encouraged support of the American Tract Society, the American Sunday School Union, and the creation of temperance organizations.

Although the different denominations in Virginia were active in a variety of interdenominational enterprises, they were also engaged in developing more effective and sophisticated denominational machinery. In 1823 the Baptists formed a statewide General Association, and by the 1830s each of the major denominations in the state, in cooperation with their co-religionists throughout the nation, had established domestic missionary organizations and foreign missionary societies. Among the Baptist churches there was some anti-mission sentiment. This feeling was strongest in the trans-Allegheny regions of the state and its leading spokesman to 1830 was Alexander Campbell. In 1840 there were 35 local Baptist associations in Virginia and in 12 there was significant opposition to missions; all of the latter were located in the western portion of the commonwealth.

From 1804 to 1860 church leaders or denominational organizations in Virginia initiated more than 60 publishing ventures, mainly weekly newspapers. Less than 20 percent of these experienced a life of ten years. Although the casualty rate was high for religious newspapers and journals, all of the major denominations succeeded in establishing weekly newspapers. The first one established on a permanent basis was the *Religious Herald*, a Baptist weekly which appeared in 1828. This paper was followed by the *Richmond Christian Advocate* (Methodist), *The Southern Churchman* (Episcopal), the *Central Presbyterian*, the *Millennial Harbinger* (Disciples of Christ) and others. These publications contained information about the denomination and its various agencies, a digest of the minutes of ecclesiastical organizations, several columns of secular news including excerpts from foreign newspapers, assorted advertisements including those for runaway slaves, devotionals, theological essays, and editorials on subjects and issues of current interest.

Prior to 1819 the only institutions of higher learning in Virginia were founded by churchmen. The College of William and Mary would be closely associated with the Protestant Episcopal Church until the early twentieth century when it became a state institution. The Episcopalians founded no additional colleges in the antebellum era; however, Virginia churchmen were influential in establishing a theological seminary at Alexandria in 1823. Although the Presbyterians established no additional colleges during the antebellum period, in 1824 they created a theological seminary at Hampden-Sydney, and a few years later (1837) added a medical school. Both of these institutions were later moved to Richmond and became known as the Union Theological Seminary in Virginia and as the Medical College of Virginia.

The Baptists and Methodists, which were the numerically dominant and more aggressive denominations, began, in the Jacksonian era, to establish institutions of higher learning. In 1830 the Methodists founded Randolph Macon College in Mecklenburg County and the Baptists established the Virginia Baptist Seminary, an institution which in 1840 was chartered by the state legislature as Richmond College. Nine years later (1839) the Methodists opened another school, Emory and Henry College, at Emory in the southwestern portion of the Valley. The first institution of higher learning in the trans-Allegheny region of the state, Rector College, was established under Baptist auspices in 1839 at Pruntytown in Harrison County. This school was destroyed by fire in 1855 and not rebuilt. The only college in that area of the state to be a permanent one was Bethany College, founded by Alexander Campbell in 1840.

The church colleges in Virginia were strikingly similar; all featured a curriculum centered on a study of the classics, mathematics, natural science, and philosophy. All were solely for males and the faculty and trustees were mainly clergymen. These institutions were small, having three to five faculty members and a student body of 60 to 125. A principal purpose of these institutions was to prepare young men for the ministry, although by 1850 more "practical" courses such as bookkeeping and modern foreign languages were being introduced into the curriculum.

Numerous participants in all denominations were active in another sphere of education: the establishment and operation of academies and seminaries. Academy was the usual designation for a boys' school; seminary often referred to a girls' school. Occasionally an institution such as the West Liberty Academy, which was conducted by a Presbyterian clergyman, was coeducational. In an era when there was no tax supported public school system, private academies and seminaries afforded the principal means of providing primary and secondary education for many Virginians.

In the colonial era many Anglican and Presbyterian clergymen conducted schools along with their ministerial duties and in the closing decade of the eighteenth century there were 24 academies in the state. After the American Revolution churchmen of all persuasions operated academies; by 1825 there were more than 300 in Virginia and in 1860 the number had increased to nearly 400; approximately 35 of these were located in the trans-Allegheny region of the commonwealth. Although not all of these institutions were affiliated with churches or denominational agencies, one student of Virginia academies claims that it would be difficult to overemphasize the importance of the part played by religious denominations in their founding and support.

Presbyterian clergymen established academies in all areas of the state, from the tidewater section to the Ohio River. From the early decades of the nineteenth century Methodist and Baptist leaders were also active in promoting education. Methodist schools were established from Brunswick County to Morgantown, and academies founded by Baptist spokesmen were scattered from Caroline County to the mountainous regions in the western portion of the commonwealth. Among the institutions founded by the Protestant Episcopal Church was an academy for boys at Alexandria and a female institute at Staunton. In the closing decades of the antebellum era (1840-1860) the followers of Alexander Campbell operated academies in a variety of places, including the counties of Orange, Albemarle, and Nelson.

In the valley of Virginia, where most of the Lutheran, German Reformed and other German groups were located, local pastors often taught in schools attached to the church. During the antebellum period

Lutheran schools were found in such places as Winchester, Strasburg, and Wytheville. In 1823 a clergyman conducted a theological course in his home at New Market, and three years later Virginia Lutherans were instrumental in helping to found a theological seminary at Gettysburg, Pennsylvania. In 1853 the Lutheran school at Salem was chartered by the general assembly as a four year college (Roanoke College). The Dunkers (who adopted the name Church of the Brethren in 1908) were affiliated with the Rockingham Academy and Cedar Grove Academy. Prior to 1860 a few schools were established under Roman Catholic auspices, among them were St. Joseph's Academy in Richmond (1834), St. Mary's Academy in Norfolk (1848), and Mount de Chantal, a school for girls in Wheeling (1848). Jewish congregations operated schools in Richmond (1848) and in Norfolk (1853). Although Jews had been in Virginia since the colonial period and had established their first congregation in Richmond in 1791, they were located primarily in the eastern region of the state; their first congregation in the west was formed at Wheeling in 1849.

Although numerous religious leaders and spokesmen were engaged in founding and operating a variety of educational institutions throughout the state in the first half of the nineteenth century, these activities did not indicate the limits of their interest in education. During the three decades before the Civil War the most articulate advocates of public education in the commonwealth were clergymen. Two of the principal spokesmen for tax supported schools were the founder of the Disciples of Christ, Alexander Campbell, and the Presbyterian clergyman from Lexington, Henry Ruffener. Although these men were joined by others, their efforts to persuade the politicians of the state to establish a system of schools available to all of its citizens did not receive a favorable response from the general assembly and a system of public education was not established until after the Civil War.

Although the opening decades of the nineteenth century witnessed considerable interdenominational cooperation in various enterprises, these were also years of emerging tension and factions within American Christianity, and these forces were reflected in the religious structure of the state. During the 1830s and 1840s the Baptist churches in Virginia were wracked by the Campbellite movement. Alexander Campbell was affiliated with the Baptists from approximately 1813 to 1830, when he and his followers embarked upon a reform movement to restore primitive Christianity. He was also opposed to participation in all cooperative societies such as Bible, tract, and mission organizations as being unscriptural. When he left the Baptist fold and established the Disciples of Christ or Christian churches, a number of Baptist congregations followed his lead and others were split. Some "Campbellite" churches were found in all regions of the state but perhaps the area of greatest controversy was in the Meherrin Association in southside Virginia. Within a decade of Campbell's departure from Baptist ranks this association ceased to exist as most of its churches became aligned with Campbell's reformation. Although most of Campbell's following was in Kentucky, Tennessee, and the Ohio valley region, he lived in Bethany, Virginia, where he operated Bethany College and published the *Millennial Harbinger*. At the time of the Civil War some of his followers were divided in their sentiments; however, unlike the older denominations, the Disciples of Christ did not split into sectional factions.

During the years the Baptists were agitated by the Campbellite movement, the Methodists experienced a schism which resulted in the emergence of the Methodist Protestant Church. This schism traces its origin to the James O'Kelly defection from the Methodist Church in the 1790s. From that date certain elements within the Methodist Episcopal Church were unhappy with the authority exercised by the bishop and the prohibition of laymen from participating in conference affairs and in governing the church. Sentiment for ecclesiastical reform which would implement these two concepts centered in the Maryland and Virginia conferences of the church but was also present in other areas. In 1828 and 1829 meetings were held in Lynchburg and in Baltimore by church leaders who wished to institute these practices in Methodism. Their efforts culminated in an organizational conference, which was held in Baltimore in 1830. At this conference the Methodist Protestant Church was organized; its constitution eliminated the office of bishop and provided for lay representation in conference meetings. At this time the Virginia Conference of the Methodist Protestant Church reported 1000 members; by 1860 it had increased to 5000. Principal churches were in Lynchburg and Norfolk but other centers of activity were in Amelia County, on the Northern Neck, and in the Monongahela valley. In 1855 Lynchburg College was founded under the auspices of this church; it was forced to close during the Civil War and did not reopen after 1865.

The Baptists and Methodists were not alone in experiencing schisms in the Age of Jackson. After several years of increasing tension resulting from growing dissatisfaction on behalf of some Presbyterians with the Plan of Union, the influence of the theology of Nathaniel Taylor within the church, and the emergence of an activist abolitionist element in Presbyterian ranks, this church split into new school and old school factions at the General Assembly in 1837. The old school faction was the dominant one and most Presbyterians in Virginia were affiliated with it; however, there were some congregations which aligned themselves with the new school faction. In 1850 the Synod of Virginia (old school) consisted of six presbyteries which reported a membership of 13,000. The Synod of Virginia (new school) at mid-century included three presbyteries and a membership of 4,100. From the beginning fraternal relations between these factions in Virginia was cordial and during the Civil War (1864) they merged to form part of what became the Presbyterian Chruch in the United States.

In the 1830s and 1840s Virginia Christians often manifested attitudes which reflected national trends or movements. The antimasonic sentiment which emerged in the 1830s was noted when the annual conference of the Methodist Episcopal Church in Virginia admonished members for joining a masonic fraternity or the Independent Order of Odd Fellows. Nativist sentiment which flourished in the nation in the 1840s and 1850s was reflected in the annual meetings of the old school Presbyterian Synod of Virginia. It was customary at these meetings for the delegates to hear a sermon "on popery," which expounded the errors, superstitions, and evils of the Roman Catholic Church. These years also witnessed occasional editorials in the Baptist press and other denominational weeklies of anti-Mormon diatribes, although there were no congregations of the Church of Jesus Christ of Latter Day Saints in the commonwealth.

The issue which caused the greatest concern for Virginia churches in the antebellum era was the one which polarized the nation and resulted in Civil War—slavery. African slavery was introduced into Virginia in the seventeenth century and by 1840 slaves constituted approximately 35 percent of the state's population. From the era of the Great Awakening all of the popular churches sought to minister to the spiritual needs of the Negro. Although some black communicants were found in all denominations, most of them were members of Baptist and Methodist churches. Slaves were accepted into church membership in the same manner as whites, upon profession of faith and relating their religious experience. Once on the membership roll they were subject to the same rules of discipline as other members. Most black and white Christians in Virginia worshipped together although the blacks were segregated to a specific seating area in the sanctuary.

From 1840 in Richmond, Lynchburg, Fredericksburg, and other cities separate black churches were formed, but all of these were "branch" churches of white organizations. Their trustees and clergymen were white and usually their deacons were selected by whites. For a few years near the close of the eighteenth and the opening of the nineteenth century a few independent black churches had been formed but by 1830 state legislation and white fears had eliminated the independent Negro church in the commonwealth.

The type of gospel preached to the blacks was designed not only to convert and keep them firm in the faith but also to make them more obedient and compliant slaves. Spokesmen of all the major denominations in Virginia prepared catechisms or instructional manuals for the teaching of slaves. The type of Christianity expounded in such publications emphasized the virtues of docility, obedience, honesty, and hard work. A bishop of the Protestant Episcopal diocese of Virginia once told a congregation of slaves that their master was God's overseer and that they were to obey him as they would God. Slaves were taught that in this world of sorrow, sickness, and toil it was their duty to work and be humble and patient. They were told that God expected them to work hard in this life so that they would better appreciate their life beyond the grave. Other teachings threatened the slaves with the fires of hell for swearing, drinking, and cheating.

Many Virginia clergymen owned slaves and some local churches accepted gifts of slaves as part of their endowment. Two of the most articulate defenders of slavery were Virginia churchmen: the Baptist Thornton Stringfellow, and William A. Smith of the Virginia Conference of the Methodist Episcopal Church, South. Both of these men wrote books expounding the "biblical" argument justifying slavery. Their writings were circulated in essay and book form throughout the nation during the last 20 years of the antebellum era.

Although most clergymen and denominational leaders in Virginia defended the institution of slavery there were exceptions. The Church of the Brethren did not countenance slavery among its members. Since the American Revolution the Quakers in Virginia had renounced slaveholding and some Quakers continued to agitate for the abolition of slavery in the commonwealth throughout the antebellum period. The Mennonite congregations in the state also forbade slaveholding among their membership, and among the major denominations an outspoken foe of slavery was William Sparrow, a professor at the Episcopal Theological Seminary in Alexandria.

Until the 1840s there were no sectional denominations; all of the major churches were affiliated together in national organizations. The Virginia Conference of the Methodist Episcopal Church sent delegates to the General Conference of this church which met once every four years and consisted of churchmen from all of the conferences in the nation. Presbyterian commissioners from Virginia met annually with their co-religionists from synods throughout the nation to form the General Assembly of the Presbyterian Church. After the old school-new school schism in 1837 there were formed general assemblies of each group but these gatherings represented a national rather than a sectional constituency. Among the Baptist churches the Triennial Convention had existed since 1814. This was an affiliation of Baptist churches throughout the United States and was the agency for promoting Baptist foreign missions, conducting the home mission program, and sustaining a publication enterprise. Most Virginia Baptists were active in all of these programs.

Tensions associated with slavery precipitated the destruction of national ties in the two largest denominations in the 1840s and resulted in the formation of sectional ecclesiastical organizations by the Methodist and Baptist denominations. At the General Conference of the Methodist Episcopal Church in 1844 a southern bishop was admonished for being a slaveholder. This action resulted in splitting the denomination and creating the Methodist Episcopal Church, South. Clergymen, churches, and conferences were free to affiliate with either the northern church (Methodist Episcopal Church) or the southern church (Methodist Episcopal Church, South). Following the schism most of the Methodist congregations in Virginia became affiliated with the Virginia Conference of the Methodist Episcopal Church, South. However, portions of the commonwealth, including most of the trans-Allegheny region, a few areas in the Valley and in the northern portion of Virginia, and some congregations on the eastern shore affiliated with the Methodist Episcopal Church. In some places controversy emerged between congregational factions concerning the control of church property and resulted in civil suits and court action. It is estimated that in 1860 there were approximately 47,000 communicants in the Methodist Episcopal Church, South, in Virginia and approximately 22,000 members of the Methodist Episcopal Church. The two Methodist factions were reunited in 1939.

The same year that the Methodist Episcopal Church split along sectional lines the Baptist Triennial Convention met in Philadelphia. The convention discussed slavery but adopted neither antislavery nor proslavery resolutions. However, when Baptists in Georgia and Alabama failed to receive approval for mission candidates who were slave owners, many Baptists in the South were ready to sever connections with the convention. Baptist leaders of the Virginia Foreign Mission Society called for a convention of southern churchmen to meet in Augusta, Georgia, in May 1845 to form a southern Baptist missionary organization. This suggestion received a favorable response and in the spring of 1845 the Southern Baptist Convention was formed. The Virginia Baptist leadership which was instrumental in creating this convention represented a constituency of 84,000 members.

The mid-1840s also witnessed the formation of the Southern Christian Association. Until 1844 the Virginia Christian Conference, which represented approximately 2,500 communicants, maintained formal relations with various Christian conferences in the north. In this year the New England Conference of Christian Churches adopted an antislavery resolution which prompted the Virginia Conference to sever relations with their Northern brethren. Virginia churchmen then invited their coreligionists in North Carolina and elsewhere in the South to form an organization of Christian churches in the slave states. The Southern Christian Convention would reunite with their Northern brethren in 1922, and in 1931 the Christian Churches would merge with the National Council of Congregational Churches to form the Congregational Christian Church.

Twenty years after the old school-new school schism in the Presbyterian Church (1857), the new school General Assembly repudiated slavery and slave owning. This action prompted the New School Presbyterian churches in the South to form a separate organization, the United Synod of the Presbyterian Church. New School presbyteries in Virginia affiliated with the United Synod until this synod merged with the Old School church in the South in 1864.

After secession and the beginning of the Civil War the Old School Presbyterians in the South formed the Presbyterian Church in the Confederate States of America; the board of publication of this denomination was located in Richmond. In early 1861 leaders of the Protestant Episcopal diocese of Virginia and other dioceses of this church in the south organized a national church under the appellation of the Protestant Episcopal Church in the Confederate States of America. At this time leadership of the Lutheran synods in the south also formed sectional ecclesiastical bonds and the Lutheran churches in Virginia became affiliated with the Lutheran Church in the Confederate States of America. At the close of the Civil War the southern dioceses of the Protestant Episcopal Church were reunited with their coreligionists in the nation, and in 1917 the Lutheran schism was healed; the Presbyterians in the nation (as the Baptists) still constitute two major factions or sectional organizations.

During the secession crisis of 1860-1861 most Virginia Christians counseled moderation and decried the spirit of "fanaticism" which was present in some areas of the South. Robert L. Dabney, a prominent Presbyterian and moderator of the Synod of Virginia, expressed the sentiments of most when he declared that the election of Abraham Lincoln was not sufficient cause for secession. He also denounced the hasty action of South Carolina in adopting an ordinance of secession. Dabney as well as the *Religious Herald* (Baptist) and the *Richmond Christian Advocate* (Methodist) urged compromise measures to preserve the Union until after the Fort Sumter incident.

Once fighting erupted in South Carolina, churches in Virginia supported public opinion and the action of the state's politicians. Secession was justified on constitutional and economic grounds and blame for the disruption of the nation and the war was placed on zealous and fanatical northerners. Only a few clergymen opposed the course of their state and migrated to other regions; in Halifax County an Episcopal rector retired from the ministry because his unionist sympathies were unpopular with his congregation.

During the Civil War most church leaders declared that the struggle was a just and righteous one. Virginia clergymen, in patriotic sermons and orations, urged young men to join the army and some assisted recruiting agents in enrolling men for service. Clergymen often set the example for others by abandoning their profession for military action. In the spring of 1861 the Rev. J. M. P. Atkinson, president of Hampden-Sydney College, was elected captain of a military company and the Rev.

William N. Pendleton, rector of Grace Church (Episcopal) in Lexington, joined the Rockbridge Artillery with the rank of captain.

During the war denominational leaders directed their attention and resources to the spiritual needs of the soldiers. Numerous ministers served as chaplains and others visited the army as evangelists and missionaries. The activities of these clergymen sparked a series of revivals in the Army of Northern Virginia; they were also active in forming army churches and Christian associations among the soldiers.

Throughout the war Virginia church members of all denominations made valiant efforts to provide Bibles, tracts, and religious newspapers for the men in military service as well as for their constituency at home. Some these efforts were by denominations acting alone, but most were cooperative undertakings with other churches. The Virginia Baptist Publication and Sunday School Board printed more than 100 different tracts and distributed over 50 million pages to soldiers and civilians during the war. The Virginia Conference of the Methodist Episcopal Church, South, organized the Soldier's Tract Society; it published tracts and the *Soldier's Paper*, a religious newspaper for distribution in the army. The society also distributed hymnbooks and Bibles to soldiers.

Virginia Baptists, Methodists, Presbyterians, Episcopalians, and others supported a number of interdenominational agencies which were formed during the war to minister to the religious needs of the men in military service. Among these were the Bible Society of the Confederate States, the Evangelical Tract Society of Petersburg, and the General Tract Agency of Raleigh. Virginia churchmen also sponsored a project to provide education for soldier orphans, and in Richmond they formed a society to furnish artificial limbs for maimed soldiers.

Most of the programs of the churches were interrupted by the war. Foreign missionaries were stranded, educational institutions were impoverished as their trustees invested endowment funds in Confederate securities. Scores of church buildings in eastern Virginia and in the Valley were destroyed by the contending armies and others were used for hospitals and stables. Many congregations were scattered and ecclesiastical bonds were weakened. Methodist Bishop John Early was unable to supervise and visit the congregations in his area, and some local Baptist associations did not meet during the war. After Appomattox churchmen urged the citizens of Virginia to accept the result of the war as "part of the workings of Providence," to prove themselves loyal citizens of the United States, and begin the task of rebuilding.

The emancipation of the slaves had a pronounced effect upon the religious structure of the state. In 1860 churches of all denominations contained slave members, but the largest number of black Christians were members of Baptist churches. After the war practically all of these members left their former churches and formed separate and independent congregations. The formation of black churches began prior to 1865 at such places as Norfolk and Alexandria and was encouraged by missionaries from Northern churches. After Appomattox Baptist, Congregational, Methodist, Presbyterian, and other missionaries and teachers from the North entered the state to care for the spiritual and educational welfare of the freedmen, and by the close of 1866 Negro Baptist and Methodist congregations had been formed in most of the towns and cities in the commonwealth.

Agents of the American Baptist Home Missionary Society assisted freedmen in forming the first black Baptist association in the state (1865). This organization, the Shiloh Association, consisted of churches in the Richmond, Manchester, and Petersburg area. In 1868 the Virginia Baptist State Convention was created; it consisted of associations which embraced all regions of the state. This convention was the principal organization of black Baptists in the commonwealth. American Baptist Home Mission personnel were also responsible for founding a school in Richmond which later developed into Virginia Union University. In 1883 black Baptists established the Virginia Theological Seminary and College in Lynchburg, and by 1900 the membership of black Baptist churches in Virginia was approximately 200,000.

After the Civil War the black membership of the Methodist Episcopal Church, South, left that denomination and entered one of several branches of Methodism. Some affiliated with the Methodist Episcopal Church but most of them became members of either the African Methodist Episcopal Church or the African Methodist Episcopal Zion Church. Both of these were autonomous black organizations which had been formed in the early nineteenth century and had their headquarters in Philadelphia and New York. Agents of these denominations came into Virginia in the wake of Federal forces and found a responsive following among Methodist freedmen. Another body was formed in 1870, the Colored Methodist Episcopal Church, consisting mainly of freedmen who wished to maintain a close relationship with the Methodist Episcopal

Church, South. The various black Methodist churches in the state reported a combined membership of approximately 30,000 at the close of the nineteenth century.

Although the black membership of the Presbyterian and Protestant Episcopal churches in Virginia was small in the post-Appomattox decades, these members were organized into separate congregtions. In 1878 leadership in the Episcopal diocese of Virginia was instrumental in founding the Bishop Payne Divinity School, a theological seminary for blacks at Petersburg, and twelve years later the diocese helped to establish a vocational school for blacks at Lawrenceville (St. Paul's College). In the closing decades of the nineteenth century other industrial high schools for Negroes were founded at Christiansburg, Lynchburg, Manassas, and elsewhere under the auspices of the Society of Friends, the Methodist Episcopal Church, and the United Presbyterian Church.

The formation of separate black congregations in the state was not entirely because of the influence of missionaries from the north. The attitude of white church members in the state toward their black co-religionists reflected a paternalistic and white supremacist approach to race relations and stimulated the formation of independent congregations by freedmen. In the scattered congregations which permitted blacks to worship with whites—mainly rural Protestant and urban Catholic ones—the few blacks who attended services were seated in areas of the sanctuary "reserved" for them as in antebellum days.

Although the white controlled churches in Virginia lost nearly all of their black members after the Civil War, relations between black and white Christians were not hostile. A number of white Baptists served as trustees of the black school at Richmond and the *Religious Herald* urged its constituency to contribute to the school's support. Black and white ecclesiastical organizations frequently welcomed each others' "fraternal delegates" at their annual meetings and invited them to attend the proceedings. The white religious press deplored the lynchings of blacks and urged that whites treat black citizens with respect and pay them fair wages for their labor. The white denominational press was sympathetic to the establishment of public schools for blacks but demanded that they be segregated. White churchmen were not supportive of black suffrage and they applauded the actions of the state constitutional convention of 1901-1902 which virtually abolished black voting in the state.

Although some church leaders had advocated the establishment of a state system of tax supported schools prior to the Civil War, such schools were not established until 1870. From its inception denominational leaders were some of the firmest and most articulate supporters of the public school system. The *Religious Herald*, which represented the largest group of church members in the state, applauded the establishment of public schools and frequently urged the general assembly to appropriate increased funds to extend the school year and to establish a normal school for the training of teachers. Church leaders, however, were not unanimous in their support of public education. The Presbyterian Robert L. Dabney and the Baptist spokesman Bennett Puryear disapproved of public schools. They viewed them as extravagant and a misuse of tax funds, as tending to weaken family bonds, and as promoting "godless" education. These men, nevertheless, represented a small faction of the citizens and church members in the commonwealth.

Since most of the public schools in Virginia prior to World War I were limited to the elementary grades, the churches remained active in operating institutes, academies, and seminaries to provide secondary education for young men and women. Throughout the closing decades of the nineteenth century and the early years of the twentieth century all churches sponsored secondary educational institutions for boys and girls. In the 1890s Baptists in Virginia were operating 15 schools for boys and 18 for girls. Secondary schools were also established by Lutherans, Methodists, Presbyterians, Episcopalians, Roman Catholics, and others. Some of these denominational schools were privately owned and operated but others were governed by a board of trustees responsible to a local association, synod, presbytery, or conference. All of the schools solicited funds from churches and individuals within their area. Church oriented schools flourished until the second decade of the twentieth century, when the commonwealth began to devote attention and resources to the establishment of public high schools.

Denominational colleges in the postbellum years faced an enormous task of rebuilding destroyed or damaged property, replenishing their endowments, and reviving interest in higher education. All of the principal colleges had suspended classes during the war but by 1866 most had resumed operations. Within the next 50 years a number of new church colleges were founded in the state. Three of these represented small groups which had been in Virginia since colonial days. In 1875 the United Brethren established Shenandoah College at Winchester and six years later the Dunkers (Church of the Brethren) founded Bridgewater College, and in 1917 Eastern Mennonite College at Harrisonburg was chartered by the state legislature as a four year institution. Lynchburg College, a Disciples of Christ school, began operations in 1903.

Virginia church leaders were in the forefront of the movement to provide higher education for women. For decades the churches had been active in the operation of institutes and seminaries for young women but it was not until the closing years of the nineteenth century that women were given the opportunity to receive a college education. By the 1880s some denominational leaders in the Baptist, Methodist, Presbyterian, and other churches were keenly aware of the need to provide higher education for women and they were urging that the church colleges become coed or else separate ones be established for women. Despite the opinion of a few that educating women would "take them out of their sphere" and make them independent of their husbands and contribute to family dissension, the advocates of higher education for women received a favorable hearing in the state. In some instances a female seminary was transformed into a college; the Augusta Female Seminary at Staunton, a Presbyterian school since 1842, became a junior college for women and later obtained a charter as a four-year college (Mary Baldwin). Hollins Institute, founded under Baptist auspices in the antebellum era, was also transformed into a four-year institution—Hollins College.

In 1898 the board of trustees of Richmond College approved the admission of young women to that institution, but in 1914 the board established Westhampton College, a four-year liberal arts resident college for women on the campus of the University of Richmond. However, the Methodists were the first group in the state to found a high quality four-year liberal arts college for women. In 1893 the Virginia Conference of the Methodist Episcopal Church, South, sponsored the founding of Randolph Macon Woman's College in Lynchburg. All of the principal denominations also operated junior colleges for women; these institutions were located in Blackstone, Danville, Bristol, Marion, Abingdon, and elsewhere in the state.

The denominations made valiant efforts to provide higher education for women but church leaders were not supportive of the movement to extend the franchise to women. Prominent spokesmen in all churches opposed woman suffrage, claiming that political activities would degrade women and deprive them of their modesty and charm. Not only were women denied political rights until 1920, they were also denied full church member status. Until the 1890s congregational business meetings and programs were conducted by the male members, and the church's representatives to meetings of the synod, conference or association were males. Although males dominated ecclesiastical affairs, women were assuming an increasingly important position in the life of the church during the years 1880-1920. Prior to the close of the nineteenth century a few Baptist churches were permitting women to attend and participate in the monthly business meeting of the congregation. In a number of churches women served on a variety of committees including music, visitation, or hospitality, Sunday school, finance, and communion. From the 1880s leadership in the women's missionary organization in all of the denominations became more active and aggressive and they achieved the right of their representatives to have time on the program of the annual ecclesiastical meetings of the different denominations. It would be another fifty years, however, before the widespread prejudice against the ordination of women would begin to wane; this prejudice was less prevalent in the Methodist Church than in other denominations.

Throughout most of the nineteenth century the churches' concern for youth was manifested in the formation of Sunday schools. However, from the 1880s on church leaders were active in promoting a distinctive ministry to their youth. Organizations such as the Baptist Young Peoples Union, the Luther League, Christian Endeavor, and the Epworth League were created to minister to youth. The purpose of these societies was to encourage and train young people to participate in the life and programs of the church, to promote their spiritual development, and to detect potential leadership for the church. These organizations were popular and by 1902 BYPUs were organized in 202 churches in the state, and they had a membership of 10,700. Within a few years these youth organizations would sponsor retreats, summer encampments, and a variety of training programs. In 1921 the Synod of Virginia purchased Massanetta Springs for use as an assembly site and retreat for Presbyterian youth groups. For many years the Synod permitted its facilities also to be used by other denominational organizations within the state. An important aspect of the ministry to youth was the establishment of campus ministry programs for students attending state colleges and universities. Although all of the denominations formed such programs, the first one in Virginia was established in 1901 at Blacksburg by the Presbyterians.

Among the various benevolent activities which occupied denominational leaders in the decades from 1880 to 1920 were the establishment of orphanages and homes for the aged. During these years all of the principal churches established such institutions at Richmond, Lynchburg, Salem, Covington, and elsewhere. In 1919 the Baptists received a charter for the Virginia Baptist Hospital and began the construction of this facility at Lynchburg. The Baptists and the Roman Catholics are the only two denominations to establish hospitals in the commonwealth.

The decades following Appomattox were ones characterized by intellectual, economic, social, and political ferment. Many of the concerns, problems, fears, and aspirations of American society were shared by Virginians. Although Virginia was not a major industrial state the tensions and violence characteristic of labor-management relations during these years were not unnoticed by Virginia church people. Throughout the 1870s and 80s church spokesmen espoused laissez faire paternalism as the ideal relationship for harmony between employer and employees. Baptist, Presbyterian, and other church people maintained that all attempts on the part of trade unions to regulate the price of labor were unsound and injurious. It was claimed that labor unions created ill feelings between employees and employers. Labor sympathizers were labeled foreign-born anarchists, socialists, and communists. However, by the close of the century some church leaders were advocating the eight hour day for industrial workers and were expressing concern about the type of occupation and the hours of employment required of women and children. When the Federal Council of Churches was formed in 1906, all of the major denominations in the state except the Baptists became affiliated with this organizaiton and church leaders expressed sympathy with many of the social and economic reforms proposed by the FCC. Although the Baptists never joined the Council, spokesmen for this denomination in Virginia were sympathetic to many of its aims. Prior to 1914 the *Religious Herald* and prominent Baptist spokesmen advocated effective child labor laws, mine safety legislation, and supported the direct election of United States senators.

Between 1880 and 1920 the nation received a large influx of immigrants from southern and eastern Europe. In Virginia this immigration was responsible for the marked increase in membership of two groups which had been present in the area since colonial times: Jews and Roman Catholics. During these years the Jewish population of the state increased from approximately 2,500 to 25,000, and Roman Catholic communicants increased from an estimated 12,000 to 38,000. Also during these years Greek immigrants established the first Eastern or Orthodox congregation in the state.

The increase of immigrants from southern and eastern Europe into the United States stimulated a revival of nativist sentiment throughout the nation. Although nativist feeling and activities were not as prominent in Virginia as elsewhere in the country, such attitudes were reflected in the religious press and in the statements of some church leaders concerning foreigners, labor sympathizers, and Roman Catholics. On one occasion the *Religious Herald* referred to the immigrants who were "flooding" into the United States as the "dregs of society" who should be excluded from the country. Labor disputes, urban crime and violence, and political corruption were blamed on foreigners.

Since most of the immigrants to America were affiliated with the Roman Catholic Church the anti-foreign sentiments of Virginia churchmen often manifested a hostility to this church. Although anti-Catholic bias was prevalent among all Protestant groups it was most aggressive in Baptist churches. The Catholic Church was often referred to as "the mother of harlots" and as a tyrannical institution which kept its people in ignorance. The dogma of papal infallibility was described as an incredible and monstrous assumption. Baptist spokesmen maintained that their denomination had existed as a separate group since the time of Jesus Christ and that they had never been affiliated with the church at Rome. Apprehension that Catholic immigrants would overrun the country and the belief that foreigners were responsible for a variety of social and economic problems in American society prompted churchmen to espouse federal legislation which would restrict immigration into the United States.

In the half century following the Civil War and Reconstruction a variety of intellectual forces helped to produce an era of controversy and tension in American religious life and thought. Among these forces were the evolutionary concept of the development of life and the theories of geologists concerning the formation and age of the earth, the critical study of the Bible in universities and seminaries, and the emergence of theological liberalism. Virginia churches were keenly aware of these intellectual forces and spokesmen in all denominations, at one time or another, denounced the evolutionary theory as atheistic and "utterly worthless." However, in 1900 the Baptist weekly published an article which declared that the evolutionary hypothesis enabled man to interpret God as a vital and abiding force. Evolution, it maintained, made possible a noble review of society and confirmed the teaching that man was the acme of creation. In the twentieth century denominational leaders in Virginia became more tolerant of the evolutionary theory and Virginia was the only southern state in the 1920s which did not adopt a law to prohibit the teaching of evolution in the public schools. Virginius Dabney claims that the reason Virginia followed this course was because of the influence of church spokesmen, especially Baptist leaders, who opposed the passage of a law prohibiting the teaching of evolution.

The critical study of the Bible and church history, and the concepts of theological liberalism received a mixed reception in the state. Generally, church leaders maintained that Almighty God was the author of the Scriptures and that people should read and accept the Bible rather than question it. An exception was the Baptist scholar Crawford Toy of Norfolk. Toy had studied at the University of Berlin and was professor of Old Testament at the Southern Baptist Theological Seminary. He was dismissed from the faculty because he denied that Moses wrote the Pentateuch and claimed that one should not use the Scriptures to affirm or oppose the facts of history or the knowledge of modern science. A few years after the dismissal of Toy, who was subsequently a faculty member at Harvard University, a professor of church history at the same seminary was forced to resign because he claimed, in a published article, that Roger Williams had probably been sprinkled rather than immersed, that the Baptist denomination originated in the seventeenth century, and that the earliest Baptists did not practice immersion. Although this professor, William Whitsitt, was dismissed, his opinions were not offensive to Baptist leaders in Virginia and he was immediately employed by Richmond College as professor of philosophy.

Neither Baptist nor Presbyterian churchmen manifested any sympathy for the doctrines of theological liberalism or the New Theology. Proponents of liberalism were accused of being indifferent to the truth and to the Christian doctrines of the trinity, the atonement, revelation, and the incarnation. The late Hunter D. Farish maintained that Methodists were friendlier to liberal thought and concepts than others. More alumni of Randolph Macon College and other Methodist schools in the South studied in German universities during these decades and the exposure to different ideas and approaches to learning made them more tolerant of ideological changes than some of their colleagues in other denominations. Unlike some in other areas, no Virginia clergyman was the subject of a doctrinal or heresy proceeding by his peers during these years (c.1880-1920).

The one sociomoral issue upon which church people in all denominations were united was the issue of temperance. The most aggressive and forceful leadership in the fight against "the liquor trade" was provided by the Methodists. Leadership in this church and in the state centered in the Reverend James Cannon, Jr., president of Blackstone Female Institute and later a bishop in the Methodist Episcopal Church, South. Cannon, the Women's Christian Temperance Union, and the Anti-Saloon League became a national force for prohibition and were instrumental in promoting the Eighteenth Amendment to the Constitution of the United States.

Throughout the period 1880 to 1920 the church in Virginia presented a united front against what was termed a "secular" Sabbath. Baptists, Methodists, Presbyterians, and others were opposed to business establishments remaining open on Sunday. Church members favored legislation to prohibit railroads from operating on Sunday, to prevent athletic contests such as football and baseball from being played on the Sabbath, and to forbid theaters and fairs to open on Sunday. Not until the 1930s would opposition to a secular Sabbath begin to subside, and then mainly in the urban areas of the state.

The influence of the institutional church program, associated with the Social Gospel movement, was reflected in a few metropolitan churches in Virginia by the end of the nineteenth century. Perhaps the Broad Street Methodist Church in Richmond developed the most extensive program of activities of any congregation in the commonwealth. It sponsored a recreation program of games for the youths and adults, conducted adult education classes, and maintained a visitation ministry to the city jail, home for incurables, and homes for the elderly. This church operated an employment bureau to assist the unemployed to find work, and inaugurated a program to care for unwed mothers. The congregation also sponsored mission work among the city's black population, conducted summer camps for children, and maintained a day care center for children of working mothers. By the close of the 1920s other urban churches had developed institutional type church programs similar to the one at the Broad Street Church.

During the twentieth century the churches in Virginia have maintained their commitment to education and the number of denominational schools has increased, one of the most recent being the first Roman Catholic college in the state, Marymount College (1950), located in Arlington. Since 1945 some denominational junior colleges, in Bristol, Bluefield, Ferrum, and Danville have been transformed into four-year institutions. Church leaders have manifested an increasing interest in the home and foreign mission programs of their denominations and in trying to minister effectively to the religious needs of the church's total constituency: those of all ages, of both sexes, and from diverse ethnic backgrounds.

The Pentecostal churches, which emerged as distinct entities in American Protestantism in the early twentieth century, were organized in Virginia by 1916. The membership of the different Pentecostal groups in 1936 was reported as being less than 4,000, and although these churches have experienced a steady growth since the Second World War the oldest and largest representative of these churches in the commonwealth claimed only 6,000 members in 1973.

The churches in Virginia, as those throughout the country, generally have reflected the prevailing national sentiment on national issues. At the time of World War I prominent clergymen and the denominational press declared that the war was justifiable because it was defensive in nature and was a contest between the forces of righteousness and barbarism. Ecclesiastical organizations endorsed America's entry into the war and the peace aims of President Woodrow Wilson. Most of the churches placed the flag beside the pulpit and many clergymen aided government officials and civic leaders in the sale of war bonds. Denominational leaders urged clergymen to enter the chaplaincy and churches cooperated in programs to minister to the needs of the men in military service.

In the presidential election of 1928 church spokesmen in Virginia were active in the campaign to elect Herbert Hoover and save the country from the pope and the saloon keeper. Although Methodist leaders in the state were more active politically than others, prominent church members in all denominations supported the Republican candidate and advised their constituencies to vote for Hoover. During the Great Depression of the 1930s Christians generally expressed sympathy for the reforms of the New Deal which were designed to aid unemployment, guarantee savings accounts, aid home owners in retaining their property, stimulate the economy, care for the needy and provide old age assistance and security.

At the time of the Second World War church leaders were more restrained in their support of the conflict than they had been in 1917-1918. Although many churches again placed the flag in the sanctuary and some congregations invested in war bonds, vocal support for the war was muted and respect and toleration for the convictions of conscientious objectors was much greater than a quarter century earlier. During the conflict churchmen in all denominations expressed sympathy for the idea of creating a United Nations organization to preserve peace, justice, and order in the world once the war ended. Clerical criticism of war was more pronounced during the Vietnam conflict. By the late 1960s a number of Virginia clergymen were critics of this war. One of the most widely publicized of them was the rector of Bruton Parish Church in Williamsburg, who denounced the war in a sermon when President Lyndon Johnson was in the congregation.

The civil rights movement, which entered its most activist phase in the 1950s, attracted the attention of all churches in Virginia. Although the leadership of this movement in the state was provided by black clergymen in Farmville, Hopewell, Richmond and other cities, a number of white church members and ecclesiastical organizations were not unsympathetic to the goals of the civil rights leader Martin Luther King, Jr. Indications of increasing awareness by white Christians of racial concerns antedated the 1954 Supreme Court decision in Brown versus the Topeka Board of Education. In the 1930s the diocesan council of the Protestant Episcopal Church in Virginia voted to give the Negro membership of the church representation on the council. In 1940 the Baptist General Association of Virginia assisted a group of black Baptists in building an orphanage at Fredericksburg, and also entered into cooperation with the black Baptists of the state in home mission activities. In the early 1950s Negro students were admitted to the Presbyterian's Union Theological Seminary in Richmond and the library facilities of that institution were made available to the students of Virginia Union University—a black Baptist school nearby.

When the Supreme Court's decision on school segregation was announced in 1954, it received favorable comment from the Presbyterian Synod of Virginia, the Baptist General Association of Virginia, and various white church leaders in the commonwealth. The reaction of the state's political leaders to the court's decision, however, was a policy of "massive resistance" to compliance with the court's order. By 1959 this

policy was repudiated by the courts. Although there were some exceptions, by the mid-1960s blacks were welcomed at worship services in
formerly all-white congregations and black students were enrolled for the
first time in such institutions as Hampden-Sydney College, the University of Richmond, Lynchburg College, Randolph Macon College, and
other church-affiliated educational institutions. Sympathy for Negro
rights was also expressed by the students at Union Theological Seminary
when they joined blacks in picketing department stores in Richmond to
protest segregated eating facilities in those stores.

One religious phenomenon of the post World War Two era in which
Virginia churchmen have assumed leadership is the "electronic church."
Two men of national prominence in this area are Jerry L. Falwell and M.
G. "Pat" Robertson. Falwell in Lynchburg and Robertson in Virginia
Beach direct religious organizations which have an international clien-
tele, and each are alleged to receive contributions in excess of one million
dollars a week. The religious operations of both of these men are non-
denominational or independent. Although Falwell's church and college
are Baptist in name neither is affiliated with the Baptist General Association of Virginia. Both of these electronic evangelists expound a theology
which appeals mainly to the Fundamentalists or Pentecostals, both are
active in the political arena and each preaches a political philosophy
which attracts those on the right wing of the political spectrum.

The history of religion in Virginia has reflected the problems and
issues of American society throughout its history and only incidentally
indicated any distinctive Virginia concern or trait. And as the nation
enters the closing decades of the twentieth century the concerns and
problems of the church in the commonwealth are not unlike those of the
church generally. Virginia Christians are concerned about the ultimate
effect of the Electronic Church on the traditional churches and their
programs and ministry, the emergence and acceptability of the charismatic movement in some of the main line denominations, the influence
of the various liberation movements upon the structure and composition
of the churches, and how the church can cope with or direct the ideological and behavioral changes which accompany a revolution in morals.

Bibliography

Reuben E. Alley. *A History of Baptists in Virginia.*

Charles H. Ambler and F. P. Summers. *West Virginia: Mountain State.*

James H. Bailey. *A History of the Diocese of Richmond, The Formative Years.*

Kenneth K. Bailey. *Southern White Protestantism in the Twentieth Century.*

Sadie Bell. *The Church, the State, and Education in Virginia.*

Myron Berman. *Richmond's Jewry, 1769-1976, Shabbat in Shockoe.*

Katherine L. Brown. *Hills of the Lord: Background of the Episcopal Church in Southwestern Virginia, 1738-1938.*

George M. Brydon. *Virginia's Mother Church*, 2 vols.

Israel L. Butt. *History of African Methodism in Virginia.*

Dick Dabney. "God's Own Network, The TV Kingdom of Pat Robertson," *Harpers* 261 (August 1980).

Virginius Dabney. *Liberalism in the South.*

H. Jackson Darst. *Ante-Bellum Virginia Disciples.*

John L. Eighmy. *Churches in Cultural Captivity, A History of the Social Attitudes of Southern Baptists.*

William E. Eisenberg. *The Lutheran Church in Virginia, 1717-1962.*

Hunter D. Farish. *The Circuit Rider Dismounts, A Social History of Southern Methodism, 1865-1900.*

John O. Fish. "Southern Methodism in the Progressive Era: A Social History," unpublished Ph.D. dissertation, University of Georgia, 1969.

Louis Ginsberg. *Chapters on Jews of Virginia, 1658-1900.*

Cornelius J. Heatwole. *A History of Education in Virginia.*

Robert R. Howison. *A History of Virginia From Its Discovery and Settlement by Europeans to the Present Time*, 2 vols.

The Negro in Virginia. Compiled by Writers' Program of the Works Progress Administration in the State of Virginia.

Otis K. Rice. *The Allegheny Frontier, West Virginia, 1730-1830.*

Dale Robinson. *Academies of Virginia.*

Roger E. Sappington. *The Brethren in Virginia: A History of the Church of the Brethren in Virginia.*

Rufus B. Spain. *At Ease in Zion, Social History of Southern Baptists, 1865-1900.*

Durward T. Stokes and William T. Scott. *A History of the Christian Church in the South.*

Herbert S. Stroupe. *The Religious Press in the South Atlantic States.*

William W. Sweet. *Virginia Methodism, A History.*

Vinson Synan. *The Holiness-Pentecostal Movement in the United States.*

Ernest T. Thompson. *Presbyterians in the South*, 3 vols.

West Virginia, A Guide to the Mountain State. Compiled by Workers of the Writers' Program of the Work Projects Administration in the State of West Virginia.

Sister Mary A. Yeakel. *The Nineteenth Century Educational Contributions of the Sisters of Charity of Saint Vincent de Paul in Virginia.*

West Virginia

Manfred O. Meitzen
West Virginia University

When West Virginia became a state on 20 June 1863, more than a century of Christian religious history had already elapsed within its borders; and previous to that, centuries of native American religious history had already transpired. The famous West Virginia Indian burial mounds at South Charleston and Moundsville are witness to those centuries of history.

Francis Asbury had already made his way into many corners of what was then western Virginia in the late eighteenth century, inveighing against drinking and the violence which accompanied it. He organized the Rehoboth Church in Monroe County in 1786. He also visited Morgantown and the Tygart Valley. At Clarksburg Asbury became acquainted with and ministered to Stonewall Jackson's grandmother and great uncle. The energetic missionary work of the well-known first American Methodist bishop had a notable effect on the history of religion in western Virginia where the Methodists, among all the organized Christian Protestant denominations, became preeminent. Until this day there are more Methodist churches in West Virginia than any other kind, and Methodist clergy and laity have supplied a steady stream of political, social, and educational leaders for the state.

West Virginia was early predisposed toward Protestantism, there being virtually no Roman Catholic immigrations or missionary activity until well into the nineteenth century. East of the Alleghenies, except in Maryland, an overwhelmingly Protestant world prevailed. Second only to the Methodists in West Virginia were the Baptists, organizing their first church west of the Alleghenies in 1773 at Bridgeport in Harrison County. Soon to follow were their churches at Stewartstown in Monongalia County and at Alderson in Monroe County. A bit later Presbyterian churches also were founded west of the Alleghenies. Episcopal missionaries too came to western Virginia at an early time.

By statehood, the work of Thomas and Alexander Campbell had been all but finished. A new denomination, the Disciples of Christ, had been inaugurated by them in nearby Washington County, Pennsylvania. The Disciples founded churches in the northern part of western Virginia, also Bethany College, which continues until this day at Bethany, at first the headquarters of the new denomination.

It should be added that Presbyterian, Episcopal, Baptist, and Lutheran churches had been planted even earlier in the three counties of western Virginia which lie east of the Allegheny Mountains, namely, Morgan, Berkeley, and Jefferson.

Civil War and Statehood, 1860-1864

A principle formulated by Paul Tillich that "religion is the substance of culture and culture is the form of religion," fits the history of religion in West Virginia from its origins as a state amidst the furor of the Civil War. There is little doubt that Protestant churches were a major contributing force in the abolitionist movement which preceded that conflict. This force also operated in the lands of western Virginia which were to become West Virginia. The abolitionist struggle in America had been prefigured by the emancipation of slaves in England. There, the prominent evangelical Christian William Wilberforce, had agitated for emancipation. Likewise in western Virginia, there was much sentiment for emancipation among Evangelicals. The Methodists, in particular, were in solid majority against slavery. Consequently, two-thirds of all residents of western Virginia opposed secession.

Not all leaders in the churches were explicitly for the abolition of slavery as an institution; but almost all of them were for the humane treatment of slaves. Alexander Campbell, for example, saw nothing wrong with the master-slave relationship. He respected the United States Constitution which allowed slavery; and he disdained the prospects of war over slavery. Though his own sentiments were against slavery, he tried to ameliorate the growing national crisis by suggesting that the South be allowed to practice the ownership of slaves. He also felt that the nation should abide by the Compromise of 1850 which allowed new territories to decide the question of slavery for themselves, and concluded that he had to accept the Fugitive Slave Act. With this complicated dialectical position, Campbell's great influence prevented the Disciples from splitting into northern and southern churches as a result of the slavery issue. It is of interest to note that Alexander Campbell's nephew, Archibald Campbell, editor of the *Wheeling Intelligencer*, used this influential medium to herald abolitionist views in the years just before the Civil War.

A number of religious factors contributed to the ultimate emancipation of slaves. As a result of slaveholder's encouragement to their slaves to be Christians, the intimate relationship of Christian to Christian prevailed between owners and slaves, at least in moments of soul searching and self-reflection. There was a consequent undercurrent of guilt about slave ownership. Also, the slaves had been encouraged to form their own independent churches. Allowance of this one dimension of independence generated in the slaves both a special love for their churches and a vision of greater liberties for themselves.

Thus the church (mainly Protestant in those days) introduced several important ingredients which moved the nation toward emancipation. Love of God and fellow human beings—the keystone of Christian theology—helped to form cultural results, though, as is always the case in human affairs, that love was broken and imperfect. This general picture applies directly to western Virginia in the pre-Civil War scene.

Religion combined with other cultural forces to move the nation to the emancipation of slaves. Nonreligious egalitarian thought springing from the Enlightenment and the French Revolution played a big role. The belief that slave ownership was no longer a viable enterprise was a postition held by still others.

Unfortunately, violence and emotion kept the rational resolution to the issue from coming to full term. Among other events, John Brown's raid at Harper's Ferry (in West Virginia) and the attack on Fort Sumter moved the nation toward the devastating Civil War. In an effort to avert bloody conflict, most church people in the pre-Civil War days were willing to stop short of demanding the obliteration of slavery as an institution. However, when war came, such restraint was useless. Consequently, views were expressed more candidly thereafter.

All of the friction which results from candor was experienced in the territory which was shortly to become West Virginia. It must be remembered that the line dividing the North and the South went right through western Virginia; therefore, the drama of the times was amplified in this territory. While all the denominations of West Virginia provided chaplains for the Civil War, some of those supplied the South while others served the North. The churches rendered services of mercy to the sick and wounded on both sides.

Laymen were expelled from the Methodist Church in Mannington for being rebels. Father Malone was driven out of the Roman Catholic Church in Grafton because he was thought to be a rebel. Father Becker in Martinsburg would not pray for Union soldiers. One Protestant church simply closed for seven years until the political climate became less volatile. Other churches invested no great stake in the political and ideological struggle of this time. A few churches ministered to unionists on one Sunday and rebels on the next. No doubt, many laymen had little ideological investment in the war. They only regretted that they had been forced to become involved in the struggle.

Even before the Civil War, the Protestant denominations had divided themselves on a national basis into northern and southern churches respectively. Many churches in western Virginia sided with the North or with the South primarily on the basis of the loyalty of the constituency or out of loyalty to synodical affiliations. Thus the Lutheran churches in western Virginia, which had been originally organized by Virginians and which consequently belonged to the Virginia Synod, showed loyalty to the South. Episcopalians, all of whom were closely attached to the Episcopal Church of Virginia, usually showed loyalty to the South. Roman Catholics were aligned with both sides. Residents along the Baltimore and Ohio Railroad so tenaciously held by the North were usually Unionists (whether Christians or not). Residents of southern West Virginia were often rebels mainly for geographical reasons, the church playing no significant role. Often enough in western Virginia, it was true as elsewhere that culture shaped religion more than religion gave substance to culture.

Western Virginia produced the great Civil War hero, Thomas Jonathan "Stonewall" Jackson. General Jackson did not join the cause of the South merely as the result of geographic or social gravity. A devout Presbyterian, he spent much time in prayer deliberating on whether he should fight with the Confederacy or for the Union.

In general, once the Civil War began, churches tended to be loyal to their territories and the majority convictions of their constituencies. The church was more influential in molding public opinion before the Civil War than it was destined to be afterwards. In the 1850s, some church people had managed to seed the idea of abolition in the ground of Christian belief in such a way as to provide major influence on the American culture. Of course this implies also that the church was one important cause of the Civil War, though usually not intentionally so. Perforce, the church is a major cause of the formation of West Virginia as a state since the immediate cause of the formation of the state was the Civil War.

From the outset, the sentiment of western Virginians leaned in the direction of the Union. The secular reasons for such a stand include the following: (1) Western Virginians in trans-Allegheny country had long been resentful of the government of Virginia in Richmond. They felt that they had not received their share of benefits in proportion to taxes collected. (2) Western Virginians had few slaves by comparison with Virginians living east of the mountains. (3) The mountains endowed western Virginians with a social and political insularity which made them want to go their own way.

The details of how West Virginia became a state during the period 1861-1863 need not be recounted in this religious history. It should be noted that, in the pre-statehood conventions, representatives were frequently clergymen. One such representative was Gordon Batelle, a Methodist minister, who strove to have the new constitution of West Virginia provide for the gradual emancipation of slaves. He with others succeeded in having the constitution provide for the prohibition of any movement of slaves into West Virginia. Once statehood was achieved, the leadership of the new state was Methodist. Arthur I. Boreman, the first governor of the state, belonged to that denomination, as did the first two senators sent to Congress from West Virginia. Waitman T. Willey, one of those two senators, was also a temperance crusader.

Spirituality ran very high during the Civil War years. It was characterized by biblical literalism, fundamentalistic morality, revivalism, and the preeminence of Protestantism. The ministry was the most respected of the professions, as reflected in the commonly held fond hope of families that their sons would become ministers.

Reconstruction, 1865-1872

Many religious conflicts and lawsuits followed the Civil War in West Virginia as those who had been rebels sought equality for themselves in the church and as lawsuits over ecclesiastical property held by split congregations were settled. Those who fought with the South were even disfranchised for a time; in other words, considerable bitterness existed.

In the early years of statehood the churches influenced culture in several significant ways. Many clergy continued to hold elective office. In so doing the Protestant values of the time made their way into the formation of state laws, especially at the outset when the first constitution was written. This influence can be felt in West Virginia until this day though laws have gradually been modified. The second constitution, adopted in 1872, was actually written in a Methodist church building in Charleston.

In education the church influenced culture in most significant ways during Reconstruction. The fledgling state had to initiate policy for public education. Virginia, of which it had been a part, had no free, public schools. In the new state public education was to take a radical turn in large measure because of ecclesiastical influence. The churches had long engaged in establishing academies throughout western Virginia. By the time of the Civil War, there were three in Morgantown, for example, two for girls and one for boys, all established by Methodist leaders. Lutheran ministers, as well as those of other denominations, had often served as school teachers in pre-Civil War days when the church buildings had also served as schoolhouses.

In the new state, the ministers joined the cry for free schools. Alexander Campbell had advocated free education for all to be supported by state revenues. The movement to create free public education succeeded. The state's very first constitution provided for public schools. A Methodist clergyman, William R. White, became the first superintendent of schools in West Virginia. He also played a major role in the establishment of normal schools in the young state.

West Virginia also had to establish a state university. At the time of statehood the only public institution that Virginia had bequeathed to West Virginia was an insane asylum in Weston. Morgantown was finally selected to be the site of the state land grant university established under the Morrill Act. That town had acquired the reputation of being a quiet place with good educational facilities because of the three academies already established there by the Methodists. Once the decision was made to establish the university in Morgantown, the three academies were sold to the state. One of them, the Woodburn Female Academy, became the site of the new university, founded in 1867. The first two presidents of the university, Alexander Martin and John Ray Thompson, were Methodist ministers. In this and other ways, the educational dimension of early West Virginia culture was very much the result of the influence of the churches. The interconnection between the Methodist Church and higher education was so great that, when Alexander Martin was fired as first president by Democrats who were at the time carrying out a purge of Republicans at the university, Methodists boycotted the University for a time.

Industrialization and Unionization, 1872-1914

The period of industrialization saw the transformation of West Virginia from an agricultural economy to an industrial one. In the northwest, centering around Wheeling, manufacturing flourished. In the rest of the state industry was based primarily on lumbering and the extraction of coal, salt, oil, and gas. The railway system was greatly expanded during these years.

Labor was needed to staff all these enterprises. Immigrants filled this need, and with their coming the demography of the state changed noticeably. Besides those moving in from Europe, many Negroes came into the state from the South to help fill this need. It was during this period that the most famous of these, Booker T. Washington, grew up in West Virginia. This resident of Malden was to become both a devout man and a prominent public figure.

A large percentage of the immigrants were Roman Catholic. At the beginning of the Civil War there was a fledgling Roman Catholic diocese in western Virginia, having been founded in 1850 with Wheeling as the seat. In that same year Roman Catholics opened in Wheeling the first hospital in what was to become West Virginia. A Jesuit accompanying a French expedition, probably offered the first Mass on West Virginia soil somewhere along the Ohio River in 1749. The small company of some 5,000 Roman Catholics in western Virginia in 1850 had swelled to 50,000 by 1914. Under Bishop Donahue (1894-1922) many Catholic mission churches were founded to accommodate the enlarging constituency.

The Jewish population also was increasing slowly. No Jews had lived in western Virginia until the 1840s, the first Jewish community being established in Wheeling in 1849. Records reveal that seven Jewish men from West Virginia served in the Civil War with Union forces. In 1873, in

Charleston, the first Jewish congregation was organized and by 1903 there were about 1,500 Jews in West Virginia. From 1910 until 1915 the Industrial Removal Office, which was a part of the Jewish Agricultural and Industrial Aid Society headquartered in New York City, functioned to help settle a few of the many Jewish immigrants in the state, to prevent further overcrowding in New York City and other eastern metropolises.

The Protestant churches also grew in numbers. Many white clapboard churches still found across the hillsides of West Virginia were built during this time. The more urban Episcopal Church organized its first West Virginia Diocese in 1878 and elected George W. Peterkin its first bishop.

The Protestant churches contrived to maintain considerable social and political influence during this period. It has been observed that as late as 1904 Daniel B. Purinton, president of West Virginia University from 1901 to 1911, inaugurated a program within the university for the preparation of Sunday school teachers. This course of study met with much approval and general success. This is likely the only time in American history when such a program has been sustained at a state land grant university. Purinton himself was a devout Baptist often travelling to attend international conclaves of the Baptist denomination. He also authored several theological publications.

The Baptists and Methodists and other Protestant groups as well promoted the temperance movement during this period. They stood behind the Anti-Saloon League and the Women's Christian Temperance Union. The influence of the Church on this issue was keenly felt in the cultural life of the State. These crusades also contributed to the ratification of the Prohibition Amendment. It should be remembered that the temperance movement was closely associated (albeit tacitly) with the question of women's rights. Remedying the injustices done to women when drinking husbands beat them or abandoned them to care for the children was a primary goal of the temperance movement. On these issues especially the churches were much involved in social causes.

In 1892 one of the state's most famous citizens was born in Hillsboro. Pearl Buck's Presbyterian parents—her father was extremely pietistic—soon left for China where they were missionaries for many years giving their daughter the rich experience of a Chinese upbringing and creating the soil from which her novels were to arise.

The Sunday School Movement in the Protestant churches wielded great influence in the state. Sarah J. Jones of Putnam County was famous far and wide for her Sunday School stories. Best known were her *Words and Ways, Rest and Unrest,* and *None Other Name,* all published between 1885 and 1893. Song books for Sunday schools prepared by M. Homer Cummings were broadly used. The Bible was the object of intense study by adults and children alike. Moral values were fashioned by the Sunday schools. The result was a prevailing morality and view of life that served to hold society together. The family was held in high esteem; neighborliness was considered a cardinal virtue; individuals were regarded as extremely important. Such virtues as these were taught throughout the Protestant churches from the Baptists on the left to the Lutherans on the right.

Modesty, presumably a virtue of much value in heaven, would seem to have less worth in the kingdoms of the earth. Had West Virginians been more cautious in dealing with the timber, coal, and steel interests which bought their land, they would have been better off financially in the long run and the state would have had more capital with which to work. Individualism may have been prized to the extent that the owners of small strips of timber land and of mineral lands could not cooperate in resisting the pressures of big business to buy them out at low prices.

Neither the Protestant nor Roman Catholic churches did much to resist the exploitation of West Virginia resources by outside interests. The social concern of the churches was oriented toward upholding basic individual morality. The churches wanted to do what they could to make the world safe for Christians to live in; and they wanted also to make the world less destructive and less tempting for non-Christians in the hopes that such people might finally find their salvation in the church. It was for this reason that the Wheeling Committee of One Hundred, an antivice committee, was founded. (Incidentally, the labor union movement regarded the work of the Committee of One Hundred as unimportant.) The churches did not think of morality as having to do with political and economic dynamics. Relying on the New Testament promise that the meek are the blessed ones, the churches spent little time fretting over the injustices perpetrated by the very rich. They trusted that in this transitory life the humble sawyer or miner had the potential of reaping as much happiness as the industrialist. As for eternal life, they were certain that the meek would be blessed.

Nor did the churches devote much attention during this period to the labor movement. Atheistic, pre-Bolshevik socialists played the major role here. The labor movement was therefore in the main a secular movement. There were some eccentric exceptions, however. The Irish-born Mother Jones, who played so prominent a role in organizing miners at the site of the violent Paint Creek and Cabin Creek confrontations between laborers and owners, was an itinerant preacher of socialist persuasion. She had worked and taught at Roman Catholic convent schools earlier in her life, but she was not an active communicant of the Church during her activistic years in labor organization. (Later in her life, she resumed being an active communicant of the Roman Catholic Church.) At all events, Mother Jones could not be counted a representative West Virginia religious spirit; for her influence consisted of crusading appearances to the state from another cultural world.

From the archives of the Diocese of Wheeling we know that Bishop Donahue served on a committee of three appointed by Governor Glasscock in 1912 to investigate the violence at Paint Creek, and we have his personal conclusions. Diplomatically, he criticized the miners and the owners in equal proportion. On the side of the owners, he allowed that they had a right to protect their property. He criticized labor for not wanting to work for more than four days a week and noted that the wages of these still nonunion miners were as good as union wages. He was critical of the miners for being careless with regard to their health. On the other hand, he was censorious of the guard system of the owners and noted that the company stores overcharged. He made a number of other observations on both sides, including the judgment that the United Mine Workers of America were the main source of the trouble at Paint Creek.

World War I—World War II, 1914-1945

West Virginia flew its patriotic colors by contributing nearly 50,000 men to the armed forces during World War II and oversubscribed the war bond drives of that era. Such patriotism and willingness to sacrifice for the cause of the nation was to be seen again in each of the wars later to be fought by the United States in the twentieth century. This love of country, which extended even to the Vietnam war, sprang in part from that Civil War tradition of loyalty to the Union out of which statehood originated.

By and large West Virginia followed the national trend of less ecclesiastical influence on secular society during this period. Not surprisingly, the churches did make special impact on the presidential election of 1928 in which prohibition was a major issue.

Rural West Virginia and urban West Virginia became ever more distinct during this period. The urban sector followed the trends of the nation in almost all regards including religious ones. Mountainous, rural West Virginia stood back from these developments to form, along with contiguous areas in other states, a special cultural entity known to the nation as "Appalachia." During the next three decades the phenomenon of "Appalachia" became the state's distinctive and most famous subculture.

Between 1914 and 1945, many sectarian movements sprang up in the rural sections. This meant a turning away from mainline religions. Private chapels, led and sometimes even owned by charismatic figures in the community, rose up. To them and this subject, we shall return.

During this period the number of churches increased to 4,968 in 1926. As in all periods of West Virginia history, the number of Methodists was the greatest. One newcomer tradition appeared. There had been no Orthodox Churches in West Virginia at the turn of the century, but seven Greek and Russian Orthodox churches had been founded in the state by 1926. Jewish congregations increased from three to 23 in the same period. Black churches too were increasing, doubling in number during these years.

The Roman Catholic Church grew tremendously from approximately 50,000 to about 80,000. Bishop Swint, who served the diocese from 1922 to 1962, is especially remembered as a builder and as a promoter of Catholic education. Considerable mission work in the state resulted from his vision and leadership.

Perhaps because of the increasing number of Roman Catholics residing in the state, noticeable anti-Catholic feelings surfaced during this period. Fear of papist intrusion into American affairs was widely expressed. There are reliable reports that qualified Roman Catholic lay people encountered obstacles in seeking to get teaching positions in public schools. The anti-Catholic Ku Klux Klan was quite active in the state in the 1920s, its national meeting was convened in 1925 on the campus of West Virginia University. The burning of crosses on the hill overlooking Morgantown was no uncommon occurrence during those troubled years.

The Great Depression had a devastating effect on West Virginia, economic conditions there bering worse than in many other parts of the nation. As a result, the state became a prime recipient of New Deal welfare and was, it is said by some, to become addicted to it. Even the infusion of massive public welfare was not enough to meet the needs of the economically devastated state, however. The private sector worked to bring in food and clothing, an effort in which the churches joined.

Pat Withrow's Union Mission in Charleston was one of these Christian commissaries of charity. Founded in 1911, the Mission had come to full maturity by the time of the Depression. The homeless and hopeless were physically sustained while they were spiritually fed by revivalistic religion. The achievements of Withrow's mission exemplify the growing urban dimension of West Virginia from 1911 on; for it is similar to other missions which had been founded everywhere in larger American cities. The Union Mission continues in a variety of ways to serve Charleston, a city of 60,000 population today. Withrow's motto was "soap, soup, and salvation." A licensed Methodist minister, his work was independent of the Methodist Church.

The Great Depression and the new presence of the federal government in West Virginia provided grounds for a renaissance of the labor unions in West Virginia. In this climate, the United Mine Workers of America under the direction of John L. Lewis built the base for its all-pervasive influence in West Virginia. Although everywhere, the churches had little to do with this important transforming development of its state's history, for better, for worse, or both.

Appalachia as a Problem Area, 1945-1970

World War II saw another record of gallant, patriotic service on the part of West Virginia. However, the unprecedented economic expansion which was to shower great wealth upon the nation for thirty years after the war was not so generous to West Virginia, especially in the rural areas. At least three major reasons can be given for this economic misfortune. (1) The market for coal diminished somewhat between 1945 and 1970. (2) As the result of the further mechanization of the coal mines during this period, many jobs in the mines were abolished. (3) The mountainous terrain of West Virginia makes the interior of the state unpromising as an area for heavy industrial transportation. As a result, while the river valleys remained fairly prosperous during this period, the mountainous regions languished economically.

It was in these ways that the much publicized territory of "Appalachia" came about as an economically identifiable phenomenon. The rural, mountainous areas of West Virginia became more isolated in spite of the modern age of rapid communication and they became distinctly poor. In the 1950s more people were out of work in West Virginia than in any other state. Thousands of welfare checks were distributed to citizens of the state. Many residents moved away to the river valleys or to other states to find employment. (Others were not psychologically bold enough to leave.) As a result of this process the population of the state dropped by several hundred thousand.

The rural folk of Appalachia showed little discontent about their poverty—to the frustration of social activists. Their lives seemed to transcend a "dollar culture." On the one hand, much of the Christian ideal could be discerned in their life style; on the other, the question arose for many whether these people had been so benumbed by circumstances as no longer to have earthly ambitions. The real situation of these people was to remain a conundrum much analyzed by assorted writers and by the news media, especially in the activist decade of the 1960s.

The religion of Appalachia is made up of variations on Protestantism ranging from the mainline churches to myriad sectarian churches. Some groups are no larger than a cluster of local people in a single valley or "holler" revolving about a charismatic lay preacher. Much of the religion of Appalachia is extra-institutional. That is, many who are involved in such religious expressions are not counted in state and national membership statistics. A number of groups are too small and amorphous to be codified as separate denominations. Consequently, the current data which indicate that 51 percent of West Virginians are unchurched is deceptive. That enumeration has missed much of the busy religious activity back in the mountains of the state.

Assorted aberrations of Christian orthodoxy can be found among these sectarian Protestants. Most sensational are the snake handlers and the fire handlers, with both standing as examples of Christian holiness groups. The snake handlers base their beliefs on two verses in the New Testament book of Mark. (Biblical scholars think that the verses in question are a later addition to Mark's Gospel.) The relevant text reads:

> And these signs will accompany those who believe: in my name they will cast out demons; they will speak in new tongues; they will pick up serpents, and if they drink any deadly thing, it will not hurt them; they will lay their hands on the sick; and they will recover (16:17-18, RSV).

For this tiny but intense band of Christ's followers, the serpents serve as verifiers of the faith that Jesus Christ has overcome death in victory. The faithful can symbolically handle the poisonous serpents (usually rattles-nakes or copperheads) without dying. It is true that snake handlers are bitten from time to time and usually recover. When recovery happens, this miracle is seen as another symbol of the power of Jesus Christ to overcome death. The Holy Ghost is believed to infuse the practitioner with such holiness as to prevent any harm from resulting from the venom of the serpents.

Similarly, fire handlers verify their faith by handling fire without physical injury. Being biblical literalists like the serpent handlers, their practices are based on passages that suggest trial by fire, such as Isaiah 43:2, Daniel 3:20-27, and Hebrews 11:34. To be able to handle fire without physical injury is viewed as a mark of holiness.

The holiness sects also take note of the phrase in Mark 16:17, " . . . and if they drink any deadly thing, it will not hurt them . . . " Poisonous mixtures are concocted for purposes of testing faith and experiencing the exalting protection of the Holy Ghost. Often the same Holiness people who have submitted to one kind of these ordeals have submitted to others.

In general, Holiness groups hope to channel to their members the power of the Holy Ghost and a sense of holiness. A part of the strategy is to keep apart from the secular world. They are anti-intellectual, depending rather on the spontaneity of the Holy Ghost to exalt them in this transitory life. This exaltation is manifest in such phenomena as glossolalia, healing power, and ecstatic dancing. More extreme results are sometimes seen: elements of witchcraft; many superstitious acts and practices that must be described as magic.

To obtain a further overview of Appalachian religion, the reader might well refer to James M. Kerr's fine essay, "A Pastor's View of Religion in Appalachia," found in *Religion in Appalachia*, edited by John D. Photiades. Appalachian religion is distinctly Protestant and of the stripe stemming from Puritanism. In church polity the Baptist form is the chief organizational heritage of the mountain religion of West Virginia. This is a heritage of dissent. It has gone hand in hand with the proclivity of isolated populations the world over to be separatistic. Many of the original settlers of West Virginia were Scotch-Irish, it is instructive to recall. These people had come to America in the first place in quest of individual freedom. Continuous with those beginnings is the Appalachian churches' tendency to be individualistic, often having no connection with big denominational groups. Furthermore, they concern themselves very little with social and political issues, with public matters of any sort.

This individualism can be observed, by way of illustration, in the congregations of American Baptist churches in West Virginia. These local churches even today remain affiliated only with that Northern denomination, spurning the covenantal membership that body has with the National Council of Churches and the World Council of Churches.

In general, Appalachian churches lean heavily in the direction of puritannical ethics. The separatistic element of the Puritan heritage makes it easier for Appalachian residents to keep their distance from national trends in ethics. Ministers usually have not been to seminaries and have no peers to criticize their views or their performance as ministers. In the manner of the Baptist tradition's opposition to centralized control, most Appalachian churches are accustomed to having unsupervised clergy. The spontaneous open-air revival remains a principal mode of worship. It was the kind of religion which nurtured frontier people as far back as Daniel Boone, for example, and which dominated nineteenth century developments.

Since the educational level of Appalachian society has been low, the historical critical method of study of the Bible has not been applied, though the Bible is read or heard a great deal. The Bible is taken exactly at face value. Consequently, biblical literalism—in many different forms—is common among all the Appalachian church people.

On the subject of eschatology, a dim view is taken of the worsening world. Salvation is finally beyond the world. The Kingdom of God will be fulfilled transcendentally, not on earth. Social action and social programs cannot better the world, fallen as it is. The Devil, who is taken seriously in this religious understanding, has control of the secular world.

The Holy Ghost pervades all aspects of Appalachian religion. Baptism by the Holy Ghost is the rite of passage into mature Christian belief. Glossolalia is considered a desirable gift of the Spirit. So is unabashed willingness to testify freely to one's faith and to witness to the wonderworks of God which the believer has experienced both in his own life and in that of others. Preaching is fervent and under the influence of the Holy Ghost. The nature of this kind of preaching has been portrayed dramatically by Aaron Copeland in the frenetic dancing of the preacher in his *Appalachian Spring* (1944).

The phenomenon of baptistry paintings, which have come into use in Appalachian churches only during the last half century, is most revealing.

While Protestant baptistries are not typically adorned with paintings in other sections of the United States, in Appalachian West Virginia they frequently are. Usually the paintings are landscapes with a river or lake central to it. Sometimes the rivers are painted so as to portray the River Jordan in Israel; more often, the landscapes are inspired by Appalachian scenery. Most of the time no human beings are involved in the paintings. When they are, John the Baptist and Jesus are usually the figures. Often a luminescence in the background of the scenery suggests the transcendent. While it is difficult to account for this phenomenon in West Virginia, it is likely that the paintings emerged to recall the days more than 50 years ago when baptisms were regularly done outdoors. The impression persists that baptisms are more valid when done in natural surroundings with flowing water.

Politicians and the news media declared Appalachia a problem area in the 1960s, suddenly plunging this forgotten world into the limelight. Residents were astonished at the rising tide of newsmen, sociologists, social workers, Vista workers, and OEO agents, who came to observe them and work with them. This focusing of national interest on Appalachia seems to have been triggered by the presidential primary campaign of 1960 when John F. Kennedy, a Roman Catholic, ran against Hubert Humphrey. The question before the nation was whether a Roman Catholic candidate could be successful in a presidential election since none ever had been before. National commentators saw West Virginia's decision in the democratic primary as an accurate indicator of whether a Roman Catholic could now be elected president of the United States. The reason for this calculation was that West Virginia as late as the 1920s and 1930s had shown considerable prejudice toward Roman Catholics. West Virginians were still, in large majority, of Protestant persuasion; and the geographic isolation of West Virginia was believed to insulate the still predominantly rural residents of the state from the new ecumenizing tolerance which was sweeping the rest of the nation.

Appalachia became a showpiece of the media; many ugly scenes met the eyes of affluent Americans. Paradoxically, however, the newly disclosed backwardness of West Virginia was offset by the apparent up-to-date ecumenicity it showed in preferring Kennedy. Campaign promises in the area of economics and the lavish campaign expenditures of the charming candidate, however, might have been the real reason for Kennedy's victory in the primary. It should also be remembered that Alfred E. Smith in his bid for the presidency in 1928 won the Democratic primary in West Virginia even though he was a Roman Catholic. He did not carry the state in the national presidential election mainly because West Virginia at that time was controlled by Republicans and because strong prohibitionist sentiments in the state could not tolerate Smith's stand on the abolition of prohibition.

While there was social friction between Roman Catholics and Protestants in the 1920s, deep political envy between the two religious groups in West Virginia never did materialize. Roman Catholics have always been a minority group. The traditional abrasive issues of parochial school support and birth control were never important in West Virginia. Only in recent years has abortion been a public issue in West Virginia. (During the period 1945-1970 Roman Catholics continued to grow in numbers until there were about 105,000 communicants in 1970. Anti-Catholic prejudice had all but vanished.)

Whatever the significance of the results, subsequent democratic presidential administrations rewarded West Virginia with a vast outpouring of aid which ranged from the construction of beautiful new roads to myriad programs for making mountaineers more up-to-date. Activists, who hoped to revolutionize life in Appalachia, as they were partly to succeed in doing in the nation's great cities, were disappointed. Appalachian religion was too individualistic and unconcerned politically for that. Roots for revolutionary social activism were not embedded in the religious soil, nor in the culture at large, at least not enough deep roots.

The civil rights revolution also occurred during this time. In 1950 Negroes comprised about six percent of the population of West Virginia. Integration was achieved quite easily in the years 1956-57, with only a few incidents of friction. It is unclear whether there were special characteristics of West Virginia religion which contributed toward this easy social transition. It should be noted that Negroes were more willing to leave West Virginia for a better economic climate than were whites. By 1970 only four percent of the population was black.

New Awareness and New Opportunities, 1970—

The growing revival of the coal industry marks the beginning of a new era in West Virginia history. This was correlated with the energy crisis which brought a new prosperity to the state. Just as West Virginia had been economically out of tune with the nation from 1945 to 1970, energy-rich West Virginia now hoped that the fortunes of the state would surpass those of the rest of the nation. This hope has not been altogether justified because a concurrent development, the sagging national economy, has also struck West Virginia. Furthermore, the chronic and prolonged labor strife in the West Virginia coalfields may yet bring the greatest economic benefits of the energy crisis to the non-union open-pit mines of the western states. Nonetheless, the economy of West Virginia has become less negatively out of phase with that of the whole country than it was between 1945 and 1970.

Church life continues to thrive along established Appalachian patterns in the mountains. The experience of urban churches of the state approaches that of urban churches in the rest of the nation. The mainline churches have all enlarged their vistas of social concern in the last decade. Predictably, this pattern has not had much effect on the churches in the mountainous districts. Bishop Joseph H. Hodges of the Roman Catholic diocese of Wheeling has joined other Appalachian bishops in issuing a joint pastoral letter entitled "This Land Is Home To Me." The letter speaks to the problems of current Appalachia, but ironically has taken shallow root, at most, among the mountain peoples.

Almost every current denomination and movement within Christianity is now represented in West Virginia in either the urban or rural scenes. Once isolated and peculiar, it is not so any longer. The more urbane Fundamentalism now flourishing in America can be found in West Virginia towns and cities. For example, the Christian and Missionary Alliance Church is thriving in West Virginia towns. Also, the charismatic movement can be found in the ranks of all mainline denominations in the state.

The Church of Jesus Christ of Latter-day Saints has enjoyed considerable growth in West Virginia during recent decades. Now 7,000 members strong, the Mormon church made its first impact on the state by baptizing 40 converts in Cabell County in 1832 long before statehood days. Joseph Smith, the founder, had visited Wheeling in 1832 to buy the paper on which was later printed the *Book of Doctrines and Covenants* which contained many of his revelations. Most nineteenth century converts were persecuted, however, subsequently moving to the West.

The most sensational incident involving religious life in West Virginia during the last decade was the Charleston book controversy of 1974-1975. In this encounter, West Virginia's urban religion clashed with its rural religion. The controversy touched on such issues as whether sex should be taught in the schools and whether textbooks which termed Bible stories as myths (a term left undefined) should continue to be used in the schools. By and large the sometimes violent controversy ended with the conservatives gaining more spoils. Just the same a lack of confidence in the educational philosophy of the public schools resulted within the conservative ranks. As a consequence, since the book controversy Christian day schools have cropped up in the Charleston area.

During the last decade, West Virginia has experienced some cosmopolitan religious growth. The Korea-originated Unification Church now carries on work in West Virginia with headquarters in Huntington. The Krishna Consciousness movement earlier established a commune near Moundsville where it has recently built a formidable national temple which has attracted much attention and brought many visitors to the area. International students have brought together a number of adherents of assorted world religions to the university and college towns of the state. In particular, there has been a Muslim presence. Since West Virginia continues to suffer a shortage of physicians in rural areas and in its mental health institutions, a number of foreign physicians have come to practice in the state. With them has come a variety of religious practices and beliefs. Until recently West Virginians have shown little interest in world religions. Perhaps, this pattern will now gradually change.

Religion is an inextricable dimension of human existence and West Virginia culture is no exception. Though religion has always been institutionally weak in West Virginia, its spiritual influence has been very deep and pervasive in the cultural life of the state. This influence may be manifest in part by the relatively low crime rate which the state enjoys. The amiability of its people is another sign of this spiritual influence. Tillich's dictum does hold true in West Virginia as elsewhere: "Religion is the substance of culture and culture is the form of religion." Even as religion has greatly influenced the substance of West Virginia culture, West Virginia in turn has given a unique form to its religion.

Because generalities are always dangerous, one must be particularly cautious when discussing the religion of West Virginia. There must always be at least two parts to the discussion, namely, religion in the towns and the cities and religion in the Appalachian areas. Even as the heretical Albigensians who lived in the Pyrenees during the high Middle Ages were deemed eccentric by the Christian orthodoxy of their time, the mountain folks of West Virginia have maintained expressions of Christian faith aberrant to American urban ideas about normative Christian belief. Even so, as we have seen, the gap has narrowed within the past two decades.

Bibliography

Charles Henry Ambler. *A History of West Virginia.*

Louise Bing. *"Soup, Soap, and Salvation," Goldenseal* 6 (July-September 1980).

Phil Conley and William Thomas Doherty. *West Virginia History.*

Harry W. Ernst. *The Primary That Made a President: West Virginia 1960.*

John D. Photiadis, ed. *Religion in Appalachia.*

Abraham I. Shinedling. *West Virginia Jewry: Origins and History*, vol. 1.

Paul Tillich. *Systematic Theology*, vol. 3.

Jack Welch. "A Heritage of Regional Landscapes: Appalachian Baptistry Paintings," *Goldenseal*, 6 (April-June 1980).

John Alexander Williams. *West Virginia: a Bicentennial History.*

A SURVEY OF
SOUTHERN RELIGIOUS HISTORY

SAMUEL S. HILL
UNIVERSITY OF FLORIDA

As its history has unfolded, the religion of the American South has departed somewhat from the religion of its foundings and founders. That is not particularly surprising in the case of the very first settlement, on the peninsula called La Florida by the Spanish when they planted the cross in the sand of San Agustín in 1565. For the population was very small and the territory not American until 1821; its Roman Catholic faith was of limited consequence in that large expanse and of scarcely any significance across the borders nearest to it.

The point is somewhat more surprising with reference to the founding of the Virginia colony in 1607. Its people were English from the beginning; its established faith was Church of England or Anglican (Episcopal from 1785). After all, a real continuity can be traced from that founding, of Virginia in 1607 by English Protestants, through subsequent decades and centuries to the present day. If La Florida was not ever to be "the South," Virginia was to be its veritable quintessence. But some funny things have happened on the way from the early colonial period to the 1980s.

If one wanted to pinpoint the salient beginning, he would turn to the 1750s or perhaps the years just after 1800. That is far from misleading even if it is not accurate to a fault. Southern religion as it has been for the past 150 and more years reflects continuity from those developments. But that is to anticipate our story rather than tell it. Even so it is well to keep in mind how abrupt the changes were between the founding generations and the late colonial and early republican ones, as well as the degree of continuity from 1800 to today.

Any serious treatment of southern religious history must consider how religion is related to developments in other aspects of southern life, intellectual, moral, political, social, and economic, as time passes. Has continuity been as prevalent in politics, say, as in religion? Is the intellectual or social history of the South of a piece with its religious history? And we may raise, but not deal with here, a third question: What has been happening in the South's religious life which marks it off from that of the North (and *vice versa*)?

The English settlers who landed at Jamestown in 1607 were all baptized Christians of Church of England variety. A priest accompanied them and a chapel was soon constructed for their worship. While life turned to the immediate and urgent necessities of building houses, planting and harvesting crops, dealing with their Indian neighbors, and arranging for their common public life, it did not do so outside the context of Christendom. The teachings and framework provided by the Christian religion were taken for granted as true and as socially necessary. Especially down to 1624, when Virginia ceased being a royal colony and became a proprietary one, the Church served as a basis for the comprehensive life of the settlers, legal, political, social, as well as the formally religious. It is the case that their fellow countrymen who sailed 13 years later and landed 600 miles farther north, and who were followed by a large and active immigration force, made New England a more unitedly, vitally, conspicuously, and self-consciously Christian commonwealth than Virginia ever was. But it may not be inferred that religion was of minor importance to the more matter-of-fact Virginians. Their settlement was, as Perry Miller made amply clear, an outpost of England. Accordingly life in the new world was established on English foundations which included a vision of life as existing *sub specie aeternitatis*. They saw themselves as God's people in an expanded Christendom, there by his providence, sent there to do his will. In Richard Beale Davis's words, the "southern colonist established himself with religion strong in his conscience and consciousness." The promotion and exploration literature attests to that throughout the period. "From Maryland to Georgia, one of the repeatedly avowed purposes in colonization was the spread of Christianity."[1] Their sense of mission required that they do more than enlarge; additionally they must impinge, impinge on the heathen native peoples in the name of Christ and his Church. Especially before the bloody massacre of 1622, the colonists sought to introduce the Indians to Christianity, with limited success however.

Another opportunity for mission was presented to them by the arrival in 1619 of the first African slaves. It is of course truer to the facts to see that as an opportunity they created for themselves by the (enforced) immigration of the slaves. Jumping ahead, we may note that as late as the *end* of the colonial period minimal efforts and still meagre success characterized the dealings of Christian whites with heathen blacks. But that kind of hindsight does not alter the awareness on the part of many white Christians of their responsibility to these non-Christian people. In sight, on mind. The presence of the slaves from Africa early came to be an influential, very nearly a controlling, factor in Virginia society (and soon the other southern colonies as well). They were all about. Everything about their residence in a colony settled by white Europeans required special attention; communication, labor, housing, regulations—and religion. But the difficulties involved in instructing a people who spoke little or no English, had been accustomed to worshipping pagan deities, and were relegated to an outcast status were immense; also energy and time for enlightening them into the Christian way were in limited supply, as were experience and know-how for doing so.

The history of religion in the South before it was the South—rather only a geographical territory of colonies and people until the Revolutionary era—is, in all candor, not very impressive. Only after the 1740s does a culturally feasible pattern of religion emerge, and it does not take hold with strength until after the Revolution. The problem lay partly in the unsuitability of a Christendom-oriented understanding of and approach to the social conditions of the southern colonies. There the population was small and scattered. The traditional parish system was hardly viable since it presupposed a baptized, settled, and compact population with an ample supply of clergymen available. Moreover, the Church of England, like most churches in the early decades of assuming responsibility for working outside Christendom to convert the heathen, had neither vigorous incentive nor proven methods for reaching beyond Christian civilization. The Anglicans in the southern colonies knew they were supposed to spread Christianity in those climes; that was to be done by the multiplying of white civilized Christian families, and also through instructing red and black peoples in the faith. But a welter of conditions militated against

Anglican effectiveness: that Church's history; the social and demographic situation; and the obduracy of Indians and Negroes.

Not that nothing was done, or that the impact was nil. As each of the colonies attained that status, it recognized the Church of England as the Establishment. This occurred in Virginia in 1619, North Carolina in 1701, Maryland the next year, South Carolina in 1706, and Georgia in 1733, and all (save Maryland which is only a partial exception) had been effectively Anglican from the first day. While the exact power of the Church varied from one colony to the next, we may note some representative features of Establishment: tax revenues were collected to help support the Church; marriage ceremonies were not legal unless solemnized by an Anglican clergyman; all school teachers had to be members of the Church. Considering the fact that by the middle of the eighteenth century dissenters outnumbered Anglicans in every colony, this made for a somewhat incongruous and often irritating situation. But Establishment was law, nevertheless, and its influence considerable.

Moreover, organized efforts were made to energize the Church's evangelization program. Indians and Negroes, and white settlers as well, were the intended beneficiaries of the formation of the Society for the Propagation of the Gospel, organized in England in 1701 for the purpose of increasing the number of clergymen going out to America. The S.P.G. did often have dedicated leadership and rather clearly focused aims, but its appearance was too little and too late. Indeed, as intimated earlier, the conditions of life and society in the southern colonies probably would have prevented the Church of England from becoming a vital and dominant force, no matter what.

This is not to say, however, that the Anglican presence did not make its mark, long term and short term. For one thing, there it was, a continuation and reminder of the Christian tradition of Western civilization of which this was an extension and a providentially promising appendage. Perhaps as many as a third of the people held membership in it down to 1750, itself no minor datum. Moreover, what was happening within the Established Church in the colonies, by reflecting social attitudes developing there, opened the door and made the way easier for the denominations which were to attract larger followings. Specifically, in Davis's words, "a civil-ecclesiastical local government of great importance which intended to keep that independence" emerged quite early.[2] In other words, parish vestries held much power. Local rule by laymen was

paramount to clergy authority and, most importantly, to episcopal jurisdiction. To be sure, these people were Anglicans, held together by the
Book of Common Prayer and acknowledging the necessity of the priestly
office. But they soon became low-church in their orientation. The fact
that there was no American bishop fostered this spirit; but, in turn, this
spirit contributed to a contentment with the fact that there was none.
Most of the lay people were pleased with the ineffectuality of an episcopal
power seated in England, many weeks away. Such an attitude of independence had affinity with the polity of Congregationalists, Quakers,
Presbyterians, and Baptists, all upstart and trouble-making groups, in
varying degrees and ways, and had become something of a hallmark of
southern (and general American) church life before the War for Independence. To those groups we will return shortly by way of observing
how the future was to lie on their side.

Roman Catholicism was planted in the southern colonies with the
founding of Maryland in 1634. That strange (as it may seem in retrospect) occurrence resulted from the Calvert family's grant by the crown of
the land of the upper Chesapeake. This English family which had converted to the Catholic faith a few years earlier aspired to spreading that
Church's work. The faith of the first Lord Baltimore and most of the other
upper-class families notwithstanding, most of the Marylanders were
Anglicans from the very beginning, and the Catholic Church was never
legally established. The influence of their Catholic faith was manifested
in the toleration act of 1649 which declared liberty for all "Trinitarian
Christians," all Catholics and Protestants, that is. Some Catholics and
non-conformist Protestants suffered disabilities, even so, but officially
Maryland brooked more diversity than Virginia. In Virginia, however,
where conformity was policy but more difficult to enforce owing to
capacious space, there were Catholics and non-conformists who lived
their own lives with a minimum of interference. Maryland's history of
Catholic beginnings, Protestant dominance, and legal toleration eventuated in the legislation which established the Church of England in 1702.

Eighteenth century developments in religion were destined to lead
directly toward the future shape of the South. In chronological order, the
Presbyterians, the Baptists, and the Methodists became the popular
religions. While these forms of Protestant Christianity are distinguishable theologically and ecclesiastically and had separate, sometimes competitive, identities in the colonies, they ranged within two related families
of Protestantism, namely Evangelical and Classical. The displacement of

the Liturgical family by these two spelled a significant alteration in southern society. Whatever the formal traditions and theologies of these latecomers, however, it was their attitudes, values, and approaches which brought about such a difference. It goes without saying that this "American" takeover of hitherto "European" patterns is part and parcel with shifting political and social sentiments. Away from British rule to American; away from centralized government to local; away from traditional values to functional ones; away from conformity toward pluralism and tolerance; away from standardized forms to personal perceptions and convictions; away from conventional morality to conscience; and so on.

What religion's roles in these social changes may have been is a moot and not very critical question. Of far greater significance is a major religious event, the Great Awakening, as symptom and symbol of the change. It took place from the 1740s onward for another three decades with the flames of fire being lit first by Presbyterians, next by Baptists, and latest by Methodists. Once the heat had been generated, it could cool and then kindle itself again, of course; revivals of religion are not predictable or controllable and their very occurrence presupposes the waxing and waning of faith, including that which they generate.

Other kinds of Protestants than Anglicans had traveled through or lived briefly or even permanently in the southern colonies from the second generation forward. There were New England Puritans, "Congregationalists," in Virginia in the 1690s. Quakers were present and forceful in northeastern North Carolina in the last quarter of the seventeenth century. Baptists were organized in coastal South Carolina by the 1690s. A few Presbyterian congregations achieved stability in Maryland and Virginia in the 1690s led by Francis Makemie; Scotch-Irish immigrants were "pouring in" by 1732. Smaller trickles of Lutherans, French Huguenots, Moravians, Mennonites, Dunkers, German Reformed, and even Deists and Jews had appeared in the southern colonies, earlier or later. By a later date some, like the Moravians of Wachovia in the western piedmont of North Carolina and the Mennonites and Dunkers of the Shenandoah Valley in Virginia, formed settled lakes of population rather than trickles. Most such people, however, created ethnic-religious communities and stayed pretty much to themselves.

It has often been remarked in the twentieth century that the South was the Presbyterians' for the taking—if only they had done so by the middle third of the eighteenth century. From all indications, they had the best chance. Their greatest contribution, as it has turned out, was through inspiring the Great Awakening which ironically destined them to a subordinate position; ranking second is their bequest of themselves as a solid and considerable company which has often anchored southern Protestant life through such provisions as outstanding preachers and theologians, excellent colleges, and influential lay people. But they failed to follow through, or "cash in", on the early successes achieved by Presbyterian leaders and congregations in the countryside north of Richmond in the 1740s. The populace was to become populist in its religious tastes through the popular denominations, Baptist and Methodist, more than the Presbyterian. Summarizing this discussion, Davis agrees with those who judge "the southern mind . . . a religious mind." And, he continues, "in one sense it always has been," that is, beginning with the colonial period.[3] But "religious" refers less to Anglicanism than to

> what the people of the first Great Awakening thought it was, and made it. This set or frame of mind, most obvious in the ordinary people of the South but clearly part of all manner of Southerners, has probably remained firmer in this region than in any other part of America. That it originated as a general American reaction or response and that it had particular and immediate origins in the southern colonies are equally true.

Somewhat curiously, although the Great Awakening caught on because it was attractive to the settled people of the South, it was instigated by people who had come only recently from outside the area. The Rev. Samuel Davies hailed from Delaware where he had been ordained by the Presbytery of New Castle, after training at William Tennent's "school of the prophets," the so-called Log College near Philadelphia. The Rev. Shubal Stearns came from Connecticut with a small band of "Separate" (more evangelistic) Baptists to piedmont North Carolina in 1755 where they generated a zealous fervor that built into a rapidly spreading conflagration over the next two decades. The Methodist cause was established by the Rev. George Whitefield, Wesleyan Anglican from Oxford, who visited Georgia in 1738 and was back in all the Southern colonies several times between 1739 and 1769. The Rev. Devereux Jarratt, Church of England priest with clear Methodist leanings, had come into middle Virginia from old England and the Middle Colonies only a few years before his enthusiasm became a public contagion around 1770. Of special importance was his planting incipient Methodist congregations, which could attain that full standing after the denomination was organized in 1784.

What was this Great Awakening? What are its characteristics and values—hence its legacy? Most fundamentally we may describe it as a movement promoting vital religious experience, appropriated immediately, that is, with assurance in the believer's heart and without manmade mediation. By contrast with, and partly in reaction to, the formal liturgical services of Anglicanism and the scholastic theological sermons of the older-style Presbyterianism, the Great Awakening preachers told passionately and imploringly of the love of God for every individual sinner. These "preachers" were the backbone of this movement. While services might be quite decorous and make some use of ordered forms, as most Presbyterian and some Methodist services at the time would have, everything centered in the proclamation of the biblical message that all had sinned and come short of the glory of God: that Christ had paid the sin-debt for each and every person; that saving grace was immediately available to all who would open their hearts to receive it experientially; and that the person so converted could rely on the Lord's promise of everlasting life in heaven and a constant sweetness of presence every moment of every day. The biblical message, preaching, the conversion experience, and earnest discipleship—these are the marks of "experiential faith". "Im-mediate" is indeed the key concept. Just as nothing comes between the sinner and the Savior, except what the sinner throws up as an obstruction, so no intermediary is needed, neither priest nor sacrament nor formal training nor brainy comprehension nor liturgy. This is religion of the heart, a kind received by the person quite consciously. This is popular religion; it is for "whosoever will" to respond to the preaching of the good news about the salvation offered to every lost soul. This is assuring religion; you are granted the gift of knowing for certain that Christ has saved you for eternity.

This "democratization" (or "Americanization") of religion struck home with a people whose ties with the European culture had been stretched almost to the breaking point by the passage of time, diverging interests, novel cultural conditions, and new political institutions. A new nation was soon to be forged on the battlefield and in human minds. A new social-cultural situation (with religion as a basic ingredient) had already surfaced. The Great Awakening of 1747-1780 participated in that as cause and effect, symptom and symbol, and reaction and assertion. Closely tied in with the spirit of social revolt building among southern colonies, against authority that was Anglican, English, and governmental, it was "indicative of real strains within the society." Rhys Isaac speaks of the awakening in Virginia (and by implication elsewhere) as an effort to reorganize society—not just religion—on different principles. It was "a popular response to mounting social disorder."[4] The conversion experience which was "at the heart of the popular evangelical movement," relieved the people of the burden of guilt laid on them by their antagonism toward the authorities. It may also have played a part in furthering their dissatisfaction. At all events, time had run out on the old order. There are few better examples of the birth of the new than religion, which shifted from conservative, objective formality to experiential, personal faith. In Donald Mathews' words, "the community created by personal experience, baptism, and discipline was a reproach to the old order and a promise of a new one."[4] Thus, the severe decline of Anglican (Episcopal after 1785) numbers and influence was inevitable even before the War against and new independence from Anglicanism's home nation. Nevertheless it is important to recall that the former Established Church not only underwent disestablishment, but, further, suffered dramatic losses in size, influence, and prestige.

The new order which emerged with the birth of the Republic spelled at least three major developments in religion: the demise of the old; the surge of those evangelical faiths which had surfaced a quarter century or more earlier; and the prominence of the moral-religious question about the Negro slaves in the population. Church membership statistics from 1792 help show this. The three Evangelical churches had about 100,000 white members, with Methodists numbering 38,000, Baptists second, and Presbyterians third. These three denominations also claimed somewhat fewer than 25,000 black members. The remaining denominations, Anglican, Catholic, Lutheran, Moravian, Mennonite, and so on made up another 50,000 all together. Best estimates show that within the total white population of some 1,140,000, 27 percent of those over 16 years of age were church members, most of these (82 percent) being Evangelicals. Probably some three percent of the black Southerners were church members and most of these were in the Evangelical denominations.

It is suggestive to note the sharp disparity between the 97 percent of blacks who were outside the church fold and the 75 percent of the whites who were not members. With the former, the huge percentage figures refer to a segment of humanity largely uninformed and uninstructed in the meaning and ways of Christianity. It is true that no other religion presented itself as an alternative, not even African traditional religions, of which minor ritual and modal vestiges survived. A quite different picture obtains among the unchurched whites. The largest proportion of them fell within the sphere of Christianity; the South was Christendom in transition or in disrepair, rather than a non-Christian or post-Christian society. Many of those who were not church members were prevented or discouraged from an affiliation by the sheer distance separating them from a place of meeting or even a concentrated population. In other words, southern whites were still within Christianity's orbit and were, in many cases, ripe for the plucking. The Methodist and Baptist churches were primed for the task. What is novel about church policy and opportunity in this era does not refer to the white population, really, but to the black. For the first time now in any concerted and aggressive way, the white denominations reached out into the black population with a view to converting, instructing, and churching.

Institutionally, the chief developments had to do with organizing the denominations. The Methodist Episcopal Church—Methodism administered by bishops (*episcopoi*)—came into being in Baltimore in 1784. The next year witnessed the formation of the Protestant Episcopal Church in the United States of America. Synods and presbyteries were being organized in Presbyterian ranks west of the mountains as well as in the old stronghold territories. Several Baptist groups had agreed on an informal alliance by 1788, although the independent spirit among the Baptists left the alliance short of being an official, centralized body. The other denominations on the scene continued to be largely self-contained as with the Moravians, Mennonites, and Quakers, or tied more closely to their Northern-based units, the Roman Catholic and Lutheran, for example.

A few new and indigenous Protestant groupings appeared between 1794 and 1810, two of them soon to be tributaries feeding into the "Christian" or Disciples of Christ or "Campbellite" stream which took well-defined shape by the 1830s. Both the O'Kelly movement and the Stoneite movement expressly reflected the "Americanization" or "democratization" of religion we have talked about earlier. Led by James O'Kelly, a Methodist minister in Virginia and North Carolina, and Barton W. Stone, a Presbyterian minister from Virginia and Kentucky, they determined to throw off hierarchical organization in favor of freedom, liberty, and republican values. By 1794 O'Kelly had become fed up with the "ecclesiastical monarchy" in the Methodist Church of which he had been a stalwart leader. Stone renounced Presbyterian church organization in favor of members being simply "Christians" and of according authority only to the New Testament. Both of these pioneer spirits also had had their fill of formal theology, preferring instead "only what the Scriptures teach." Any good Methodist, Calvinist, or Baptist would have said much the same. But O'Kelly and Stone exchanged concepts for texts, creeds for verses, and reflection for subscription and practice.

On the western Kentucky and Tennessee frontier, Finis Ewing gathered a company of fellow Presbyterians into a new Cumberland presbytery, which soon made its way into independence. These devout souls were less concerned with organizational matters than with the relation between doctrine and piety. For them the accomplishments of the camp meetings and revivals demonstrated the truest character of religion, vital piety, the direct experience of the Lord in one's heart. Failing to convince theology-minded Calvinists of the need for reform in this direction, they went into business on their own by 1810.

Thus in the early years of the nineteenth century, the popular Southern denominational spectrum was deployed: on the right the Presbyterian Church, the "Christians" and Baptists on the left. In between ranged the Methodists and Cumberland Presbyterians. That is to look at the situation organizationally. If, instead, the interest is beliefs and experience, the Presbyterians and Christians were conservative and the Cumberlands, Baptists, and Methodists, least to most radical, were the innovators, all stressing the primacy of personal experience. By mid-century, incidentally, the Methodists had pulled in their horns a bit, leaving the hitherto more doctrine-concerned Baptists as the radicals among those emphasizing religious experience.

The greatest single event in the era between the founding of the Republic and the Civil War was the Second Great Awakening, and it was of course no single event, strictly speaking. An avalanche of revivals of religion occurred between 1799 and 1810. There had been an "acceleration of Evangelical tempo" (Mathews) between 1785 and 1792, and a general elongation of the aftermath of the first Awakening as well. But marvelous things began to happen on the western side of the Appalachian mountains, in Tennessee and Kentucky. In 1799 a revival erupted in Logan County, Kentucky, near the Tennessee line, sparked by the fiery preaching of James McGready, Presbyterian minister recently arrived from North Carolina. The most spectacular outpouring of the Spirit occurred two years later and 200 miles farther north, at Cane Ridge in Bourbon County, Kentucky. Great numbers of people flocked to the weeks' long exercises that summer and hundreds joined churches of the three major denominations. Over the ensuing decade, enthusiastic religion flourished, spreading the Christian cause back every road, up every "holler", and into every settling community on the frontier. Somewhat surprisingly, the contagion scaled the mountains in an easterly direction. It is a point of real significance that the mountain range intervening did not manage to sunder what was from the beginning a single culture despite distances and formidable difficulties in travel. The Evangelical soil on the east was nurtured by seeds sown on the west, and the harvest of souls was great in both areas.

In one sense there was nothing very noteworthy about the Second Awakening, beyond the fact that it happened and where. A similar mode of dynamic Christian expression had occurred a generation and more earlier, after all. But some differences, mostly evolvings perhaps, should be observed. For one thing, the social setting in the west between 1800 and 1810 differed from the earlier circumstances back east. Out there it could not be taken for granted that the Christianization of a scattered, unsettled, truly pioneer population would take place. When the Great (Kentucky) Revival occurred, it did not vitalize the lethargic or renew church members in their churchmanship; instead it relocated them from life outside the influence of the church and Christianity—there being few of the former and little of the latter—into the fellowship, inspiration, and teachings of meetings and congregations of Christians.

A second new wrinkle attendant on the later trans-Appalachian developments was the institutionalization of programs for converting the lost and sustaining the joy and discipline of the Christian life. Two types of meetings came into being, "camp meetings" and "protracted meetings," which succeeded in ushering in a new day, lasting until the present, in regional Evangelicalism. The eighteenth century revivals had been less programmed and more spontaneous and, most important, associated with existing congregations as a general rule. Moreover, among the Presbyterians and Methodists especially, traditional churchmanship with its emphasis on theology and the sacraments had continued. Out west, once the effervescence had begun, the meeting was the thing. It happened at a designated place, usually outdoors in the summer, on an announced schedule, through what came to be a routinized style, liturgies of singing, praying, testifying, preaching, and altar calls. Paradoxically, the more rough-hewn form of religious exercise was also the more systematic. Camp meetings attracted immense crowds to outdoor summer seasons of revival. Revivals (protracted meetings) emerged as more localized versions. They occurred between or after crop seasons in churches, usually lasting two or three weeks.

Just how successful they were is illustrated by the enlargement of Methodist ranks, from 38,000 in 1796, to 55,000 in 1803, all the way to 80,000 by 1807. While rates of growth moderated after that phenomenal decade, they were far from stagnant or stabilizing. With this occurrence, it was empirically certain, not merely predictable, that the South was Evangelical country. Methodists retained the camp meeting as their strategem, also sponsoring revivals, while the Baptists soon largely restricted their efforts at ingathering to revivals. Presbyterians withdrew from both, opting instead for a more gradualistic, theological, and churchly way. It was over that issue, of course, that the Cumberland Presbyterians broke off, but their presence was to be felt in minor ways only and almost exclusively in western Tennessee and Kentucky, though later in Texas. The conquest by the "big three," numerically the "big two," was complete by 1810.

This Evangelical dominance of the Southern religious scene was more than numerical, however. Its theology— more precisely, its way of understanding Christian meaning and even everyday reality— became normative for an entire region's notion of the truth. This was little less true of the unchurched and of Episcopalians (who began to grow again after 1825), for example, than of those who formally promoted it. Clement Eaton summarizes this development thusly: "By 1830 the Southern people had become thoroughly converted to orthodoxy in religion; the skepticism that had existed among the gentry of the eighteenth century, the age of reason, had virtually disappeared. . . . The religious belief of an overwhelming majority of Southerners in 1860 was of a type that would today be called fundamentalism, resting on a literal interpretation of the Bible."[6] (Eaton's summary is more helpful for seeing the larger religious situation of the region, it should be noted, than for describing the message proclaimed and believed.)

The Evangelical message took as its premise that reality in its distilled essence consists of two units, the eternal, morally perfect and demanding God, and the sinful, punishment-worthy individual. Every person is thus in a desperate condition. But, all credit to the sacrificial, atoning death of Jesus Christ, the Son of God, hope for pardon abounds. The gifts of new life here and of heaven after death also are offered. By opening your heart to receive Christ as Savior and Lord, you can be "born again," made a "new creature." This happens in a conversion experience, which is typically regarded as a conscious, one-time, memorable, and datable event. Through this process, Christianity is viewed as preponderantly a religion of salvation—of the individual from guilt and condemnation for pardon, new status before God, and everlasting life. While revivals, camp meetings, and evangelistic sermons are concerted efforts toward bringing about conversion, they do not exhaust the enterprise. The whole of church life is directed toward the goal of saving souls.

It thus becomes necessary to see what such a proclamation of the message does not do, in addition to what it does. It does not present a theology of community or of social justice or of the stewardship of the natural order, for example. Beyond that, it is a simple formulation, identifying the tenets of the faith definitively in a problem-solution rhythm. Also it sees no need to wrestle with such issues as authority or tradition, taking the Bible as solely authoritative and its teachings as self-evident, and regarding tradition as limited to that of the New Testament delivered in pure form to the present day without any significant intervening history.

Such descriptions are accurate; but they are also misleading. On the question of social justice, to take one example, the Evangelical churches turned their converts into morally very sensitive people. To be a converted Christian, a saved person, was known to entail appropriate demeanor in gratitude for forgiveness and as worthy of one's new status and identity. Obedience to Christ's teachings was held up as essential. In the context of Southern society, that meant honesty, familial integrity, sociability, and neighborliness on the affirmative side. It also necessitated "abstaining from every appearance of evil," interpreted as cursing, gambling, breaking the sabbath, dancing, and (especially later) drinking. Totalled, the moral impact was toward a disciplined life. One is attentive to what he or she does and does not do, indeed even scrupulous. The instincts of the flesh must be bridled and full run given to the leadings of the Spirit. This made for a people who were morally serious about work and secular values as well as about godliness. Strictly speaking, though, this kind of religion did not promote or result in "social justice." As William McLoughlin says: "What the southern church-goer came to consider social reform (the only kind of reform appropriate to the Christian qua Christian) was the personal moral reform that brought order to the community by restraining violence, strengthening self-discipline, and encouraging familial and neighborly responsibilities for good behavior."[7] Concerning themselves with political or economic matters was considered to lie outside their obligations or even proper sphere of duty.

Something of the same can be said about describing Southern Evangelicalism as "simple" in theology and "programmed" in method; those are descriptions, not charges, and they are accurate. Confusion arises if one takes them to mean that southern churchmen were anti-intellectual or, less extremely, disinterested in education. The historical record supports such suppositions in some cases on certain subjects. For example, it is true that among many Baptists and in some Methodist circles, a polarity existed between an "educated" and a "called" ministry, with the former regarded as superior. In general, however, the commitment to the education of young men, ministers, lawyers, physicians, and other leaders of society was substantial, as borne out by the number of colleges founded and supported by the denominations. When the fact of their relative poverty and lack of centralization is kept in mind, their accomplishments are the more striking. The Baptists contributed Meredith, Wake Forest, Georgetown, Richmond, Mercer, Howard, and Furman between 1820 and the Civil War, a staggering output for a folk people. Methodists expressed their commitment to education through Randolph-Macon, Emory, Emory and Henry, and several other colleges which later died out or formed the nucleus of institutions which evolved with changed names. Hampden-Sydney in Virginia, Oglethorpe in Georgia, and Davidson in North Carolina resulted from a predictable Presbyterian interest. It should also be noted that the education of women was regarded as appropriate and the object of financial and leadership support. The founding of Salem College by the Moravians, Newberry by the Lutherans, Erskine by the Associate Reformed Presbyterians, and Transylvania by the Christians (from an earlier Presbyterian establishment) serve to remind us that other Christian bodies were about in the South and that they too were interested in the education of the young and the quality of the civilization. To be sure, these denominational schools were self-serving to a considerable degree. But higher education has a way of leaping its defined boundaries, generating critical inquiry, and demanding that risks be taken. The fact that these pious servants of God took pains to provide education was demonstration that they had already outgrown piety narrowly conceived in the process of moving from a sectarian vision toward becoming an "enlightened and refined people." Through their colleges (and also theological seminaries) they contributed to the maturing of a frontier society becoming steadily more settled.

We can delay no longer in touching on the "central theme" of Southern antebellum history, its religious dimensions no less than political, economic, and social. The predominant influence of racial matters was apparent from 1800, strong from 1820, and overriding by 1830. How was slavery to be defended against Northern and European criticisms? How to justify slavery on constitutional and religious grounds? What to do in discharging responsibility to and for slaves? How to bring Christianity to them and include them in the churches' life? How to correlate slavery as an institution with personal relations to slaves? How to adjudicate between slaves as people and as property? These and dozens more related questions plagued the Southern (religious) conscience, preoccupying leaders' minds, and upstaging all other agenda items at denominational gatherings. The best clue as to their disposition is provided by the fact that the three major denominations fell out with their Northern colleagues and acted to form separate regional denominations. The Methodist Episcopal Church, South, was organized in 1844. The next year saw the birth of the Southern Baptist Convention. The Presbyterian Church in the United States came into formal existence in 1861, after three decades of strained relations. Slavery was the divisive force in all three cases.

We have noted previously how early Afro-Americans were brought to the Southern colonies and that the moderate efforts to Christianize them were rewarded proportionately. Under the loose arrangements that made up colonial society, slavery was a fact but not much of a public issue and problem. It did not become so until there were legal norms by which to assess its legitimacy and a political entity to raise questions about it, and later to call it into question. Once judicially defined and politically enforced institutions had appeared, however, slavery and Negroes emerged as a central issue for the South. Accordingly, their Christianization became, to white perception, politically and socially as well as theologically, both possible and necessary.

But this change was more an evolution than an abruptly new condition. The Methodist Church provides us with the standard case. In the 1780s Methodists formulated their leaders' antislavery views into definite rules. Circuit riders were required to free their slaves; pronouncements were made which declared slavery to be "contrary to the laws of God, man, and nature, and hurtful to society, contrary to the dictates of conscience and pure religion." In 1784 their founding conference was so bold that it "promised to excommunicate all Methodists not freeing their slaves within two years." But that decision was highly controversial—in fact it threatened to shatter the infant church—and had to be rescinded within six months. Beginning with this response, that Church came to terms with the realities of Southern society, particularly as regarded economics. One adjustment after another was made, compromise following compromise. By 1800 any keen observer could tell which way the wind was blowing, by 1816 conservative policies were in force, by 1820 the Methodist Church was at one with its culture on the issue of race. "From emancipation to evangelization" is the way Mathews captions the evolution of attitudes and policies. Methodist leadership had begun with the zealous dedication to eradicating slavery and making free people of the Afro-Americans. Little by little that social ethics fashion faded and the society's more individualistically religious type of interpretation was applied to a fragile social condition.

Plans to evangelize Negroes soon became more than policy statements. Among Methodists, after 1830 especially, a veritable crusade was mounted. It was called "Mission to Slaves" and was well organized rather like a foreign mission society. Baptists also went about the task with vigor, indeed with characteristic aggressiveness, but chiefly through the agency of local congregations or the activities of slave owners who saw to it that their Negroes heard Christian preaching. White Evangelicals had taken on this responsibility with some success from the 1790s, actually, there being some 140,000 black members in Evangelical denominations by 1830. But the decade beginning with that year was pivotal. Conflict was heating up in the nation over the issue of slavery. The South's political energies were being expended more and more in the defense of slavery—and its moral passions too. But down home the dangers were if anything yet more ominous. The Vesey conspiracy of 1822 in South Carolina and the Nat Turner insurrection of 1831 in Virginia struck terror in the hearts of white leaders. Although most blacks probably were little affected by these dramatic instances of rebellion, a number were. In any event, whites were fearful, not only for their own lives and investments (in slaves), but for civil peace and the preservation of the South's economic and political way of life. Every state legislature in the region acted promptly and peremptorily to muzzle the black revolutionary spirit by imposing laws curtailing the right to assemble, worship, become literate, and much more, except under strictly supervised circumstances. An enormous crescendo of concern to make Christians of the slaves occurred as a part of the same push.

Impressive energies were devoted to the condition of Negro souls. Well organized Methodist evangelization activities appeared across the South, especially in the plantation areas of the seaboard states. Congregations of the Evangelical denominations stepped up their appeals and refined their approaches to Negroes, urging them to fill the gallery and special section seats reserved for them. Plantation owners saw to it that "praise houses" were constructed on their land and Negro preachers assigned to stir their people in the Lord's name (with a white foreman present for surveillance). Large slave-holders like (the Rev.) Charles Colcock Jones worked thoughtfully and diligently for years to compose catechisms expressly for the slaves, then to instill the teachings of such a Christian primer in them. In sum, a variety of missionary enterprises, ranging widely in type, manner, and immediate objective, appeared as response to the portents of revolution and as preventive measures. Whites' motives were not limited to these more publicly attuned ones, however. In addition, a number of white people cared about blacks, both as a lot and as friends with names. Others viewed the Southern American situation as a stage in the divine government of history in which Christians were commissioned to convert the heathen from one dark continent. In a different vein, many slave owners took measures to bring Christianity to their human property in order to pacify and comfort them, defer their gratification until life after death, or make them more dutiful and servile. Needless to say, within the breasts of many white Southerners motives were mixed. Often there was some genuine recognition of their human needs, but hardly ever did a member of the ruling race overlook the unique caste and economic status of black people.

It would be difficult to determine whose religion, blacks' or whites', was more profoundly affected by the preoccupation with racial issues in the antebellum period. On the surface, the religion of black people was. But of course both were, profoundly, and the conundrum is finally more playful than helpful. The truth is that the white church attempted and accomplished very little from 1830 until after the Civil War which was not dominated by racial and interracial considerations. Despite theological intentions and official disengagement, it was much mixed up in secular affairs, in the economics and politics of the region and the nation. It will have to suffice to say here that such items as these set the agendas for southern churches for more than a generation: how to convert and instruct Negroes in the ways of Christianity; how to structure, next maintain, then sever, relations with their co-religionists in the nonslaveholding states of the country; how to deal with the Negroes they knew or were responsible for, as property, as friends, as acquaintances; what, if anything, to do about public policy concerning Negroes, taking into account their being persons, property, the backbone of the region's economic system, and, alas, even potential revolutionaries.

The religion of the South's black people shared much more with the Evangelical Protestantism of the region's whites than it diverged from it. Most obviously, both were Evangelical. After all, it was Evangelicals among Southern white Christians who were motivated to bring Negroes to the Christian faith; naturally their manner of Christian expression is what they imparted to the slaves whom they instructed and who participated in the services of worship they provided. When blacks held their own services, whether those were approved and overseen by whites or held clandestinely, they added their own flourishes and unique styles to the white religious legacy; still, the similarities were marked. The "invisible institution" too was Evangelical. Much the same can be said for the independent black congregations, usually Baptist, composed of free Negroes which arose in Petersburg and Richmond, Charleston and Savannah, Lexington (Kentucky), and several other places between Independence and the 1840s. Formally continuities outnumbered discontinuities by a wide margin; but the differences too told for quite a lot.

An expressiveness of spirit came to characterize black religion. (Actually many white Baptists and Methodists had earlier given vent to comparable manifestations of "enthusiasm.") For Negro Christians the message was presented unvarnished and the response was uninhibited. Such bad news as one's eternal damnation called for a groaning and bewailing befitting one's anguish and sorrow. Such good news as God's gracious proffer of forgiveness through the love of Christ's sacrificial excruciation quite rightly issued in shouts of joy and praise for blessed release. As Negro Christians had opportunity to develop their own styles of preaching and singing they did so. The preacher may have been unlettered but his preaching was far from theologically illiterate. He knew all that was needed, the biblical message of personal salvation and a rich intimate knowing of the Savior who lived in the believer's heart. The spiritual music composed and sung was similarly direct, heart-felt, and expressive. Black religion dealt with life as blacks lived it, as much in its demonstrative modes as in its content. It was all about pain and sorrow, sin and shortcoming, pardon and joy, praise and thanksgiving, grace and hope. This version of religion provided great benefit; it accomplished things in the Christian's life, accomplishments which were known, felt, registered, and not infrequently shouted about.

We have noted the variety of motives which prompted white Christians to share their religion with their black fellow Southerners. Now we are observing that, whatever the level of purity or the specific quality of the incentive, the religion they shared "took." For a large minority of Negroes conversion, baptism, instruction, worship, and the dedicated life became central aspects of their oppressed human condition. The institutional development of Negro Christianity had to await Emancipation and War's end. However, the character of that religion had been formed and its power unleashed. There were many thousands of Negro Baptists and Methodists by 1850; church life had become a more important regular feature of slaves' existence than family life. Of course that notation tells us as much about the high barriers that the system of slavery erected against the realization of life in family units as it does about religious life. But when one recalls how small had been the Christian impact on the southern black population only a third of a century earlier, these cultural inroads are seen as impressive indeed. Thus, when twentieth century observers regard southern blacks as a generally religious people, they are pointing to developments that are relatively recent, dating from the three to five decades before slavery was brought to an official end.

Let us recapitulate in order to see how the religious scene appeared in the American South on the eve of the Civil War. The colonial Establishment, for a long time now the Protestant Episcopal Church, had been rebounding from its desperate straits since about 1825 and was once again a presence to be reckoned with; its constituency, however, was largely confined to traditional families with conservative instincts. The Presbyterian Church had become a substantial force, standing firm for proper doctrine, often taking the lead in promoting traditional regional views on the place of the races. Its membership totals left it in third place, but its inclinations were to minister to its own people and its own kind of people, those from the more privileged, better educated classes of society. This meant that while its presence and influence were strong, its growth in size would accord with natural increase. In neither of these two denominations was Negro membership very large. The formerly established church, the church of the colonial planter class, did continue to hold small numbers of Negroes in parishes wherever that kind of society was perpetuated. So, while Negro Episcopalians outnumbered Negro Presbyterians, neither group belonged to the religious mainstream in black society.

Baptist and Methodist figures were impressive, to say the least. These churches had managed to attract the rank and file of Southern whites from the era of the Second Awakening and were in commanding positions well before 1860. Their aggressive, warm-hearted, certain approach to Christian faith compelled an evangelistic outreach and attracted an immense following. Much the same can be said for the black religious scene. Accordingly these two denominations accounted for a large proportion of the sizeable minority of Negroes who owned church membership.

After these, the list of religious organizations carries only minor importance. Liberal Christianity showed some signs of promise from 1800 to the 1830s but its views were too radical for Unitarianism or any deistic philosophy to achieve permanence. Jews comprised a long-standing and influential minority in such cities as Charleston, Savannah, and Richmond; otherwise there were very few to be found. A comparable tale can be told about Roman Catholics. Where they were numerous, they were strong, as in New Orleans, Mobile, St. Louis, and Louisville and the area just south of it. Elsewhere Catholics were few and far between. The attraction of this most traditional form of Christianity to any besides birthright Catholics was virtually nil; as a matter of fact, most considered this no Christianity at all and beyond that a menace to all things noble. But there were birthrights Catholics, it should be remembered. Wherever French missionaries had penetrated or French settlements established, Catholicism was alive—in Louisiana, just after 1700, in Arkansas and Missouri a century later. Similarly the Spanish presence in La Florida (as noted), Mobile, and most of all Texas. Irish and German immigrants to the river basin towns of Missouri and Kentucky also contributed to a permanent Catholic population. In the latter state, the removal of Maryland Catholics to the area south of Louisville had occurred before 1800.

Most other religious groups parallelled the Episcopal and Presbyterian churches, and more formally the Jewish and Catholic communities, in having an involvement largely limited to an ethnic or quasi-ethnic population. Several sorts of German Protestants maintained size and strength in their specified locales. Germans moved in strength to the hill country of central Texas between 1840 and 1860, typically split in religious affiliation between Lutheran and Roman Catholic. Lutherans flourished in the valleys of Virginia and in some piedmont counties of South and

North Carolina. In the latter area, the Evangelical and Reformed tradition also enjoyed strength. Dunkers and Mennonites made out a sturdy existence in their own coves near the Shenandoah. Moravians built such villages as Salem, Bethabara, and Bethania in their corner of heaven on earth.

Congregationalism survived in certain areas of tidewater Virginia and eastern piedmont North Carolina. It also turned up in Missouri as one-time New Englanders moved westward to the Old Northwest and some on farther. Quakers who inhabited some parts of those same areas were partly enabled to compensate for lost population—which moved to the Northwest Territory because of revulsion over the persistence of slavery—by adopting a revivalistic style which attracted new members. But the only other bodies with much general appeal were the Cumberland Presbyterians and the Disciples of Christ. Neither was identified with particular ethnic or class groups and, during the pre-Civil War years, both aggressively sought to convert the public. Their influence was geographically restricted, however, the Cumberlands rarely ranging outside western Tennessee and Kentucky, the Campbellites proving successful west of an imaginary line connecting Cincinnati, Lexington, and Nashville. The line did have a northern extension, however, so that the Disciples were becoming a midwestern as well as southern phenomenon. The deep southern (Tennessee and northern Alabama) Campbellites were carving out their own distinctive positions by the 1850s; although they did not become the "Church of Christ" movement until the turn of the century, their direction was being set before the Civil War.

The relative simplicity and homogeneity of southern religious patterns around 1860 was quite pronounced. It stood in real and ever sharpening contrast with the Northern scene where the Anglo-Saxon Protestant churches were rivalled by infusion of German-Scandinavian strength, Roman Catholics in frightening (so it was viewed) proportions, Jews emigrating from western Europe, and emerging sects such as the Mormons and Adventists. Missouri alone among the Southern states showed any tendency to parallel these Northern patterns. Beyond what we have noted, the new Mormon faith in the 1830s had staked out claim to Daviess County as its kingdom—the place where the Garden of Eden was located. The South was to spawn and adopt its own sectarian communities but not until the years around 1900. Never were its patterns to be affected by the immigration of different kinds of people. It grew its own diversity in the enclaves of black people, mountain people, and a frontier society.

"Homogeneity" was at least as important as "simplicity." As the Confederate States of America was being born in the Spring of 1861, Protestant orthodoxy prevailed. Everybody knew, or knew he should and would know, that the Bible was the exclusive authority for all truth that really mattered, that life is made up of a few earthly years and an eternity for which the former is a critical preparation period, and that the Southern cause in liberty, economics, and ethics was a matter of great moment to the Almighty. The South's cause was not just its own; it was God's, hence a righteous one. The teachings of the Bible, the preservation of the Southern way of life, and the region's convictions about the good society were seen as closely linked. Not often under conditions of religious liberty has a "nation" been so unified in a common commitment by the ruling classes (the white race) on a religious position which reached out to embrace a political and economic philosophy as well.

Any discussion purporting to treat the "religious history" of the Civil War period is bound to refer to more than the career of organized religion. From the pulpit, Southern congregations heard appeals for sacrificial involvement in the great cause and divine justifications for the struggle. It was God's will that South and Southern way of life survive. A moral watershed had been reached in the nation's history and God's faithful were being called upon to advance the cause of righteousness. Imbued with these passions, lay people provided generously for the physical needs of the troops. The troops themselves entertained little thought but that the homeland and its values should be defended. Clergymen promoted the Confederate program, in a great many cases through service as military chaplains. Often the most loyal Confederates and the most devout churchmen were the same people. The role of the chruches was not to provide leverage for Southern self-criticism; on the contrary they made legitimate and even holy the defense which the divine Providence had given over to them. Beside this quality of concern and activity—a genuine preoccupation it was, the institutional life of the churches was relatively insignificant. Revivals of religion were frequent, however, both in churches and among the troops; in that sense the churches grew. But times were hard for the religious institutions of the embattled Southland as for all the others. As the war intensified and spread, buildings were destroyed and weekly practices effectively disrupted. As if matters were not bad enough already, Secretary of War

Stanton confiscated much church property and wrested congregational life from the Southern people, turning it over to Union ownership. At War's end, all was reclaimed, but severe dislocation had occurred and a deep bitterness engendered. Denominations already divided now became alienated.

Somewhat curiously, perhaps, the Christian cause did not suffer as a result of the belligerent conditions which lasted for four long years and the animosity provoked by it. In fact, church life was resumed—in reality, continued—and its contributions to the regularization of life were indispensable for the people and the culture as they sought to put back together the fractured pieces of a shattered existence. Their theological interpretations as to why a holy war should have been lost may look strained and contrived to later generations, but those which were advanced succeeded in satisfying Southern men and women in the decades when the Lost Cause was being celebrated. In actual fact, religion was to become an even more dominant dimension of southern life than it had been in the previous era when it was a forceful element in the region's righteous cause.

The biggest news of the immediate post-War period, religiously speaking, had to do with the recently emancipated Negro people. Literally within weeks they were forming independent congregations, usually Baptist and Methodist. They chose to go their own ways, but in the context it was inevitable that they would do so. Having their own churches both symbolized and galvanized the new freedom. Lacking much experience in business and political enterprises, they could not turn to those areas for identity, creativity, and security. Religious experience, having been a vital aspect of their culture for a number of decades, lay ready to hand to provide the qualities of life they sorely needed in this revolutionary time. In the first place, a church could be their own. (One of the reasons for the greater attraction of the Baptist faith than the Methodist was the local autonomy enjoyed by each congregation in the former as against the connectionalism of the latter.) Here self-government and free rein to practice their own styles and tastes could be experimented with. Secondly, the church was not only something familiar in the Negro community; it also enjoyed a good reputation. It had sustained a great many people during hard seasons. More than that, for many it had helped make bearable their lot of subjugation. Third, it bade fair to become the center of the social life of the black community. The church offered fellowship, education and training, provision for welfare needs, and opportunity for men to enter the one profession open, the ministry. Various denominations, principally Northern and including several not strong in the South, founded colleges and other schools for a population which had been systematically prevented from acquiring a formal education. In other words, for a variety of reasons, the church was a living and self-recommending option at a time when hardly any other institutional agency was accessible. It was not only not absent or forbidden, it was available and participation in it feasible. In time, as seems inevitable with all institutions in society, a tendency toward formal organization occurred. In the 1880s and 1890s that process produced the National Baptist Convention, the cooperative organization which bound Negro Baptist congregations together in the interest of such concerted activities as foreign and domestic missions, colleges and schools, and mutual nurturing through fellowship. The Methodist tradition also took on more visible shape. Membership was spread among: the Colored Methodist Episcopal Church, which was founded in 1870 as the Negro branch of the Methodist Episcopal Church, South; and the two traditional Negro Methodist denominations, the African Methodist Episcopal Church and the A.M.E., Zion, Church, dating back to 1816 and 1821, respectively, of Northern origins but with some membership and influence carrying over from the antebellum South.

Within the Christianity practiced by Southern Negroes, the dominant cadences were those of excitement, adventure, novelty, promise, and challenge. Among whites the Christianity of the postbellum decades was characterized by rapid growth and expansion, sectarian proliferation, and a tightening and hardening of positions, theological, moral, and social. On the important subject of growth in membership, John S. Ezell has written: "Before the Civil War, scarcely twenty percent of the Southern people were affiliated with any church; yet after 1865 the Southerner soon found it difficult to believe that any person could be decent in morals and manners who was not a church member."[8] In other words, while many were joining, most others were just as positive about the value and necessity of church membership. Not only were there no alternatives, there was little criticism of the church and scarcely any rejection of Christianity.

This was less true of the population moving westward from the "old southwest" across the river to Arkansas, Oklahoma, northern Louisiana, and Texas, but it was true for them as well. Settled sparsely before the Civil War, those areas attracted larger population plantings between

1870 and 1900. Soon the same denominational hegemony was to prevail, although the Churches of Christ were to be strong throughout, as were the new sects in Oklahoma, Arkansas, and Missouri, and Catholicism in Texas.

Already the largest denomination, the Southern Baptist Convention, experienced dramatic increases in membership, income, property values, and cultural influence. Its centralization and bureaucratization were not to take place until the 1920s, but its blanketing of the region was an accomplished fact before the turn of the century. Furthermore, its quantitative growth was matched by a qualitative dominance of regional religious life, and beyond that to the accepted values and truth-claims of the society generally. It won the status of normativity; probably no other institution typified the culture more accurately or influenced it more profoundly.

During this era, it expanded its efforts through establishing a press to publish Sunday school materials, strengthening the role of its colleges, developing a foreign missionary enterprise, founding theological seminaries, and much more. Organizationally vigorous and progressive, the white Baptist ranks were quite conservative in ideology. An earlier spirit of ecumenical openness gave way to a denominational self-consciousness and provincialism. A competitive attitude developed on the subject of doctrinal teachings. The Southern Baptists also boasted of Southern purity, a point of view which did align Southern Protestantism generally against the compromising postures they saw being taken by Northern churchmen, but without attendant ecumenical cooperation.

On the ethical front of Southern religious life, two issues loomed largest, the liquor question (so referred to) and the place of Negroes in the society. The making and consuming of alcoholic beverages had been routine in the colonial and antebellum South; as a matter of fact these activities continued largely to be taken for granted down to the 1880s. Many have observed that the South was the heaviest drinking section of the country down to the Civil War; celebrations of all sorts, including weddings and funerals, were marked by the loosening of inhibitions provided by whiskey and rum. Baptists and Methodists were as apt to enjoy spirits as Episcopalians or Presbyterians; similarly no distinction existed between the customs of the clergy and the lay people. But all this changed, owing to a complex host of factors, with the beginning of the Jim Crow era (in the 1880s). Complicity in the liquor traffic, whether as user, manufacturer, or retailer, came to be regarded as rank evil. One's behavior on this all-important moral issue went far toward identifying him as Christian practitioner or not. Organized efforts to control or even outlaw the entire liquor business consumed a large proportion of Baptist moral energies, a program which contributed a great deal to the achievement of statewide prohibition in most of the Southern states by 1919 when the Eighteenth Amendment made that a national policy.

The racial question competed with the drinking issue for first place in the Baptist conscience. What to do with, about, and for the once enslaved people in their midst was an item white Southern society could not avoid in those years. But the forms this concerns took were quite distinct from the direct approach made to the question of drinking where it was thought easy and necessary to identify the Christian position. With reference to racial ethics, the ordinary mode was more often political than ecclesiastical. The churches did act in a number of ways. One was by not acting to integrate congregations, another by supporting Negro colleges and domestic missionary efforts. Most fundamentally, they quietly encouraged their members to accept the culture ethic that Negroes were inferior, that all institutions and facilities were to be segregated along racial lines, and that Negroes had special need for personal services which compassionate white people should be sensitive to provide, in roughly the manner of adults' treatment of children. Directly this affected the churches through the day to day assumptions and practices of the membership, rather than through energetic or tortured or persistent activities in church meetings and decision-making councils. Even so it is accurate to describe this as "direct" inasmuch as the church finally had to take moral responsibility for a human situation—and problem—bulking as large as this one did in a Southern society shot through with a Christian commitment to the true and the right. In summary, we may turn to Ezell's interpretation that in general the churches "buttressed a conservative social philosophy with an orthodox theology."[9]

What this amounts to is that the history of black religion in the last third of the nineteenth century heavily implicates the white churches in whose company blacks were not welcome. The names were the same, Baptist and Methodist (overwhelmingly), but the communities were far apart. In a variety of subtle and not so subtle ways, the white churches saw to that. There was some intercourse between them, but the traffic flowed only one way. There was indeed more than a modicum of concern and compassion, but it was expressed through a structure that placed white over black. If the names had not been the same, if history had not converted the former progenitors to forcing withdrawal and separation, the story would not have been so complex—or so sad.

In this discussion of the two great moral issues facing the Southern Baptist people, we have really been reciting facts applicable to Southern church life generally. That denomination both epitomized and shaped Southern society. However, the story of the Methodist Episcopal Church, South, is astonishingly similar, and its culture-fittedness and influence also very great. On the matter of the use and sale of alcoholic beverages, the Methodists were equally as determined. Every General Conference of that Church addressed the issue, always in forceful tones, until by the 1896 sessions it could be declared that "we are a Prohibitionist church." Likewise on the subject of race, the Methodist Church went along with its culture, showed much concern for personal service to Negroes, and acted by not acting. Nevertheless some features did mark off this denomination from its sister groups. For one thing its connectionalist system and a residual sense of catholicity kept it somewhat aware of kinsmen elsewhere. This produced two quite opposite effects, one its retaining a degree of contact with the Methodists of the North, the others its developing a keener sense of comparing and contrasting. More than the Baptists even, the Southern white Methodists thought to rate themselves on a scale of Christian purity—highest, of course. They were not reticent to declare that in doctrine, vitality, and moral rectitude their performance outshone other companies of Christians outside the South, the heartland of God-fearing, Bible-believing, and warm-hearted people.

Such regional self-esteem was not seen as tainted by the presence of some quite negative and even destructive impulses. The Ku Klux Klan had emerged in 1869 to defend against intruders, first Negroes, but later Roman Catholics as well, in the first two decades of the twentieth century. Churches did not sponsor, or often overtly approve of the program of, the Klan. However, many of the leaders of the Klan were preachers and convinced lay churchmen. Moreover, much of the message and symbolism drew from Christian sources and, by default, much of the Church's action by inaction helped promote the Klan's programs of intimidation, hate, and violence. The whole of Southern culture, with religion as a fundamental ingredient, generated a climate of contrast between the ruling and the subservient classes, between the religiously authentic and the insidious. At a time when the Negro people, as vitally a part of Southern society as anyone else, were struggling to lift themselves from severe deprivations, everything about white society strove to fix them in a lowly estate. In the public arena, Jim Crow laws prevented them from advancing to dignity and opportunity. The churches wrote them off as a people who, while incurably or at least needfully religious, had exotic and quaint tastes, peculiar sensibilities, and inferior capacity for understanding. In such a climate the overtly demeaning policies of the Ku Klux Klan were quite predictable. When a little later another alien group of human beings, Roman Catholics, came in view—not really into sight—an inhospitable reception greeted them. Paradoxically and in a pathological manner, the Klan, the Southern Baptists, and other Southern voices warned against a foreign take-over, the disruption of a solid, sober, and straight-thinking society, when it became clear that the North had been irretrievably altered by the immigration of millions of Roman Catholics from Europe since 1880. Few Catholics had actually moved to the South, not even in response to lures dangled before 1905 by some deep South states in hopes of landing new cadres of industrial and agricultural workers. It was the report of Catholics up north, and the paranoid fear of their settling in the South that gave rise to the anti-Catholicism articulated by religious voices between 1900 and 1920. This was an age of the denunciation of "isms," not just Roman Catholicism, but also the likes of Bolshevism, labor unionism, and federalism—and sporadically, Judaism.

This period of Southern history is not attractive by very many standards respected by high democratic civilizations. But those were "tough times," what with defeat in war and dissolution of the traditional society, a Reconstruction which was as harshly received as imposed laws and "occupation troops" always are, bitter economic depression, and an awareness of the region's reputation as benighted and reactionary in the midst of a nation hurtling progressively forward in an optimistic era astir with unprecedented growth, development, achievement, and world acclaim. The churches would have faced an insurmountable task had they produced a united prophetic front under such conditions. Alas, instead they were part of the problem; more accurately, the religious institutions were threads in the large, intricate bolt which comprised the fabric of Southern society and culture. In their behalf, it can be said that they did provide millions with challenge, assurance, hope, a sense of destiny, both earthly and heavenly, and guidelines for meaningful existence. Their contributions were made all the more impressive by the difficult, often desperate, conditions prevailing in the South.

Not surprisingly, such conditions helped give rise to some dissenting strains. In specific ways for a limited population, these sought to relieve the monotony and uniformity of a struggling existence, providing a fresh vitality and grounds for optimism. The three most prominent were: several sectarian offshoots from the conventional denominations; the creation of an alternative theological outlook, "liberal" or "incarnational", by the Sewanee (Episcopal) school of thought; and some southward sallies of the "social gospel" which was enjoying quite an inning in Northern Protestantism between 1890 and 1925.

As the turn of the century approached, some severe dissatisfaction was setting in among clusters of Methodist and Baptist people, especially the former. This had to do in part with the sheer increase in size, sophistication, and complexity of local congregations. As towns and cities grew and the qualities of living characteristic of a frontier-rural society receded, church life lost touch with the needs and tastes of many in the lower classes. Theological concerns also contributed to the rise of new conservative groups. Especially among Methodists where the craving for "holiness" had never been too far beneath the surface, new independent congregations arose which gradually evolved into organized sects in the half-dozen years before and after 1900. There were several of these, most famously, the Church of God (Cleveland, Tennessee), the Pentecostal Holiness Church, and the Church of God in Christ (a black organization). By the years of World War I, the Assemblies of God had come into being and northern and western-born comparable movements began to attract a following in the South. The obvious point must be underscored that the Southern plain-folks were part of a national development and even that organizations from beyond the borders were making some impact on Southern life, more in the sects than in the denominations. Religious importations had scarcely happened on the Southern scene since the colonial period. The beginnings of a cultural reintegration of the South into the national culture, thus, can be faintly detected in some religious happenings of the early twentieth century among the lower classes. The "pentecostal," "holiness," and "millenarian" movements have been smaller respecters of region than virtually any other religious traditions.

The "holiness" impulse was toward entire sanctification, or moral and spiritual perfection. The possession of one's life by the Holy Spirit was deemed a real possibility and a spiritual attainment to which every genuine Christian should aspire. It should be accompanied by the renunciation of all evil moral practices, most particularly drinking, smoking, cursing, dancing, gambling, and playing cards. Some Holiness people also adopted the "pentecostalist" distinctive, namely, the conviction that the ability to "speak in tongues" proved that a person had been possessed (or baptized) by the Holy Spirit. In being so endued, one was transposed into a higher key of spiritual existence where he or she emitted sounds deemed meaningful while also unintelligible. Both the Holiness and the Pentecostal Christians believed in the reality of physical healing by faith through prayer and the laying on of hands. It is important to add that thousands of Southern Negroes embraced these sectarian practices and that, quite remarkably, a number of interracial congregations grew up around these practices. In other words, a religious development apparently so conservative displayed some radical traits in addressing both regional and racial provincialisms.

Brief attention must be focused on another emergent communion of this era, one which is neither Holiness nor Pentecostal. The Churches of Christ had been taking informal shape since the 1850s as the Southern segment, usually rural and poor, of the Campbellite movement. The 1906 *Census of Religious Bodies* identified them as a separate body—they prefer "movement" or "brotherhood" to "denomination" since they reject general organization in favor of radical congregational autonomy. While their strength has been largely limited to Tennessee, Alabama, Arkansas, Oklahoma, Texas, and Florida, it is formidable where it exists. They are distinguished by their peculiar system of biblical interpretation which they insist is not an interpretation, the conviction that they perfectly embody New Testament teaching and practices, and by the absence of musical instruments from church services and of any centralized organization. These Southern Campbellite sectarians, instead of being holiness or pentecostal, are scholastic and legalist. In being so, they depart from the huge majority of popular Southern Protestants, but they too blend easily into the Southern landscape, and they and their fundamentalist kinsmen number several million in the South.

From the opposite end of the Protestant spectrum as well, some innovations were stirring around 1900. In the Protestant Episcopal Church, which had long since reestablished itself in the economy of Southern religion, a tradition of theologians, with William Porcher Dubose of Sewanee as the central figure, had formulated a theological alternative to the sin-guilt-crucifixion-pardon preachments of the mainstream. Without discarding this complex of classical Christian themes, they nevertheless worked out an "incarnational" theology. This too had antiquity on its side, but any prevalence it might have enjoyed in the South had been prevented by the evangelical temper which characterized

Episcopal as well as more truly Protestant belief. For these men, clergymen trained by them, and parishioners affected by their outlook, Christianity was a part of the natural order of things; it had continuities with general human experience and with other world religions. Theirs was a less catastrophic, less tragic, less supernaturalistic view of things; taking this approach put them closer to the spirit of the liberal theology sweeping the continent and the American North. In emphasizing the world as God's creation and God's becoming a part of our historical situation by his incarnation in Jesus of Nazareth, they drew a more optimistic bead on the human condition and the future of civilization. Their perspectives told for little in the actual functioning of Southern society, but their work is worth noting because it highlights the diversity, moderate though it was, in Southern religion and the capacity for transcending regional conventions which showed up here and there.

The final deviation to be referred to has some connections with the second. For Edgar Gardner Murphy, Dubose's most famous pupil, epitomizes the Southern expression, such as it was, of the "social gospel"tradition. The South's version of this famous and influential form of American Protestantism was carried out by a few people, both clergy and laity, in each of the major denominations, and in Alabama quite often. The issue or problems in society which were addressed ranged across a rather wide span: prohibition, child labor laws, workmen's wages and hours, education for Negroes, working conditions for women, and much more. Since this was an era of industrial expansion in the region, particularly in textiles, and since state legislation seemed to be required if any effective results were to be achieved, a significant minority of religious leaders devoted energies to improving the lot of workers. Deprivations in Negroes' lives also came in for some organized efforts. A third area was dealt with less directly and formally, namely, the desire of farmers to organize in the interest of forming cooperatives, alliances, and groups. A few of the leaders in behalf of this cause were churchmen, again both clergy and lay, who construed it to be their Christian responsibility to implement the declared concerns of the farmers. Typically, Southern social gospellers drew back from espousing federal intervention; the region's tradition of localism and states' rights had outlasted the demise of the Old South, indeed it had been exacerbated by the ravages of the Reconstruction era. Notwithstanding the damper put on their activities by Southern political and social customs, a large handful did devote themselves to the social application of Christian values for the sake of alleviating human distress and assuring basic rights.

By the 1920s patterns of religion in the American South had become essentially fixed. Things had changed somewhat from three decades earlier with the introduction of the sects, most but not all of them natively regional; also Negro church life, especially among Baptists by so far the largest group, had become more organized and cooperative. Otherwise the basic designs remained remarkably constant from the pre-Civil War days: few Catholics and fewer Jews, with neither exercising much influence; white Baptist, Methodist, Presbyterian, and Episcopal churches large and dominant, even normative, for the religious—and cultural—life of the region; here and there the presence of Eastern Orthodoxy, Christian Science, Theosophy, Baha'i, Jehovah's Witnesses, and some of the new (actually or functionally) religions which had begun to make a mark on society north of the South. Patternlessness had come to characterize America from Massachusetts to Pennsylvania, New York, and New Jersey westward to Ohio, Wisconsin, and Minnesota, thence to the West Coast, in most places. The South's span had widened a bit, but Evangelical Protestantism retained its remarkable hegemony. And what was true in terms of denominational patterns was, if anything, even more characteristic of the mind-set of Southern people, white and black, male and female, old and young. It was a latter-day version of Christendom.

To most appearances very little was to change in the decades of the twenties and thirties. Some significant developments did occur, however. The denominations were ready for fresh agendas. Consolidation had already occurred, issuing in unprecedented institutional strength. In this sense "modern society" was arriving in the South. Complex organizations, bureaucratization, and large-scale denominational cooperative undertakings were now possible and actual, owing to much better transportation and communications. No longer was the South a rural and village society or a post-rural and village society, inhabited by people who found gatherings a major ordeal and were not conditioned to attending meetings at some remove from their homes or to receiving appeals from stated clerks, bishops, or executive secretaries. Their various mission enterprises, foreign and domestic, were well under way and needed additional promotion and support. Similarly, their colleges, and increasingly, the newer agencies such as orphans homes and hospitals. The social gospel as such was not a commitment but far-flung institutional enterprises were beginning to acquire sizable proportions. This undramatic but profound shift in denominational life was scarcely any less reflective of the classic "centralized" churches such as the Presbyterian, Methodist, and Episcopal, than of the historic "free" churches, the Baptist in particular, and the sects. Nearly all were entering the mainstream of "modern" life; only a few balked, with the Churches of Christ and some hyper-localist Baptist bodies, principally in the mountain areas, managing to keep their skirts relatively clean.

The 1925 trial of John T. Scopes symbolized in several ways the social changes which gave rise to these religious changes we are noting. For one thing communications were such that people knew about the court room activities in Dayton, Tennessee, where the young biology teacher was being tried for teaching the Darwinian theory of evolution. That is to say, all kinds of people knew, Northern and Southern, educated and illiterate, liberal and conservative, as symbolized in turn by the presence of H. L. Mencken of the *Baltimore Sun* and two of America's most famous citizens, William Jennings Bryan of Nebraska, a two-time presidential candidate, and Clarence Darrow of Chicago, the greatest trial lawyer of the age. As the North came south and the South's public affairs became both its own and the nation's, the communications achievements which made all that a reality beamed it to the whole world. With high drama, a religious question had brought Southern culture into the modern era. But it was the prior infiltration of a modern idea, Darwinian biology (which had kicked up a fuss in the North between 1880 and 1900), to a small, remote Southern town that had created the stir in the first place. Not many contemporaries could see this event for its deeper layers of significance, brushing it off lightly as an example of the South's benightedness or, if they were Southern conservatives, applauding this show of determination to prevent the "acids of modernity" from eroding religious purity. What it demonstrated was that Southern culture could no longer stop the flow of alien ideas into its citadels; in truth, that "alien" was no longer a meaningful concept. And, as we have noted, the introduction of complex modern organizations into the Southern framework now made possible the dissemination of ideas and programs, proevolution or anti-evolution, and pro- or anti-anything else. Informal networks of communication were now augmented, often surpassed, by increasingly more sophisticated devices for getting the word out on any subject by means of radio and mailed literature.

The so-called Fundamentalist-Modernist controversy of the 1920s was more a Northern phenomenon than a Southern. Up there conflict was widespread and clashes often bitter, leading to the fracturing of denominations. As if to be part and parcel with that tumultuous decade, the churches showed their seamy sides. The same high seas buffeted the Southern church though less destructively. The main issue down here was indeed the evolution controversy. Concern over the teaching of biblical criticism had been felt in fullest force in the 1870s and 1880s— simultaneously with similar developments in the North. Not that that issue did not surface in the 1920s (and before and since); but the mainline Southern denominations worked out their respective compromises, typically opting for a circumspect advocacy of critical interpretations of the biblical texts. Evolution hit with full force in the 1920s. It produced heroes and villains, alternatingly vigorous defenders of the integrity of scientific research and persistent critics of the heresy of placing scientific theories ahead of the plain teaching of the Bible. Church colleges often got caught in the middle. The more progressive of them thought of the cause as having academic life-or-death significance, hence fought valiantly to guarantee their freedom to pursue the truth wherever it led. Most others too refused to turn back the clock, but worked out a different balance between piety and learning, that is, between their accountability to the sponsoring churches and their academic responsibilities. The schools operated by the sects on the whole stood above the fray; the fact that many of them were not accredited made it easy for them to avoid coming to grips with this divisive issue. As a matter of fact they felt themselves confirmed in their disengagement from the world where such things go on. As corollary to this, true Fundamentalism, the position which equates the truth with certain indisputable truths that are officially defined and tenaciously defended, appeared on the Southern scene with force for the first time in the 1920s. Its most representative appearance came with the founding of Bob Jones College in 1927.

Summarizing, the 1920s were a time of consolidation and fragmentation, of coming together and of taking sides. Sectarianism was inheriting causes which made its message more distinctive and attractive. The religious mainline managed to withstand erosive forces; on the positive side, they began to function like large business concerns. Both classes of religious institutions continued to grow, with astonishing speed really. The black churches likewise retained their fundamental place in that community, also growing by leaps and bounds. The ethnic and quasi-ethnic communions remained roughly what they had always been, but they too showed signs of vigor. Catholics and Jews were still anomalies in the Southern setting, except for those customary locales of strength, which, incidentally in the Catholic case, had become quite large by that time.

Whereas the North had lost any normativity or clear-cut patterns well before World War I, owing to immigration and the encroachments of modern ideologies, the hold of religion on the Southern mind had been intensified. That had not occurred without some new wrinkles, several concessions, and some reactions, however. The world was becoming with the South—if not yet too much, nevertheless much. The most famous book in Southern history, *I'll Take My Stand*, was published in 1930 by twelve Southern intellectuals who were endeavoring to say just that. While hardly provincial, much less reactionary, they plead for the South to avoid going the way of the rest of the western civilized world, that is, toward urbanization, an industrialized economy, a rationalistic, post-mythic imagination, and large scale bureaucracies. They were assessing the burgeoning situation accurately; the churches, which many of them had grown beyond, were one of the culprit factors whose modernization they deplored. Yet, the very religious institutions that devoutly intended to be conservative and were judged by many to be the essence of the South's backwardness were, in their own ways, at the forefront of change.

A few liberal instincts too were stirring from their slumbers in the post-War I decades. The Commission on Interracial Cooperation, the Southern Tenant Farmers' Union, and the Fellowship of Southern Churchmen are examples of agencies brought into being by church leaders for the sake of bettering the lot of blacks, the poor, farm and factory workers, and other oppressed peoples. Officially and in practice, the churches were most reticent to involve themselves in such radical causes. Only a tiny percentage of Southern Christians saw this kind of enterprise as an aspect of their calling. Nevertheless the leadership of most radical social programs in the region was provided by church men and women, including clergymen. In a majority of cases, however, the clergymen who did participate in these kinds of movements either renounced their orders or went ministerially inactive, or they were asked to resign from denominational affiliation. It was the rare case indeed in which the teachings of the church accorded with the message of these social reformers, either from the church's or the dissenting minister's perspective. Down to the 1970s the churches found it trying to give reforming spirits ample space in which to move about for fulfilling their special vocations. It is almost equally as true that such people found the South's orthodox religion distasteful and were nearly as anxious to pull out as their judges were to be rid of them. By the 1970s matters had changed enough to accommodate a reasonable amount of healthy tension.

The era of World War II and its aftermath has proved to have a significance for Southern life surpassed only by the Civil War and the years in its orbit. The details of the two impacts are dramatically different, of course, but what the 1940s did to the South was monumentally significant. In a nutshell, the concerted national effort entailed in the waging of that war unified the whole nation spelling the end of the South as a separate region. Never again, we may confidently conjecture, will the South be regarded as an imposter or stepchild or regard itself as a stranger in the context of an alien culture. Of course ever since 1789 the Southern states had been as much as integral a part of the political union as any others; similarly it was clear that Southern society was American society, notwithstanding its charming or reprehensible distinctiveness. Yet it stood apart, to its own eyes and others', as a unique even curious culture. From the 1940s forward, there was a blending of general national and Southern regional concerns, problems, programs, peoples, and cultures. The "solid South" was breaking up not only politically but also culturally.

At bedrock the "civil rights revolution" is what brought the separated South to a close and the integrated South into being. The military barracks and the crews' quarters of World War II had been no respecter of persons. Also the Axis powers' threat to the free world was so grave that the war effort captured the imagination of the entire country, calling forth a massive dedication to victory which brooked no regional (or other) reservations. Once the War was over and the nation reaped its legacy in the social arena, "civil rights" became a governmental concern. By 1954 it was a legal concern as well, as manifested in the Supreme Court's ruling against the racial segregation of any and all public facilities. The die was cast.

The Southern churches had not really prepared the way for this social revolution—most of the churches, that is. Among sectarians there was at least some history of doing church together. It was black churches which led the way, although by no means a majority of them. Black Baptists and Methodists were in the vanguard, thanks chiefly to a cadre of padres with such names as King, Abernathy, Walker, and Shuttlesworth the most prominent. A respectable minority of white church people joined hands with their black fellow Christians and helped play a part in dislodging *de jure* if not totally *de facto*, racial segregation which had prevailed in Southern society for over three centuries. Church buildings, organizations, and ministers provided the platform from which the non-violent revolution was conducted. Never had its role been more significant nor its reputation more eminent.

Yet, in what turned out to a weighty irony, the very revolution which did so much to improve the lot of black people occasioned the defection of many from the institution which sponsored it. By the troublesome times of the late 1960s in American society, a number of younger blacks taking up the cause divorced religion from social change and the good life, choosing an altogether secular style of life. Insufficient time has elapsed for us to be certain what the future of the black church will be. Regarding the past, there is abundant evidence that it was a powerful agent for social transformation in the 1950s and 1960s.

Although things could never be the same in the South for any race, group, or individual, the white churches directly were affected relatively little. Some integrating of a small minority of congregations began to occur. Few are visibly upset about this or adamant to prevent its spread any more. But the absence of violent reaction has not been matched by an eagerness on the part of either whites or blacks to build genuinely interracial congregations. What has come about is far greater mutuality in the form of respect, actual cooperation in church-related and other constructive causes, and an interaction as two races of people hitherto unknown in Southern history. It remains the case that certain sectarian bodies lead the way in actually practicing interracial church life.

On a quite different front, the 1970s witnessed the outbreak of different sorts of Evangelicalism in unpredictable quarters. When viewed against the long history of the South as the very heartland of Evangelical Protestantism, this announcement is startling. The new development is, for one thing, taking place in the more classic, staid traditions, Episcopal and Presbyterian quite noticeably, as well as within the much enlarged Roman Catholic population of the South. It is also turning up among the young on university campuses through interdenominational Christian groups—typically Northern in base and style—which have not enjoyed a great deal of popularity in the past. Still another manifestation of this new Evangelicalism comes in the women's and businessmen's fellowships built around weekly meetings largely given over to personal testimonies. These are para-church movements; that is to say, they are not affiliated with any denomination and in fact are sometimes perceived by the churches as rival organizations which claim more loyalty than the traditional institutions do, even when individuals belong to both.

What is this new Evangelicalism? Whatever it may be, is not the South so saturated with approaches of that sort that little room should be left for another? At the outset we must note that it is Evangelicalism, not evangelism; the latter refers to the activity of aggressively seeking to win outsiders to the Christian faith, which in the South has meant saving the lost. Spiritual status—whether one is lost or saved, hell-bound or on his way to an eternal heaven—is not the orientation of these new movements. Instead the focus is on sober acknowledgment of the authority of the Bible and serious study of it and on the (usually) quiet but always deep-running sense of God's presence in and direction of one's life. In most of its forms it is more intense, sober, strong, than expressive, joyous, and uninhibited. Some of the last qualities do show up in the more charismatic or pentecostal forms, however, especially among members of the more formal liturgical churches. In that context it is necessary to note that this phenomenon is not the same as Evangelical Protestantism nor are its manifestations limited to that species of Christian believers. That continues to be the dominant form of Christianity in the South, nevertheless. The two principal roles of the new Evangelicalism would appear to be: first, renewal of a religious tradition which is difficult to renew on its own terms because it lives on "a high"; and second, attracting people for whom the regular churches seem to have little appeal to a vital and earnest form of Christianity.

As the 1980s open, little has changed and much has changed. On the side of the continuities, we note that the long-dominant denominations retain their positions of supremacy, in numbers and influence alike. Among black and white Southerners, as for so long, Baptists rank a strong first trailed by the Methodists as a second majority communion. The various sect groups multiply in membership and, of late, have acquired more standing among the better classes. Among the most vigorous, rapidly growing, and widespread are: Assemblies of God, Church of God, Churches of Christ, the United Pentecostal Church, Seventh-Day Adventists, and of the less traditional groups, Mormons and Jehovah's Witnesses. The Presbyterian, Lutheran, Disciples of Christ, Congregational, and Episcopal churches remain forces to be reckoned with, but down south as well as nation-wide, they are experiencing a gradual but ongoing decrease in membership. Jewish percentages are little higher than ever, except in peninsular Florida and in the more cosmopolitan communities of the region. Roman Catholic numbers and proportions have increased some especially in those same metropolitan centers.

Those changes in the Jewish and Roman Catholic situations symbolize the considerable discontinuities now characteristic of Southern religious patterns. We have earlier noted that a form of high-intensity Christianity more associated with traditional Northern tastes than Southern has begun to make impact. That is a discontinuity tending in the traditional direction, however. Looking the other way is the ever enlarging company of secularists, people, that is, who are rarely atheist and not necessarily agnostic but for whom religious belief and practice make very little difference because they are accorded very little importance. In pursuing this course, the South reveals its consonance with what is happening in the nation at large.

In the juxtaposition of continued and revitalized traditional religion with an unmistakably secularist turn, the South perpetuates its distinctiveness. A remarkably high degree of homogeneity still prevails. An extensive commitment to religion continues despite the western worldwide demystification of reality. But inroads have been made by that perspective into the once alternative-less Southern culture, and the gap between belief and unbelief widens and deepens there too, presaging a profound heterogenizing effect. Much does remain the same; but the sameness is more dynamic owing to the presence of tension as a factor. Much changes and changes take some of the Southern people beyond any traditional pale. The religious South is distinguishable from other sections of the country, but day by day the distinctiveness weakens as events draw the South closer to emulating developments occurring in the rest of the nation.

Footnotes

[1]Richard Beale Davis, *Intellectual Life in the Colonial South, 1585-1763*, vol. 2 (Knoxville: University of Tennessee Press, 1978), p. 629.

[2]Ibid., p. 669.

[3]Ibid., pp. 687-88.

[4]Rhys Isaac, "Evangelical Revolt: The Nature of the Baptists' Challenge to the Traditional Order in Virginia, 1765 to 1775," *William and Mary Quarterly* 31 (July, 1974):368.

[5]Donald G. Mathews, *Religion in the Old South* (Chicago: University of Chicago Press,77), p. 24.

[6]Clement Eaton, *The Growth of Southern Civilization* (New York: Harper and Row, 1961), p. 314.

[7]William G. McLoughlin, *Revivals, Awakenings, and Reform* (Chicago: University of Chicago Press, 1978), p. 133.

[8]John Samuel Ezell, *The South Since 1865* (New York: Macmillan 1963), p. 346.

[9]Ibid., p. 348.

MUP RELIGION IN THE SOUTHERN STATES

designed by Margaret Brown

composition by Omni Composition Services, Macon, Georgia
    typeset in Garamond by Joan McCord on an Addressograph Multigraph Comp/Set
    phototypesetter 5404, and paginated on an A/M Comp/Set 4510

design and production specifications:
    text paper—Warren's Olde Style, 60 pound
    cover (on .088 boards)—Joanna Arrestox B book cloth
    dust jacket—100 pound enamel, printed two colors and varnished

printing (offset lithography) by Omnipress of Macon, Inc., Macon, Georgia
binding by John H. Dekker and Sons, Inc., Grand Rapids, Michigan